Whatever Happened to the IBM AS/400?

Is It Stuck in the Big IBM Vault of Unwanted Treasures?

Whether IBM likes the AS/400 or not, it is clearly the best kept secret and AS/400 or Power i Users for years would rather swear an oath to the AS/400 rather than swear an oath to any political party.

BRIAN W. KELLY

LETS GO PUBLISH

Referenced Material : The information in this book has been obtained through personal and third party observations and copious reading over many years. Where unique information has been provided or extracted from other sources, those sources are acknowledged within the text of the book itself. Thus, there is no formal footnotes or bibliography section.

Published by: **LETS GO PUBLISH!**
Brian P. Kelly, Publisher
P.O Box 621
Wilkes-Barre, PA 18703
brian@brianpkelly.com
www.letsgopublish.com

Library of Congress Copyright Information Pending

Book Cover Design by Michele Thomas

ISBN Information: The International Standard Book Number (ISBN) is a unique machine-readable identification number, which marks any book unmistakably. The ISBN is the clear standard in the book industry. 159 countries and territories are officially ISBN members. The Official ISBN For this book is:

ISBN 978-0-9977667-0-7

The price for this work is : $22.95 USD

10 9 8 7 6 5 4 3 2

Second Printing Release Date: August 2016

Dedication

To My Wonderful Neighbors

Angel Mrs. Mercedes Leighton
Mrs. Jeanne and Mr. Joseph Elinsky
Mrs. Carol and Mr. John Anstett
Dr. Dwaraki Bai and Dr. Haragopal Penugonda
Angel Mrs. Maxine and Angel Mr. Simon H. Coblentz
Mr. Ozzie Kroll

The day that my neighbors, who are all professionals and business people in their day jobs, understand the elegance and desirability of the IBM AS/400 from having heard IBM's message, is the day that the AS/400's chances of survival as a relevant business computer begin to increase.

Acknowledgments

I would like to thank many, many people for helping me in this effort to produce my 68th book.

To all the people that I have ever mentioned in the Acknowledgments of any book, I continue to appreciate your contributions. For those new to the experience of helping me bring in my book projects and/or who help me in my life, I want to thank you all from the bottom of my heart.

Please check out www.letsgopublish.com Acknowledgments to read the latest version of what once was the largest acknowledgments in the world, though the rigors of the Guinness Book were too time consuming for us to apply.

You are listed online and if not please send me a spirited, yet irritated response. I do appreciate your great work in my publishing efforts.

God Bless all the helpers!

Thank you so very much!

Table of Contents

Preface:

For quite a few years, my friends in the computer industry and I have been confused by IBM's failure to highlight its single best product, the AS/400. I can remember saying to members of this group of AS/400 aficionados that only IBM could create the AS/400 and only IBM could destroy the AS/400. No company besides IBM could have invested as much capital on the technology that was necessary to create the AS/400, and no other company could intentionally destroy the product of its efforts, as the finest computer system ever built.

After many years spent telling customers that it was planning to promote the AS/400, the plan never came. IBM's AS/400 customers are now in a private revolt against the company. IBM has not done a good job in its vital roles as caretaker and life-sustainer of this system, upon which many large and small IBM customers run their businesses. If IBM were doing a good job, one of the most asked questions in the industry would not be the following:

"Is the AS/400 Dead?"

Most people see IBM as a very successful company that is really great at making big computers. That is IBM's legacy for those who drink from the fountain of public knowledge. Unless you work in the computer industry, you would naturally be unaware of all the ventures over the years in which IBM was less than successful.

For the record, today's IBM is the same IBM that lost the PC business, the relational database business, the telecommunications business, the application software business, the satellite communications business, the Unix business, the word processing business, the video disk business, the computerized branch exchange business, the disk drive business, as well a number of other businesses in which you and I would have made millions. Yet, without learning a lesson, the new IBM is behaving as arrogantly with its AS/400 customers as it did during these other great losses. So what are we to expect?

IBM's AS/400 customers are not completely unaware of IBM's poor track record with groundbreaking technology. Moreover, they are very aware that the very same IBM is doing nothing to help them after ten years of requests to keep the AS/400 as IBM's lead business system.

Anybody who is paying attention to the problems that IBM is having with its AS/400 would not be surprised if Big Blue pulled the plug on its AS/400 box? Folks that is the antithesis of trust. Many see IBM heading down a path in which it will become known as the company that lost the entire small to midsized production business computer marketplace, even though it had the finest products.

I am paying attention and I am mad as hell at IBM for what they have done to the AS/400 and the Power i. I fight back with words but IBM often does not want to listen. So, I write a lot of books. My latest which I finished tonight is a reflection of a trues story, a dream more or less that I rally had. Based on the dream, I was compelled to write the book before this titled, *I Had a Dream that IBM Could Be # 1 Again.* That is a comforting thought for we IBM and AS/400 lovers but we have to get IBM on-board.

Rather than waiting until it is too late, IBM's AS/400 customers have been quite outspoken to IBM and to the industry. These customers are adamant that the company should do something to promote the machine. However, "IBM knows best" remains the huge computer company's mantra as it continues a forced march against an undisclosed plan that seems to include taking down the AS/400. Let me repeat, I recently completed a how-to manual for IBM to become # 1 again. The name of this book is *I Had a Dream that IBM Could Be # 1 Again.* I am not kidding!

In order to make my points in this book, not the last, I reach back through a lot of IBM history. Some of the history I lived through as an IBM branch office systems engineer, some I lived through as an IBM customer, and some as an industry consultant. Though I have not seen it all, I've seen enough to know that sound marketing logic is not the prevailing thought in the new IBM. Think Signs and Think Pads are not seen very often today in IBM, and there is good reason. Where is the thinking IBM?

With a book size well over five hundred pages, you may think that I told every story about IBM that ever was. Yet the cutting room floor is filled with another five hundred pages that just would have made this book too long to enjoy reading. Maybe another day! I would love it to be about how IBM rescued itself in 2017. Hey let it be 2020 and that still is OK!

For the most part, this book reads as a series of thirty-nine essays. Each of thirty-nine chapters is built as a story unto itself, with the sum of the chapters telling the IBM AS/400 story. For the most part, you can pick up any chapter and read it without having to read a prior chapter. However, you may want to read the first set of chapters first to get a perspective on what the AS/400 computer is all about and its relevance in IBM history.

This book presents the IBM product, the IBM problem, the IBM customer reaction, the IBM past history, the IBM propensity to do the right and wrong thing, the IBM preoccupations, the IBM current history, the IBM biases, the IBM probable future, the AS/400's probable future, and the terms under which the AS/400 as a viable, relevant system can survive the IBM that has been working so hard for so long to destroy it. Now that's a sentence! I will take the award, please!

This is not a technical book. However, there are a few chapters in which I do get just a little bit technical, hoping that I can show the reader in reasonably simple terms how the AS/400 is a special machine with a long and successful tradition. Though this book is nonfiction, there may be some areas in which my analysis of a situation differs from IBM's. Moreover, there are surely areas in which my recollection of facts and actual events may be different from IBM's.

Of course, I believe that my analysis and my recollections are accurate and fair, and that's why I wrote the book from my perspective, not from IBM's. My AS/400 customers and I believe that we have already had enough of IBM's perspective.

IBM did not help me at all with this book. I would have liked to have had some IBM help, and I asked a few important IBMers along the way for some help, but I got none and so I did not persist in my requests. In a subsequent edition of this book, I would be pleased to include a rebuttal from IBM about some of the facts, analyses, or conclusions that Big Blue may dispute.

However, I think I am 99$^{44/100}$ % correct. Right! If IBM provides me incontrovertible evidence that I am wrong, I would be happy to add IBM's story to my own, to get a complete story. I'll print the response and highlighted it on one of my many web sites. You'll also get my rebuttal of IBM's rebuttal unless they show me they are on our side.

When you finish reading this book, you may think that I have treated IBM and its management team quite harshly. I ask for your indulgence. That I was motivated to write a book of this length on the survivability of IBM's AS/400 gives you an idea of how harshly that I believe IBM has treated its AS/400 customers and consultants. I can appreciate that IBM would want the gloves kept on when it is the object of reproach.

However, from my eyes, IBM has not been fair to its customers.

I have taken every opportunity in this book to show how and why IBM has not been fair. I am fair in this book, but I am definitely not balanced. IBM does not look good in the end, because IBM has not behaved well with its AS/400 product and now its Power I product. The balanced part of this book will come from IBM's corrective action or perhaps its rebuttal.

At any rate, I hope that at the very least, along with learning a number of things, you enjoy reading this book. I sure have enjoyed writing it.

Brian W. Kelly
Wilkes-Barre, Pennsylvania

About the Author

Brian W. Kelly retired as an Assistant Professor in the Business Information Technology (BIT) program at Marywood University, where he also served as the IBM i and midrange systems technical advisor to the IT faculty. Kelly has designed, developed, and taught many college and professional courses. He is also a contributing technical editor to a number of IT industry magazines, including "The Four Hundred" and "Four Hundred Guru" published by IT Jungle.

Kelly is a former IBM Senior Systems Engineer. Over the past twenty years, Brian Kelly has become one of America's most outspoken and eloquent technical authors. Besides this book, his titles about IBM include *Chip Wars*; *Can the AS/400 Survive IBM? Thanks You IBM:* The story of how IBM helped today's technology billionaires and millionaires gain their vast fortunes, *The All-Everything Machine, The All-Everything Operating System, Whatever happened to the IBM AS/400? Besides these,* many other Kelly books are available at www.bookhawkers.com

Endorsed by the Independence Hall Tea Party in 2010, Kelly, a Democrat, ran for Congress against a 13-term Democrat and, took no campaign contributions, spent enough to buy signs and T-shirts, and as a virtual unknown, he captured 17% of the vote—www.briankellyforcongress.com.

Chapter 1 The Little Lab That Could

Clandestine Activity

Once upon a time, in a small IBM laboratory in Rochester, Minnesota, there was a team with a big mission. Their job was to build a more modern set of unit record equipment. The Rochester team was blessed with the electrical and mechanical engineering know how that could make the project a success, but they realized that because it was the 1960s, electromechanical machines were not in high demand. After all, the IBM System/360 already had been shipped, it was a huge success, and computers were really catching on in the marketplace.

The Rochester team was well aware that the mission to build computers rested elsewhere in IBM, yet they earnestly believed that they should use computer technology, not electromechanical circuitry, in the new machine. They also knew that if they called their machine a computer in its internal project stage, they would not gain IBM's approval to build.

However, Rochester was approved and had the budget to build the next generation of card processing machines. Officially, that's what they began to develop. Unofficially, however, the team knew they were designing and building a new computer system. The machine that flowed from this work would be called the System/3. It would change IBM forever, offering ease-of-use IBM computing to small businesses for the very first time.

Once the System/3 was introduced, the Rochester team was no longer able to hide the fact that it had built a bona fide computer. The System/3 would be recognized in the industry as a computer system. It may not be nice to fool Mother IBM, but the Rochester team knew that there would be no project if it were not clandestine. So they forged ahead, using chicanery and secrecy as two favorite allies.

Some say Rochester is a land where all there is to do is think. The opportunity to think in the cold while enjoying more than 250 days of sunshine each year made Rochester the perfect site for the conception of a new generation of computing. Though the System/3 was simple, it was very capable and innovative. A picture of a later-model system, which looked almost the same as the announced model, is shown in Figure 1-1.

Figure 1-1 IBM System/3 Model 10 with MFCU (Right) and Printer (Left)

Photo Credit for S/3: Jim Watt
http://www.kroytech.com/siteinfo/persbackgr.htm#IBM_System

One-Third Size, 20% More Data

The first innovation at Rochester was the introduction of the 96-column card (see Figure 1-2). It was one-third the size of the 80 -column punched card forms, in which many people over the years had received their paychecks and income tax return checks. The main input unit for this card on the System/3 was a device called the 5424 multifunction card unit (MFCU). It is located on the right side of the picture in Figure 1-1. This name came from IBM's System/360 Model 20, which had a similar, but much larger, multifunction card machine (MFCM) that processed 80-column cards. The two other pieces of card gear built by Rochester were the 5496 data recorder and the 5486 sorter.

Figure 1-2 No Holes, 96-Column, System/3 Punched Card

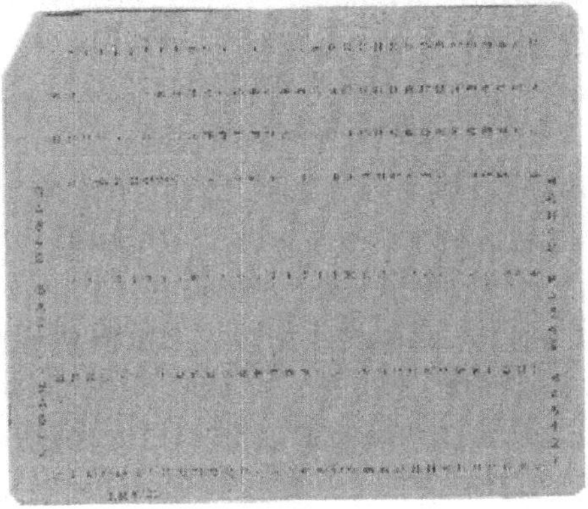

By any other name, the 5496 data recorder would be an intelligent *keypunch* machine. It was the source of original entry. Its purpose was to permit an operator to create 96-column punched cards that represented either master records or transactions for the business. Combinations of holes in the three-tiered card represented numbers and letters. Together, these were the data elements that provided input for the system.

Before being processed in the MFCU, the data often would be sorted using the 5486 sorter. This was a two-tiered desktop device and was necessary in order to resequence cards for processing. IBM provided a sort program for the System/3 to companies that believed that they could not afford a 5486, and they could sort their cards using the two hoppers and four stackers of the MFCU.

Unlike other unit record incarnations over the years, there was no separate collator unit available that could be used to merge two decks of sorted cards. There was no interpreter that could be used to print the meaning of the holes on the top of the cards. There was no reproducer that could be used to duplicate card decks. There was no big calculator that could be used for computations. And there was no 96-column accounting machine that could list the cards and provide, for example, invoices, orders, or management reports. The System/3 would provide all of these unit-record-like functions.

The MFCU, instead of a collator, was used for merging card decks. Special card programs were provided that enabled two columns of cards to be merged into one. The 5496 data recorder was used as an interpreter. Another special card program permitted the System/3 MFCU to reproduce cards by reading one deck on the left side and punching out a duplicate deck on the other side of the MFCU. The CPU of the System/3 provided calculations and report formatting. (The CPU is the highboy column in the middle of the picture in Figure 1-1.) Finally, the System/3 complex included a choice of printers. The 5203 Printer (shown on the left side of Figure 1-1) printed several hundred lines per minute.

There was no disk on the original System/3 computer system, and it came with just 8k of memory as standard. That's 8,096 memory positions. The System/3 card system did have an operating system. It was provided in a stack of cards less than an inch high. This deck of cards was called the System Initialization Program (SIP), and its job was to "boot" the system. After powering up the unit, an operator would place the SIP deck in MFCU1 (the first hopper of the MFCU) and press the Start button. When the deck was read, the System/3 was ready for business.

RPG for the Business System/3

Another major innovation for IBM at the time was the perfection of the RPG (Report Program Generator) programming language. This language was built for very old IBM computers in the 1950s, such as the IBM 1401, but it had not yet been perfected and had a poor reputation. The RPG II for the System/3 was a real programming language. It was rich in business function and thus made the System/3 a real business computer. The language was instrumental in making the System/3 an instant success. It was simple. It was somewhat English-like, and it was not verbose or intimidating for new programmers, as COBOL was. Most of all, it was easy to learn.

Since there were not many for-hire programmers back then, the lucky folks tapped to learn RPG in the 1970s with System/3 were often young, bright, and trustworthy. They held other positions in their companies and seemed like the right candidates. Most of these programmers have grown up to become the gray-haired AS/400 professionals who often complain to IBM about not marketing their favorite system.

Eventually, IBM added disk to the System/3. In the area under the MFCU, the company provided space for four disk drives, known as 5444s, stacked two in each of two drawers. Each drive could hold 2.45 million characters of storage. Later, IBM attached its old 2319 drives to the System/3, calling them the 5445 Disk System, when attached to System/3. Each of these drives could hold 20.48 million characters of storage. Eventually, faster printers, such as the legendary IBM 1403 (with 1,100 lines per minute), were added and the System/3 became a very popular small business computer. It was very successful and profitable for IBM.

IBM rewarded Rochester for its clandestine accomplishments by permitting Rochester to continue making these computers.

The biggest and most powerful System/3 was introduced in 1973. It was known as the Model 15D. Other System/3 models included Models 4, 6, and 8. During this period, IBM moved from card-oriented processing to floppy disks in eight-inch packages. The later System/3s were "cardless." Therefore, the unit record façade for Rochester was over but the plant continued to make these System/3 machines, which everybody referred to as computers.

Made for Humans, Not Machines

In addition to RPG, one of the factors that made the System/3 easy to use was its control language, known as the Operator Control Language (OCL). All computers preceding the System/3 required humans to learn cryptic languages, such as Autocoder, SPS, or JCL, in order to communicate with the machine. Rochester knew the old way was not going to fly with a machine destined for small businesses and run by non-professionals. Programmers at the time who recall their first look at OCL for the System/3, especially those who were mainframe-trained were amazed by its simplicity.

IBM made the System/3 language easier for the programmer in the business environment, rather than for the software engineer in IBM who had to write the complicated routines that would scan the cards and interpret their meaning for the machine. Before the System/3 existed, the control language used on IBM machines was very cryptic and quite difficult for a normal human to read, and even more difficult to write. A control language statement for a mainframe disk drive, for example, might look like the following:

```
// Dlbl,,3,,42,,sys0022,,39,payroll,,,,99999, end
```

There was nothing easy about writing this type of mainframe statement. If you are an old mainframe person, you know that this is not exact but it is representative. Mainframe job control language (JCL) was quite difficult to master and it took forever to get this stuff to work. It was almost impossible to know how many commas were needed in between parameters. If you were off by one comma, the statement would mean something entirely different, and the mainframe machine was very unforgiving and not very helpful. System/3 OCL was much different. It was English-like. A sample statement might look as follows:

```
// File Name-Payroll,Unit-F1, etc.
```

The purpose of showing this is not to teach about old computers, but to give a perspective as to how much simpler the new System/3 made computing at the time. The "Unit=F1" part of the S/3 statement was needed because the system had more than one disk drive. Just like a PC with multiple disk drives uses one-character symbols, the letters A through Z, to distinguish the drives, the System/3 used two-character symbols. Instead of A, B, C, or D drives; the System/3 drive names were F1, F2, R1, and R2. The F's were for the two fixed drives, and the R's were for the two removable drives. Today, other than diskette, CD, and DSD drives; disks are "fixed" in all computers and are non-removable, or fixed in place. The day of the removable hard disk passed when System/3 technology made its exit from the marketplace.

Terminals for System/3

During the mid-1970s, IBM developed a program on mainframes called the Customer Information Control System (CICS). This program ran in one part (or partition) of a mainframe and permitted many terminals to be used simultaneously with the machine. CICS was difficult to use. The IBM 3270 terminal was the terminal of choice at the time.

So that System/3s could also support terminals, after disk drives were introduced, Rochester built a program called the Communication Control Program (CCP) between 1971 and

1972. I can remember learning this and announcing it to the IBM office in Scranton, Pennsylvania. CCP was very similar in function to CICS. Along with the new capabilities, CCP added a degree of complexity to the System/3 environment for terminal processing, but nothing close to the degree of difficulty brought forth by CICS. Nonetheless, CCP was not for the casual System/3 programmer..

The IBM System/32 Is Introduced

With all of this innovation, the System/3 became a big hit in businesses all across the world, and Rochester became a big hit within IBM because it was making money for the corporation. In 1975, IBM Rochester was at it again. The Lab introduced a System/3-like machine that was desk-sized. Notice I did not say desktop. Desk-sized was about as small as it got back then. This unit had a keyboard and a small monitor, and had a printer attached to its back. It was an all-in-one computer called the System/32 (see Figure 1-3).

Figure 1-3 System/32 – Circa 1975

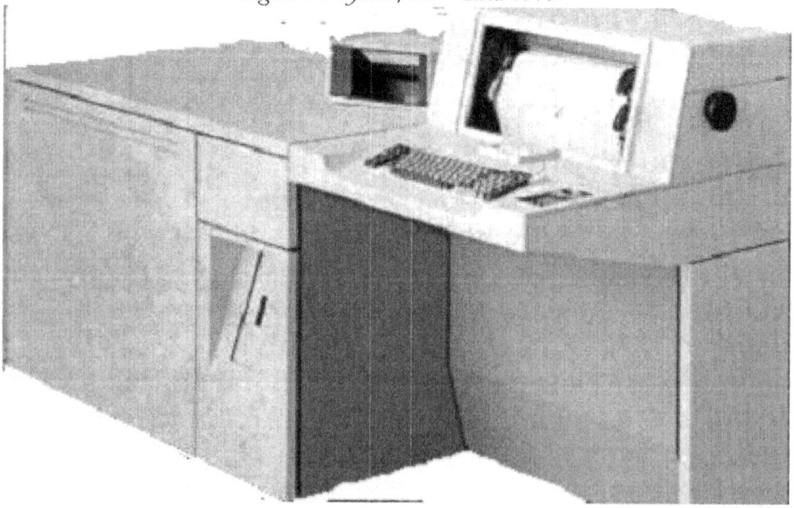

The System/32 used the same notion of OCL, as did the System/3 disk systems—shown in the example above.

However, since there was just one big disk drive on the left side of the unit, the OCL was even simpler than that of the System/3. There was no need for the R1, F1, R2, and F2 designations in OCL. The System/32, however, came with one major disadvantage. It had just one input keyboard. Though key to diskette units, such as the IBM 3741, could be used to help with the keypunch load, and the System/32 did have a diskette reader, the one keyboard proved to be the major disadvantage of the box. As such the System/32 lasted just two years before IBM improved the design.

In 1977, Rochester announced the new and improved System/32. It was a boxy computer called the System/34 (see Figure 1-4). It used Operator Control Language, just as the System/3 and the System/32 before it. Therefore, the System/34 was also easy to work with, and OCL was a big reason.

By using terminals instead of a built-in keyboard, the System/34 solved the "one keyboard" problem of the System/32. The big difference between the two systems was that the new System/34 was a multi-station, multi-user system. By introducing the notion of multi-programming with the System/34, IBM enabled each user to have a piece of this one computer system as if it were his or her own machine.

Figure 1-4 IBM System/34 Multi-Station Computer

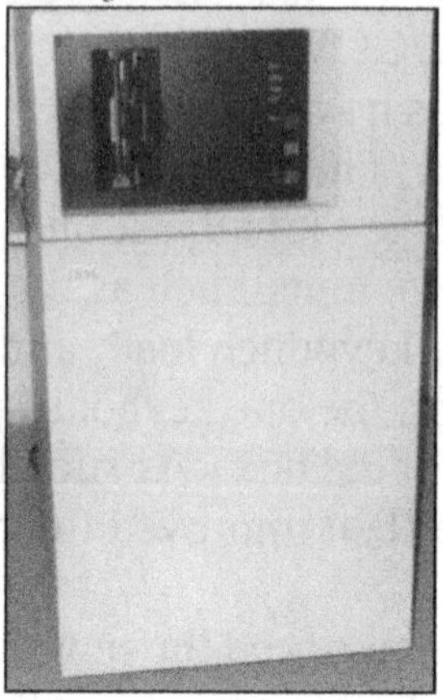

System/34 used terminals, but did not need the complexities of System/3 CCP. Terminal management was built-into the System Support Program (SSP) operating system. It was an industry first. You could attach a number of semi-intelligent, high-speed terminals to the system over a local wiring type called twinaxial cable, without the need for modems. The new terminal that IBM invented was big and square, and it was called the IBM 5250. See Figure 1-5. Each of these terminals, at the time, could be purchased for about $4,000. Though 5250s are no longer sold, the green-screen 5250 legacy continues today through PC products that emulate the 5250 terminal's data stream.

Figure 1-5 IBM 5250 Type Terminals

The 5250 terminal had been built for the Rochester designed and developed System/38 computer system, which was to be the follow-on computer to the System/3 Model 15D and the entire System/3 line. The System/3 had used the IBM 3270 terminal, which is still popular on mainframes today and is an often-emulated device. Back in the 1970s, however, Rochester could not convince IBM to allocate enough 3270 terminals to meet the demand of System/3 users. The delivery schedules of 3270 family terminals were as much as two years out for mainframe customers. There were two reasons for the long delivery. The 3270 devices were very popular, and IBM had underestimated the demand.

Without the corporation's assurance that it would supply enough 3270 terminals for the shipment of each of Rochester's new small business computers, the Lab could not depend on a supply that was adequate for new computer customers. The System/34 could do nothing without a terminal. Rochester knew that two years for a terminal would mean many lost sales.

IBM cared more about its mainframe products than the reasonably new endeavors in Rochester. Rochester did not matter as much to the corporation, and the management at Rochester knew it had to plan for success, rather than depend on the corporation and face failure. Though it was a small matter at the time, having two terminal lines in one IBM created an even greater wedge between the wares of Rochester and the wares of the mainframe division. IBM customers with 5250-based systems and 3270-based systems had continual cross-operating issues until IBM stopped selling terminals several years ago.

In retrospect, IBM executives should have stepped up to the challenge and solved the problem at the corporate level. The company would have been better off permitting Rochester to build its own 3270s, rather than have them create a completely new terminal line.

Rochester management was very concerned that it: could not trust the rest of IBM for a supply of 3270-type terminals. Without terminals, Rochester could not sell its computers. It is also a documented fact that mainframe plants in IBM were not happy about Rochester making computers in the first place.

Rather than risk being taken down from within, Rochester created its 5250 line of terminals. Better management at the top of IBM would have separated the competing teams and ensured that Rochester would not be put out of business by mainframe-controlled plants not supplying terminals. Without top management's assuredness, however, Rochester had to do its own thing.

In 1977, when the in-process System/38 was taking much longer to complete than originally anticipated, Rochester decided to announce the System/34 and to use with it the terminals and printers that were designed for the System/38.

Tough to Get a System/38

In this book, you will learn lots about the System/38, the direct predecessor of the AS/400, and its origins and unique attributes. The System/38 was a well-designed system, using the best that IBM knew about computers. Rochester had never really built a sophisticated computer before. Therefore it was difficult to know how difficult it would be to achieve the major technical advances brought forth with the System/38.

When IBM announced the System/38, in October 1978, Rochester knew that the machine was not working well enough but felt that it would be ready in 1979, in time for the first customer shipment. System/3 Model 15D customers, as well as many others, enamored by the outstanding specifications of the System/38, signed up in droves on the day it was announced for an early shipment of this new box.

There would be no early shipments. IBM seemed to take forever to give customers a ship date, and when they got one, it was two years out. This created a big public relations problem for the company. There also were big problems in making it all work. In 1979, Frank Cary, CEO and chairman of IBM at the time, appeared before IBM's customers and the world, and asked for forgiveness for delaying the System/38 for 11 additional months so that it would be ready for business use.

The System/38 finally arrived in 1980 to a mostly welcoming customer set (see Figure 1-6). It was the best system that IBM had ever built. Its underpinnings were so advanced that no machine, besides its direct descendents, the AS/400 and Power i, has ever reached the same level of hardware and software technology and integration.

Figure 1-6 IBM System/38, Announced in 1978

System/34 Was Available

Because of the delays, as well as the remarkable popularity of the System/34, total sales for the System/38 never surpassed 50,000 units. There are unofficial estimates that the total of

System/38 shipments was even as low as 20,000 units. Yet the System/34, with its 5250 workstations, caught on like gangbusters and shipped well over 100,000 units.

In the early 1980s, the mainframe division of IBM became concerned that there were too many IBM systems aimed at the same customer. Company executives were never happy that Rochester built computers, and felt that that job should be done in a mainframe plant, such as Endicott or Poughkeepsie.

Mainframe-oriented IBM spent hundreds of millions of dollars coming up with a new system that would do everything that the System/34 and the System/38 could do. The System/36 replaced the System/34 in 1983 (see Figure 1-7). By 1985, the systems convergence project, called Fort Knox, sponsored by the mainframe plants, had failed. (See Chapter 15, "The Fort Knox Project.")

Figure 1-7 IBM System/36, Announced in 1983

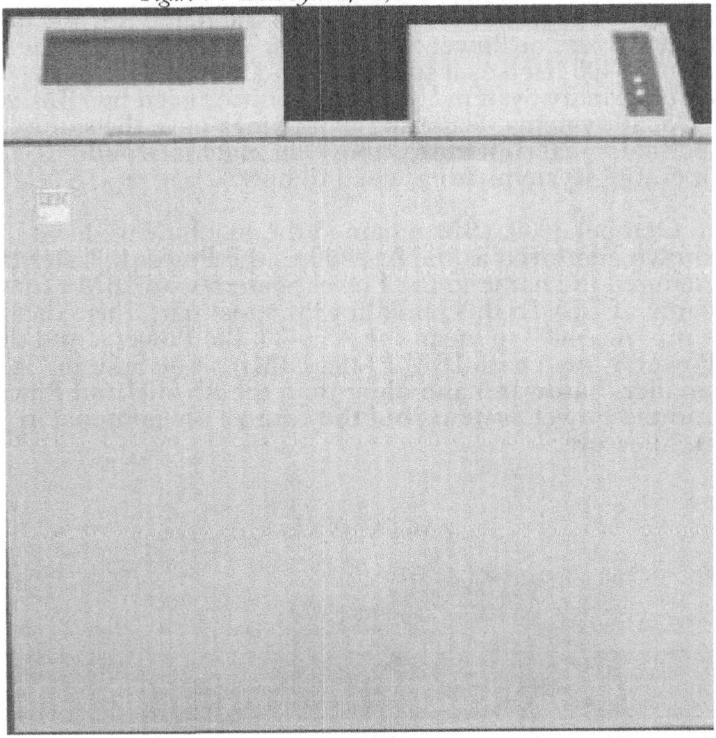

One of the secret goals of Fort Knox was to minimize the impact of the Rochester Lab on the company so that mainframe plants and labs could take over their system work. This also failed, but the disdain for Rochester and its products persisted in important parts of the corporation.

Finally, the AS/400

The Silverlake project was initiated at Rochester in the mid 1980s to create one replacement box for both the System/38 and the System/36. After little more than two years, in June 1988, IBM announced the results of Silverlake as the Application System/400, or AS/400 (see Figure 1-8). In many ways the box was a repackaging of the System/38, but it also ran System/36 programs untouched.

Note: Though this book title uses the name AS/400 rather than Power i or Power System with IBM i as the name of the AS/400 itself as a successor and a derivative of the revolutionary System/38 that was introduced by IBM in 1978, all systems, reagradless of names have the same technological superiority above all machines and operating systems from when til now.

In October 2000, IBM renamed the machine we have known and loved as the AS/400 as the Power i. Later IBM changed the name to the Power System with IBM i (new name of OS). In this book, for the most part, I use the term "AS/400" to mean the AS/400, the Power i, and the Power System with IBM I (aka IBMi). The System/38 is smaller (hardware) and older than the AS/400 and Power i and the Power Systems but they are all phenomenal in architecture.

Figure 1-8 Modern AS/400 RISC Box

The AS/400 was a resounding success by all measurements but one. System/36 customers were not too happy about it. They expressed their displeasure by keeping their old System/36 boxes as long as they could, and when they upgraded, they would buy either a second used System/36 (same size) or a bigger used System/36. It took a long time for IBM's System/36 customers to warm up to the AS/400. However, there was enough new AS/400 business at the time from the former minicomputer vendors, such as DEC and

Data General, that IBM did not have to care about not fully pleasing its own System/36 installed base.

AS/400 Evolution

In 1995, IBM changed its AS/400 hardware to 64-bit RISC from 48-bit CISC, yet the company chose not to rename the system, as it had done when the AS/400 replaced the System/38. (See Chapter 8, "No Risk with RISC" for a better explanation of CISC and RISC architectures.) At the time, IBM made some additional changes to the box, and the new chips permitted the System/36 operating system to run natively on a RISC version called the AS/400 Advanced/36.

This machine did very well, and IBM's System/36 customers rewarded IBM for giving them what they wanted by purchasing lots of these new boxes. Eventually, IBM was able to place the entire System/36 instruction set, as well as the AS/400 instruction set, on newer and better 64-bit chips. With this change, the company was able to withdraw the Advanced System/36 from marketing several years ago. Today, the AS/400 can perform both System/36 and AS/400 operations.

In 1997, IBM spent a little money on the AS/400 image by adding an "e," for *e-business*, to the AS/400 name, thereby making it the AS/400e. IBM renamed the AS/400 again in 2000, as the eServer Power i 400. This name change affected only new shipments. AS/400s that were already installed in customer locations were not renamed. From this point forward, both the AS/400 name and the shortened name Power i applied to the AS/400 server.

Since 1995, with the introduction of the 64-bit RISC processors, IBM has boosted the power and the number of processors that are usable on the AS/400 product line. In 2004, IBM introduced the Power5 series of microprocessors and doubled the number of processors that could be packaged as one AS/400 from 32 to 64. The company also changed the name again to the eServer i5 and changed the operating system name to i5/OS. Power 5 is bringing with it the capoability of having sixty-four high-speed computers operating simultaneously in one machine. That sounds a lot like a mainframe. The AS/400 is now recognized as a mainframe-class machine.

With all of the enhancements over its 16 years, the AS/400 is clearly the most architecturally elegant and capable machine in the industry. From the ground-up, it was built as an integrated machine. When you add this internal elegance to the powerful engines (64-way Power5) that are now available with AS/400 technology, the box is clearly the best and most powerful computer of all time.

So, with that as its billing, a reasonable person might wonder, "If the AS/400 is so special, why is there a problem?" The real problem is IBM.

The IBM Problem

In my experience in teaching AS/400 courses to IT professionals coming from other platforms, I have found that those coming from real computing platforms, such as DEC VMS, HP3000, Unix, Linux, and mainframe, do not have positive feelings about the AS/400. They do not know what to expect, but they think it will not be good. It does not take long for them to become impressed with the awesome architecture and innate capabilities of the AS/400. Most wonder why they have never heard from IBM that transitioning to the AS/400 can be such a positive experience. They wonder why IBM keeps the AS/400 such a secret, and why IBM thinks it is okay that the public is not aware that the box exists. IBM just doesn't get it.

These people are not alone. AS/400 professionals continue to beg IBM to advertise the machine. They ask IBM every chance they get--at users group meetings and in letters to forums and magazines--to make the public aware that the

AS/400 is the best computer in the marketplace. They want their bosses and the decision makers of their firms to have a positive inclination toward the AS/400 machine that provides the essential services to their organizations. They don't want to have to continually defend their AS/400 against the Microsoft initiative du jour that is always on television. Because IBM is silent, IT shops must continue to justify their decision to maintain an expensive AS/400 box instead of a nice Microsoft/Intel box. IBM just doesn't get it.

I reference my neighbors in this book as the type of people who should know that IBM's AS/400 is built for their businesses. In fact, I feel so strongly that IBM should be marketing to my neighbors that I dedicated this book to them. At the bottom of the dedication page, I placed this little note explaining why:

> **The day that my neighbors, who are all professionals and business people, understand the elegance and desirability of the IBM AS/400, from having heard IBM's message, is the day that the AS/400's chances of survival as a relevant business computer begin to increase.**

My neighbors have heard about the AS/400, but not from IBM. They know of the AS/400 only because I am their neighbor, and they know that I am an AS/400 consultant and author. They have concluded that an AS/400 must not be right for their businesses; otherwise, they reason, surely they would have heard about the machine from IBM. My neighbors have never thought that any of IBM's marketing initiatives were directed at their small businesses. They are right. IBM just doesn't get it.

One of the reasons why the survival of the AS/400 is in question is that IBM fails to market its finest server. It is not the only reason, however, and to give the full picture, there are 39 chapters in this book. But before getting to that, I'll briefly cover the perspective of the AS/400 as a computing platform and introduce some recent IBM actions that have done more harm than good to the AS/400 platform's chances for long term success.

Is It Really That Nice?

If the AS/400 were as easy to explain as it is to use, the public would already be aware of its nuances and ramifications. Knowing about the wonderful systems that came before the AS/400, from the Rochester Lab, and recognizing that the AS/400 is the follow-on to all those wonderful technologies, it is easy to surmise that with an AS/400 at the heart of your computing infrastructure, life could not be much easier. And that is very true.

Most of this first chapter has depicted the renegades at IBM Rochester as the creators and sustainers of the AS/400 product and all its System/3-like predecessors. Now it is time to move on from learning how the AS/400 came into being to understanding the many threats that must be overcome so that the AS/400 will survive.

"Can the AS/400 Survive IBM?" There is a lot buried in that little question. "Can the AS/400 survive, period" would be a much larger question. Though there may be other threats to the well-being of the AS/400 product line, such as competition from Microsoft, most AS/400 insiders and customers agree that IBM itself is the main threat to the AS/400 and its OS/400 operating system as a viable business computing platform.

She Was Only Sixteen

The AS/400 was just sixteen years old when I wrote the first version of this book. Like most adolescents, the machine depended on the good will of its parent, IBM, for its future well-being. Like any good parent, IBM decided that its three other children, just growing up at the time, the PC server,

Unix boxes, and the venerable mainframe, should be treated equally to the AS/400.

So, in 2000, IBM gave all of its servers the same surname, eServer, and changed their unique names to line up better with their new surnames. The AS/400, for example, became the eServer Power i. The mainframe became the eServer zSeries. The RS/6000 became the eServer pSeries, and the PC Server Line became the eServer xSeries.

How can one find fault with the notion that IBM is treating all of its children equally? The answer lies in the fact that the notion of parenting is an improper analogy for IBM's product lines. However, IBM seems to believe that it is a good analogy, and that is at the heart of the AS/400 survival question. No matter what IBM thinks of the AS/400 and all its products, IBM is not human and its products are not children. Its products are products. The AS/400 is a product, just like the three other series in the eServer line.

Moreover, *eServer* is not really analogous to a surname. It is more analogous to the notion of a **kingdom** in the classification of species, as in the animal and plant **kingdoms**. Just because all these IBM machines may be animals does not mean they are all the same kind of animal.

Moreover, it is an axiom in the animal kingdom that there can be just one human species. Upon inspection, one would find that the eServer xSeries (PC Server) walks on four legs and needs each of those legs to minimize reboots. A four-legger is definitely not human, so the PC Server can be summarily dismissed from the "who's best?" lottery. However, the PC Server's parent, IBM, is too fair with this "child." It's thought of as one of the kids even though it has four legs. We all know that without all four legs in operation, the PC Server clan often fails, forcing a reboot. It is not IBM's best "child," and it certainly is not as elegant and powerful as a human.

Though the pSeries and zSeries can most certainly walk on two legs, they, too, are not as capable as humans. They're powerful enough, for sure, but their "brains" are not fully developed and they do not have built-in facilities for self-management. IBM does not explain it well, but there are only four choices in its eServer line. So far, I've discussed three of the four eServers, none of which would be classified in the animal **kingdom** as human.

The AS/400 is the only system that is analogous to human. Its brain is much more developed than the other eServer systems. The others may be able to grasp things and speak in terms that sometimes are understandable, but they do not come close to the overall human-ness of the AS/400.

Despite these major differences, IBM attempts to make all IBM servers equal to the AS/400. Since the others are not human, this simply cannot work. The AS/400 is the only human-like system, no matter what IBM tries to make of its other servers.

One would think that IBM would want to highlight its most special system. Think again. IBM chooses to do no such thing. In fact, it appears that IBM is somewhat embarrassed that it is forced to admit that it owns the rights to the AS/400 and its got the most elegant, most human-like system ever invented in its product line. IBM behaves as if the company is embarrassed that its AS/400 is not as minimally capable as all of the other servers in the marketplace. In a nutshell, that's it. It is an enigma for sure. Big Blue is the problem with the AS/400. IBM just does not get it.

The First E-Business AS/400 Models

Though in 1997, Rochester seemed to find a few marketing dollars to add the "e" to the AS/400 box, making it the AS/400e, the fanfare was short lived, as corporate IBM called back the Rochester advertising dollars and it rang up its own ad campaign about magic boxes for all of the company's server lines. AS/400 customers complained about the magic box campaign burying the AS/400 in obscurity, but IBM chose not to listen. That's where the timeline shown in Figure 1-9 ends. In many ways the corporate control of advertising started much sooner than the year 2000, but by thc time the year 2000 arrived, with the new Power i, the name AS/400 disappeared from IBM's sales manual.

Figure 1-9 AS/400 Timeline System/3 to Power i

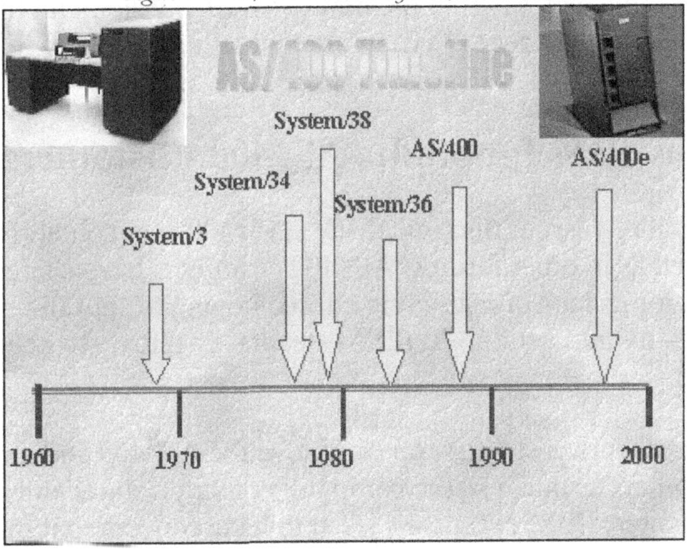

Near the end of the 1990s, IBM's RS/6000 line (Unix) and its new beefed up Netfinity line (PC Server) were competing in many cases for the same customers as the AS/400 line. Rather than further differentiate the AS/400 as the business system of choice, IBM tightened control of its advertising and its overall message so as to not cast aspersions on the other two product lines. AS/400 customers have been upset with IBM ever since, and have challenged it to "let the AS/400 go!"

Few knowledgeable industry experts would deny that the AS/400 is the finest commercial system ever built. And

AS/400 customers think IBM should advertise it as such, especially to executives, who are most often the ones making purchasing decisions.

Unfortunately, it does not appear that this will happen. Many who work with the AS/400 every day see that the old mainframe IBMers, who once tried to kill the System/38 and dismantle the Rochester labs with the Fort Knox project, are in control of IBM's advertising dollars, using their influence to weaken the status of the AS/400's future within IBM. And some may say that the new software division and the new Global Services Division are their allies.

Does IBM Ignore Its AS/400 Customers

Year after year, at the COMMON AS/400 user conference, as well as in other forums, AS/400 customers have chided IBM for its lack of marketing efforts, hoping to spur the company into action. Yet IBM steadfastly refuses to help them.

IBM executives do not appear to love the AS/400 and its customers as much as the company's other products and customers. IBM executives seem to have concern that the superiority of the AS/400 would be too obvious to the masses if the company chose to inform the public. That would raise the bar for IBM's other platforms, and would hurt its profits. It would hurt by reducing sales of IBM's other products, including PC servers, Unix servers, consulting services, and generic software.

In 1997, IBM believed that it had answered the pleas of AS/400 customers by adding the little "e" and including the AS/400e in its obscure magic box ad campaign. In those ads, however, IBM never gave the world one reason to think about an AS/400e as a viable solution for running a business, other than that it was a magic box, and that IBM made the box. The fact that IBM also had three other magic boxes (mainframe, Unix box, and PC Server) in the product line made the magic box message imprecise. The message was that IBM's got you covered, but nobody learned anything about the AS/400 from the message.

Because not all computers are equal, and the AS/400 is the best business computer ever introduced, treating the AS/400 the same as all other IBM computers buried this superior machine in a sea of uniformity and inhibited its uniqueness from being noticed. When all things are equal, price becomes the differentiator. With the AS/400 being the highest-priced box (other than a mainframe), the Unix and Windows platforms became the obvious choices among IBM's customers.

In the late 1990s and in early 2000, while IBM was pooh-poohing the lack of acceptance of the magic box campaign and its lack of marketing to its AS/400 customers, the company was simultaneously promising a great new marketing push at COMMON to its AS/400 customers. It previewed the push with the code name Mach1. This kept AS/400 customers at bay, until they found out how abysmal the Mach1 campaign would be when it was announced in October 2000. The only good thing about the campaign was that the magic box theme was gone.

IBM not only buried the AS/400 further into its server line, the company also took away its name. As noted above, IBM rebranded its entire server line as eServers. The AS/400 brand was gone. Mach1 had taken it away. There would be no more AS/400 in IBM. IBM eliminated it and buried the idea of an AS/400 under a big umbrella of "eServer." There was no longer a way of differentiating the AS/400 from the other new series members, other than the small letter in front of a series designation. The AS/400, for example, became the eServer Power i. But the AS/400 was not a mainframe. It was not a PC server, and it was not a Unix box. What was it, and what is it? IBM still has not explained.

So that Rochester would be unable to breathe some life into the AS/400 after IBM had buried it, Big Blue took the entire remaining advertising budget, minuscule as it was, from the AS/400 Lab and gave it to its new eServer group. It was a gift with nothing in return. The only eServer ads that anybody I know remembers are those that highlight PC servers and therefore benefit Bill Gates and Andy Grove (Intel founder) far more than IBM. After its inaugural splash in June 1988, the AS/400 has remained a forgotten stepchild of IBM, but in 2000, with the server division taking control of Rochester, even the lab that once kept it alive has had its means slashed by the corporation.

The reaction to the eServer announcement by IBM's AS/400 customers was predictable. They felt that IBM had betrayed them again, and Big Blue had done just that. Though IBM continues to take it on the chin from customers for its poor AS/400 marketing, there is still no movement to correct the problem. It is clear that IBM does not see its AS/400 marketing as a problem. That's just a case of poor vision.

Maybe IBM Listens

As you can see in this little history of the AS/400, IBM has enhanced the machine to make it a technology leader in many areas. However, until May 4, 2004, the company priced AS/400 hardware substantially higher than the same hardware in other systems. IBM announced the new Power5 based eServer i5. With this, the company signaled that a big part of the hardware cost premium for acquiring an AS/400 was being eliminated. With May 4th's tremendous jump in power and capability, coupled with a substantially lower price, if IBM would only let the world in on its secret machine, its stockholders such as yours truly would be able to live high on the hog again.

IBM Makes It Tough for CIOs

In their daily work, IT directors must fight Windows ads every day. The preponderance of Windows in the home has made business managers and PC people in the company biased toward Microsoft and against IBM, and especially the "legacy" AS/400. IT directors and CIOs know that an AS/400 is several times more productive and reliable than any other system, but they get sick of being the only ones telling their company that an AS/400 is worthy of its investment. They would appreciate IBM speaking up in advertisements to help vindicate them for having chosen the IBM box.

IBM says, "I hear you!" but consistently chooses not to help AS/400 loyalists. IBM's lack of help does not sit well with AS/400 professionals on the front line. As AS/400 IT directors are getting older themselves, they are more likely to give up than to spend time defending an IBM that won't speak up for itself.

IBM's lack of public advertising support for its own product paints a murky future for the AS/400 product line. Why does IBM behave so strangely? Even those who think they have the answer to this question are confused. While researching for this book, I learned that most AS/400 shops believe that if IBM knew the right thing to do for its AS/400 customers, it would do it. I do not fully share that opinion, and in this book, back it up with facts.

To come to proper conclusions about the viability of the AS/400 over the long haul, it helps to separate Rochester IBM from corporate IBM. Rochester IBM, the "Little Lab that Could" is the good guy in this picture, and corporate IBM is clearly the bad guy. The question that continues to ring with the AS/400 faithful and industry analysts is a simple one: Can the AS/400 survive IBM?

With announcements like IBM held on May 4, 2004, I am beginning to think that the company may again want the AS/400 to succeed.. And, that ladies and gentlemen, is good news for the AS/400 and for AS/400 shops. Now, if only my neighbors were told.

Chapter 2 Being There!

IBM Was a Great Company!

IBM was a great company to work for until the last few years of my career in the late 1980s and early 1990s. When rough times came, the IBM that had always been successful seemed to have no clue about how to continue to do well. In 1993, less than a year after I took a leave of absence from the company, John Akers, the IBM CEO at the time almost caused IBM to go out of business. The company's financial position became so fragile that the board of directors was left with no choice but to hire its first CEO from outside the company since 1914, Tom Watson Sr.

Ironically, Thomas Watson Jr. accompanied Louis V. Gerstner Jr., IBM's new CEO and Chairman to work on his first day. That says something about how the Watsons felt about what the successor CEOs had done with their company. Gerstner took the reins from John Akers on April 1, 1993, less than a year after I departed. I was very lucky to get into IBM, but didn't know it at the time. I was also lucky to get out of IBM on the best terms that I could have imagined for being a foot soldier in the corporation and not an officer.

Joining IBM

By the time I reached my senior year at King's College, in Wilkes-Barre, Pennsylvania, I realized that the warm fuzzies were about over and I would have to get a job. I took several interviews per week at the placement office and made a number of visits to companies I had written to. I had done reasonably well in college and had a large number of job offers, including one from IBM.

I had worked in the computing center at King's College for several years, and the IBM people that I met gave me a wonderful impression of the company and what it would be like to work there. The King's systems engineer, Tony Opalski, suggested that IBM's education in the first year alone was worth more than graduate school. I was not sure I wanted to work for IBM, since I did not know enough about many other companies. After I took my share of interviews, however, I felt more and more comfortable with giving IBM a try.

In February 1969, IBM sent a recruiter from Syracuse to King's College to conduct interviews. I signed up and eventually received an invitation to visit the IBM branch office in Utica, New York. In an apparent cost-cutting move, I was asked to contact George Mohanco, a fellow student at King's, to see if he would accompany me on the interview. No company had asked this of any of my fellow classmates. It seemed weird., but George and I took the trip

Note: On the trip to Utica, George and I completed the questionnaire to a computer dance that we were running for St. Vincent's High School in Plymouth, PA. George and I wrote a big program in 1620 Assemble Language (S.P.S.). The last bug in the program was fixed the night before the dance while George and I were at a King's College Friday night mixer. As I recall the King and Queen that the IBM 1620 selected were going steady

We met with Jim Harper, the systems engineer manager, Warren Reichlin, the branch manager, and Ken Cloud, a systems engineer. Ken took us to a number of customer accounts and showed us enough about the type of job we would be doing that George and I both decided we wanted to work for IBM. We were assured that we would soon be getting job offers as IBM systems engineers by mail, and we did.

IBM's Unbundling

Mohanco and I arrived in Utica, New York, and checked into the Travelodge Hotel. IBM was putting us up for two weeks, before our first big seven-week training school in New York City. The next day, George and I arrived on time for our first day of work. It did not take long to figure out that it was an important day in IBM history. It was June 23, 1969, the day IBM announced "unbundling."

Until now IBM had given away all services, including programming, to its customers. As long as you rented a computer from the company, you got everything else for free. On June 23, all of that changed. IBM systems engineers, who formerly provided services free of charge, were to bill customers for all time spent on customer premises and in researching customer questions in the office.

Additionally, formal classroom education, self-study guides, IBM manuals, and all other IBM services that had been provided to customers at no charge were no longer free. And they were not cheap, either. On June 23, 1969, IBM unbundled all of these services from the price of the hardware rental. Each customer received a token 3 percent rental discount and was told that by January 1, 1970, all mutually planned free services were to end. IBM would accept contracts for services from then on. The minimum rate for services was $22.00 per hour, for very basic work, to $66.00 per hour for large systems activities. In 1969, that was a lot of money.

George and I were hustled down into the Utica branch office classroom, where the meeting was conducted. There was a ton of donuts and coffee galore, so it was obvious this was going to be a long meeting. Lunch was provided, followed by more coffee. One thing I noticed immediately was that the IBM folks in this meeting were not happy with what was being announced.

Dick "Bucky" Flint was very vocal. He was the star salesman in Utica and handled all the bigger accounts. He was angry, and let management know that unbundling was not a good idea. Jerry Cybulski, Walter Cybulski's brother, was also in the meeting. Walter had graduated in data processing from King's College just a few weeks earlier with George and I, but chose not to join IBM. Several years later, the three of us would be working for IBM in Scranton, Pennsylvania.

Early IBM Training

My first assignment after the first seven-week training school was with Unit Record equipment at D'Arcangelo and Clarke, C.P.A. in Rome, N.Y. They needed some major work in order to agree to keep their rental IBM 402 accounting machine. After spending a month wiring an aged trial balance board for the company, it still was not enough to justify the machine rental, and the company canceled the unit and shipped it back to IBM. Bucky Flint was not too happy about that.

While I was at my first training class, the System/3, the predecessor of the System/38 and eventually the AS/400, was pre-announced. This was late in August 1969. None of my former IBMer friends can remember the exact date, though Ed Schmidt thinks he's got the official date pegged at September 15. He may be right. Besides unit record machines, my training was in programming languages, such as COBOL and RPG. When the System/3 was announced, it was an RPG-only machine, so I was ready to meet the challenge.

In the same IBM school where Bill Eisenhardt taught unit record concepts, Arnie Norden taught us all about the IBM 1130 and its new RPG II language. This first school was before the System/3 was available. The RPG that was announced with the System/3 was also an RPG II flavor. Just like new and improved Tide, it was obvious to all of us that the "II" after RPG meant that it was new and improved. When I came back to the branch office in between schools, I was writing RPG programs and wiring unit-record IBM 402 accounting machine boards.

Off to Scranton

I was in Utica for two years when I had a chance at a position in Scranton, PA. I had had enough of 10 months of snow each year and living in motels. I applied for a position at Marywood University, close to my hometown of Wilkes-Barre. Marywood offered me a job as a data processing manager at its campus just outside Scranton. I was 23 years old and ready to leave IBM to come home. Rather than accept the job immediately, however, I brought it to the attention of my IBM manager, Jim Harper, who asked if I would prefer to work for IBM in Scranton. Since I had a formal request for transfer on file, I knew that he knew what I wanted. Within a few days I interviewed in Scranton, and in a few months I was working for the IBM Scranton branch office.

There is an old saying about Scranton that goes back to the Vaudeville days. Players from New York would say, "If you could play Scranton, you could play anywhere." They probably had never played Utica. Though I had met a lot of wonderful people in my two years, I was glad that my playing days in Utica and Ogdensburg were behind me. Ironically, my first account as a systems engineer in Scranton was Marywood College. (The school had yet to apply for university status.) The Sisters accepted my declining their wonderful job offer graciously and welcomed me as their assigned IBM systems engineer.

For 21 years, until the end of May 1992, I worked for IBM in Scranton as a systems engineer. At that time, I took advantage of the IBM Individual Transition II offering, giving me a leave of absence from IBM, which led to a no-penalty retirement. During the leave, IBM paid all my benefits. The company also gave me a wad of money at the outset. In 1999, as part of the leave agreement, I formally retired from IBM, and now IBM obligingly drops a retirement check into my bank account every month.

Post-IBM

Upon leaving IBM, I accepted a position as a consultant at a local college and began a private consulting and education practice. I have also traveled the country, mostly in the Northeast, to teach classes that I design, and have performed various consulting activities for a number of clients.

Since leaving IBM, I have had the pleasure of writing the first book on AS/400 Data Warehousing (1996) and the first book on the AS/400 and the Internet (1997). I am both a student of computers and a teacher of computer technology. For many years, I have been a featured speaker at COMMON conference, the major users group for IBM midrange computers, and have presented at IBM and industry seminars on advanced AS/400 topics such as queuing theory, data warehousing, and the use of the AS/400 on the Internet.

Before restarting this book again in the fall of 2003, I completed my ninth technical book on the AS/400 for Lets Go Publish, a company that I kicked off in 2002, along with my partner, Joe McDonald. I continue to maintain my technical competency through reading, seminars, conferences, and hands-on work. This is the 21st book that I have written. I can assure you there are a few paragraphs in a number of prior books in which I tell IBM what I think it needs to do to make the AS/400 a continued success. I have also shared my thoughts with many IBM managers over the years. I hope that one day IBM will listen.

From my first experience with a System/3, at the A. Barton Hepburn Hospital in Ogdensburg, New York, where Carolyn Skelley, the self-proclaimed "shade provider" served as business manager, to my current role as Power i technical advisor to the IT faculty at Marywood University, I have always been an IBM midrange computer advocate and a specialist in the technology. In 1988, at Marywood University, my love affair with the AS/400 product began. I had the pleasure of presenting IBM's new AS/400 to a crowd of well over 300 people in Marywood's beautiful Center for the Performing Arts, and I have supported the AS/400 ever since to IBM customers, and now as a consultant and educator in my own business.

I am convinced that the AS/400 is the finest computing machine that any company has ever built. Over the years, I worked with hundreds of companies on many machines. I have most often assisted IBM's midrange customers in installing new AS/400s or System/38s from scratch or by helping them migrate their existing machines to AS/400 technology. There is nothing like an AS/400.

Max Miller Pilots AS/400

During this time, I have never met an AS/400 customer who did not fall in love with his machine. One customer in particular, Max Miller, from Bloomsburg Mills in Bloomsburg, PA,: was amazed by the power and facility of the system. I helped Max convert from a System/3 to a System/38. Max was a Navy pilot during the Korean War and was accustomed to high tech in the form of jet machinery. Several months after going live on the System/38, Max bought me a machine-brewed coffee on one of my regular visits, and he shared with me his awe for the System/38 in these words: "This machine still humbles me." The machine humbled a lifetime pilot and computer specialist. He added that he had never seen a machine that was so powerful, yet he did not have to understand it all to make it run well. Max is not alone in his awe for the System/38, the AS/400, and now the Power i.

AS/400: Work Less, Get More Done

The AS/400 helps IBM's midrange customers to get their jobs done as quickly and as productively as possible, with little breakage. AS/400 customers are loyal to the AS/400 because they know there is no better business tool. They do not want anything to impede their ability to continue using an AS/400 to solve the business issues of the day. They do not see an advantage to working harder to get less done than they can with their AS/400.

Because of this, they are wary at what they see coming from IBM. In fact, as IBM becomes more and more of a services company, many fear the company will either change the AS/400 so that it is no longer relevant or abandon the AS/400 altogether.

They are very concerned right now about their choice of an AS/400 as a platform upon which their businesses can depend. They perceive a threat that becomes more and more real year after year. As difficult as it may be to believe, the threat comes from IBM itself, not from its competition. IBM's indifference and lack of effort in promoting the AS/400 product line gives them an uneasy feeling about the future of the machine they use to run their businesses. IBM treats the AS/400 product like a stepchild that it would just as soon have go away. There are many reasons why IBM's actions and inactions are threatening the AS/400's ability to survive as a viable computer system. But what's puzzling is that IBM behaves as if it does not care.

Getting IBM on the Stick

IBM is a stubborn company, staunch in its own righteousness. Yet I do have a small hope that if IBM executives read this book as a self-analysis, such as the "Man in the Glass," they may conclude that the company should do more with the system, and in so doing, help itself in the process.

I also have hope that IBM stockholders who really know very little about IBM's product line will better understand the opportunities that IBM squanders on a daily basis by not supporting the most advanced technology of any of its computers, including mainframes. Finally, there is an active computer trade press out there, who may pick up on the theme. Though they have no reason to particularly love IBM or the AS/400, some little guy like me picking on big IBM makes for a good story. I hope to give them enough information so that the trade press can prod IBM into doing the right thing, for the company, its customers, its stockholders, and for the AS/400 product line. There is always hope, but there is not unlimited time. While IBM sleeps, Bill Gates has insomnia.

This book, then, is about the AS/400, how it came to be, IBM's reaction to the product, and whether the AS/400 has a chance of survival. For 23 years inside IBM and 11 outside, I lived through what is in this book. Even while with IBM, I was not sitting back, quietly watching what was happening. I spoke up as needed and submitted many suggestions to the company about ways to improve. IBM actually paid me for a number of the suggestions that I made. After I left the company, I stayed active with the product. I wrote a number of articles and was a constant in the feedback areas to keep the awareness of the AS/400 at peak and to prod IBM to do what it should to keep this special machine successful.

My role in this book is as a keen observer, a reporter, an analyst, and to some extent a concerned complainer. As you read this book, you will be introduced to a lot of substance about IBM as a company, the AS/400 as an IBM product, and the viability of the AS/400 as an IBM product. Can the AS/400 product line survive the lack of care and feeding from its parent, IBM? That is the very question tackled in this book

This chapter began with a little background on the author. The reason I introduce myself to you is that the story is told from my eyes. I am an active player in the computer industry and have much experience with the AS/400 and its introduction as a product. Because I serve as a consultant in the AS/400 marketplace, I also have a big stake in its success. I want every AS/400 story to be positive. If we can convince IBM that the system is worthwhile, perhaps Big Blue can make AS/400 technology shine and become recognized as the best in the industry.

Where the Rubber Meets the Road

Most of the stories and perspectives that I share in this book are original, while some may have been told before by somebody else--but not from the same perspective. For example, nobody knows about the IBM and AS/400 internal decision-making process better than Dr. Frank Soltis, the AS/400 Chief Scientist and the major architect of the system when it was conceived in the early 1970s. To tell his story from inside the lab at IBM, Dr. Frank wrote two books. My story does not come from inside the labs of IBM, however. It comes from where the rubber meets the road. It comes from where IBM meets its customers.

I spent my career working with IBM's AS/400 customers, so my perspective comes from meeting the customers and selling IBM systems. I'll highlight the things that IBM is doing right and present very definite ideas about many things I think the company is doing wrong. Moreover, I'll explain how the company strangely repeats its mistakes with impunity while the IBM board does not seem to notice. Finally, I will offer suggestions about what IBM needs to do to be right with itself and its customers, and to be right with its most elegant product line, the AS/400.

Every day for 35 years, I have worked with IBM's small and midsized business customers, who depend on IBM to do the right thing. Today, most of these loyal IBM customers think that IBM's game plan does not include them. From my observations, I think they are right. I too am waiting for IBM to tell us to stand up and be counted. Once you finish reading this book, you may feel more like we do, and you, too, may have a hard time understanding why IBM management doesn't make it better..

During my career at IBM, I was in the company of the best of IBM's best--from the chairman to the parking lot attendant--in various settings. The people I met were very special and very capable. I see myself as ordinary, compared with many in IBM I have come to admire.

While at IBM, I found myself displeased with a number of decisions that I observed, and I would challenged the decisions of upper management, both informally, in peer meetings, and formally by speaking up using IBM's "open door policy" or the company's internal "Speak Up!" forum.. I can recall being reprimanded by local management for responding truthfully to questions asked by distinguished IBM visitors in meeting forums. Unlike many IBM folks who learned that this could be damaging to one's career, I did what I thought was best, and sometimes I paid the price. Thankfully, local managers turn over every two years in IBM posts like Scranton. Besides those managers who were not so good, I had the opportunity to work for a number of fine managers who permitted wild ducks to operate with just a few restrictions.

I have learned that IBM does not always know what is right for its customers. Moreover, in IBM's toughest times, I learned that the managers are concerned first about their personal careers, then IBM, then the customer, and then the employees. The IBM playbook is not written that way, but it was not until the early 1990s that IBM ran into tough times. Nobody in the company was prepared to deal with adversity. When pressed, I have seen IBM too often choose not to do what is right for its customers, for policy reasons or for the good of IBM or its management team. That is what is wrong with the AS/400. IBM executives have stopped doing what is right for the AS/400 customer base for reasons that they have not fully explained.

The AS/400 Name Is on the Way Out

Since October 2000, when the company changed its name to the Power i, one could argue that there is no longer an AS/400, and that it has not survived. The phenomenon of the renaming to eServer Power i 400 is covered in detail in Chapter 17, "The Rebranding of the AS/400 as the Power i." Most of this book was written while IBM referre to its AS/400 models as the Power i before the company changed its name again on May 4, 2004. The AS/400 is now known in IBM's sales amterial st the eServer i5. At the time of this writing not much has been reported about customer reaction to the new name. It may still be an AS/400 world.

The AS/400 and the Power i both use the same operating system, Operating System/400 (OS/400). However, with the introduction of the i5, the operating system also was rechristened to i5/OS. Whether the OS is called i5/OS or OS/400, it is such an important point that is noted throughout the book. It is the one factor that differentiates the AS/400 hardware machine from all other computers. So, in this book, when we say AS/400, it is because that is what AS/400 customers call the machine, regardless of what IBM calls it. Additionally, the AS/400 is the machine that runs the OS/400 operating system or i5/OS and not Windows.

The Perfect Company

One of my IBM friends gave me some top-secret counsel about my book well into the production cycle. This person was very concerned about all the issues that I had presented and wanted me to know that there is a lot of good in IBM. Part of the note follows: Of course the names are omitted to protect the innocent

> **Note; But for the record.... in general this is the finest company I have ever worked for. (I worked for other LARGE companies ...prior to IBM) because of the integrity and the goodness that is in the hearts of the majority of the IBMers... and THAT is a very big deal for me. So I don't mind the frustrations of them making mistakes because of our size and scope.... and with the help of wonderful partners and customers like ... and ... maybe we can all make it better.**

Of course, my objective for this book is to help make it better, not to just grumble about how it is. No, IBM is not the company that it was in the 1960's and 1970's, and maybe it can't be. In many ways that was a perfect company. The new IBM is not a perfect company. It's certainly not a bad company either. In fact, overall it is a fine company. I sure hope that IBM will use the information and opinions in this book to make IBM and the AS/400 even better. I would love to see the company that makes the perfect machine again become the perfect company. Never say never.

The Perfect Machine

One of my industry friends did me a few favors as I was fine-tuning this book for its big release. He told me that my biggest problem from his eyes as seen by reading this book, is that I think the AS/400 is a perfect machine. He said, from his perspective, the System/38 was as close to perfect as any machine has ever come. He does not think that the AS/400 is quite as perfect as the System/38 with its pure function and simple elegance.

Maybe he is right. I do think the AS/400 is a perfect machine. I'll correct myself on that. I think it is as close to perfect as a machine can get. You'll see in this book that there are some things that I think IBM needs to do to improve the AS/400's competitive position and there are some things of which I am aware that were implemented too hastily and perhaps still are not perfect with this offering. However, that being said, there is no machine in existence, from my experience, that completes as many error free productive machine cycles that real computer users can depend on as an AS/400.

It may not do spinning globes and dancing bears as good as some toy computers out there, but if you want a machine on which to run your business, you can stop your search. Just like Ivory Soap, the AS/400 may not be 100% pure, but it's far closer than anything else I have ever seen, and I am encouraged to think that it will only get better… as IBM permits that to happen.

Introduce the Neighbors

This book is dedicated to my neighbors, who are all successful business people. Looking out my front door, on my right, is the home of Simon Coblentz, a recently retired owner of the Coblentz Store in Berwick, Pennsylvania. On my left is Mercedes Leighton, a retired Wilkes-Barre City Controller. Across the street on the left are Jeanne and Joseph Elinsky, owners of Roscoe Advertising and Noble Furniture. Directly across the street are Carol and John Anstett, who have a real estate brokerage firm. Across the street on the right are Doctors Dwaraki Bai, a children's specialist, and Haragopal Penugonda, a urologist.

They are fine neighbors who have no idea what an AS/400 is. Yet they are representative of the small business community who own businesses and sit on the boards that make decisions about IBM products. They would only know an AS/400 if they owned one or heard IBM making a big fuss about one on TV.

If one day my neighbors come to hear about an AS/400 machine from IBM, I will know IBM has gotten the message carried in this book. If that day ever comes, IBM will have made the right turn and the AS/400 will prosper.

At the end of this book, after 39 chapters of facts and anecdotes about IBM and its AS/400 product line, you will be well qualified to form your own opinion about whether IBM's approach is proper for its AS/400 product line. In order to get to that point, you will pass briskly through many interesting chapters.

Chapter 3 Who's on First?

The Best Computer Ever

The AS/400 is the best and the most special computer ever built. That is why it is inconceivable that the company that owns the rights to the machine does not seem to try to earn a huge profit from it. For you music lovers out there, it may help to know that the AS/400 is to computers what Bose is to great sound. Bring on the music.

As the direct descendent of the System/38, the AS/400 is even more wonderful. The older System/38 line was not as well endowed performance-wise. In fact, it suffered from capacity constraints imposed by IBM's own mainframe division. However, it was built with the same advanced architecture, and thus, by design, is the same high tech machine as the AS/400. Therefore, I would argue that the AS/400 and the System/38 are singularly the finest computers that any company has ever made.

AS/400 Becomes eServer Power i

In the fall of 2000, as noted in Chapter 2, IBM changed the name of the AS/400 to the eServer Power i 400. Many who earn their livelihoods from AS/400-related work have chosen to recognize the Power i not as a different computer but a branding change. That change, unfortunately, has done more to hurt the prospects of attracting more computer users to the AS/400 platform than to help it. The corporate rumor mill suggests that a new name may be in order for the platform in the near future. That would be a good idea. Hopefully, the corporate "namers" will buy a few thinking caps before they try again.

Tell Somebody!

IBM's legions of AS/400 customers have been crying out to the company for some help in giving the AS/400 product line some name recognition among regular people. They are not happy having to do IBM's marketing job in their own IT shops. Having to continually justify the AS/400 as being more capable than Windows and Unix is a tiring chore.

IBM has reacted indifferently to its customers' plea for help, and the rebranding is a major manifestation of that lack of concern. When IBM placed the eServer brand on each of its four server lines, it made the AS/400 appear as merely another horse in IBM's eServer stable. The new branding message is that the AS/400 (Power i) is no better and no worse than any of IBM's other horses. But that is not true! Nothing in the branding or the message gives a prospective new computer an idea about whether the box is a packhorse, a thoroughbred, a workhorse, a show horse, a mule, or a plain old jackass.

Anyone who takes the time to look would see a machine that is the embodiment of all that IBM knows about computers, implemented with an elegance unparalleled in the computing era. The reason why IBM chooses to downplay its finest system is an enigma. The fact that IBM minimizes the system, however, is indisputable.

Only IBM Could Create an AS/400

Only a big company with such huge resources as IBM could have conceived, designed, and built such an elegant machine. For this, I must thank the IBM Corporation. But the thanking ends at the moment of its birth. The record shows that the AS/400 has narrowly escaped death a number of times from the hand of its very creator, IBM.

> **"....the only thing I can say about IBM and the AS/400 is that it never would have been built without IBM ...no one could have afforded to build the S/38 and subsequently the 400. Granted it will never get its due from IBM because of the "eating your children" scenario...even now it would not survive without IBM technology behind it. It is stuck in a "hardware neutral world" with ever increasing "software neutral" components... ...UDB, SQL, TCP, Unix, SAP, Lotus etc...it will lose its uniqueness...It already has in hardware ... fortunately, I have my retirement and all I need is for the AS/400 to remain viable for the next 2 years and then for all I care it can disappear...."**

That says something, doesn't it?

Credit for each word above is given to George Mohanco, who, like myself, began his IBM career on June 23, 1969, the day IBM announced "unbundling." And, like myself, when given the opportunity to leave IBM, protect his pension, get a nice financial send-off, and pursue another career, he took the first train out, in 1992. George retired from the Pensacola, Florida, branch office when it existed in the early 1990s. And, like myself, on July 1, 1999, George finally began to collect from the IBM "eagle" each month, and we both expect this to last for quite a while, until we reach that place above, where we expect to find the AS/400 in charge of all operations, and to see some confused former IBM executive wondering why he hadn't thought of that while he was still on earth.

IBM Has the Server Bases Covered

What a blessing IBM has today! It has all the computing bases covered. When you consider that Microsoft has just a piece (though a reasonably large piece) of just one base, PC software, you can readily conclude that IBM has the armaments that should power it to victory in the computer marketplace. Unfortunately, it does not have the keen Microsoft marketing generals leading it in battle, and IBM has so many rules of engagement that it gets itself tangled up all the time in a mess of its own creation.

First Base -- Mainframe

In the traditional mainframe system arena, IBM's leadership in commercial hardware technology is unquestioned. Mainframes are the types of computers that General Motors and Chase Manhattan and Prudential Insurance and other large companies use as their main processors to run their businesses. IBM's System/390 product set (now called the zSeries) competes against relatively few. The players in the large mainframe and supercomputer marketplace include Fujitsu, Hitachi, Cray, and not many others. In this period of resurgence for the power of mainframe computing, IBM is doing very well for itself. For sure, you can get to *first base* with a zSeries.

Second Base – PC Servers

In the personal/micro/X86 space, IBM has *second base* well covered with its industry-heralded ThinkPads, its appealing and inexpensive ThinkCentres, its NetVista line, and its high-function, high-speed Netfinity Servers (now called eServer xSeries.) The xSeries servers compete head on with all PC Network servers running Windows NT, Linux, Netware, and OS/2 LAN Server. Most of IBM's success in this space is shared with Microsoft and Intel, who provide the bulk of the software and processor hardware in this system area. However, today, there is no question that IBM has very formidable offerings in this area.

Third Base – The Unix Box

In the multi-user and workstation Unix spot, IBM is well positioned on *third base* with a rugged "taken no prisoners" submission. It has developed a mature offering with its RS/6000 hardware (now called eServer pSeries) and its highly stable Advanced Interactive Executive. Dubbed AIX by IBM, this is the company's Unix operating system offering. If you want to buy Unix from IBM, you would buy its AIX offering.

Efforts to move the Linux operating system to the pSeries only strengthen the product line in the Unix marketing space. The eServer pSeries offers AS/400-level hardware facilities to system customers who prefer the personality and the unique applications of a Unix machine.

Home Run – AS/400

In the business solutions spot, IBM has hit a home run with its AS/400 (eServer Power i) product line as it stands on home base as the obvious winner. Its biggest problem is that since the work an AS/400 does so nicely can also be performed on the other three bases, though with far greater difficulty, IBM has a problem in understanding where the AS/400 box actually belongs in its product mix. The company also has a problem making its purpose for the AS/400 clear to its IBM computer prospect list. Unless one already knew, it would be hard to tell from what comes from IBM these days. Other than the silly name they gave to such a phenomenal offering, IBM is well positioned on home plate for the big score of the millennium. But it has to want it.

It's the Revenue Sam?

As you look at all the bases, for each server sold, it might help to speculate how much money IBM takes in, component wise, when it sells a particular server model. Of course, the server choice all depends on which base the prospect winds up on when it enters the IBM ballpark.

Mainframe - zSeries

If a mainframe is sold, there is little question that IBM is happy, for more reasons than the millions in revenue that come with each mainframe. That's because IBM gets most of the money. The company gets paid for the hardware and the peripheral equipment. It gets paid for the operating system, the database, the transaction processor and all of the expensive software that is required to run a mainframe. Microsoft and Intel get none. Color me with a happy face.

PC Server - xSeries

For each IBM PC sold--xSeries or otherwise--Intel gets the booty for the processor and perhaps even the motherboard. Dell or some other assembler gets the money for the frame and the assembly work. Microsoft gets the money for the operating system and the productivity applications. Is it no wonder why this business is not profitable for IBM? Yet the company keeps pushing PCs as if it is. Of course, IBM gets no revenue if the customer buys from Dell or another vendor. This is the case 19 times out of 20. Color me with a sad face.

Unix Box - pSeries

For each RS/6000 (Unix Box - pSeries) sold, at the same capacity as an AS/400, IBM gets the hardware dollars, but not as much as if it really were an AS/400. After all, other than the controller cards that take care of the disks, etc., the system is so identical to the AS/400 that you might even call it an AS/400 box. In fact, for the last few years the pSeries has been made in Rochester, on the same assembly line as the AS/400. However, there is no IBM-built operating system. Instead, IBM uses the Unix operating system with its own brand, Advanced Interactive eXecutive (AIX), to power the box. Linux is also supported on the RS/6000, or as IBM now calls it, the pSeries.

Once you put AIX or Linux on one of these boxes, the rest of the software revenue is up for grabs. In other words, the dollars do not necessarily flow into IBM's coffers. Oracle, for example, steals database revenue from IBM. Tuxedo steals transaction-processing revenue, and a host of other software vendors are on call when they see IBM selling a Unix box.

Once Unix or Linux goes on the machine, IBM cannot be sure that it is going to get the rest of the loot. Let's face it, the way IBM markets its products today, depending on the benevolence of its distribution channel, and the willingness of the customer to accept an all-IBM solution, you can bet that Big Blue does not get much of the spoils. Color me not sure: sad, but less sad than Wintel.

AS/400 Business Machine - Power i

If an AS/400 is sold, there is no question who gets the revenue. Just about every penny--from the hardware to the database software to the transaction processors to the communications support--comes IBM's way because it is built into the price of the system. Because the AS/400 provides all of this as part of an integrated architecture, the customer pays up-front when buying the machine itself.

Though IBM should be happy, often it is not, because there is a secret society in the company that apparently does not want the AS/400 to succeed. Over the years, it has done its best to get in the way when the AS/400 was doing "too well." The mainframe heritage managers are not happy because Rochester tricked its way into selling computers, and the Systems Products Division, the manufacturing arm of mainframe IBM, had previously built all of IBM's computers in Endicott and Poughkeepsie.

If, say, a reasonable, prudent person were placed in charge of IBM, he would be more than happy when an AS/400 sold. Other than parts that IBM chooses not to make anymore, the AS/400 is all IBM, just like the mainframe. When an AS/400 is sold, IBM makes real money. Color me happy, yet agitated by IBM's lack of staying power.

Lineup Should Be Highlighted

How can it be that with such an all-star lineup, with all the bases covered, IBM is struggling with brand recognition? It is because IBM looks like it doesn't know what it should do next. IBM's AS/400 customers tell the company executives loudly and clearly: "It's the marketing, IBM." There is nothing wrong with the AS/400 that a good marketer such as Bill Gates or Michael Dell would not be able to solve post haste. IBM's marketing is clearly the problem with AS/400 sales.

Surely, if HP, Dell, Sun, Microsoft, or any other computer and operating system vendor had the all-star system lineup that IBM has in its front line, well positioned on each base, it would not try to homogenize all of them into a big blurry blob on the infield. These companies would help their ticket holders (customers) understand all of the players on their relative merits, and they would sell all four solutions. They would thank their God for their blessings every day on the way to the bank. Lots of people would come to the ballpark to see the AS/400 play if somebody told them that it was going to get in the game that day. For some reason, IBM seems to look at having everything that everybody else wants as a big marketing problem.

Chapter 4 System/3 to System/38 to AS/400

Protect the Mainframe

Because of major internal pressures, with the System/3 onward, the Rochester Lab had to struggle to get its computer products out the door. Having worked for the same IBM, I am reminded of my own experience working for this wonderful company, founded by great and honorable people. It is too bad that the Watsons had to turn IBM's business over to lesser souls.

As successful as IBM Rochester was with its System/3 line, IBM would not permit the Rochester Lab to design and build its System/3 successor product constraint-free. In the mid-1970s, small and midsized businesses were pleading with IBM to give them a bigger and more powerful and much better System/3. There was little interest from this group of customers in becoming small mainframe customers. They liked the notion of ease-of-use that came with the System/3 line.

Knowing full well that Rochester needed a follow-on product that was several times faster and promised more growth over time than the System/3, IBM still placed major performance and capacity constraints on the new system. It was obvious that IBM's mainframe division was paranoid that the small systems in Rochester would one day take down the mainframe. Rochester was therefore expressly prohibited from building a system that could in any way make a mainframe look like a lesser system.

To Dream the Impossible Dream

In the spirit of "The Little Engine That Could," a children's book that teaches the power of a positive attitude, Rochester was always "the little lab that could." It took nothing less than a yeoman job to overcome the corporate constraints and ultimately succeed in building the most advanced computer ever built. Looking back, it was next to impossible to create a system that was as architecturally elegant as the System/38, given the performance and capacity constraints imposed by the mainframe-biased IBM executive team. The machine as prescribed by the mother ship would be nothing more than a performance dog.

Before the Rochester designers and engineers had their pens out of their pocket protectors, IBM had given them a seemingly impossible task. The bad blood between Rochester and the rest of the corporation was so intense that the mainframe management team did not care if Rochester completed its project successfully. If Rochester failed, the mainframe division would get tapped for building the next small business machine, and that would not be all that bad from its perspective. To certain IBM players, the possibility of Rochester's influence in computers being minimized would be a major advantage of a failure to produce a follow-on product.

Mainframe-Imposed Constraints

The more risky side for mainframe-centric IBM would be if the project were successful. That's why all the constraints were necessary. The last thing that mainframe IBM needed was a system to be developed that was better and faster and cheaper and had more capacity than a mainframe. By keeping the constraints in place, Rochester could not build something outside of the governor specs without its management suffering severe repercussions from within the corporation.

IBM was making it difficult for Rochester right from the beginning of the Pacific (System/38) project. The IBM management team had a mainframe perspective, and thus was not at all pleased with Rochester building IBM computers, period. The purpose of the performance and capacity constraints was to ensure that the new system would not be a threat to the small mainframe systems that the mainframe division had begun to build. Mainframe IBM was poaching on the territory of "the little lab that could," hoping to grab the same customers for which the System/38 was intended.

Somebody living outside of the cold and bright days in Rochester, with something else to do with his life, would have just given up. A reasonable person might have concluded that the superior specifications of the Future Systems Project (Chapter 13) could not be built within the hardware constraints that had been imposed on the Rochester Lab.

The Biggest Spoof of All

However, the often snow-bound Rochester planners and engineers were very clever. They devised ways to permit the System/38 operating system to believe that it would be running on hardware that was substantially bigger and better than what IBM would permit it to build. In other words, Rochester built low-level software to spoof the rest of its software into thinking that the hardware was much more capable than it actually was permitted to be. In so doing, they also spoofed IBM into thinking they were building just another toy system.

Not only did Rochester practice chicanery in scamming IBM to be able to build the original System/3, but it also used its clandestine expertise to fake out the System/38 into thinking it was something that it was not. The word ingenious fits in there someplace. It was a marvelous hoax.

Over 30 years ago, as the System/38 was being conceived, IBM's AS/400 Chief Scientist, Dr. Frank Soltis, then working in IBM's Rochester Laboratory, provided the underlying computer science expertise for many of the advanced notions incorporated into the System/38 machine. Through a process called hardware abstraction, Soltis, along with the Rochester scientists, engineers, and developers, were able to free the operating system from depending on the actual hardware of the machine. That's what is meant by spoofing. (This notion is described in more detail in Chapter 6.)

The System/38 was a remarkable achievement on many fronts. A little lab in Rochester, under duress, defined a system with a more powerful architecture than any IBM system ever built. In addition to their own skull power, they benefited from the abandoned Future System project (Chapter 13) that was supposed to provide the specifications for the mainframe to beat all mainframes. In October 1978, Rochester felt that its Pacific Project work was close enough, since its new hardware was all finished, and the new machine actually IPLed. (IPL stands for initial program load, and that's like Microsoft saying "boot.") So they announced the IBM System/38, with first deliveries scheduled in mid-1979 (Chapter 1).

Could Not Deliver

Though IBM had promised its customers a 1979 delivery, it was not going to happen. The System/38 was buggy, unstable, and slow. Though I had never seen a Microsoft product at the time, the System/38 behaved in many ways like some of the early Windows machines that I used back in the late 1980s and early 1990s. It was not ready for prime time.

I got the call to ship out to Rochester in January 1980, over a year after IBM had told the world that the AS/400 would not be delivered in 1979. After a few moments on the machine, I saw why IBM had to delay the system: "Function Check!" The system that I worked on would continually blow up with these messages. The function check was the System/38's unfriendly error message. When it had no clue what to do next, it gave the function check message.

For a machine that was supposed to be advanced and user-friendly, the function check was an intimidating message to receive. What did I do? Many of the function checks were so severe that they brought the whole operating system to a Microsoft-like grinding hang. They forced an IPL. As noted previously, an IPL is called rebooting in Redmond, Washington. In Microsoft terms, rebooting the system took about a half hour, and in my first experience, there were not many moments between the function checks. With each new operating system build that the lab produced, however, the function checks and hangs appeared less frequently. In just a few weeks, I could see that progress was being made.

Rochester had taken much of the good from the FS project (IBM's Future Systems "FS" Project – fully explained in Chapter 13) and had developed its own-patented algorithms to achieve many of the defined advanced functions. With all this computer know-how and hard work, the Little Lab That Could deserved success with the last part of the Pacific Project. However, Rochester had never taken on an impossible project before. Obviously, when it let IBM announce the System/38, it did not realize it was impossible. But it takes just so many operating system crashes before a "little lab" has burned out of ideas.

The System/38 put a big black mark on IBM that it had not seen since the System/360 had to be delayed. The corporation was not going to get smudged again by the System/38. Like it or not, in 1979, any person who could program and withstand the rigors of a four-drop flight to Rochester got to see most of the seasons there that year. Though the Rochester stalwarts might even suggest that the newbies got in the way, IBM ensured that the System.38 was going to live, rather than bear the embarrassment of a premature death.

In the summer of 1980, I received my formal IBM systems engineer training in Philadelphia by the pioneering masters, Skip Marchesani, Don Wickham, and Paul Lambert. Skip is a long-time friend and is still very active in AS/400 circles, and I have not seen Don since the Philadelphia days. I talk to Paul every few years. Though no longer with IBM, he is still teaching AS/400 topics in on-site classes on demand. By the summer of 1980, when my local office got its own test System/38, we were not seeing as many function checks, but there were just enough to cause some chagrin among the ranks.

The Sinking Flagship

One of my systems engineer cohorts from Baltimore captured the feeling about function checks in a training lab while I was in Philadelphia for this in-depth System/38 training. He had written a snappy little program in RPG that was very clever, and the story it told hit us between the eyes. He defined a screen panel and drew a ship with a flag saying “S/38” waving above. It was the System/38 flagship. It was a neat-looking screen panel. Of course, the wave and the waving were simulated with slashes and blob characters, since none of us were good enough at that time to program the ship to move. Or so I thought.

The panel invited the terminal operator to position the cursor on the ship to see if he could blow it out of the water. Of course, I had to give it a shot. Position and press--boom! When response time was good, the next scene would happen immediately. It showed the same water, but where the ship had been, there was just the little flag with "S/38" written on it. The message was clear. The flagship had sunk. All shots sunk the ship! We all soon learned that no matter where we aimed, the flagship would sink. Again, it was very revealing and somewhat chilling. Before those emotions set in, however, there were many belly laughs.

The System/38 Has Left the Building

By August 1980, we received our own System/38 in the Scranton branch office. We had a number of clients who had the boxes on order. After we got the operating system installed (it was not preloaded in the beginning), we began to bring in real customers, with their real programs, to see if we could get them to run on the new machine, the System/38.

On a happy day in November 1980, in Scranton, three IBM customers received the first System/38 shipments from IBM on the very same day. Miraculously, all systems were ready at the exact same moment. Marywood University, The Scranton Times, and St. Joseph's Hospital were installed at the same second of the same day in November 1980. To this day, they all brag that they were first. None of us in the Scranton office would ever tell them any differently.

Some Had to Make Do

Some customers were not lucky enough to be early in the queue, even if they needed the box desperately. One of my clients, for example, Kay Wholesale, ran out of gas on its Sytem/3 Model 15D, the biggest Rochester machine that IBM could make in 1979. The 15D was not cutting it. The local office had convinced the IT manager at the time, Al Komorek, a very savvy programmer and DP manager, that he could not wait for the delayed System/38. The company moved its online order entry to a System/34 and transferred completed orders to the 15D over communication lines (no LAN) for invoice, accounts receivable, and inventory control processing. This trick kept them alive while waiting for the System/38.

Because of continuing constraints from the mainframe division, IBM did not grow the System/38 fast enough to stay in front of many of its customers whose applications and businesses were growing. The mainframe influence kept the specifications down lower than the lowest mainframe box, and for the same machine instruction, small customers paid about twice the rate of larger customers. When emerging businesses, such as Kay Wholesale, grew from $7 million to $400 million, they did not want to rewrite their programs, so they did not want to move to the mainframe, no matter how big it could get. Additionally, they did not want to go from several to 20 or 30 IT people on staff just to support a mainframe. By imposing these artificial hardware constraints, IBM gained little and lost a lot of confidence from its emerging large customers at a time when these customers needed IBM the most.

No New Accounts Solves the Problem

In recent years, IBM has solved the problem of new customers growing too rapidly by not getting any of the new business that is available. Ironically, now that AS/400s are the size of mainframes, and the AS/400 name is gone, IBM has no marketing vehicle in place to capture new companies that might ever grow that large.

Elegance with Missing Pieces

For eight years in the midrange, the System/38 was El Supremo. The biggest problem, as noted in the stories above, was that it did not grow fast enough for its customers. There were a few other intentional inadequacies built into the machine to impede its ability to be the system of choice in certain circumstances. For example, IBM refused to give the system a number of capabilities that reasonable people expected to find on a business machine of its era. These included cheap ASCII terminal support, Structured Query Language (SQL), Ethernet, and Token-Ring LAN support. If a customer needed any of these, IBM could not propose a System/38 as a solution. The mainframe division, however, had all these facilities and stood ready whenever a customer crumb fell off the System/38 table.

System/38--Unloved by IBM

In the early to mid 1980s, the System/38 was doing well from a functional standpoint, but the spoofing was over. Corporate IBM knew it was a computer, and knew it represented trouble for mainframes. If you were a systems engineer working with small businesses that used System/34s, System/36s, or System/38s at this time in IBM history, the handwriting was becoming clear. Systems engineers were encouraged to increase their skills to not be left out in the cold when advanced technology was introduced that would replace the System/3X line. A number of field technicians jumped ship and joined the mainframe division to ensure a living and to feed their families.

By the mid-1980s, some systems engineers had become reasonably good at working with System/38 relational databases, and IBM needed DB2 (corporate relational database) expertise in the mainframe arena. In a personal survival move, I took the bait and went through the full complement of DB2 for MVS (mainframe) courses. I can still recall Dick Morris from Leslie Fay and Big Ed Godleski from Harper and Rowe staring at the DB2/MVS demo as if they had wanted DB2 all along. Dick Morris went so far as to tell me that he had defined relational database as a solution for Leslie Fay long ago, perhaps even before the late Tedd Codd (its inventor) had even thought about it.

It kept me going. I knew I would not get fired if I knew something that was needed by the mainframe division. The word inside IBM was that the System/38 was going to go, and possibly the other small systems. After I was DB/2 trained, things actually got better for the System/38 and for systems engineers of small systems. The word came down that the System/38 elimination project had fallen through and that Rochester had gotten the okay to replace the System/38 with a machine that could run both System/36 programs and System/38 programs. When that day came, in June 1988, and the AS/400 was revealed, I tore up my MVS DB2 card for good. Thanks, but no thanks.

System/38 in AS/400 Skin

The AS/400, introduced in 1988 as the follow-on product to the System/38, was not at all revolutionary. That was okay. What was revolutionary was that IBM was most interested in selling this new box even though it was developed and manufactured in Rochester. Before the company changed its mind, I wanted the branch office to know that I was in on the new deal.

As unbelievable as it may sound, no other computer had caught up to the System/38 in its 10 years of existence. In 1988, at the time of the AS/400 announcement, no other computer vendor, including IBM (mainframes), had 48-bit hardware, and none came close to having 128-bit program addressability. During this time, IBM's mainframes were upgraded from 24 to 31 bits with a new version of the heavy-duty operating system called MVS/XA. Yet even at 31-bits, this was a far cry from the inherent 128-bit facilities of the System/38. (See Chapter 6 for more machine details.)

The most notable hardware announced with the AS/400 system was a Local Area Network (LAN) adapter. The System/38 was never equipped with the hardware necessary for it to work on a LAN. At the time, IBM was a proponent of the Token-Ring style LAN adapter, and this was made available with the original AS/400. Later, as Token-Ring became irrelevant, the company made Ethernet available. The other notable hardware announcement was an optional ASCII workstation adapter that permitted the system to directly attach cheap non-IBM terminals.

Among the recognizably new software capabilities put forth on the new AS/400 were three products that were ported from the System/36. These included a programmer development facility called the Program Development Manager (PDM), as well as two user products, known as the Data File Utility (DFU) and the Query Product. In addition to these products, the biggest new software capability offering for the new AS/400 was its support for SQL, a facility that had been conspicuously absent for 10 years from the integrated relational database provided with the System/38.

In addition to limiting its hardware growth, IBM had withheld certain software facilities from the System/38. It was obvious to outsiders and well known to IBMers that the mainframe crowd did not want the System/38 or the AS/400 to appear to be a fully capable computer. The idea was that if IBM's larger customers did not think that the System/38 or the AS/400 was fully capable, they would not be tempted to trade in their mainframes for one of those renegade systems.

DEC Killer

During its heyday in the early 1990's, the AS/400 did its job as IBM's midsized systems weapon. Though IBM's System/36 customers never really embraced the system, the company's small business marketing force was able to leverage the capabilities of the box to win new business. The AS/400 was heads and heels above the competition of the day, and for IBM, it won the day.

Problems for a Grown Up AS/400

Having few friends in corporate IBM has not and will not play well for Rochester, especially if it ever really needs a decision to be made in its favor. Most of the decisions coming from corporate today have relegated the AS/400 to an irrelevant status in the new server division. When all your friends are gone, it's tough to survive. That is a big risk for the AS/400 today. It seems like a lot of people in IBM are gunning for the "little lab." Will an unfriendly IBM executive management team permit the AS/400 to hang on? So far, yes, but they have destroyed IBM in Rochester, Minnesota.

Though I sincerely believe that IBM could race back to the top, its achievements most recently indicate that that it is more interested in share buybacks than being a technology leader. We like to call the machine and operating system combo, the AS/400 rather than the IBM Power System with IBM i. We all know what AS/400 means and IBM's technology refreshes never affect the main attributes of the system enough to cause AS/400 users to think a new name is appropriate.

One time, all of the good of IBM's AS/400 systems came from an obscure lab in Rochester Minnesota, someplace close to the Mayo Clinic. IBM began building the Rochester campus in the mid-1950s, hiring modernist architect Eero Saarinen, who covered the buildings in blue panels—a nod to Minnesota's skies and IBM's "Big Blue" nickname.

Eventually this campus grew to more than 3.6 million square feet and it provided work for over 8,000 employees living in proximity of the City. Besides the AS/400 system, The City of Rochester became a manufacturing hub for some of the IBM Company's most powerful supercomputers.

But IBM kept looking overseas for a better financial deal than Rochester's team of technology innovators could give them. It is well documented that these best of the best gave IBM 80+ hours a week for years while getting paid for just 40. Big Blue, a company that in recent years would be pleased to find a buyer for the Tin-Man's heart years earlier, had moved much of the manufacturing and development operations out of Rochester before in 2013. In 2013, it was sharpening its paring pencil.

IBM was planning to cut back even more. The company suggests its new focus is on cloud and "cognitive computing." IBM chooses not to say how many employees are left in Rochester, but estimates range between 2,000 and 3,000. When we talk about Rochester accomplishments over the decades, we see both a great manufacturing facility but also a highly motivated and innovative software laboratory that developed one of a kind breakthrough IT produces. The System/38, AS/400, and many other phenomenal systems came from Rochester's elite brain trust.

.

IBM had already decimated its Endicott facilities over the years. This is where IBM built the minicomputer sized mainframes that competed internally against the Rochester products. As it cut back in Rochester, just like in Endicott, IBM has begun to lease out space in the campus to companies such as Charter Communications.

All good things must end. And, so even good things like IBM in Rochester, Minnesota, home of the AS/400, must also end. In many ways, the purpose of this book is to relive those IBM glory days in which Big Blue could do no wrong. Those were the days before the current era in which IBM has a difficult time doing anything right.

If the spirit of the AS/400 era somehow can be reborn, and IBM can get itself to choose to be the best again instead of simply working on its share value, I believe in my heart, that the once best company in the world can gain respect again and can again reach the top. After all, Microsoft, Intel and Apple did not beat IBM in the IT marketplacc. IBM handed it to them by never fighting back even when Big Blue had the best product set that had ever been built.

For now, Rochester's demise is being looked upon as the end of an era – the minicomputer era to be precise – for the

IBMers who wonce worked ork in the company's sprawling Rochester, Minnesota facility. Their jobs have moved mostly to Mexico.

In 2013, Big Blue solidified the deal by meeting with approximately 2,800 employees in the facility on a Tuesday afternoon and told them it would cease manufacturing operations. IBM in Rochester, with a facility originally built in 1956 with many expansions over the decades is no longer IBM Rochester. IBM in Rochester was designed to make unit record (Tab) equipment, processors, systems, disk drives, main memory, operating systems, and various systems software aimed at SMB customers. If it were a company by itself, its commitment to excellence would have assured that it would become the top computer company in the world.

The move for IBM from Rochester is another step in a long, slow slog toward irrelevancy for the storied facility in the Land of 10,000 Lakes. Those left at IBM to market systems that the company no longer enhances rapidly enough to keep pace, have a tough job for sure. Sometimes pundits see the IBM Company as an entity with a death wish. Not much news comes from IBM Corporate HQ.

For example, IT Jungle recently offered some comments about IBM's AS/400-type Business Executive, Scott Forstie. They noted his tremendous energy and abilities but acknowledged his major handicap was working for an IBM that is always downsizing. They see Forstie as a guy who has the keys in the ignition of a car that isn't allowed out of the garage. IBM has permitted its AS/400 technology to be successful from the day it was invented.

Chapter 5 It's a Beautiful Day in the Neighborhood?

Automatic Transmissions 'R' Us

From the very beginning, the AS/400 was designed to be simpler than all other systems. To this day, no other platform has such a good a balance between "easy-to-use" and "powerful." Unlike Mainframes, Windows, and Unix, the AS/400 comes without a clutch. It's got a fully functional automatic transmission. In fact, when you drive an AS/400, you would find that for the most part, you are not needed; the system drives itself.

You can know enough to run an Power i or an AS/400 when you know less than a few percentages of what there is to know. Max Miller found that out quickly. With the AS/400, for example, much of what you want to do is already set up with default values, and thus, you do not have to think out each piece of a command. You just run it. With a minimal amount of training, one person can in fact know enough to run an cntirc company using an AS/400. It's done all the time. That's why once people have worked with an AS/400, with OS/400, they are spoiled and resent working again with other machines.

In basic no-frills form, the AS/400 is hard to beat for a new install of a reliable system at any new customer location. PCs are still for fluff things such as e-mail clients, drawings, and things requiring really cheap connectivity. You may not yet want to surf the Net on an AS/400, but you surely would not want to trust a fully audited, transaction-controlled, mission-critical invoicing application running on behalf of 100 users if it were written in a PC-oriented kids language, and if it were running on a farm of Windows PC servers with 20 label printers in multiple plants. For this, you need a nice sized professional staff if the application is for a PC-based system. Why would anybody do this with a PC-based system? If the system were an AS/400, just one person would be able to handle the mission, and the person would also be able to take lunch.

Part of how the AS/400 is able to get lots done in a reliable fashion is that it is much easier to use, and its rules are stricter than any other environment. Hackers don't like rules, so for the most part, they stay clear of the AS/400. On other platforms, for example, you can write a program that destroys the system itself. You can do it intentionally as a hacker, or you can do it by error, unintentionally, because you did something wrong.

Most of us have seen the ease with which viruses can be created on Windows systems and how hackers break into Windows and Unix boxes all the time. AS/400 prevents this within its architecture. It prevents users from killing themselves. It is not unimportant that the techno-geeks don't like it as much as they like Unix or Windows. They get stopped at the door. They can't hack the AS/400 and bring it down successfully--and they don't like that one bit!

Ease of Use for Technical Staff

AS/400 professionals love the ease with which they can manage the AS/400 system and its relational database facility. On mainframe computers and Unix boxes, and even Windows boxes, it is not quite so simple. For example, on all three of the non-AS/400 flavors, the database is not integrated. That means that you get to install it, apply the patches, and ensure that it is fully functional. You get to make sure that it works, and get to integrate it with everything else on your machine. Moreover, with mainframes, in order to have a database, you have to hire an expensive extra person to your staff. This new person is called a database administrator (DBA) and he comes with a price tag of about $80,000 or more per year.

A DBA is not just needed on a mainframe. When A PC server is used for real business applications, a DBA is required on this inexpensive platform as well. Moreover, on the PC platform, you always install in pairs, in case one goes down.

So you get to do the installation work twice. If you know of any advanced PC shops with databases that do not have a DBA, you know they're not doing too well. Though the AS/400 is a database machine, you need no DBA, because the database is built into the machine. Most programmers discover that they have been using a database long after their applications have been using it successfully with the AS/400 for years.

The AS/400 Keeps on Ticking

Internet and AS/400 oriented magazines have many wonderful stories about how AS/400s just go ahead and get their work done, regardless of the level of feeding and caring the systems get. The AS/400 is very much like a good old Timex watch. Sometimes, however, AS/400s keep on ticking long after they are forgotten. For example, this story relayed by Mark Villa of Charleston, South Carolina, is one that brings the ease of AS/400 operations picture well into focus.

> **"There was an AS/400 in a plant that was doing its thing on a regular basis, and it was basically unnoticed out in the plant. Unknowingly, the company built a wall in the area during some construction, and someone went hunting for the AS/400 months later, and found it was enclosed."**

Runs Many Applications At Once

Unlike Windows Servers, AS/400s run many applications at the same time. Windows servers do not do well when used for more than one function. That's why a single-server PC grows into a small farm of PC servers almost overnight. An AS/400 can be a Web server, a Domino Notes server, a Java Virtual Machine, a Windows NT server, an OS/2 server, a firewall, an invoice machine, an accounts receivable machine, and so on--all on the same single-processor box, without even having to partition the unit. More industry analysts are noticing this facility and giving the AS/400 very high marks in their total-cost-of-computing analyses.

The AS/400 can actually be a server farm under its one set of covers with just one server box. It can also provide the same facility for Windows servers as a storage area network (SAN). Because the AS/400 is so many machines in one, sometimes it gets no credit for being any, when it is actually all. Today, IBM seems to have a problem with the identity of the AS/400. Back in 1988, the company had no problem spelling out exactly what an AS/400 was all about. The company highlighted the AS/400 as its workhorse of midrange servers. IBM called the AS/400 its midrange business system. It still is, but since the name change, IBM has forgotten.

Technical Note: A SAN is short for Storage Area Network. This is a modern notion involving the separation of the data storage elements from single computers and the centralization of that data on a central server, the role of which is storage management. A topology would show many servers all accessing data from the same set of disk drives managed by the Storage Server in the Storage Area Network. Because many Intel servers can be installed as blades in an AS/400, the AS/400 box itself serves as a SAN for Windows Servers at 10 to 15% of the cost of a typical SAN approach.

Today the AS/400, or Power i, or Power System with IBM I is still alive and kicking, with an installed base of more than 400,000 and perhaps as many as 750,000 systems in about 250,000 businesses around the world. Between 30,000 and 90,000 new systems are sold each year, according to some published statistics. The AS/400 survives because many of its customers buy a new one every four or five years, and because IBM has chosen not to eliminate the box--yet!

AS/400 Staying Power: Bring on the Clones!

There are serious concerns by some industry analysts about the AS/400 platform's proprietary image and what is perceived by most AS/400 customers as IBM's failure to aggressively promote the platform. AS/400 customers want the box to be successful, and they don't want to have to explain to their management why they have an AS/400 each time the lease is up. The fact that the AS/400 is still selling to its existing customers flies in the face of long-standing predictions about the demise of the platform. IBM's biggest AS/400 problem today is that its customers are upset by the way the company markets the box.

Today, no other company makes AS/400s. More than being worried about AS/400 clones coming into being, IBM's AS/400 faithful are concerned about IBM trying to abandon support of AS/400's operating system, OS/400. Just as Windows brings life to hundreds of millions of PCs, OS/400 is the lifeblood of the AS/400's midrange technical capabilities.

IBM does not seem to like OS/400 (now IBM i), and in old boxing terms, the company seems to have a favorite "bum of the month" for the AS/400 to run against. At times IBM favors Unix, and at other times it looks like Linux or Windows. Rather than any of these has-beens, AS/400 shops would welcome some smart and savvy competitor coming along with an AS/400 clone. If OS/400 is worth cloning, this would be viewed as a long-term positive prognosis for the platform.

The AS/400 constituency is not happy with IBM and its homogenization tactics and the "bum of the month" club. If a company, such as HP or Sun, appeared on the scene with a reasonably reliable copy of any hardware box running OS/400--a clone, if you will--you'd need to bring in MPs to direct traffic during the migration flow.

Old Reliable

The most cited reason behind the continuing popularity of the AS/400 is its reliability. The unprecedented ease of use and the low cost of management follow right behind. The AS/400 continues to be an out-of-the-box product with bundled applications, communications software, and its own integrated database. No system requires the small amount of care as an AS/400.

Ease of Migration

The system provides the ability to integrate new technologies with very little disruption to business operations. AS/400 users have been benefiting for many years. For instance, Pagnotti Enterprises of Wilkes-Barre, Pennsylvania, a holding company for some mining and insurance businesses, replaced its old AS/400 CISC architecture system with a 64-bit RISC system in 1999. The company's RISC machine is now old, and they are looking again. Despite the magnitude of the 1999 shift, resulting in a major performance increase, no changes were required to the application code or logic, according to Betty Carpenter, IT director for the company.

"The conversion to 64-bit was as simple as restoring the objects on the new system," said Carpenter, who has worked on AS/400s for more than a decade. That's why AS/400 customers do not want to switch.

In 1988, IBM launched the AS/400 to replace its aging System/38. Over the years, IBM has kept many of the original features but adapted the overall system to the technology changes needed for the times. Over these 38 years, counting the System/38 years, IBM also has succeeded in making the platform far more open than anyone ever would have expected. For instance, the AS/400 today offers native support for mail and messaging technologies, such as Lotus Domino and ERP, from companies such as SAP, PeopleSoft, and Baan.

The AS/400 has become a mainframe in size at the large end, and a mainframe in capability on all models. Super mainframe capability can be seen in a concept called logical partitioning on the AS/400. This feature was borrowed directly from the mainframe. Using this facility, an implementer can define one AS/400 as if it were many AS/400s, and each one can behave as a separate machine. Moreover, one AS/400 may be running OS/400, Linux, or IBM's AIX at the same time. The future is wide open. In private meetings, IBM has announced that Bill Gates would like Windows to run on an AS/400, and IBM has not ruled it out.

How Popular Is the AS/400?

Besides my little cadre of customers in Northeastern Pennsylvania, there are several hundred thousand others. Of course, I think they all should be my consulting customers, but I am happy with what I have got. A few national and world-class IBM AS/400 customers, last time I checked, include the following:

Enterprise Rent A Car,
With over 40 AS/400s, 20 of which are dedicated to handling an application with 1.3 million transactions each hour.
Ball-Foster Glass Container Co.
In Muncie, Indiana.
J&L Fiber Service
In Waukesha, Wisconsin, a materials supplier for the paper industry.
Cornerstone Retail Solutions
In Austin, Texas.
Bergen Brunswig Corp., a pharmaceutical distributor in Orange, California.
Saab Cars USA,
Inc., in Norcross, Georgia (U.S. headquarters).
AppsMall
(AppsMall.com) in Rochester, Minnesota.
CoreMark, (formerly Klein Wholesale)
In Pennsylvania, the fifth-largest candy and tobacco wholesaler in the United States. Also significant in Canada
Marywood University,
Liberal Arts institution in Scranton, Pennsylvania.

Better than half of all AS/400s are installed in countries outside the United States.

You'd have to pry an AS/400 away from its users with the biggest crowbar ever invented in order to create some separation. Check out this comment from a leading AS/400 news company, NewsWire/400, of Penton Media:

> **"We've been running our Web site on Domino on the AS/400, and we're not even running on the latest and greatest platform. We're running on a 50S. The beauty of it is, the thing never goes down. Our maintenance on it is almost nil. We don't do anything with it; it just runs."**
>
> **--Terry Bird, principal, Appsmall.com**

It's not just the AS/400-biased media that pump the AS/400 from time to time. In an *InfoWorld* article on July 31, 2000, just before the rebranding of the AS/400 to the Power i, Maggie Biggs, writing for the "Enterprise Toolbox" section of

InfoWorld's e-magazine, noted that the industry perception of the AS/400 seemed to be changing.

In her article, Biggs discussed the changing perceptions as the AS/400 morphs into what she calls a powerful, dynamic e-business server. The article was published a few years after IBM had stuck the little "e" on the back of the AS/400, making it the AS/400e. While writing the article, as a matter of course, Ms. Biggs felt compelled to slam IBM for keeping the AS/400's capabilities a secret:

"Actually, the AS/400 has been e-business-ready for several years, but it's nice to see the marketing folks at IBM finally catching up with the platform's technological advances."

Biggs continues:

"Our experts from the Test Center and Info-World Review Board (made up of our free-lance writers) examined the newest release of the AS/400 and its operating system, OS/400, and expressed frustration at how under-marketed this platform is.

"After more than 10 years of advances and a metamorphosis into a beefy e-business server, the majority of people still view the AS/400 as a legacy platform. This is a shame because the AS/400 is a multifaceted server capable of fulfilling a myriad of business needs regardless of the size of the enterprise or the tasks that are thrown at it. And the AS/400 continues to be one of few platforms that can simultaneously support legacy, client/server, and Web-based computing.

"...what kind of ROI you might expect to gain by adopting the AS/400... found the costs low when compared to the software and hardware capabilities of the platform, which stand out favorably in many ways when measured against competing servers...

"These servers can be configured to meet the requirements and budgets of businesses both large and small. IBM has enabled technologies that let you run both Unix-based applications and Windows NT and Windows 2000 applications within your AS/400 environment. You might use these technologies to consolidate servers, reduce expenditures, or to improve business process integration...

"From what we experienced during our testing and analysis, the AS/400 appears ready to provide some stiff competition for its server rivals. You may not hear about the AS/400 as often as you might hear about other platforms, but just ask any of your colleagues who have worked with the platform and I think you'll hear a positive response."

Amen!

As the client/server revolution went sour and Windows server farms began proving to be more and more difficult and expensive to manage, despite IBM's stoicism about advertising the platform, there has recently been a definite resurgence of interest in the AS/400 server, fueled by word of mouth. Businesses seeking a reliable, scalable platform are starting to notice that out of all the technology that is inside the AS/400, the bottom line is that it works and for the most part, it does not go down.

Though not happy about IBM's AS/400 advertising, one thing that aficionados are not complaining about is the seventh generation, 64-bit architecture of the AS/400, in that it continues to benefit from Big Blue's ongoing, multi-billion-dollar investment in AS/400 technology.

Perhaps it would help if IBM knew that when and if the marketing really starts, the customer complaints would stop.

AS/400 Waiting to Be Successful

The AS/400 is poised to become the flagship for IBM once the company chooses to hoist the flag. Besides having the most elegant packaging of computer basics, its features include enterprise e-commerce applications, native support for key Web-enabling technologies, such as Web servers, Java, Lotus Domino, and IBM's WebSphere server.

Not to be outdone by the big jobs, the server also boasts support for Windows NT, Windows 2000, Windows XP, and Windows 2003 application serving.

The free operating system shipped with the machine is on duty from the moment you turn it on. The Windows process of loading the base operating system and then adding all the Windows fixpacks is not necessary. The AS/400 operating system, known as Operating System/400, or OS/400, is pre-installed, and is tested for hours before shipping. As you would expect, like the Spaghetti ad, as you list features that an operating system should have, when you talk about the AS/400's operating system, you'll find yourself saying, "It's in there!"

Before I close this chapter, I would like to present a quick laundry list (Figure 5-1) of some of the advanced facilities that you will find in your average AS/400. If you are not technical at heart, it may not be too meaningful. However, the list at least gives an idea of the AS/400's full capabilities to solve business problems and to provide solutions in many areas that might not at first be obvious

Figure 5-1 Some AS/400 Capabilities

- 64-bit Power5 RISC-based architecture-IBM's most powerful RISC processors.
- 128-bit software architecture.
- Spooling and job management for multiple users/separate queues.
- Performance management for allocating resources.
- Single level store (AS/400 unique).
- Technology-independent machine interface (AS/400 unique).
- Integrated DB2 Universal Database (AS/400 unique).
- Capability-based addressing for integrated security (AS/400 unique).
- Object oriented (AS/400 unique).
- Clustering--integrated.
- Apache Web Server (HTTP) Server--integrated within system.
- Web search engine.
- Enhanced TCP/IP stack and utility--integrated within system.
- Encryption.
- File serving and client/server integrated features.
- Logical partitioning--advanced system facility.
- GUI application development tools for client/server and Web.
- Intel integration--Windows under the covers.
- Etc., etc., etc.

It is amazing that with a box like the AS/400 in its stable, IBM has chosen not to let my neighbors in on the secret. In their daily lives, my neighbors, who I introduced to you in chapter 2, either operate or are retired from successful businesses. Here's a picture of Carol Anstett of John Anstett Realtors and Jeanne Elinsky of Roscoe Advertising and Noble Furniture at their party best (Figure 5-2).

Figure 5-2 Neighbors from John Anstett Real Estate, Wilkes-Barre, PA, and Noble Furniture, Nanticoke, PA -- Never Met an AS/400!

None of these fine neighbors ever met an AS/400! This must change. IBM has to figure out a way to tell ordinary citizens about its prized system.

Chapter 6 The All Everything Computer

AS/400 Can Do It!

From legacy code crunching to Web services support to Linux, Unix, Windows, and even autonomic computing, the often-underestimated AS/400 platform can match any IT environment. This truly all-everything operating system IBM i, with the Power 8 computer chip can do it all. By the way, my personal shortcut for the AS/400 of today is the Power i. IBM has not adopted it yet but they sure should.

If you strip from the new Power i all of the fancy new stuff the press seems to be enthralled by, such as client/server, ODBC, Linux, Windows, logical partitioning, AIX, PASE, QSHELL, and Java, you are still left with the most elegant, most functional, and most powerful server in the world. It is just waiting to be loved. Along with a number of other graying AS/400-lifers who worked with the advanced technology of the System/38 after its announcement in 1978, and saw it become the AS/400 and now the Power i, I know that there is no computer that can top the AS/400 for pure architectural elegance, with or without a GUI (see Chapter 33, "A Town Without GUI").

There is no reason not to love the AS/400, if you really know it. So I might be so bold as to suggest that the Teddy Bears, a musical group from the 1950s, would have taken notice of the AS/400 in 1988, if IBM marketing had let the non-IT world in on its AS/400 secret. They would have been able to capitalize on a great theme to reenergize the group for a new hit tune for the times. The Teddy Bears could have taken Phil Spector's hit tune and enjoyed singing, "To know, know,

know the AS/400 is to love, love, love the AS/400!" If only they knew.

Twenty years after the song, from 1978, with the introduction of the System/38, the AS/400, and now the Power i, this not-so-well-known IBM server parlayed **advanced systems architecture** while never abandoning the notion of **small system ease-of-use**.

The purpose for this duopoly is to enable powerful customer-oriented applications to be built that would last long into the future, without reengineering. If there is any legacy that the AS/400 possesses, this is it. However, because software code runs forever and for better on this platform, competitors and the Windows-dominated press have chosen to call the AS/400 a legacy system (see Chapter 12, "Is the AS/400 a Legacy System?"). Yet, if called to task, no industry expert could deny that the AS/400 is an "all-everything" computer, the best all-around commercial system ever conceived.

AS/400: Six Advanced Principles

The AS/400 is the only server in existence that offers six major advanced architecture facilities as part of its standard, integrated offering. The purpose of this book is not to teach the AS/400. However, along the way to presenting survival issues, in order to gain an appreciation of this splendid computer system, some things are helpful to know. There is no other commercial system or server that has been able to deliver even one of these advanced properties. At the core of the AS/400's machine and software architecture are the following six advanced principles:

1. Integrated system functions
2. Highlevel machine
3. Single-level storage
4. Object-oriented architecture

5. Capability-based addressing
6. Integrated relational database

These features provide a platform that is renowned for flexibility, large system function, ease-of-use, and non-disruptive growth. To help you get a better appreciation for what these mean, without hurting the non-technical brain along the way, let's take a quick peak at each of these principles in turn.

Integrated System Functions

The traditional approach to gaining computer function is to use add-on software. If you need a database, you buy one. If you need a transaction processor, you buy one. If you need compilers, you buy them. The traditional approach is an ala carte approach. You never get a full dinner. Most vendors, including IBM with its other server models, found it easier over the years just to add software function patches, rather than start over and design the system the right way. The System/38 and its successor products changed this paradigm.

To put the patchwork quilt puzzle into perspective, it helps to know that there still exists a function in IT called systems programming. In many ways, systems programmers finish the computer vendor's work in the IT shop. When 40 or 50 essential products have to be installed, tailored, configured, and continually monitored, there is a high-paying job available for a highly technical person. To a degree, you can even see this type of person in Windows shops. They don't write programs or add value in any way to the IT shop, yet they are essential because they take piece parts and build and maintain operating systems and software applications on the IT shop floor. Without their efforts, there would be no completely installed servers to work with. Only in the most complex, multi-system environments is such a position required in an AS/400 shop.

Unlike the Windows and mainframe piece parts approach, one of the major design criteria for the System/38 was to ship a complete product to IBM's customers. The System/38 was designed not to need additional time, effort, or skill for its completion. That's integration. And only the largest IT shops, with multiple systems, have a need for an AS/400 systems programmer.

Using IBM's famous Future Systems (FS) project design concepts as a basis, a little IBM lab in Rochester spent most of the 1970s building the System/38. IBM had studied the best possible architecture and ingredients for a new system replacement for its mainframe processor line. After being rejected by the mainframe division, this advanced architecture became the foundation for the most advanced computer system ever built: the System/38. If announced today, the System/38 would undoubtedly be the third-most-advanced computer ever built. It would follow the AS/400 and the Power i.

When you build a computer system in which the hardware, the operating system, and all of the support programs for program development and operations are all built together, you can build a system in which function is distributed to the proper layers and components. You can achieve integration, smaller code paths, better performance, better stability, more productivity, and less functional redundancy. Everything a developer needs in order to be productive can be built together. IBM announced and made available the most advanced system of its time with the introduction of the System/38.

No longer did system programmers have to spend hours determining what versions of what products could be built together in a complex system generation process. For the first time, every system model in a computer product line had all of the functions. From top to bottom, every System/38 could be used to build and to run the same application programs. It was in there! It still is with the AS/400.

High-Level Machine

Quite simply, a high-level machine implementation works in favor of the user, rather than the computer designer. Low-level machines, such as Unix or a mainframe, operate with languages and interfaces that are machine-oriented, not people-oriented. If you like talking in ones and zeros, you'd like the lowest level language--machine language. A high-level machine is another way of saying that user functions are built into the machine without having to worry about the machine itself. In many ways the result on the System/38 and its successors is a system-managed system, rather than a user-managed system. A high-level machine is like a high-level language, in that you talk to it in all ways at a level far away from the ones and zeros and the bits and bytes. Thus, this advanced notion brings with it a tremendous increase in operational and system productivity.

Access to the vast array of advanced system functions is provided by a powerful, consistent interface, or **high-level machine interface**. IBM calls this interface the **Technology Independent Machine Interface (TIMI)**. Computer scientists would label the high-level machine interface as an **abstract machine**, since the architecture of the machine that you believe you are working with is only visible at the high level. The actual low-level hardware looks substantially different, but the user or programmer never interacts at the lower levels with the machine.

AS/400 programmers love the notion of the TIMI, and they don't want to give it up, because they don't want to have to learn cryptic machine code and silly names for normal functions. Anything less is inferior. Even the machine instructions are more like the spoken word, or as we say in the United States, English-like. The interface is at such a high level (more human than machine) on the AS/400 that machine instructions, not add-on packaged programs, are used to retrieve and update database records, perform multiprogramming, handle storage management, query database files, or create indices over DB files.

Having said all that, one of the biggest benefits from a high-level machine interface comes when you are changing hardware. For example, when IBM changed its AS/400 hardware in 1995 from a technology known as Complex Instruction Set Computing (CISC) to the IBM-invented, industry-leading Reduced Instruction Set Computing (RISC) model, even though the hardware was completely different, the company needed to rewrite just a small portion of the operating system to work with the new hardware.

No OS Rewrite Necessary

Only the very-low-level microcode (IBM calls this licensed internal code) had to be touched, and this represented less that 5 percent of the operating system. The microcode portion presented the machine personality to the operating system. Rochester had written the AS/400 operating system, called Operating System/400, or simply OS/400, using the high-level machine interface. Since OS/400 spoke to only the high-level TIMI, it remained virtually unchanged even though the processor type had changed.

Immediate 64-bit RISC Processing

OS/400 knew nothing of the processor architecture. So when the processor architecture was changed from CISC to RISC, and the hardware instruction set was redesigned, and the architecture shifted from 48 to 64 bits, the operating system programs did not have to be modified. They ran the same after the hardware change because they were always shielded from the actual look of the hardware. They were based on the high-level interface, and therefore continued to run. More importantly, for IBM's AS/400 customer programmer community, the millions of System/38 and AS/400 compiled programs, written by IBM customers across the world, were enabled to run, unchanged with the new AS/400 RISC platform.

While IBM changed its hardware to RISC, it did one more thing at the same time that is historically significant. The company introduced 64-bit processors. Suffice it to say these were much bigger than the Windows and Unix and mainframe 32-bit processors, and that the more bits one instruction can carry in one machine cycle, the faster the machine. All this happened in 1995, and the technology was immediately available to AS/400 customers without even having to recompile their programs.

IBM achieved this in a very short time because of the TIMI. It took Intel until the year 2000 to create a 64-bit processor. The processor did not run well until later in 2001, and Windows still cannot use all 64-bits. Windows is still saddled with using 32 of the 64 bits. Windows 2000 will never be 64-bit; though it is still possible that Microsoft will eventually get its 2003 offering working with 64 bits. By then, it may be Windows 2004 or 2005. As a point of note, IBM's mainframe division finally got its 64-bit processors out in late 2001.

TIMI Saved IBM Lots of Time

All of the time it took other companies and IBM's own mainframe division was saved in the AS/400 implementation because of the TIMI. Though all of the technology changed, the interface to the existing operating system remained constant. That is a significant advancement and will be the same as IBM and other vendors move toward 128-bit hardware implementations in the future. The TIMI gives the AS/400 a big edge.

Therefore, in addition to making everything on the system easier to work with, the high-level machine interface protects the programming investments of software companies and IT shops by enabling existing programs to run on new hardware without having to be rewritten. Try that with Windows or Unix!

Single-Level Storage

Many readers may already understand the notion of virtual storage. It has been used in computer systems since the very early 1970s. Virtual storage permits computers to run programs that are bigger than the memory of the machine itself. It does this by permitting memory to be over-committed, running many different programs. It uses the disks on the system to store pages of programs that are not being used at a particular point in program operation. This has many advantages, including not being shut down when the system has inadequate real memory resources. **Single-level storage** takes the notion of virtual storage one step beyond.

Single-level storage, as with all of the advanced techniques being discussing, was first introduced with the System/38. With single-level storage, a System/38, through the TIMI, believes that all of its objects exist in a 281-trillion-byte memory continuum (based on just a 48-bit hardware address). That's pretty big!

It does not matter with single-level storage whether the data actually resides on disk, bubble memory, or bubble gum, though today the storage devices are limited to disk technology. In 1979, I recall giving my first presentation about the System/38 as a systems engineer with IBM. The presentation guide suggested that the 281 trillion bytes represented the sum total of all of the disk drives that had ever been built at that time. I was impressed, for sure. It took mainframes 20 more years to reach this level of addressability.

At the high-level interface, the single-level storage mechanism delivers an image that is unaware it has disk drives. Memory is viewed as one big continuum, with objects addressed by name. All objects get an address in the continuum. The microcode worries about where the objects and object pieces actually reside on disk. This saves programmers and systems managers (in larger installations) tons of time managing system resources.

Unlike a PC system, there is no C, D, or E drive. Therefore, the C drive never gets filled up, and a D drive is never needed. All the data appears as if it resides on one disk drive, though it is spread evenly across as many as several thousand disk drives on the largest systems. Think about all the time that saves a person having to decide which disk or disks something should reside upon in a large system.

The Car Analogy

To help gain an appreciation and form a proper perspective for the hugeness of single-level storage, this next example uses the analogy of a car and miles per gallon, or better yet, inches per address.

If a car could go one inch per address, then mathematically a car with a 24-bit address space would be able to go 264 miles. Say the address width is doubled to 48-bits. Without doing much work, you might conclude that you should just double the number of miles to 528. But that would be wrong. A car with a 48-bit address space could in fact go 4.5 billion miles. You don't double it once, you double the cumulative value 24 times to get the 4.5 billion value. In other words, the car could go to the Sun and back about 24 times. Can you imagine where an AS/400 RISC system with its 64-bit hardware address would take you? How about a 96- or 128-bit address? This would basically cumulatively double the 64-bit address, 32 to 64 additional times. We can all agree that the result would be a very big number. Anything more would be nothing less than extra very big.

Experience teaches the popular adage, "software is not written, it is rewritten." Many of the costliest mistakes in computer history have come from software that broke when someone tried to change it. If you can let it be, and it works the same before and after a hardware change, then your investment in software is better preserved. Too bad Bill Gates' company has not learned this.

Wouldn't Microsoft like to be able to say "puff!" and have Windows XP, 2003, or its derivatives be able to work with the 64-bit Intel Itanium chips? Sorry, only 32-bit chips need apply. Windows is not object-oriented and has no high-level machine interface. It thinks the hardware has 32 bits. It actually cares about that. Therefore, Windows can't use the 64-bit facilities in the Pentium IV. However, it can use 32 of the 64-bit capabilities. So it wastes half of the chip!

Yet, somehow, way back in 1995, IBM's AS/400 operating system, OS/400, and all user programs were able to use the 64-bit facilities of the new IBM PowerPC 64-bit RISC hardware--from the day the AS/400 RISC boxes were available. In one of its better ads at the time, IBM bragged, "64-bits, no buts!" Windows has lots of buts, nine years after the AS/400 began using 64-bit hardware to its fullest potential.

If your neighbors knew about this, would there be a higher or lower chance that if they needed a computer, they might consider an AS/400? Then again, only somebody trying to differentiate the advantages of a computer system would be inclined to tell them. Why not IBM? Why is IBM so silent? This is discussed in a number of other chapters.

Object-Oriented Architecture

In 1978, IBM systems engineers spoke of the AS/400 as having an object-oriented architecture, though technically the system at the time was object-based. Only in the late 1980s and the 1990s did the term object-oriented take on real meaning with the use of new programming languages such as Smalltalk, C++, and Java. These used what is known as the object-programming model. As hard as it may be to believe, even the 1978 model System/38 was an object-based system. Much of what everyone has learned about object orientation over the years is contained within the notion of an object-based system.

In 1995, IBM's Rochester Lab rewrote the rules of how far object-oriented programming could be taken. In a major redesign and reprogramming effort, Rochester rewrote the under layer (microcode, low-level code) of the AS/400 operating system (the microcode or licensed internal code) as an object-oriented project.

The 95 percent of OS/400 that ran above the TIMI continued to work just as before, after some cosmetic changes. Even more importantly, all of the user code (RPG and COBOL programs) that had been compiled over more than 15 years, continued to work.

IBM used an object-oriented methodology and object programming tools. No other system had ever been written in this fashion. It was a first: new hardware and a new orientation. Somehow, though a major technical achievement, it did not make the national news. The AS/400 in-crowd knew about it.

However, IBM seemed more concerned about appeasing PC server, Unix, and mainframe divisions than touting such a renegade accomplishment. When you consider that Windows is getting a lot of press because it is working toward running on a 64-bit platform, the AS/400 accomplished this long ago and yet does not get a fair shake from the press.

Today, the AS/400 and Power i are the only object-oriented, object-based systems in existence. It's too bad that IBM marketing never told your neighbors about this. If they knew, when their businesses need a computer, they could seek out the best.

Capability-Based Addressing

Security is the process of controlling access, preventing access, limiting access, granting access, and revoking access. Capability-based addressing, implemented in the System/38 in 1978, is acknowledged by the experts as the best way to achieve system security. With the AS/400 family, it is built in.

Of course, you are not going to buy a computer just because it has capability-based addressing. But once you have an idea of what it is, you'll want your computer to have it. You will then see all other systems as inferior. This advanced notion is worth discussing. Way back in the 1960s and 1970s, computer scientists were planning the future of computing. One of the first advanced capability-based system designs from Carnegie Mellon was called the Hydra. Interestingly enough, Hydra also was object-oriented, and was built with a machine abstraction layer (high-level machine interface), along with a single-level store and tons of integrated functions.

The KeyKOS micro-kernel operating system emerged in the mid 1980s and was an improvement over the Hydra. In the mid 1990s, yet another improvement operating system arrived, with the help of the University of Pennsylvania's Extremely Reliable Operating System (EROS) project. EROS releases sound much like the story of Linux. Now on Release 0.6.0, with prerelease 0.8.3 already shipped, the EROS project, spearheaded by Jonathan Shapiro, has taken the concept of capability-based systems yet another step toward the ideal.

None of these implementations--Hydra, KeyKOS, or EROS--are implemented on a system that you can buy. The AS/400 in many ways is the only commercial embodiment of capability-based systems. The Hydra, the KeyKOS, and the EROS efforts are computer science research projects at their best. They may very well be the wave of the future for all other machines, but they are not out there today. The System/38 was introduced as a capability-based system in 1978. The AS/400 and Power i are even better implementations for the 21st century.

Though capabilities pertain to objects, the way the concept is implemented on the AS/400 platform is unique, in that the hardware and the software are designed together. As mostly software implementations, the Hydra, KeyKOS, and EROS, (DEC, Motorola, IBM S/370), even if successful, could not achieve the unparalleled performance and scalability advantages of hardware and software integration and abstraction as done by AS/400 processors. Again, the AS/400 is the only commercial machine that offers these unique capabilities.

If you are as intrigued by the notion of capabilities as I am, read *What a Capability Is!* by Jonathan Shapiro, available on the EROS Web site at http://www.eros-os.org/essays/capintro.html.

After taking an informal survey, Shapiro concluded that none of his friends, not even the technically savvy, who worked in the computer field, understood what he did for a living. So he decided to help folks like you and me understand the notion of capabilities by starting from scratch. His article is well written, light in spirit, and assumes little knowledge. It takes the reader on a journey toward a real understanding of the concept of capability-based systems.

Because Jonathan Shapiro has already done a great job in defining the notion of capability, I have chosen not to paraphrase, but to include three paragraphs from his work. I repeat them below, for the technically inclined. If you have no concern for the technical aspects, feel free to skip these.

"Dennis and Van Horn introduced the term capability in 1966, in a paper entitled 'Programming Semantics for Multiprogrammed Computations.' The basic idea is this: suppose we design a computer system so that in order to access an object, a program must have a special token. This token designates an object and gives the program the authority to perform a specific set of actions (such as reading or writing) on that object. Such a token is known as a capability.

"A capability is a lot like the keys on your key ring. As an example, consider your car key. It works on a specific car (it designates a particular object), and anyone holding the key can perform certain actions (locking or unlocking the car, starting the car, opening the glove compartment). You can hand your car key to me, after which I can open, lock, or start the car, but only on your car. Holding your car key won't let me test drive my neighbor's Lamborghini (which is just as well--I would undoubtedly wrap it around a tree somewhere). Note that the car key doesn't know that it's me starting the car; it's sufficient that I possess the key. In the same way, capabilities do not care who uses them.

"Car keys sometimes come in several variations. Two common ones are the valet key (starts, locks, and unlocks the car, but not the glove compartment) or the door key (locks/unlocks the car, but won't start it). In exactly this way, two capabilities can designate the same object (such as the car) but authorize different sets of actions. One program might hold a read-only capability to a file while another holds a read-write capability to the same file.

'As with keys, you can give me a capability to a box full of other capabilities..."

Capability-based addressing is a notion that uses the address to provide the capability that permits or denies access to an object. Again, because the AS/400 is a hardware/software hybrid, this advanced security notion could be explored and implemented within the address scheme of the AS/400's high-level machine. The AS/400 uses this advanced computer science notion as its object-level security implementation. AS/400 object addresses are really not known above the machine interface, and thus even security is enforced below the machine interface (TIMI).

IBM was so proud of its implementation that in 1981, at the International Conference for Computer Architecture, Frank

Soltis, a well known IBM scientist and the main architect of the System/38, along with Merle Houdek and Roy L. Hoffman, presented the notion of capability-based addressing as implemented in the IBM System/38 to the Association for Computing Machinery (ACM) Special Interest Group on Computer Architecture.

The System/38 therefore, in 1978, was the first commercial machine that used a capability-based model enforced by capability-based properties. On the System/38, the addressability pointers were built to be 128-bits wide, of which 96 bits are the address, and the remainder represents the authority (capability). The System/38, AS/400, and Power i hardware use an architecture known as "tagged," which makes it virtually impossible to counterfeit a system pointer.

The AS/400 therefore handles all security by object through its capability-based addressing. Everything on the system is an object. Everything can be secured very easily at this base level, using the capability-based architecture. Before an object can be used, a capability (authority) must be established to use the object based in the user profile and the object description itself. Security checking takes place at the time you attempt to reference any object on the system. If you are authorized, you get a "key" to it. If not, you are excluded.

The beauty is that it is extremely functional and fast, since it was not built as an afterthought. It was built into the machine architecture itself. It's done within the base of the system. In other words, it differs from all other commercial implementations, since it is not an add-on provided only by software.

Does this sound like a legacy machine?

Integrated Data Base

The System/38, in 1978, was the first computer ever built with a relational database that was integrated within the hardware and the very framework of the system. Integration is a common theme in the AS/400 architecture. The integrated relational database was and continues to be a hallmark of the AS/400 and the Power i. There is no other commercial machine in existence, even today, which comes with a built-in relational database. Can you imagine how far ahead of the competition the System/38 was in 1978, when DB2, IBM's mainframe relational database product had yet to be announced? And with a System/38, it was just there! You got it with the machine. With AS/400 and Power i, you still do.

Moreover, since the notion of relational database was part and parcel of the architecture of the AS/400, a number of often-used relational DB facilities were built right into the hardware instructions set. Consider that one of the most frequently used operations in a relational database is index creation. The AS/400 has implemented this function as one hardware instruction. That is why the System/38 would outperform all competing systems of its size in the relational DB area.

In fact, to run as well as a System/38, the competition had to execute its benchmark with sequential and indexed file processing to avoid the overhead of the add-on databases. The System/38 had just one performance number. It could run database as well as non-database applications with no degradation.

AS/400 and Power i Break DB Rules

Most relational databases use mathematical set theory and set oriented operations, implemented through the Structured Query language (SQL). Simple features such as the ability to link a compiler read and write operation to the database are not part of the deal. Language compilers on other machines know nothing about databases. In fact, "compiler reads and writes to a database" are anathemas to the spirit of the original relational database model.

Rather than worry about upsetting the late Tedd Codd, the inventor of relational database, the System/38 pioneers in the Rochester labs chose to create a relational database that could support set theory but, more importantly, could work naturally with the problem and procedural programming languages of the day. Back then IBM did not care if it was different, if different was better than the standard. Therefore, the System/38 developers built a relational database that could not only read and write naturally to the database, but the language compilers were written as database-aware.

Since the one and only System/38 relational database would always be present on every System/38, the compiler writers and the utility writers did not ignore the opportunity to enhance the productivity of the integrated database within their own software offerings. In fact, they built their products to take advantage of the presence of the database, and to make their compilers and utilities, as well as the database, easier to use.

Oh, sure, the Tedd Codd database purists hammered the System/38 as not being true to the relational model, since it permitted record-level access. Other relational database implementations were plagued with jury-rigged, unnatural facilities (for the times) within their high-level language (HLL) compilers. For example, to read a record, the programmer would have to call a program and pass it parameters. Moreover, the programmer would have to fully describe the input and output in the program.

System/38 COBOL and RPG programmers had life easy. Since the System/38 compiler writers knew about the database, they enabled natural operations in the language, such as READ and WRITE, to access the database with no special operations.

Programmers did not have to code unnaturally to get their job done, so they got many more jobs done than on non-integrated database systems. Moreover, the data descriptors for input and output popped right into the programs at compile time without the programmer having to code them, saving an additional ton of coding time.

The traditional Tedd Codd databases were often very difficult implementations, requiring high-priced database administrators to manage the systems. Moreover, at the time, databases were either all or nothing. All programs had to use the database if a major file were converted. This created major implementation difficulties. The System/38 database worked first time, every time, with no database administration required.

If a file were defined to the database, programs still could use their System/3 or System/34 or System/36 or System/370 internal RPG or COBOL data descriptions without having to convert the program to use the new database field descriptors. This meant that cutover was a snap and that adding database files was not an issue. All of this permitted programmers to build systems faster and bring them online faster than ever before in computer history.

Rather than making it more difficult for programmers, by forcing them to use set theory in their program logic, IBM created the easy to learn data description specifications (DDS) language to accommodate the way programmers actually worked.

This helped the programmers who used the database be even more productive than those who chose to continue to use auto report, copy books, or hard-coded input/output program specifications. In its product-excellence slide presentations that I delivered to System/38 and AS/400 prospects over the years, IBM suggested a five-to-10-fold increase in programmer productivity would be achieved over traditional methods, using these powerful, integrated tools.

It was real. Actually, it still is. The only difference today is that IBM has stopped saying it. Why? Rex Harrison would surely call it a "puzzlement!"

The System/38 got away with breaking the big relational database rule that data must be processed in a set, rather than one record at a time. Instead, Rochester chose to make programmers more productive, not less productive, by giving them a database that worked the way they worked. It was not until the AS/400 was announced that SQL even made it into the product line, and then, as now, it was an optional facility.

No Name Database

In the early 1990's, IBM did a survey of its AS/400 customers. It is a fact that many AS/400 customers feel they need no IT staff or a small staff to keep their systems running. IBM polled its AS/400 accounts to see if they knew they that there was a database on the system. IBM reported that half of the AS/400 users surveyed did not know their machine had an integrated database. That's when IBM decided to use its DB2 brand for the AS/400 integrated database.

Of course, that ruined one of my favorite pitch lines that I always felt put the AS/400 DB in perspective. Once I was able to say, "If it has a name, the machine knows nothing about it. If it has a name, it is not built in; it is an add-on software package." Consider the plethora of databases that fit this mold: DB2 for all other platforms, Sybase, Informix, and Oracle, for example. They all have names. With these databases, no compilers have any built-in hooks. There is no read or write interface from a compiler to any other database on any other system. Now the AS/400 database has a name, DB2/400 Universal Database, but it is still integrated.

Future System Today

When the System/38 was developed in 1978, and deployed in 1980, it was dubbed the "future system today." An honest appraisal by the Windows-loving trade press of the underpinnings of the AS/400 and Power i, which still uses the advanced System/38 technology, would render a far more complimentary identifier than their current label, "legacy."

In recent years, IBM's PowerPC architecture has entered what is called the POWER5 generation. Though these boxes were not to appear until later in 2004, IBM did enough early testing to know that the new chips are again going to blow the socks off the competition. At the same time, the baby PowerPC chip that IBM is developing for Sony PlayStation is to come on board.

Though many of us define the AS/400 through OS/400 or IBM i, its operating system, AS/400 hardware itself has become the acknowledged best in the industry. In fact, IBM calls the system a mainframe for the masses, which is the most complimentary thing IBM has suggested about the AS/400 in years. The fact is, the power of the system today is mainframe-class, if not faster.

Today's AS/400 has logical partitions that enable it to run programs on multiple virtual or real processors in one AS/400. I am not talking about multiprogramming, but rather a technique that actually provides each of the "partitions" all of the services of the machine, while separating each partition from the others. The partitions behave as separate machines. Thus, the system can run a Linux firewall in one partition, Domino in another partition, WebSphere in still another, and have 29 or more partitions left to run the business applications.

Insider rumors indicate that IBM is merging the mainframe onto the POWER5 processor architecture with its Mach5 project. Theoretically, an AS/400 or AS/400-like machine will be able to run Unix, mainframe, AS/400, and PC applications in the same box. The AS/400 sure is an all-everything machine.

In addition to IBM being tops on the large side of computing with its AS/400 offering, the company has a chance to revolutionize the small business area with the PowerPC Chip built for the PlayStation. One would expect that a wary and conscious IBM would build no technical reason into the new PowerPC chip that would prevent it from running OS/400.

IBM therefore should be able to mass produce these inexpensive chips and use them in small PC-sized AS/400 computers, thereby reducing substantially the entry price of AS/400 business computing. And wouldn't that be a grand day!

The Best of the Best

The AS/400 and Power i architecture represents everything IBM knows about computers and wishes it could have placed into mainframes over the years. The AS/400 is the most technologically elegant machine within IBM, and in the entire computer marketplace. It is certainly not well understood, and IBM does not market it in a way that comes close to the distance separating this system from all others.

Develop Applications Five to Ten Times Faster

Application development on the AS/400 is five to ten times more productive than on any other platform. Somehow over the last 10 years or so, IBM has forgotten what made the AS/400 the DEC killer. Programmer productivity and easy-to-build applications brought the AS/400 to its renowned position in the industry. AS/400 programmer productivity not only killed DEC as a company, but there was also some friendly fire. The IBM 9370 and the IBM 8100 also suffered from the success of the system. The latter deaths did not well endear the product to the mainframe chieftains who spearheaded their development, and who, by the way, have always run IBM.

AS/400 Makes Mainframes Look Bad

Thus, in a company ruled by mainframe bosses, with all products seemingly examined for their mainframe affinity and friendliness, and their abilities to generate services revenue, the AS/400 has not received much help from the corporation. Ironically, the AS/400 today is a mainframe, but completely unlike the mainframe that IBM understands and builds in mainframe plants.

It is time for IBM to take a hard look at why an AS/400 might make a mainframe look bad. The company should not punish the AS/400 for being better, and it should not reward the mainframe for being inferior. IBM should position the AS/400 and OS/400 as the mainframe of tomorrow. We all know what that means: In the long term, the inferior mainframe would have to go.

There is nothing like this all-everything, "Swiss-army knife" machine. It would be nice for stockholders if IBM had the guts to tell your neighbors something about it. It is the best computer technology available. But, just like beta and VHS, the best technology does not always win. IBM will have to tell your neighbors, if the AS/400 is going to survive. I hope the new IBM executives can find the intestinal fortitude to do the right thing.

Chapter 7 Bill Gates, Steven Jobs, and Otto Robinson

AS/400 Users Love the Machine

Show me a business with a computer shop that runs the AS/400 with a reasonably competent staff, and I'll show you a set of very pleased IT professionals. AS/400 people love the AS/400. It is a modern-day phenomenon. In one independent survey after another, AS/400 users, display more computer bias and are downright bigots regarding their machine, compared with all others. They have very good reason.

David H. Andrews is one of the most respected consultants in the AS/400 marketplace. As proprietor of the D.H. Andrews Group, he tests the attitudes of AS/400 customers periodically. Through his consultancy, based in Cheshire, Connecticut, over the years, Andrews has conducted countless surveys of IBM AS/400 customers and others in the industry. Andrews' work offers powerful insights for customers to examine and for IBM to evaluate in making future plans for its product set.

Ironically, in the survey mechanism and its ultimate reporting, part of the encouragement for the customer-survey takers to work through the survey mechanism was a caveat that the only way that the AS/400 culture can be preserved and extended is for IBM to get a clear message of its customers' plans for the platform.

The results of the year-2000 Andrews survey have long been available for analysis, and they reflect the same attitudes that AS/400 customers have today, and for many years. AS/400 users are arguably the truest and bluest of all IBM's customers, and are perhaps the most loyal customers in the 30-plus-year history of the midrange computer.

This is not to say that the customers who are firmly lined up in the AS/400 camp are as firmly entrenched in the IBM camp. In fact, because of the way IBM is holding this group hostage today, extorting larger fees for those who choose to use an AS/400 as an AS/400, there is considerable discontent with IBM as a company within the ranks (see Chapter 24, "The Dead Goose That Once Laid Golden Eggs").

One of the least favorable conclusions that Andrews drew from the survey is that the enthusiasm which respondents show about their AS/400s, in terms of the value of the platform, is disproportional to their concerns about the level of support that IBM and its partners will put behind the AS/400 in the future.

Besides the obvious black eye, the negative for IBM is, of course, that these same AS/400 customers are increasingly looking at alternative platforms and cross-platform development technologies. Obviously, this indicates a willingness to be in a position to jump off the AS/400 platform if they feel they have to exit or find a viable alternative to the AS/400.

That said, the study concluded that the AS/400 would continue to be the primary platform for the majority of respondents for some time to come. There is no other machine that is similar to the AS/400, but the mixed results of his survey indicate a love so deep for this platform that the respondents would be pleased to take on the benefits of a similar platform from a company other than IBM.

For those of you interested in reading D.H. Andrews' information first hand, go to www.andrewscg-commerce.com/as400.html.

The Most Reliable System in the Industry

As noted previously, the most cited reason that AS/400 users continue with the platform is that it is built like a brick house. It just does not go down. It does not check out in the middle of the night for unknown reasons, forcing a business into a panic. It is stable; it is reliable; and it is there when you need it. While the average PC server experiences several weeks of down time each year, the AS/400 checks in with a measly five hours. Most AS/400 shops claim no unplanned downtime whatsoever.

No matter how reliable a machine may be, nobody buys anything just because it is reliable. My pencil doesn't go down, either, but I would not pick a pencil as the main data processor to run my business. The reason why the AS/400 gets such high marks is that it provides high-quality business solutions, which are more customizable than on any other platform. AS/400s allow businesses to react to change more rapidly than any other platform.

If you are Bill Gates, Steven Jobs, or Otto Robinson, you chose your AS/400 because it is the only machine that can give you the competitive edge necessary. With the AS/400, these three people have been able to plan for change in their industry and be leaders rather than followers in molding their computer systems to fit the ever-changing complexion of their businesses.

Three guys, two of which were techno-geeks and embarrassed that to be able to collect their A/R, they need an IBM AS/400 because it was built for the job, have a story incommon with a banking exec who had no reason to leove he IBM Sytem/38 or the IBM AS/400 but he was too smart not to do so.

Bill Gates Secretly Used AS/400s to Run His Business

Business managers and executives typically are unconsciously unaware that their production data processing systems and decision support systems are using AS/400 technology. Perhaps the most unconscious IBM AS/400 customer of all is Bill Gates, the "barbarian leader" from Microsoft. For many years Microsoft executives slept restfully at night, knowing, according to many observers, that their business was safe because it was running on 23 silent AS/400s in a back room someplace, way out of sight. Though the evidence is no longer as obvious, the rumor mill suggests that Gates and company still process on AS/400s, but they do not take D.H. Andrews satisfaction surveys.

Steven Jobs Secretly Used AS/400s to Run His Business

Steven Jobs and Apple, many years ago, when the brilliant Jobs was alive and running Apple the first time, he decided to switch from the five DEC VAX units on which they were running their highly profitable microcomputer business, to the IBM System/38 platform. The System/38 is, of course, the direct predecessor to the AS/400.

Many industry analysts, who were familiar with both the former DEC (swallowed by Compaq, which was swallowed by HP) and IBM, give credit to IBM's AS/400 box for actually taking DEC out of the midrange computing business. The AS/400 killed the DEC VAX and made the company easy prey for the PC leader of the day, Compaq, to acquire. Now, as noted, even Compaq has disappeared from the computing scene.

When I look back at Apple's decision to move to the AS/400 product set, it is obvious that there had to be a compelling reason. At the time, Apple's major product was the Mac. As a terminal to DEC machines, the Mac worked quite well. It had a natural serial interface and terminal emulation software. DEC users could just plug a Mac into the Network, and with the proper software it would just work. The same was true for Mac users. Apple was able to place DEC servers on their Ethernet networks or serial networks, and they would connect with few technical issues.

The System/38, never in its lifetime supported serial (ASCII) terminal devices, and it never supported Ethernet or AppleTalk or any other Local Area Network protocol. In other words, the Macs could not connect to the System/38. Being a renegade company, Apple saw something in the System/38 that it did not see in any other computer in the industry.

Apple knew it would be able to react to business changes more quickly with a System/38 than any previous computer system, including the DEC boxes. It was so important for Apple to use the System/38 that the company created Rube Goldberg special devices and then jury-rigged the company with the devices to enable their Macs to talk to the System/38.

When the AS/400 came out, it had what was needed. It eventually supported both serial (ASCII) and Ethernet, as well as AppleTalk, so that the Mac became a natural device. But Apple had selected the System/38 when industry observers would have concluded that there was no way for the Mac to participate. Thus, there is no doubt that Apple Computer loves its System/38s, and now its AS/400 systems. Today, there is actually more reason for the AS/400 and the Mac to be friends. They are, in fact, relatives. The underlying technology in the new PowerMacs is a similar to the PowerPC technology that IBM uses in its AS/400 and Power i line.

The early Apple says a lot for the desirability of the System/38 and AS/400 systems as IBM products. Back in the early 1980s, Apple saw that there was a definite competitive advantage in using the box as its business system, and the company made sure that it did what was necessary to allow that to happen.

Otto Robinson openly used just one big AS/400 to run his Bank's business

At Penn Security Bank in Scranton, Pennsylvania, Bank President, scientist, and entrepreneuer Otto P. Robinson Jr. was told outright by IBM that the System/38 was not to be used as a modern banking computer. IBM clearly told Robinson on numerous occasions that neither the System/38 nor the AS/400 was a banking machine, and would never become a banking machine.

IBM suggested that the Penn Security Bank president look at its mainframe line of computers. IBM did not want his business if he wanted a System/38. Mr. Robinson, a very bright individual who, besides being bank president, is also a lawyer and a mathematician, was perplexed that IBM would purposely deny the banking industry the use of what he believed to be its finest computer system of the day.

Robinson was relentless in his dealings with IBM, and he never gave up. He knew the System/38 and later the AS/400 and Power I were the best computer systems in the industry, and he could not understand why IBM would deny small bankers the use of such a paerfect machine.

Despite IBM's desire not to sell him one, Robinson ordered a System/38 for the bank. Because IBM had created an adapter for the magnetic ink character recognition (MICR) reader that the bank needed to process checks, his programming team converted his System/3-based batch banking software to the System/38 platform.

Meanwhile, Otto Robinson was actively lobbying IBM for banking devices (teller terminals and ATMs) to be natively supported on the System/38. I had the pleasure of being the assigned account systems engineer to Penn Security Bank, so I got to see all of this action first hand.

Robinson just would not take no for an answer. Eventually, his notoricty in doing things with the System/38 that nobody else was able to do brought him invitations to speak at COMMON and other computer and banking trade shows.

Ironically, the same IBM that had told him that he should not use a System/38 invited the outspoken bank president to various IBM-sponsored banking seminars across the country to demonstrate his effective use of the System/38. Operating without a muzzle, each time he slammed IBM for its lack of System/38 support to the banking industry and challenged IBM to get its act together.

Robinson did not sit still in his own shop, either. He discovered his own hardware solution for the terminal incompatibility. Just as Apple could not naturally connect its Macs, Otto could not connect IBM's leading-edge teller terminals. The System/38 supported just one terminal type. It was known as the IBM 5250. It was a green-screen terminal that at the time was more capable than the mainframe-oriented IBM 3270 terminal set.

Moreover, IBM did not even support its old time communication protocols on the System/38. These had very technical sounding names, such as the BISYNC telecommunications protocol or the ASYNC ASCII protocol. IBM supportcd its green-screen 5250s through the then new Systems Network Architecture/Synchronous Data Link Control (SNA/SDLC) protocol.

Working through all that technical mumbo jumbo, it meant that the System/38 box could not even attach the older mainframe style terminals and it could not attach the IBM's new 3600-style BISYNC banking terminals. Clearly, the System/38 had been left out of the banking picture intentionally, since this was traditional IBM mainframe territory.

Enter the Wild Ducks

Within IBM over the years, I had the pleasure of meeting and working with a number of "wild ducks." Sometimes these ducks were left alone to achieve greatness in IBM. One such duck was a talented engineer named Ed Brucklis. Brucklis worked out of IBM's Boca Raton, Florida, plant. When I met Mr. Brucklis, he had just written a program for IBM's Series/1 minicomputer that could be used to enable the attachment of unsupported terminals, such as 3270 BISYNC terminals, to the IBM System/38. In essence, Brucklis did for IBM what Apple's engineers did for Apple. Through his program, 3270 BISYNC terminals were able to talk to the IBM System/38.

Since Brucklis's Series/1 front-end creation was developed in the same Boca Raton facility that offered limited banking support to IBM's midrange customers, he was persuaded to carry his creation one step further. He added the translation for IBM 3600 Teller Terminals and ATMs. It did not take long for Otto Robinson to get word that an ATM hardware solution (through Brucklis in the Rube Goldberg vein) for the System/38 was now available. (Okay, so I told him!) Brucklis himself eventually helped make it work for the bank president.

After he realized the boxes could connect and talk, Robinson discovered an old ATM software package that had been built for the System/3 line of computers in the early 1970s. This program, written by IBM's Bill Pinkerton and others, permitted IBM's ATMs to be controlled by very old System/3 programs. Robinson worked with his local IBM systems engineer, yours truly, to research whether this package could be made to run on the System/38. I offered my endorsement and recommended how to proceed. Robinson ordered the package and some IBM ATMs, and I worked with the programming team to make sure the ATMs would light up and deliver the cash.

Before going live, Robinson once again beseeched IBM. This time, he argued for an encryption routine for the AS/400. IBM again reminded Robinson that the System/38 was not a banking machine. In frustration, Robinson ordered the BASIC language for the System/38 and wrote his own data encryption standard (DES) routine, using the BASIC programming language.

ATMs were so important to small banks around the world that Robinson opened his doors to any and all to see the marvels of the System/38 controlling a network of ATMs. From as far away as Indonesia, System/38 banking people came and were impressed, and many moved forward with their own System/38 implementations.

As nationwide ATM networks began to spring up everywhere, CashStream, Cirrhus, and Mac were the big players. Robinson contracted with CashStream, and his team then had to modify the Pinkerton ATM package even further to accept ATM cards from non-Penn Security customers. This was also a success.

System/38 Home Banking? Why Not?

In the early 1980s, banks were experimenting with some innovative notions like bill paying systems and home banking. An astute banker, Robinson saw the need to enter this marketplace. At the time, not even the big players had a presence. Robinson went to IBM again and asked about ASCII terminal support for what he termed video text. IBM again reminded Robinson that the System/38 was not a banking machine and that it supported only the 5250-style terminal data stream, and there were no plans to change this.

Robinson called over his local IBM marketing team to discuss his dilemma. He did not want to know what the System/38 could not do. He was already using ATMs on the System/38, and IBM had said that he could not do that with the System/38. I had been working with Series/1s at the time, since IBM was pressuring its branch offices to sell these systems. IBM gave me the job of seeing what we could do with this most unpopular box in our local branch office.

I introduced Otto Robinson to the idea of using another Series/1 running the Yale ASCII terminal package. This package could support any type of ASCII terminal in existence, including the RCA Videotex Terminal, of which Robinson was particularly fond. The problem was that the Yale ASCII Series/1 wanted its host to speak the BISYNC 3270 data stream. It would then convert it to ASYNC ASCII, the necessary protocol. Unfortunately again, IBM's System/38 spoke only SDLC and the 5250-style data stream.

Once again, Ed Brucklis came to the rescue. It seems that the original intent of the translation software originally written by Mr. Brucklis was to permit 3270 BISYNC terminals to attach to the System/38. This was just what the Yale ASCII package wanted. So again Mr. Robinson was pushing the IBM envelope trying to use technology that was not yet available for the System/38.

The Rube Goldberg Home Banking Solution

Long before Internet computing, in his model home-banking scenario, Robinson envisioned a bank customer with an RCA Videotex terminal dialing the Yale ASCII Series/1 at the bank. He saw the Yale ASCII Series/1 converting the ASYNC ASCII data to BISYNC 3270 for the original Brucklis Series/1. The Brucklis Series/1 would then convert the BISYNC 3270 data signals into SDLC 5250 signals and send the twice-converted data stream to the System/38. The System/38 would think it was talking to a directly attached native 5250 terminal. In reality, the connection was from a dialed-in terminal device three systems away. (Phew! If you had a hard time following that, there is no need to worry. You are not alone.) Eventually it worked, but not right away.

Not knowing if this would work, IBM agreed for Ken Lefevre, a Series/1 specialist from Philadelphia to make a house call with yours truly on Otto Robinson. Though he thought it was a very novel idea that may have unforeseen issues, LeFevre could not offer any reason for this approach not to work, and gave it his stamp of approval. Robinson then bought his second Series/1, and in short order, in the test environment, the System/38 was talking to dial-in RCA devices using the two Series/1s in between. But there was a problem.

Hang Up! Please!

Since the AS/400 had no notion of dial-in terminals, there was no way to tell the System/38 that the dial-in banking customer had disconnected. This created a big problem. If another banking customer called into the same phone line, after a prior customer had hung up, he would be connected to the same session the prior user thought he had exited. Obviously, in the banking industry especially, this compromised security. Clever as it was, it would not do the whole job.

Robinson went back to IBM, which, of course, again reminded him that the System/38 did not support banking or ASCII terminals. Otto Robinson reminded IBM that it had taken the money for the second Series/1s and the Yale ASCII package. Every now and then, the lawyer in Robinson would show his face. IBM agreed to have Ed Brucklis himself visit the bank, but did not imply that this technique would be supported or that it would ever work.

When Brucklis arrived from Boca Raton, it was snowing in Scranton, and he did not have an overcoat. Soon after Brucklis' arrival, we went to lunch about a block away from the bank. Mr. Brucklis got a taste of Scranton, Pennsylvania, winters that he would not soon forget. It was food for some gentle jabs when we sat down at Shookey's Restaurant. At lunch, there was some peppy conversation between the bank president and the software engineer. The two hit it off and formed a bond that was quite understandable. Both men would never accept the decks they were dealt, and when faced with what others would call insurmountable obstacles, they were able to devise methods to surmount them.

Robinson muses sometimes about the wild duck characteristics he saw in Ed Brucklis. They were a good team. When Brucklis saw the home banking workshop, he was obviously tickled that his work was being used so cleverly. The RCA Videotex terminals were set up using TV sets as monitors.

The Home Banking Skunk-Works Demo

Robinson demonstrated the home banking skunk-works setup and showed the problem with the dial disconnect. He asked Brucklis how the product could possibly be usable with such a major flaw? I can still remember when Brucklis stood, undaunted, and gently fired back at Robinson: "When this product was written, nobody ever thought it would ever have to talk to a Philco TV." Both men roared with laughter, and Brucklis vowed to make it work. He did. Over time, he became one of Robinson's favorite IBMers.

When the AS/400 came out, Penn Security Bank was in line for one of the first. The bank made the transition painlessly from the System/38. When IBM announced RISC-based AS/400 models in 1995, again Penn Security was one of the first IBM customers lined up to make the transition. And, again, it was mostly painless.

Otto P. Robinson Jr. is still the bank president and still uses the AS/400 to give him the competitive edge he needs in the banking industry. Thanks to Otto Robinson and his unrelenting input to the IBM planning processes, unlike the System/38, the AS/400 is able to handle the unique requirements of banking, as well as home banking.

Who's the Fool?

Bill Gates, Steven Jobs, and Otto Robinson are not fools. What did they see in the AS/400 predecessor (System/38) that would encourage them to go through one hoop after another to be able to deploy the AS/400 heritage platform in their businesses? What makes the AS/400 so special that Microsoft, with a now less than amicable relationship with IBM, and an operating system (Windows Server) that directly competes against AS/400s, persists in its use of the platform?

They did not know or care that the AS/400 or System/38 had 48-bit or 64-bit hardware. They did not know that the system uses 128-bit software addressing. In some cases, they did not even care that it did not have the hardware support to allow for essential devices to be attached. It was not hardware. It was not IBM, for sure.

What they saw in the AS/400 (and the System/38) was a machine that could help them run their businesses with minimal issues and disruptions. More importantly, in many ways they saw a system that would give them an edge over their competitors so that they could adapt their business systems to the changing times at speeds unattainable on any other system.

Otto Robinson saw it as a survival issue. Steven Jobs saw it as a business issue. I've got to believe that Bill Gates, like Otto Robinson, saw it as a survival issue. He needed a system to make his rapidly growing business survive. Quietly, the AS/400, using OS/400, did the job for all three.

AS/400 Plusses

The time from conception to implementation has always been far less with the AS/400 (System/38) product line. Some developers will say 5 to 1; others as much as 10 to 1. This ratio is the relative speed that application development and program maintenance and updates can be performed on the AS/400 compared with all other platforms.

For businesses wanting the competitive edge, there is no time to wait for the important functions and features to be rolled into the industry-standard packages. Therefore, you must build them yourself. The AS/400 plays well in this arena. Ask Bill Gates! Ask Steven Jobs! Ask Otto Robinson!

Chapter 8 No Risk with RISC

The PowerPC Is Coming

In 1994, as IBM prepared to refresh the AS/400 product line with bigger and more powerful processors, Dr. Frank Soltis, AS/400 Chief Scientist, and others freely discussed the coming 64-bit PowerPC RISC processors that IBM was cooking up in its labs. IBM's Power 8, the new engine for the IBM Power System with IBM I (aka Power i) is a successor technology system based on IBM's Power technology.

IBM had pre-announced the coming of RISC processors to its existing customers like nothing else I had ever witnessed. The company was usually very tight-lipped on future products. So intent was IBM on bringing RISC processing to the table in short order that it announced a new batch of AS/400s in new "RISC" cabinets about a year before RISC emerged.

The new black systems that the company introduced in May 1994 were dubbed **RISC ready**. The cabinets used for the RISC-ready boxes were substantially different from the white racks that had been used in prior CISC systems. The days of rack-based AS/400s had passed. When the RISC boxes did arrive, the cabinets were so similar to the RISC-ready boxes that it was obvious they were intended for a 1994 announcement of RISC boxes. But the RISC processors were not ready for prime time in 1994, so IBM did the next best thing. Even though they were not RISC-based, the new black models again energized IBM's AS/400 sales.

> **Note: RISC processing stands for reduced instruction set computing. The late John Cocke, a very bright IBM engineer who worked for the company until 1992, invented the notion of RISC. John Cocke passed away in 2002.**

> **Cocke's concept of RISC resulted from his detailed study of the trade-offs between a number of advanced notions available at the time. He demonstrated that a small (reduced) number of instruction circuits on computer chips could be appropriately defined to exploit the instruction set and thus realize very high performance with relatively few circuits. So if made correctly, each computer chip could be less expensive, and along with some additional sophistication in software compiler design, the resulting machine would perform substantially better than the complex circuitry of the day. Cocke's notion was contrary to the established direction of the functionally more complex instruction sets and machines. Once RISC was established, it was not long before the more complex notion of instruction sets was dubbed complex instruction set computing, or simply CISC.**

Advanced 36 – First RISC Box

In May 1994, the AS/400 had already been out for six years, and its interactive capabilities were beginning to look passé compared with the other exciting computing notions of the day. For example, client/server computing and the Internet had long eluded the AS/400. Additionally, over the six years since IBM had introduced the AS/400 as the replacement for the System/36, the company had little luck in attracting the bulk of the System/36 customers to its AS/400 line.

On October 4, 1994, IBM finally acknowledged that it had to take some action to bring its System/36 customers to the AS/400. This group of customers was far more loyal to its System/36 boxes than to IBM. As a group, it had steadfastly refused to move to the AS/400. In an uncharacteristic act of chicanery and benevolence, the company announced that it was using its first set of AS/400 PowerPC RISC chips to introduce a brand new System/36, built from its yet-to-be-announced AS/400 RISC hardware.

The System/36 instruction set was very limited, so IBM was able to etch the entire set on the new PowerPC RISC chips, even before the technology was ready for the more expansive AS/400 instruction set. The new box that was built on the

RISC chip was introduced as the AS/400 Advanced 36, and was an immediate success. Its constituency had waited six long years for its arrival.

With this announcement, IBM rescued its System/36 customers from the used-computer market and gave them exactly the system for which they had been asking the prior six years.

At the same time, IBM rechristened the AS/400 product line and juiced up its capabilities for the newer applications of the day. The acronym AS/400 stayed, but IBM changed the meaning of the "*AS*" part of these new **RISC-ready** units from a*pplication system* to *advanced* s*ystem* and a*dvanced server*.

RISC Is Ready

RISC-ready did not last long before RISC was ready. On June 21, 1995, IBM finally introduced its RISC line of AS/400 processors, based on PowerPC technology. In addition to being RISC processor driven, the new machines offered the industry-first implementation of 64-bit processor hardware. It would take another six years for Intel to produce a 64-bit processor and another three years after that for Windows to be able to use its power.

At the same time the RISC boxes were announced, the RISC-ready (CISC) black boxes announced just a year earlier became immediately outdated. The only thing RISC-ready about the one-year-old boxes, in retrospect, was the black frame. I found no special advantage in having fallen to the notion of RISC-ready. The black frame RISC-ready CISC Model 30S that I was using would have to last three more years. The one-year-old black boxes were no more ready for RISC than the older AS/400s. It was quite expensive, as I recall, converting a RISC-ready hardware box into a RISC box.

The new AS/400 boxes themselves were being slotted into two different environments. The "Advanced Systems" RISC-ready boxes were replaced by the "Advanced Series" machines that were fully RISC processor enabled. The name Advanced Server continued with the new RISC server models.

One more historical change occurred with the introduction of the RISC-ready models and continued with the RISC boxes. IBM had introduced what it called server models of the AS/400. These were substantially more powerful and less expensive than the typical AS/400 system models. However, the server boxes were not equipped with much interactive horsepower (see Chapter titled, "The Dead Goose That Once Laid Golden Eggs").

They were good for client/server computing and batch computing, but they could not be used for typical AS/400 applications. IBM said that it announced these to compete more vigorously against Windows servers, which had no interactive AS/400-type requirements.

With the change from CISC to RISC, IBM did not change the name of the AS/400. Despite the fact that the hardware had completely changed, there was no real name change. To an extent, the name did change, however. The "AS" no longer had the same meaning.

In 1988, the box was known as the **Application Server/400**. In 1995, the AS/400 got two new names and became the **Advanced Series** and the **Advanced Server**. The subtlety was so great that many missed the change. IBM again subtly changed the name of the AS/400 on August 19, 1997. At this time, the company was interested in squeezing in that little "e" that Lou Gerstner, IBM's chairman at the time, had fastened next to the word "business." Gerstner had coined the term e-business, and by gosh, all IBM servers were on a clear track to becoming eServers.

Lou Gerstner's notion of e-business spilled over to the AS/400 product line immediately as the faithful servants at Rochester painted the little red "e" next to the word AS/400 on all new shipments from the plant. The "new" AS/400e models were made available August 29, 1997, less than two weeks after they were announced.

AS/400s Keep Growing in Power

Sitting at the top of this new line was a model called the 650. It was a 12-way processor, a first for the AS/400, and it delivered phenomenal overall performance for systems of the day. Its relative power rating was 2340 for the 12-way (12 computers in one) in terms of the Commercial Processing Workload (CPW) benchmark measurements. CPW numbers are all relative. There is no magic to the CPW benchmark. It is simply that the higher the number, the faster the machine.

Note: A processor is the computer part of the computer. On larger systems, it is known as the central processing unit, or CPU. For example, the Pentium IV, or the Celeron, is the PC's Intel processor. The computer industry uses the term n-way to describe how many processors exist on a particular system or server model. Thus, if n=12, a 12-way system would have 12 CPU chips, each being able to process data and perform computations. There has been a law of diminishing returns regarding n-way systems on most vendors' servers. In other words, if a server delivered 120 CPW with one processor, two processors would not deliver 240. There is always overhead associated with processor switching and keeping all processors busy on a server. So a two-way might yield 220 CPW, a three-way might yield 300 CPW, and so on. As IBM and other vendors have been making n-way systems more efficient, more and more processors can be added without negatively affecting performance.

To put the CPW number in perspective, let's compare the 1997 AS/400 with the 1978 System/38. When the System/38 was announced in 1978, the fastest model at that time would clock in at less than 2.25 CPW. In less than 20 years, as you can see, the processing power had grown over 1,000 times.

With this new model set, for some reason, IBM marketing did not make a big deal out of what the "e" or the "AS" stood for, as had been done in the past. The implication was obvious. The AS/400 product line was to participate formally in IBM's notion of e-business. But IBM chose not to make a big hoopla at announcement time.

In 1998, IBM again added to the AS/400 hardware line by jacking up the power of its top-of-the-line Model 650. This was the fastest AS/400 processor at the time, coming in at 4550 CPW from the prior year's maximum of 2340 CPW.

On February 9, 1999, IBM made more AS/400 announcements. The company introduced a new RISC-based computer line call the 700 series. At the top of the model 7XX line stood the Model 740. Like the model 650, it was a 12-way machine. Also like the Model 650, the 740's top rating for a 12-processor system was 4550 CPW. The 7XX line was basically a new packaging scheme, and it introduced a new notion called interactive and batch CPW. The Model 7XX machines could act as interactive systems (standard AS/400 terminal programs) and as client/server systems. Thus, by combining the batch and interactive capabilities of the systems in one box, IBM was able to eliminate the need for two different model types: Advanced Series and Advanced Servers. The 7XX machines were known only as servers. (This notion is explained fully in Chapter 25.)

On May 22, 2000, IBM was at it again. This time, the company had introduced its 8XX series of processors. The 7XX series had lasted just over a year. The 8XX line also included 12-way processors, just like the Model 740 series. However, with the new S-Star processor, the company juiced the individual processors so that the 12-way systems were capable of firing out an amazing 10,000 CPW of computer processing power. At the same time, IBM introduced its first 24-way (24 processor) AS/400 model, known as the 840. Its CPW rating for a 24-processor unit was 16,500. This is better than 6,000 times more powerful than the original IBM System/38. The 8XX line also included low-end single-processor units that proved very attractive for small and midsized businesses.

Also, on May 22 and June 12, 2000, to help the smaller customers, IBM announced a smaller sized AS/400. It was called the Model 270 AS/400 line. The boxes were very powerful for client/server computing, but IBM limited the amount of the machine's power that could be used for traditional terminal-oriented computing.

At the same time, the company announced the smallest box in the line, the AS/400 Model 250. This is a tiny, almost portable unit that prices out at less than $10,000 for a very basic machine. This unit was a further constrained machine with a limited growth path. Its intended market was Intel server customers and IBM AS/400 developers who could not afford a large AS/400. Overpriced at a $10,000 minimum cost with no real IBM marketing force and no real IBM marketing effort to promote the machine, the Model 250 overall has not been very successful.

IBM's Total Rebranding

The year was not over. In fact, just five months had passed since the introduction of the Model 8XX, when, in October 2000, IBM held a major all-IBM announcement meeting. Every server, from mainframe to AS/400, was affected by the announcement. The company rebranded all of its computers as eServer models. The AS/400 received the dubious name **eServer Power i 400.** Many AS/400 observers note this as a turning point in IBM's overall attention to the AS/400 product line. This was such an important announcement to the overall potential of the AS/400 that I wrote a full chapter

(17), which analyzes the impact of this announcement on the machine and its customer set.

The year 2001 was not so special in terms of AS/400 hardware or software announcements, especially since the AS/400 had now become the Power i. More and more AS/400 technocrats continued to call the box the AS/400. This was partially due to resentment that IBM was trying to homogenize its server lines and partly because only the newer AS/400 systems had been renamed. As noted above, these units had just been announced in May 2000. All other AS/400 systems were not renamed, and all of these remaining non-Power i boxes, some relatively new and some very old, continued to use the OS/400 operating system and continued to be AS/400s.

On May 14, 2001, IBM had its one AS/400 announcement for the year. The company enhanced the speed of the RISC processors again. With this announcement, IBM took the wraps off its latest PowerPC processor, known as the Power4, and made it available on Power i boxes. These chips had been used successfully for about a year in its pSeries processors, which were formerly the RS/6000 product line. Power4 processors have more sophisticated technology and achieve higher speeds than predecessor RISC processors. To highlight the whopping power of the new processor chips, IBM introduced its AS/400-Power i Model 890, 24-way processor. This behemoth with all 24 processors running delivers 29,300 CPW of power.

Concurrent with the juiced up 24-way processors powered by IBM's Power4 technology, IBM stretched the processor limit of the AS/400-Power i one more time. The new 32-way Model 890 was off the charts. It delivered a whopping 37,400 CPW of power with its 32 processors. Again, that's well over 12,000 times the power of the original System/38.

IBM also introduced better and faster disk technology. With the introduction of the Model 890, the company offered over

72 terabytes of disk along with these powerful processors. For those of you who are counting, that's about one quarter of the 281-trillion-byte addressability of the 48-bit processor in the original System/38. Even at this new level of capabilities, the old System/38 hardware could address every piece of real estate on the disk drive and still have room to spare.

On January 24, 2003, IBM gave the AS/400-Power i still another facelift. New models were announced, called the 800, 810, 825, and 870. Because IBM believed it had finally solved a problem that had became known as the "interactive penalty" with these models, the announcement has historical significance. Unfortunately, the contents of this announcement were not exactly what the smaller customer set was looking for. Overall, from a confusion standpoint, the new boxes created as many problems as they solved. IBM's lack of market understanding, in this regard, is detailed in Chapters 17 and 25.

The end is not in sight with power boosts on the AS/400 hardware. In 2003, Dr. Frank Soltis pre-announced the 2004 server lineup. He said,

"Our 2004 Armada box-based, POWER5 chip-powered systems will scale up well to 64-processors. So not only is there a major boost in the n-way capability but in combination with the POWER5, the new box achieves well over 50,000 CPW."

Windows could not use 64 Bits

By 2004, three years after Intel and HP brought forth the 64-bit Intel PC processors (Pentium IV), Microsoft was still trying to get its Windows Server operating systems up to 64 bits. The first 64-bit Pentiums that came along in March 2001 were not all that usable. Moreover, in real applications, they were slow because Windows simply could not use half of the machine. By the second quarter of 2002, Intel's 64-bit CISC based Pentium IVs began to run better than their older 32-bit XEONs and AMD's Athlon processors with Windows. It did not come easy. Just about all of the performance comes from faster cycle time (MHz). Windows continues to waste half of the machine's power, since it can work with just 32 bits at a time of the 64 bits that the P4 can carry per cycle.

Let me say that again in a different way. Though the Intel P4 processor is a 64-bit processor, the Windows of today is not capable of using all 64-bits. So, Microsoft modified the P3 version so that it could run just as it did on the 32-bit Pentium III machines. Thus, it uses just 32 bits of the 64 bits that are available. In other words, when Windows moves data on the P4, it moves 32-bits at a time, not 64-bits because it has yet to be written and tested to use all 64-bits. Because half of the P4 is in effect crippled when running Windows today, without the cycle time increase (MHz), Windows programs on P4 would be running slower than Pentium IIIs, even though the hardware permits twice as much performance for the same cycle time on a Pentium III.

For the 64-bit Intel processors to become acceptable, knowing that Windows would reduce the potential speed by 50 percent, first the processor hardware had to become stable and usable. Then the processor's performance had to achieve market acceptance from the PC vendors (like Dell, Gateway, and Hewlett-Packard) and customers. Despite many setbacks, all along in this venture the press was giving Intel and Microsoft kudos.

As noted above, the AS/400 processor architecture was changed from 48-bit CISC to 64-bit RISC based in 1995. For all the marketing noise that IBM made about this phenomenal technical achievement, you would have thought Intel and Microsoft were in charge of the announcement. Seven years later, when Intel's 64-bit technology arrived to great fanfare, nobody bothered mentioning that Intel was not even close to being first in the 64-bit game. The AS/400 had been doing 64 bits since 1995, and Intel, seven years late to the party, got the kudos.

Because Intel and Microsoft are not the same company, a funny thing happened on the way to using the full power of the 64-bit Intel processors with Windows. Microsoft wasn't ready when the time came to play. Again, just as with Intel, the trade press gave Microsoft a pass. Gates and company had not designed a TIMI into their operating system. Microsoft continues to use just 32 bits of the 64 in the Intel chip. It will take some time for Windows to use the full power of the 64-bit Pentium.

A few years ago, *Power i News* snagged a quote from Frank Soltis, Power i chief architect, in the "Out of Context" section of its weekly e-newsletter. The quote was titled "64-bit repercussions."

Here is the Quote:

> **"One of the major differences between IBM [processor] technology and Intel [processor] technology is that Intel has made the decision that, in order to use their new hardware technology, you will rewrite everything--operating systems, applications, everything.**
>
> **And the ripple effects through all of the various vendors that are using that technology are going to be tremendous. In fact, it has forced some of those vendors to literally abandon some excellent systems."**

All computers are not created equal. But you've got to ask why Microsoft, with all of its programmers, can't complete the migration to a 64-bit operating system using a processor that has been available for three years. It must be a pretty tough job. It is a tough job in 2004, yet somehow IBM Rochester pulled it off nine years earlier, in 1995. Rochester made this dramatic hardware change and at the same time had its OS/400 operating system available to process all 64 bits for all of its customers' applications on the day of announcement.

To go from CISC to RISC, and from 48 bits to 64, the AS/400 went through two major architectural changes at once. Yet AS/400 programmers in businesses across the globe never had to touch their program code--not even one line of it. That is simply remarkable. The programs ran on the old 48-bit CISC system one day, and the next day they ran on the new 64-bit RISC AS/400 system. Not only does Microsoft have to finish its transition of Windows to 64 bits, but also Windows applications must be redone in order to use the 64-bit operating system and the power of the new 64-bit Intel hardware. That's a tall order, yet the press is silent.

A 64-Bit RISC, No Buts!

While Intel and Microsoft have been and continue to be praised for a partial implementation, IBM is already on its eighth generation of 64-bit RISC processors. For nine years and counting, since 1995, AS/400s have been enjoying the benefits of 64-bit hardware and software computing, and neither the press nor IBM has made a big deal about it.

Moreover, organizations across the globe have painlessly migrated their object code to the 64-bit AS/400 RISC platform from the 48-bit AS/400 CISC platform. My old IBM accounts in Pennsylvania--the Scranton Times, Marywood University, Penn Security Bank, and College Misericordia--all have their programs running on 64-bit RISC with no code conversion whatsoever.

Despite the lack of accolades from IBM and the press, the AS/400 CISC-to-RISC hardware change was revolutionary, outstanding, and worth touting. Nobody had ever done it before 1995. It was a technology first. The IBM mainframe did not get to 64 bits until 2001, six years later. For reasons that AS/400 customers still do not understand, IBM did not call attention to its own AS/400 for this major technology achievement? One would think that Intel and Microsoft thank IBM every day for its humility.

Chapter 9 MADGIC! MADGIC! MADGIC!

The IBM AS/400 Closing Seminar

When I worked for IBM, I had the pleasure of being known as an AS/400 senior systems engineer and a system specialist in the Mid Atlantic Area of IBM. As a systems engineer and Mid Atlantic Area Designated Specialist (ADS), I migrated my skills a number of times from large systems and back to the small and midrange computers that were the rage from 1969 to the present. The AS/400 was my focus area before I took my leave of absence from Big Blue in 1992. I formally retired from IBM in 1999.

In other words, and this will matter to some folks who have been in the business for some time, I started with IBM's first small business computer, the diskless System/3, and then graduated to the System/3 model 15D and its Communication Control Program (CCP). I worked with the System/34 both as a front end for the System/3 and as a machine for customers to mark time with, while waiting for the delayed System/38.

I also spent a small amount of time working with the System/36--enough time to find out it was not much more than a grown-up System/34, yet not a System/38 or AS/400 or Power I class machine.

One of my jobs as a midrange specialist was to attend national IBM product briefings and then to announce new products and significant new releases of products to the local office and the business community in northeastern Pennsylvania. On June 21, 1988, I had the pleasure of announcing the brand new AS/400 to over 300 business people at the Center for the Performing Arts Auditorium on the beautiful campus of Marywood University in Scranton, Pennsylvania (see Chapter titled: "The Silverlake Project").

It's MADGIC!

For years before the announcement of the AS/400, I had been presenting new System/38 prospects with a one-day detailed overview of the System/38. IBM's marketing representatives (salesmen) had dubbed the session MADGIC after a similar, but longer (three day), national IBM program that was much more technical than my seminar. Readers in the computer business may remember that a crew from Philadelphia--Don Wickham, Skip Marchesani, and several others--had created the MADGIC program to help sell System/38s in the early 1980s.

The acronym stands for *marketing application development generates installed customers*. It sure does. The MADGIC program worked very well for IBM. My shorter program had similar results in the Scranton IBM office, but without the three-day investment.

When the AS/400 replaced the System/38 in IBM's product line, I ran through the IBM canned "product excellence" slide sets and replaced a number of the slides to reflect what was new in the AS/400. The machines were so similar that I was able to continue the MADGIC program with just a few changes. All of the wonderful things that IBM had brought to the System/38 were still available on the AS/400 and none had yet to reach the competition.

The "madgic" show was so similar that the same databases and programs that I had used for the "live" demo ran unchanged on the AS/400, just as they had on the System/38. For the technical folks out there, the only major change that I made in my live presentation was to switch from the Programmer's Menu to the newer Program Development Manager (PDM).

Both MADGIC seminars (IBM's three-day version and my one-day session) had the same purpose: to convince IBM's new system prospects that the best computing platform for their business was the System/38, and, subsequently, the AS/400.

A marketing rep with an ongoing sales situation would invite the technical team and the management team from the prospect's organization to attend the one-day offering. The morning of the seminar was dedicated to informing DP managers and programmers about the wonders of the AS/400 system, while their management watched their eyes. The afternoon session took the information and summed it up in a "show me" hands-on demo. By the end of the day, the prospect team had built a live application using the productivity-oriented development tools of the AS/400, along with the programming language of the day, RPG/400.

The sessions were very successful. Even prospects that decided that they could not afford an AS/400 wanted one after the session. Most attendees became System/38 or AS/400 customers. They had become convinced of the "magic" of the system through the MADGIC session. Once they were convinced, more often than not, IBM received as a reward another installed AS/400 customer.

AS/400 Still Offers Rapid Application Development

Marketing application development generates installed customers. This sure is a different tune from the one heard in the industry today. The AS/400 still is a leader in providing a rapid development environment for both interactive and batch applications. In other words, fully functional business applications continue to be developed in short order using the standard tools available with an AS/400 system.

There is no database on any platform that makes coding easier for programmers. If an IBM marketing representative could get a prospect for a day to sit through a MADGIC session, the rep would more than likely close an order within one to six months of the session. A brochure could not do it then. A brochure cannot do it today. Several sales calls on the customer or prospect could not do it. Today, new prospects typically receive no sales calls from IBM, since there is no longer a real IBM sales force.

There was and continues to be too long of a story to tell about the AS/400 for any computer prospect to hear in a sales call. Moreover, there is never an ad that gives prospects a clue that they might be able to productively employ an AS/400. Because IBM makes no such investment today, its AS/400 installed base is shrinking, not growing.

I hear IBM say that its installed base is growing, but I do not see it. Everywhere I go, fewer and fewer people have heard about the AS/400, and more and more customers are giving up and moving to a platform their executives know about.

The MADGIC session took about a day to show attendees how different and better an AS/400 is compared with anything that they had ever used. It was a big investment for IBM to bring in just one prospect for a whole day. But in about 80 percent of the cases, the investment paid off with a nice sized order for a System/38 or an AS/400 system.

In the late 1980s and the early 90s (before the client/server revolution), IBM gained many new accounts. Once companies became convinced that the AS/400 system made developing applications so much easier than on any other platform, they knew they could sustain their competitive edge by climbing on board the platform. The age of full expectation for software packages had not yet arrived.

Today, there are no IBM people left to convince prospects that an AS/400 should be considered an option, and there are no prospects banging on IBM's door to find out.

The System Makes a Difference

The simple theme in the Scranton MADGIC sessions was always that "***the system makes a difference***." Many hardware vendors would set the prospect selection bar by suggesting that software solutions (available packages) should be the sole criteria, not hardware or overall system capability. When their package was the industry leader, it was tough to sell against. But it is easy to point out that the system makes a difference if you get an audience and are so inclined to make that your theme. Today's IBM does not work hard to get an audience, and the system is no longer the theme. Today's IBM takes the line of least resistance. IBM will happily sell you any IBM product that you want, and won't help you one bit in understanding which system it thinks is best.

Back when I was with IBM, I don't know how many times I heard a prospect say, "It does not matter what the software runs on as long as it does the job." I would bristle at hearing that. Of course, it was a clever marketing theme for a hardware vendor that did not have a solid hardware system and operating system upon which to run the software. It was and still is a good way for IBM's competitors to eliminate a major advantage of IBM's best solution, the AS/400 system.

A smart IBM marketing rep, however, would continue to insist that the system makes a difference. Over the years, unfortunately, IBM forgot about that message, even though it does not sell business software solutions. IBM sells hardware, middleware, and services. Independent vendors, which have loose partnerships with IBM, sell software solutions. I've seen them in action. If the customer resists an IBM hardware solution, the package vendor quickly makes the prospect comfortable with a non-IBM solution.

How clever of some vendors to take away a head-to-head system comparison by limiting choice to software. The competition was keen, but I could never quite understand why IBM rolled over so easily on this one. When IBM began to market "solutions" independent of hardware, I never agreed with this strategy, and I still do not.

IBM does not sell application software solutions, so it does not make sense that solutions should be the major selection criteria. IBM sells computer systems, such as the AS/400 system. Ask any real IT professional who has worked on a number of platforms. The system makes a big difference.

IBM mainframe and other sales people, as well as IBM's competitors, knew they would easily be beaten in head-to-head system competition. So to give the small mainframe or Unix box, or other non-AS/400 box, a chance of being the winning entry, a smart competitor would neutralize the advantages of the AS/400 by taking the hardware and the operating system from the equation.

If your competition was an AS/400, this substantially increased your prospects of gaining the business. Over time, as you will see in this book, it was IBM's own server divisions and other divisions with their own agendas for success that complained the loudest about the AS/400's unfair competitive advantage as a system. Rather than highlight its best offering, IBM acquiesced to its whining also-ran divisions and stopped advertising the AS/400 as the system to beat all systems.

How Could an AS/400 Help When a Packaged Solution Is Needed?

The raw facts indicate that no software package ever does the complete job. This is just as true now as it was in the 1960s. In fact, businesses are so complex and so different that no proposal for a solution can ever possibly have all of the software features listed that are needed by the company. Most proposals that I have seen, for example, emphasize all of the new facilities and new ways of approaching old problems that are desirable for the firm. However, very few proposals inventory the features that are provided in the company's current software. Thus, all new software implementations come with major disruptions to the business as problems solved uniquely with the prior packages need to be developed and solved again.

There is always a list of items that you learn about after installing and implementing a new package, that the package either fails to do, or that it does in a way that does not suit the organization. When companies wake up the day after the package is installed and they must run their businesses as well, if not better than prior to implementation, unknown package holes become a big issue. And there are always many issues and concerns like that, with which to deal.

Software sponsors across the organization do not want to be blamed for the holes. In many cases as I have witnessed, they try to cast blame on somebody else for not telling them that a certain missing bell or whistle or necessary y function was ever noted. When a package is implemented on a system other than an AS/400, the nightmare of missing function lasts substantially longer. You will see all kinds of acts trying to squeeze a round peg in a square hole, when it just is not going to fit.

People from your own shop as well as vendor personnel will show up with their various sized shoehorns trying to squeeze the software package into areas that it just does not belong. That's the only real solution if you do not have an AS/400 box. Short of throwing out the package when you realize that major function is missing, making do is the only solution.

It is different with an AS/400 or Power i. Instead of package caretakers, the few IT people in an AS/400 or a System/38 shop are typically capable of designing and modifying systems and programming. They are not like the Windows people, whose specialty has become rebooting. If you reboot and reboot and reboot, and the system still cannot do billing, with Windows that's where you are left. You are still out of luck. The 53rd reboot will not bring billing.

Standard Options Plus Customization Capability

Consider the analogy of building a house. Say that you discovered a very narrow hallway that could cause an accident. If you bought the house plans and had the house built as is, you would get a dangerous, narrow hallway in the completed house. That's like what you get when you choose a non-AS/400 box. To prevent an accident, you place a sign someplace to warn everybody about it or you block it off and have them go all around the house to get to the other side. When you've got an AS/400, you have the system "power tools" that permit you to enlarge the hallway without needing special signage and without having to compromise another room.

The fact is that packages do not do everything, and you will always be looking to find solutions for what the package does not do. I mean always. Often the biggest libraries in shops with package solutions are the add-and-change libraries. Without these, the business would be crippled. When you go live with a System/38 or an AS/400, you can feel better about your package because the system makes a difference. It cannot be refuted. If the package needs an adjunct built, you can build the addition with no sweat. If the package needs better integration, you can alter the system easier. If the package needs better reporting, the tools are available in the system to get the job done five to 10 times faster than on any other box. So if your system is an AS/400, your options for poor solution recovery are immeasurably increased. The package becomes reasonably easy to extend to cover the areas necessary to fully perform the job.

Suppose, several months or years later, your packaged software vendor ultimately deploys the solution that was missing when you went live. Of course, by then, your home-developed code would already be working, and probably working well. Again, the system makes a difference. The AS/400 system tools allow for the home code to be removed more easily and the new code inserted without major disruption. The system is one of a kind in the computer industry. The AS/400 system does make a difference. That's why AS/400 IT people do not want to work on anything else.

What About Down Time?

It is OS/400 and its host of integrated functions that make the big difference. However, the AS/400 gives you the very opposite of a double whammy. Not only is the operating system solid, unlike Windows, but the hardware is also rock solid, unlike the PC.

When the system goes down, it can be argued that the system makes a difference. Notice please that I did not say "if" the system goes down. Even an AS/400 box goes down, but very rarely. Windows boxes on the average are down several weeks per year; whereas AS/400 boxes go down just a few hours per year. If your system is an AS/400, chances are it will not go down this year at all. When it eventually does go down, you will be up far more quickly than on any other platform, including the single-system mainframe.

MADGIC Is Impossible Today

From homemade software to customization to lots of packages to just a little down time, the AS/400 system can make a big difference. After a day of MADGIC, the prospect would have no need for guessing. They learned and touched enough that they could actually "feel" the power and facility of the box and they sometimes liked the machine enough that at the session, they signed on the dotted line.

Today the MADGIC scenario is all but impossible. One of the problems in properly positioning the AS/400 as a desirable computing platform continues to be the amount of time it takes to do a proper briefing. But, an even greater problem today is finding a prospect. An even greater problem than finding a prospect, however, is finding a salesperson or an IBM business partner willing to invest the time to find a prospect.

In the new IBM, even if a local IBM still existed, and even if there were an anxious prospect, with checkbook in hand, ready to discover the AS/400 system, there would be nobody available to sell it to them. There is certainly nobody to present a one-day or even a one-minute AS/400 presentation. And there is no possibility of a hands-on live demonstration.

IBM did away with most of the local facilities, speakers, and foot soldiers over the last 10 years. The folks who once told the story are not there any more to do the talking. The company saw its local sales and technical force as too big of an expense and did not feel that it needed them for anything anymore. Since then, the company has not had any ability to identify new computer prospects.

In the unlikely event that a prospect were to stumble in, IBM would have nobody available to differentiate the AS/400 in any meaningful way. Maybe that's why IBM closes very few new AS/400 accounts these days. Maybe that's why IBM's server revenue is down substantially over the last 10 years.

IBM business partners may argue that selling new accounts is their job. It may be their job, but they don't get paid enough to chase new business. In the 1980s, IBM's new-account sales people sold nothing but new accounts. When IBM was IBM, it understood that new accounts are an investment in the future. They are an annuity. Because new accounts were the future growth of IBM, new-account sales people were paid handsomely for each piece of business.

The old IBM knew that if a new account sales person had to care for installed accounts, there would be few new accounts. The sales person would concentrate on the installed accounts where the dough is much easier to get. It's the same for IBM business partners. They also don't have the time. So nobody does the new account job, and nobody is looking for MADGIC.

If IBM is ever to become #1 again in IT, it will have to take a hard look at the things that helped it be # 1 when it was the unquestioned leader. Nothing happens overnight but if IBM were to change its focus on what would work, slowly but surely the magic would be back even if all of the MADGIC were not. More Sooner than late, IBM's back end would be the only view the competition could find.

The Unspoken Word

If nobody is telling the story, how does anybody learn about the existence of an AS/400 or the good qualities of a new IBM? Quite frankly, I don't know. Other than the AS/400 experts who write for the trade press, former AS/400 IBMers, and AS/400 battle scarred customers, there is nobody out there telling people who don't already know that an AS/400 would serve them well. That's just the way it is.

A little magic sure would help.

IBM must again want to be better than the rest or it will remain a slow dog in a fast race.

Chapter 10 Some Servers Are More Equal

The Watsons Were Great Skippers

Many opportunities have been presented to IBM over the years, and with impunity, the company's leaders have been able to fritter away a disproportionate share of those opportunities. Aside from the huge wager that paid off big time, when IBM bet its business on the System/360 in 1964, its finest hour came from its great work in developing and marketing its first mainframe computer system in the 1950s. Thomas Watson Jr. out-smarted his father to get IBM moving from the electromechanical devices of the 1930s and 1940s to the promise of computers.

In many ways Thomas Watson Sr., IBM's founder, was blessed in the same fashion as Apple's founder, Steven Jobs. Everything he touched was successful. His only real faux pas was that he chose to resist computers until it was almost too late. But again fortune came his way, as his son Thomas Jr. was able to put a team together quickly to gain back the lost ground.

Watson Sr. gave IBM a proud legacy and a loyal constituency. The company had been profitable for over 40 years when Tom Sr. turned the reins over to Tom Jr. Tom Sr. had accumulated lots of cash and was not about to give any of it up for a chance at a big win. Both father and son had this thing about renting machines rather than selling them. Not only was there lots of money streaming in from the long-term rentals of tired old equipment, long written off, but IBM's crackerjack field sales force kept selling more and more rentals. IBM's year-to-year sustenance was continually ensured through its rental base. One might say that even if nobody sold anything, with Tom Sr.'s cherished rentals, there would still be a big wad coming in. But, of course, standing still was never the objective in Watson's IBM.

The objective was always to make a buck, but not at all costs. Both father and son believed that "if you take care of the people, the people will take care of the business." The company thrived on new sales. The IBM that the two men passed on was so well blessed with momentum and assets; it could afford to make lots of mistakes. And it did.

Like his father, Thomas Watson Jr. did not make many big mistakes. However, he was much more inclined to take a gamble than his ultra-conservative father. On Tom Jr.'s watch, IBM achieved its first billion-dollar year, and the company was closing in on $10 billion a year in revenue when he eventually passed the reins to T. Vincent Learson, the first CEO who was not a Watson.

When the Watsons Were Gone

The caretakers to whom Watson and Learson passed the company, however, were not as vigilant with the company's assets and options (see Chapter 38, "Time for New Management At IBM?"). Having graduated to success through selling big iron (mainframe computers) to big companies and big government, the latter day CEOs had a seemingly difficult time figuring out how to be successful with any other product line but mainframes.

Lost PC Market

This mainframe predisposition, "mainframe above all," cost the company big time. How big was this cost? You don't have to go far for a counting. You may recall that IBM invented the IBM PC in 1981. At the time, as one would expect, IBM held 100 percent of the PC business and had 100 percent of the opportunity. All the company had to do was play its cards right. The results are in and have been for more than 25 years. IBM failed big time in the PC marketplace. It had great cards, but its mainframe-oriented executive management team played them poorly.

The company lost well over 95 percent of the PC market by being a mainframe company instead of a computer company. They lost the rest because it was too expensive to maintain such a small market share. The cost was monumental. If one were to make a new company, for example, by combining the revenue of just the big players in the PC and microcomputer industry--HP, Microsoft, Intel, Gateway, Dell, etc.--the new company would bring in substantially more than $500 billion in annual revenue.

In fact, Apple is more than twice the size of IBM and the new HP is much larger than IBM itself. The combined company would therefore be significantly larger than IBM itself. The real value of the PC marketplace is about $1 trillon. Nobody would would win an argument that such an annual loss is not a big cost! Considering the market was IBM's for the taking, it was an unnecessary loss.

Industry experts credit IBM with legitimizing, if not creating, the microcomputer business with its PC introduction in 1981. Since the machines that were the previous best-sellers (Apple and Radio Shack) behaved differently from the IBM units, used different software, and were basically incompatible with IBM's new unit, IBM is universally credited with creating a new branch of the microcomputer industry, known simply as the IBM PC industry.

In the later 1980s the PC industry would begin to include non-IBM, compatible computers, but the marketplace in 1981 included just IBM's products. Today, as we all know, this market segment is known as PCs and nobody cares about compatibility any more other than assuring Intel Inside and Microsoft Windows on the outside.

Though most know how the story turned out, if you go back to 1981, you'd find that the PC marketplace that IBM had created was the company's to grow or to lose. There was no other game in town. Compaq, Microsoft, Intel, Gateway, and Dell would not have been able to aggressively snatch this market from IBM if the company had not been preoccupied with its mainframe business and with keeping its mainframe business from being broken up by the US Justice Department.

Poor Top Management

If you objectively analyze IBM's decisions and actions over the 20-year period since it invented the PC, you can conclude only that the company intended to give this very important business to its competitors. It is amazing that the only IBM manager to lose his job in that period was John Akers, and he was not ousted because of PCs.

Before 1981, the highly successful IBM had not earned a dollar of revenue from PCs. Perhaps this is the only saving grace in the big IBM giveaway. You might conclude that since they had not really earned income from PCs, anything in revenue they got was gravy.

Obviously, IBM, despite all the money spent on forecasting, did not see the PC market as a big deal back then. Consequently, giving this business to Microsoft, Intel, and Compaq, was of little significance. But now that the real numbers are in, history has it noted as IBM's most costly blunder, at over $100 billion per year. It may be the most costly corporate blunder of all time. Yet IBM management got a pass.

Some may buy the argument that IBM was purposely trying not to dominate the PC marketplace, hoping not to rile the Justice Department by dominating another industry. However, when the Reagan administration withdrew its antitrust actions against the company in 1982, within the PC's first year,

IBM took no recognizable action to reclaim the PC territory it had already begun to give to others. IBM still owned the PC industry, yet there was no visible marketing plan to flourish in this new business.

Intel and Microsoft had gained the most, and should have had the most to fear in 1982. IBM still ruled the day. Their affiliation with IBM took both companies from little more than "*also-rans*" in a big industry to multi-billion-dollar behemoths.

Bill Gates was a master and he learned how to play IBM as a fine-tuned instrument, while Intel gained from IBM's indifference to not having "IBM inside." History proves that IBM's losses in the PC field were caused more by a poor choice of friends and partners than its perceived enemy, Uncle Sam.

IBM's fear of government intervention and its belief that it was a mainframe company were major contributing factors to the company getting off track in the microcomputer market. But it was clearly the myopic mainframe vision that did the company in.

For years, IBM sat by as this entire industry of PC competitors came into being. IBM aided and abetted the enemy, ensuring its own destiny. The emerging PC leaders helped take the competitive edge by using IBM's own intellectual capital and original ideas. Some of the takers were partners, while others were just superior entrepreneurs. But there were lots of takers. It was not long before this burgeoning industry seceded from the IBM mother ship and became self-sustaining.

The Railroad Business and the Mainframe Business

I am reminded of the story of the fall of the railroads whenever I think of the remarkable possibilities IBM failed to capitalize on over the years. The loss of its PC business is just one of these cases. The railroads, as most know, provided the main transportation arteries and carried the most business on its lines for many years.

Railroad companies believed they were in the railroad business. The business was growing quickly and was highly profitable. Then one day, almost overnight, trucking companies began to poach on the railroad companies' business. Before long, buses began to carry passengers--the same passengers who once rode trains to all destinations.

It was more convenient, in many cases, for businesses and individuals to use the trucks and the buses, rather than head for the tracks. The trucking business began to thrive, while the railroad business began to hurt for all the business it was losing.

It was not apparent to the railroad executives that they might buy some trucks and buses and try going trackless. They were, after all, in the *railroad* business. There was no such thing as trackless in the railroad business. When the railroad companies began to die off, their autopsies showed one common but major illness. They had made a gross misassumption of the industry in which they participated.

It turns out they were not in the railroad business at all. They were in both the transportation business and the shipping business. And the transportation and shipping businesses are the two businesses they lost while they kept the railroad business. Their competitors understood that they provided transportation and shipping, not railroads. They knew that folks wanted the best transportation at the fairest price. A train was not part of the decision process.

When the railroads could not provide what the people wanted, these new transportation/shipping companies were pleased to steal their customers. They brought on the busses, the trucks, and even the automobiles. Transportation was what people wanted, and they were willing to leave the railroads, the tracks and the great impressive trains to get it.

IBM has always been, and seems like it always will be, in the mainframe (railroad) business. It executes precisely in the mainframe business. It is the acclaimed best-of-breed in the mainframe business. Everything else in IBM has always been just a sideshow to the mainframe event. Even IBM's new mission, *cloud computing*, is an offshoot of huge powerful mainframe computers.

The IBM Company found it just as difficult to believe that it is in the information technology business as the railroads found it to believe that they were in the transportation business. IBM did not operate as if mainframes were just a segment in the overall IT scheme. Thus, in most of its other business areas (non-mainframe), over the years, IBM has proven to be easy pickings for its new breed of competitors. These competitors not only picked IBM to the bone; they ate the bone.

Like a big, docile fish in a sea of Oscars and Piranha, IBM was attacked and severely beaten and conquered by just about every little company that chose to take it on. IBM had so much cash it hardly noticed for a long, long, time. From Univac to Digital Equipment Corporation (DEC) to Cray, to Intel, to Oracle, to Microsoft, to TI, to Sun, the Big Blue IBM mainframe company was clobbered and it barely survived the vicious attacks on its periphery. With each attack, IBM was left with less. But just like the railroad companies, IBM continued to see itself in the mainframe business.

Companies such as Microsoft were bold enough and successful enough to aim right for IBM's heart. Their objective was to deliver a deathblow in IBM's prime hardware business area--servers, even mainframe servers.

Perhaps IBM has survived this long from a Microsoft server attack at its heart because, as some would say, Microsoft would have a hard time recognizing a heart even if it stumbled onto one. But many of us out here watching are just not sure that IBM ever had the mettle to survive a battle with the crafty and agile Bill Gates. If there were mettle hiding someplace in IBM, it was sure kept locked up by the corporate chieftains.

It stopped being a live-and-let-live world out there when Microsoft decided that it was ready to rule the IT world, and the Gates / Balmer duo always played to win. Moreover, Microsoft always had a little product and a little plan, which it claims is big enough to take down IBM. And rather than fighting Bill Gates and Company, IBM persisted in making new arrangements to cooperate and join Mr. Gates as a "friend." It turns out Bill Gates was the most unaffordable, most expensive friend IBM ever could have chosen. With all the Microsoft baggage to carry, old and new, tough times came to IBM and if IBM is no careful such times may very well come again.

Use the Secret Weapon!

Companies that want to win who are being defeated, do not have secret weapons that they choose not to use against their enemies. Unfortunately, IBM in the railroad business failed to see that it had other tools in the product development and implementation shed that could kick the pants off the competition.

Many, including IBM itself, do not realize that the company still has its secret weapon, which is one of few products that ca help IBM win big again if it chooses to do so. It is a study object of this book in that if deployed properly this time, IBM can stage itself to become # 1 in all aspects of IT once again.

The AS/400 (Power i) has been waiting on the IBM bench for a long time hoping to get its chance to play on the first team. It has been in the game but was always removed when a mainframe player complained about the AS/400 getting too much exposure.

This complete machine, now packaged as Power i is a unique, all-IBM computer system, introduced and marketed by a rogue division (like Microsoft) within the IBM Company. It would be well known today, and well marketed, if it had started off its life as a traditional mainframe.

History credits this secret IBM weapon with bringing down the once mighty Digital Equipment Corporation (DEC). It was nicknamed the Digital VAX killer, until all of the VAX's were dead, and Compaq swallowed DEC. Then, Mother IBM put it backin the barn and locked the door.

Thus, there is a big problem with deploying the secret weapon today. IBM as a company does not believe in it and more importantly, IBM does not like it. Spawned by the biggest company in the mainframe business, the secret weapon is not a traditional mainframe. It is better and that makes the mainframers cringe.

Moreover, IBM executives, even after all their mainframe-bias-induced failings, do not seem prepared to upset the still powerful anti-Rochester (mainframe) contingent within the company. The biggest fault of this secret weapon is that it has no corporate sponsorship. Thus, it is doomed to remain a secret unless new IBM executives decide to brather some life into the battered company.

Most companies in any business would love to have a number of outstanding products to bring to its customers. For IBM, however, multiple product lines became a big burden instead of an opportunity. For a ten year period in fact, the only visible marketing from IBM revolved around coaxing all who would listen into believing that the Company had just one product line, the eServer with four sub-products.

Despite IBM's strongest wishes, its customers still saw four distinct product lines and they saw IBM as being foolish for thinking otherwise. The machine families may have had the same first names, the personalities of the four IBM servers were not at all alike. Everybody but IBM Top Management noticed.

Wishing and hoping and renaming were not ever going to make four completely different machines the same. Along with this questionable marketing strategy, at this time, the IBM Company persisted in minimizing the impact of its brightest star, the AS/400, masking and homogenizing it into something much less obvious.

Rather than highlighting its best server product, and differentiating its others, IBM's marketing group took the company's four distinct and substantially different server lines and tried to make them appear to be the same to potential customers.

(See the Chapters about homogenization and rebranding.) IBM began to call all four servers "eServers" and has designated each server line as a product series within the eServer emblem. Those who remember the days when milkmen brought jugs of pasteurized milk to the door know that you had to shake them first because the cream was always at the top. In fact, with most things in life, the cream rises to the top. The best is recognized as the best. For milk connoisseurs, a major disadvantage of homogenization is that the milk is all mixed up and any cream that there may be is scattered throughout the whole bottle or carton. Thus, all parts of the milk look the same because all the parts have been mixed together. So in the new eServer world, the chances of the AS/400 being highlighted for what it is any time soon is quite remote. Homogenization will prevent it from rising to the top.

Since the four IBM server lines are not the same, and are not even similar in personality, IBM, in effect, had merely given its products new clothes and an umbrella. The fabled emperor would be proud of IBM's recent accomplishments. But for the rest of us, it just does not work. The AS/400 masqueraded as the Power i under the eServer umbrella is difficult to distinguish from the notion of eServer.

One could have predicted that the AS/400 as the eServer Power i would be treated as a second-class server by IBM. It has always been. One could have predicted that the AS/400 as the eServer Power i would lose sales and market share after being covered by any umbrella that denotes sameness. AS/400 systems sell because of greatness, not sameness.

The AS/400 line has lost sales and is still not the major contributor to IBM that it once was. The minimalists in IBM did their trick on the AS/400, and unless IBM chose to reverse its direction, the finest system within IBM was doomed for years to wear invisible clothes, hidden under the eServer umbrella. When the umbrella disappeared, it was a good day for the AS/400.

IBM stockholders would not be proud of what IBM had done with the Emperor's new clothes. I would expect that most were never aware. I predict that history will show this as another big gift for the enemy. The most positive comment that I can make about the eServer homogenization is that it was worthy of a big thank you from industry competitors.

Any competitor that competes against AS/400 for its business for this time period could breathe a big sigh of relief. The eServer competition for a while had a fine time differentiating their products from the indistinguishable wares of the Emperor.

There do not seem to be any revolutionary ideas coming from IBM recently indicating that the IBM AS/400 story will evenrually have a happy ending. To call it as I see it, it sure looks like we can expect the same level of botching and floundering and squandering as in the past. However, with the percentage of cash reserves lots lower than during the Watson years, IBM has a new and bigger worry if it fails like it did during the Akers years. It's called survival. "Mainframe over all," along with the light-blocking umbrella, can no longer be seen as a positive marketing mantra. IBM needs to do better.

Protection from Cannibalization

When you look at how IBM executes, you might find yourself saying, "Poor little IBM." Historically, with regard to the AS/400, poor little IBM has struggled most with protecting its mainframe business from irrelevance. Yet the company is not just in the mainframe business. It still has a lucrative Unix line.

Along with its floundering PC line, IBM positioned all of its servers so that the AS/400 could not harm any of them, including Intel PCs before IBM exited this marketplace. The last thing IBM wanted was for its AS/400 to become so successful that its other server customers begin to migrate to the all-IBM AS/400.

According to IBM people, with whom I have spoken, on a per unit basis, IBM would do well profit-wise with an all-IBM machine such as the AS/400. Ironically, IBM's server management team seemed much more concerned about cannibalization of other server lines by the AS/400 than it did assuring the success of the AS/400 for IBM and its stockholders. It was like the IBM Company could not permit the AS/400 to become too successful.

Rather than use the Madison Avenue firms to come up with a plan that highlighted the various strengths of IBM's diverse servers, IBM chose to drown all of its servers in the proverbial sea of homogenization.

IBM paid Madison Avenue firms millions of dollars annually, and one would expect that in return the ad companies would come up with better ideas. But maybe IBM's internal politics prevented these firms from being creative. After all, IBM itself had been unwilling to suggest to the marketplace that it even had a really super computer because the success of that machine would hurt sales of its other server products.

Should a Company Highlight Its Best Product?

Is it possible that IBM was correct in minimizing its best product so that the others look better? What if, for instance, General Motors came out with a water powered luxury vehicle that revolutionized the entire industry and leapfrogged the competition? Let's also say that its forecasts promised huge returns at the expense of the competition.

Would GM keep it a secret because unintentionally, some of the new purchases might also come from traditional Cadillac or Buick owners? Would GM not take full advantage of the moment and position itself to win sales using its lead star? Doesn't that make marketing and business sense?

Even without a water-fuel revolution, GM does not keep its top-of-the-line Cadillac hidden because it might affect its Suburban sales. Ford does not keep its Lincoln under wraps so that Thunderbird sales are not cannibalized. Sony does not keep DVD products out of the marketplace because they will hurt CD sales. These companies seem to understand that the competition works for some other company. Your own products are not the competition. It really is time for IBM to learn this lesson.

AS/400 Was an IBM Marketing Failure

Aside from the first few years after its introduction, when all of IBM knew that DEC had to be taken out, the AS/400 has endured a long-standing marketing failure. I have to say that this is by IBM's choice. Ironically, in the 1970s and even in the 1980s, as the AS/400 was introduced, IBM was often characterized as a marketing-first organization. The company had reasonable but not necessarily leading-edge products. IBM was rarely praised for having the best technology. Industry watchers over the years credited IBM's huge successes to its marketing and sales prowess, not to its product innovation.

As noted previously in this chapter, one should not forget that IBM is out of the PC business on a de facto basis and because it sold its businesses to Lenovo.

There was a time that the more PCs that IBM sold, the more money it lost. So PCs for IBM have not been such a great business since it chose not to make them successful. Yet IBM during the eServer period advertised PCs all the time, but never the AS/400. IBM never told the world that its AS/400 was the best products its labs had ever produced.

Will IBM permit the AS/400 (now known as the Power i) to go the same way as the PC and the PC server? The Company sure does not protect its AS/400 marketplace, which still today is number one in the midrange business computer area, but others are closing hard using Windows boxes in clusters as weapons.

Will IBM wait until HP creates a clone and takes away midsized systems just as Compaq stole IBM's PC business? We can say it can't happen, but IBM's poor management of the AS/400 product and its customers, is a ripe situation for an opportunistic marketer to tap. Maybe if IBM decided to be

#1, things would be different when the Company was forced to excel.

Mainframes Come First

IBM has always been a mainframe-first company. No other server is equal to the mainframe. IBM's financial team for years believed that if it was good for the mainframe, it was good for IBM. When John Akers, Lou Gerstner's predecessor, a manager with mainframe heritage, single-handedly took IBM to the brink of financial collapse, the financial guys and the board of directors finally saw through the ruse. To save the company from financial ruin, the IBM board fired Akers and brought in Gerstner to save the company. He definitely saved the company, but the mainframe legacy was so strong that it lived on despite Gerstner.

Going back to the System/38 era, always ready to protect its mainframe business, IBM, for all of its claims to greatness, did not know how to cope with revolutionary, industry-leading technology coming from one of its small renegade plants in the Midwest. IBM's mainframe-oriented management team took the only action that seemed to fit. It tried to kill the System/38, as a company would try to kill a competitor, rather than embrace a non-mainframe innovation and learn to profit from it.

There was a lot jealousy in Poughkeepsie and Endicott, IBM's mainframe bastions. The System/38 was not invented there. It was not a mainframe project. Besides the jealousy, there was even more concern that the System/38 itself was a great concept and offered such promise that it was dangerous to the well-being of the mainframe. What if mainframe customers began to demand advanced functioning and ease of use in the same package? The fact that the System/38 was actually a better design than the patched-up mainframe architecture did not help the love affair, either. IBM's culture permitted the mainframe division to have influence over all divisions, and it was not good for the System/38 that the mainframers considered the box a threat to the viability of the mainframe.

Mainframe IBM knew that the System/38 was the only product that arose from its own future systems (FS) project of the 1970s (see Chapter titled: "Future Systems Project"). IBM's top executives had sent the mainframe contingent of the future system team home packing. They told the mainframers in no uncertain terms that they could not implement the new technology defined for the future system because it would be too disruptive for IBM's big mainframe customers.

Nobody in IBM told The Little Lab in Rochester, Minnesota, that they could not use the best of the FS project as the basis for their next system, which happened to be the System/38.

Sometimes subtly and sometimes obviously, this shortsighted management team tried to remove the System/38 from the IBM product line. The Fort Knox project, covered in Chapter 15, was a prime example of this. When the AS/400, the almost-aborted System/38 follow-on product, became successful, despite the mainframers' attempts to destroy it before it even began, corporate IBM again chose to limit its prospects for success, rather than highlight its special features.

Mainframe Reps Preferred the Competition

IBM once had a big division known as the Data Processing Division (DPD). When I first joined IBM in 1969, DPD was the only division besides the typewriter division (the Office Products Division) that sold computers.

I worked for DPD. Later, IBM formed the General Systems Division (GSD). This division was created as a buffer to ameliorate the Justice Department in case they decided to split up IBM. For years, the DPD folks sold mainframes and the GSD folks sold small computers, such as the System/3, and later the System/38. Shortly after GSD formed its field division, IBM moved most of its people who supported small systems, including myself, to GSD.

IBM was always more effective when it had product representatives in three divisions: office products (typewriters), general systems (small computers), and data processing (mainframes). However, there were some conflicts among the divisions, but that's what managers are for.

For example, DPD reps would often make a call on a larger customer, only to find that a GSD rep was already trying to sell it a System/38 or a System/36 as a mainframe satellite processor. Account control was paramount for the DPD sales team. They did not want the executives in their accounts deciding that the GSD guy was going to dictate IBM account strategy.

There are many stories about DPD sales people who boasted that they would prefer to lose to IBM's competition than to a GSD representative. From my vantage point in the field, all of the conflicts were management problems and could have been solved with proper direction, rather than by permitting sales people to run the show.

To put the internal IBM threat in perspective, at the very root of the overall marketing problem, IBM as a company was not accustomed to selling superior technology. The System/38 all of a sudden was discovered with an architecture that should have first been built for the mainframe. The larger that IBM permitted the System/38 grow, the more of a threat it was to IBM's mainframe business.

Ironically, through the years, IBM was always defending itself against superior technology. For example, Tom Watson Jr. was continually miffed that IBM mainframes could not be built to be faster than the supercomputers of the day. So the company had to develop defenses against companies with better technology. This time, it was the mainframe part of IBM defending itself against the superior wares of its own lab in Rochester. They were not interested in defending the mainframe against this "little" box from Rochester. They wanted to take Rochester out of the picture.

Even today, the mainframe has yet to catch up with the 1978 Model System/38. That's the difference between revolutions in technology (AS/400) and evolutions in technology (mainframe). This must have been frightening to the mainframe power brokers, who, among other things, wanted management power to remain in Poughkeepsie, rather than migrate to a little lab in Rochester.

Mainframe systems sold for orders of magnitude more than the System/38. Yet they were saddled with limited hardware architectures that yielded orders of magnitude less addressability than the System/38 product line. As noted in Chapter 6, with its 48-bit hardware, the total number of storage spaces that the System/38 could address was 281 trillion (addresses) at a time when the mainframe hardware was capped at 16 million addresses, by design.

No wonder the mainframe management team was concerned. It is understandable that a mainframe-myopic IBM never positioned the System/38 to receive the universal acclaim that it deserved in the computing industry. So it remained a little known stepchild. Each time IBM put down a surge from Rochester, IBM's Endicott and Poughkeepsie plants were spared to live yet another day.

Big IBM Did Not Need the System/38

Just like IBM did not need help from a PC division in 1981, the company did not want or need help from Rochester in the late 1960s to early 1980s. IBM was bowling over its competition on all fronts, or so it seemed. The company was bringing in record profits, and everything it touched was turning to gold. With or without quality products or marketing, inertia sustained the company. More than anything IBM did itself, inertia was its driving force to continued success. IBM was successful because it was successful. Yet inertia was a double-edged sword for the company. By the time the inertia let go in the early 1990s, during the last days of the Akers regime, IBM had forgotten how to be successful. The mainframe-only days of computing were long gone.

Because financial success was associated with the mainframe, and little labs really did not matter, the System/38, whose architecture was a big threat to the mainframe, fared worse inside IBM. It got credit for nothing.

The mainframe division, the source of many of the ideas that were implemented within the System/38 offering, was very concerned that if it let the System/38 grow into a big powerful mainframe-sized machine, it would pick up a big appetite and start eating mainframes for lunch. The division could not let the product succeed. And because IBM was not financially strapped, and really did not need Rochester, mainframe-sponsored protective actions were often implemented without question.

The Elephant and the Mouse

The System/38 was absolutely revolutionary, but IBM was afraid of the trump card that its own engineers had given it. The company really did not know how to deal with this awesome creation. Since the mainframe influence in corporate management was so profound, however, there was no pressure to come to any quick conclusions.

It is somewhat humorous in retrospect to consider that the big mainframe division was concerned about the little System/38. They had placed so many governors on size and speed and cost that it was a wonder the System/38 could even run. Considering the constraints Rochester's laboratory operated under, one would naturally have more appreciation for the creation of the System/38. It was a big project in IBM. In retrospect, it is a wonder that it was permitted. However, the resulting machine was not permitted to deliver adequate processing power or storage. It had to be profitable, and it had to be cheap to build. On top of the real technical constraints of doing something highly advanced for the first time, the artificial constraints placed on its development made the System/38's ultimate technology success even that much more noteworthy.

Today, the AS/400, in the form of the eServer Power i, is as powerful as IBM's most powerful mainframes. The governors are gone. Somehow, the AS/400 is becoming the mainframe of tomorrow, by default. Regardless of whether IBM lets it happen, this is not where most of us who wage war in AS/400 land see the machine fitting in.

The biggest mainframe shops already have big time power with their mainframe computers. IBM really does not have to kill the mainframe for the AS/400 to be successful. The big shops have lots of people and don't need the exceptional ease of use that is found on a powerful AS/400 box.

Don't get me wrong; I think it is good that the power of the AS/400 can continue to grow. But I would not suggest that the mainframe shops are where the new AS/400 customers should come from. The AS/400 is strategically positioned to attack the server farms of today and the farms of the competitors' Unix and Linux processors. But even that is not where the box will do its best.

The AS/400, at any size, is a business machine. It should be marketed as IBM's premiere business machine. For applications that need Unix or Linux or Windows or a mainframe operating system, that's where the other systems should come into play. From a $2,000 developers' AS/400 to a $3,000,000 production AS/400, as the business machine of the present and the future--that's where IBM can make a killing. Let's vote to spare the mainframe its death and keep it alive for traditional mainframe applications. Let's also vote out the mainframe management team that has hurt IBM for so long. Long live the mainframe *and* the AS/400!

Chapter 11 Where Does the AS/400 Fit?

What Kind of Machine Is That?

In IBM, products are slotted for particular user types when the funding is given for the development of new or upgraded machines. From the time of its earliest computers, despite IBM's best attempts, machines that have been built for one market are often purchased by another. The IBM 1620, for instance, was built in the 1950s for scientific number crunching. Yet many businesses and institutions used it for non-scientific purposes. Joe Balz of King's College, my alma mater, used his 1620 system to run the college. The machine did the payroll, student scheduling, and student billing.

The IBM 1130 is another machine that was geared for the scientific community; however, once IBM enabled it with the RPG II language, businesses and institutions were able to use it the way they saw fit. John Ardizoni of Mercy Hospital in Scranton, PA, used his IBM 1130 for patient billing, and Tom Ostrowski Jr. of Marywood University, also in Scranton, used his 1130 to run the institution. An almost perfect example of such a slotting failure is the IBM Series/1. It was designed and built to be a process control minicomputer, to do things like controlling compressors based on product temperatures and for traffic signalization, but when it did not sell in that market, IBM's resilient field force sold it to anyone who would buy it. Barbara Keegan, a programmer for one of my customers, the National Book Division of the W.W. Norton Company, used her Series/1 as a sales analysis machine.

The System/3 was the forerunner of the System/38. It was a very slow business computer, but was a great data processor. It did not even have a hardware-multiply feature. Yet IBM equipped it with the FORTRAN language, which was intended for scientific endeavors. Ken Hoffman of Owens-Illinois (now Techneglas) in Pittston, Pennsylvania, used his System/3 with FORTRAN as a number cruncher for TV faceplate data reduction to help the engineers know where to shave the glass plungers that molded glass. Jack Walsh of Cornell Iron in Mountaintop, Pennsylvania, used System/3 FORTRAN to configure steel doors for store openings and various other commercial-door purposes.

The AS/400 was built as the follow-on to the System/38, which was the follow-on to the System/3, which was built for the small business community. As the System/38 and the AS/400 grew in size, the capabilities of the machine were enough to handle even midsized businesses. Moreover, the systems made terrific distributed processors in large businesses that used mainframes for most computing chores.

Before the new millennium, when software packages made it appear that great programmer development facilities were no longer needed on a computing platform, the System/3X line and the AS/400 were the systems of choice for "roll your own" computing. A new application, such as accounts payable, could be designed and programmed with a System/38 or AS/400 type machine in as little as one or two months. While IBM had its field force in place, the AS/400 was always the lead box sold to a new business prospect as a system solution to run the prospect's business. Application software packages always came second, because with the AS/400, applications were so easy to create.

IBM has continually changed its business structure over the years. It's no wonder the AS/400 has been lost during the struggle. As recently as 1999, for example, the AS/400 began to be positioned as a “server” in the new IBM Server Division. Other products in the Server Division at the time included the PC-based Netfinity server, the Unix-based RS/6000, and the mainframe-oriented System/390.

Back then, there was no notion of a series of eServers. Instead, the IBM marketing arm positioned the AS/400 as an innocuous magic box among magic boxes, a silly notion even at the time. Of course, all of IBM's other servers were magic boxes as well. It did not matter whether the server ran Unix, Windows, OS/390, or OS/400. The magic box ad campaign did nothing to enhance the sales of AS/400 servers. This was about the time that IBM also began its campaign to strip away the identity of the AS/400 as the company's business system. After all, all of IBM's servers could handle business applications just as well as a Series/1 or a 1620 or an 1130.

Dennis Grimes, chief information officer of Klein Wholesale in Wilkes-Barre, Pennsylvania, knows that the AS/400 fits in, and hopes it always does:

> **"Old systems never die; they just fade away. Everything comes to an end, even IBM. As long as the AS/400 offers value, it will survive. Most of my staff members support business problems, not IT problems. We have our share of IT problems, but if I tried to do this with a WINTEL cluster, I would have everyone tied up with just IT support.**
>
> **"Someday someone will tell my management that we are dinosaurs and that our IT is too expensive. We will replace it with PC servers and support from India. No one will remember how we once supported business problems. Will the AS/400 go the way of OS/2? Both had terrible positioning and marketing, but the AS/400 enjoyed an installed base that it inherited from the S3X lineup.**
>
> **"If IT becomes a commodity, the AS/400 will disappear. Maybe in 2039?"**

In the late 1980s and early 1990s, before the magic box ad campaign, IBM claimed to have three major business areas: **enterprise systems**, **application business systems**, and **personal systems**. Under this three-headed arrangement, the AS/400 was clearly positioned, as IBM's application business flagship. If a system prospect wanted a business solution, the AS/400 was always the right system for the job. (It still is.) Its positioning was clear, and it was a big winner in most of its engagements. It was in this context that it seemed that the whole of IBM was behind the AS/400 in its fight to overtake the lead that DEC and others had stolen from IBM during the mid-1980s.

S/38 and AS/400 Strategic Miscues

By the time the first System/38 was shipped to customers, because of shipping delays, many who had placed first-day orders had already done something else. The System/38 delay in availability put a major dent in its prospects for success. System/38 sales amounted to less than 50,000 units over a 10-year period. (Some say as little as 20,000 units.) Moreover, the system was plagued by IBM's careful strategy of ensuring that it did not grow too big.

Thus, many businesses that had adopted System/3 and System/38 technology were outgrowing it by the late 1980s. Rather than take the IBM mainframe route when they outgrew the System/38, many businesses chose the competitive route. DEC and the band of minicomputer vendors had their best years while IBM's marketing vision was blurred by the Fort Knox project (see Chapter 15 for details on Fort Knox).

Good-bye, Minicomputers

When IBM emerged from the Fort Knox travesty, the company funded Rochester's AS/400 development as the natural follow-on for the System/38. Though it was late in coming, this work spawned the AS/400 system and positioned IBM to be the leader in business systems. From the moment that it was announced, IBM's guns were set on DEC and the minicomputer crowd. Within a few years, most DEC, HP, and Data General users, had been eliminated and the AS/400 reigned supreme.

Hello, LAN Servers

Then what? The next emerging technology was client/server and network/server systems that were pioneered by Novell. Its Netware product was hotter than hotcakes. But IBM was still looking through mainframe glasses. The company failed to admit that it had lost the PC revolution and seemed to think it was now okay that Novell use larger PCs to take small-business new accounts from the AS/400 just because IBM's PCs happened to run Novell Netware. That strategy killed the AS/400 as a new account vehicle in the 1990s. Moreover, when somebody wanted a PC, with Dell and Gateway and Compaq out there, IBM became the last place anybody would look for one. Just like today, nobody with a choice was buying IBM's PCs.

Not only did IBM keep the price of an entry AS/400 out of the range of small businesses, it encouraged the small business owner to move toward other non-IBM products. First it was Novell Netware, then it was Windows NT Server. Because Microsoft and Novell had client/servers and file/servers that ran on IBM's PCs, Big Blue decided that the AS/400 did not need these important capabilities. IBM positioned the AS/400 as a back-room business system only, which kept it from being a true server in the mid 1990s. That strategy lost IBM not only the desktop market but also the small new-account marketplace. This business community went to Novell and then to Microsoft servers. This was the business area that IBM had won from DEC, and now it was giving it to competing PC software vendors just because their wares could run on an IBM PC.

IBM refused to give the AS/400 real Internet capabilities until the mid 1990s (see Chapter 28, "Client Server and the Internet"), and the platform was not fully Internet enabled until the late 1990s. Meanwhile, small companies such as

Citrix were able to distribute the GUI of Microsoft applications to thin-client PCs, permitting the application to run on server PCs while the clients ran in thinner client mode.

IBM has yet to understand the lesson of the GUI message. To this day in 2016, a native GUI interface is AWOL from the AS/400 operating system (see Chapter titled: "A Town Without GUI"). All of these were major strategic mistakes on IBM's part. When you sum them all up, that explains how IBM's competitors grew rich into the billions at the expense of IBM stockholders.

Right now, a business needs to shell out a good $100,000 or so to afford an AS/400 style system, no matter what IBM may say (see Chapter 25, "The Dead Goose That Once Laid Golden Eggs!"). This expensive entry price keeps many companies that prefer to add a little bit here and a little bit there away from the product line.

The lack of a GUI makes the system look old (read: "legacy") and forces adopters to defend the platform at great length to business managers who think GUI is always part of what is needed. The cost of AS/400 applications at the small end is also a major deterrent for new account adoption. The good news continues to be that when installed on an AS/400 most available applications actually do the job.

The AS/400 Fits In

So where does an AS/400 fit in? It is the finest business system in existence, for any price. If you can afford one, you should want one. It does not go down. It may not provide dancing bears and spinning globes in its first course, but it sure can do that if you really want it to--and a lot more.

It fits in with any organization that is sick of two to three weeks of downtime and lost data every year. It fits in with companies that actually want to solve business problems, rather than give a few sharp college kids a neat job keeping the servers up and running. It fits in with companies that can get over the cost and tune into the benefits of having a real system that provides real business results with real business information. Finally, it fits in with companies that are so concerned about running their business that their executives are not as likely to complain to IT every day, wanting one of Bill Gates' $5.00 ideas implemented in two seconds.

Unfortunately, there is little AS/400 inertia to be found in the IT industry today. Nobody is going to ask for it by name. Your neighbors have not even heard of it. My neighbors have no idea what it is. It will emerge as the champion of only those companies that admit defeat with inferior systems and server approaches and are brave enough to move its way. The biggest challenge to the platform is that these brave souls may never learn about the AS/400 if IBM marketing has its way.

Chapter 12 AS/400 Is Not a Legacy System

Microsoft Should Provide AS/400 Inspiration

Those of us in the computer industry who have followed Microsoft's meteoric rise to success have seen the little giant from Redmond, Washington, devour some big prey on its way. Without Microsoft in the act, IBM's PC would have been successful and sustainable. But by having given Microsoft essential pieces of the puzzle, IBM now finds itself bringing in a very small portion of the spoils of a PC marketplace worth well over $100 billion per year. Considering that IBM brings in just a hair over $80 billion per year in total revenue, it is a fact that Microsoft has cost IBM several trillion dollars over the years.

Just like IBM in the 1950s and 1960s, Bill Gates wants it all. Al Zollar, IBM's AS/400 general manager, thinks IBM should stay away from Bill Gates and just let him enjoy the fruits of his chicanery. I can't make Al do what he should for the AS/400 platform, but I can unmask some of Microsoft's chicanery, even if Al Zollar might just want to let it slide.

I have been doing some work trying to find out exactly when the term "legacy" system began to be used. I find the term is as negative for the AS/400 as the brand name Windows is positive for Microsoft. Microsoft will never get rid of the term Windows, because for any product on which the company can slap that name, it needs a constant caravan of Brinks trucks to take the cash to the bank. IBM may never shed the term "legacy" from its AS/400 and mainframe ranks because executive management finds nothing wrong with the term. In fact, IBM executives use it themselves to describe their traditional computer product set--from the mainframe, to the Unix (AIX) box, to the AS/400. Gates to IBM: "Thank you, IBM, for remaining unaware!"

It's ironic that the only machine on which IBM does not slap the term legacy is Microsoft's 20-year-old Windows driven PCs. IBM uses the word *legacy* as a synonym for its traditional computer products, while Microsoft servers and client PCs get a pass. It really is the marketing, IBM, but that is another chapter. (See Chapters labeled *marketing*)

Did Gates Label the AS/400 "*Legacy*?"

Sometimes, when you can't use experiential inductive logic, you can look at the results and use deductive reasoning to come to some valid conclusions. Sometimes you need a combination and some good rounding, too. Don't worry; I am not going to hurt your head with syllogisms in order to make my point.

I still want to know the first person or organization to use the term *legacy* when referring to the AS/400. I regret that in all of the research I conducted, I was unable to find the answer. That's not all bad. An advantage of not finding any facts to support my argument is that I can beg the argument and you can call it my opinion.

Therefore, it is my humble opinion--and certainly logic to an extent supports my conclusion--that Bill Gates himself, one way or another, is responsible for using the term legacy to mean any computer system not powered by Microsoft Windows.

In my research, I found that very few people who have written about legacyware associate it with hardware. Before I found a definition that included hardware in the free

Wikipedia encyclopedia, I toyed with the idea of having a one-sentence chapter that read as follows:

> **"Since there is no such thing as a legacy system, but there is such a thing as legacy software, the AS/400 cannot be a legacy system."**

Wikipedia says the following:

> **"A legacy system (or historic system) is a computer system or application program, which continues to be used because of the cost of replacing or redesigning it and often despite its poor competitiveness and compatibility with modern equivalents."**

From a hardware and operating system perspective, the AS/400 is undeniably the most advanced system in the world. Therefore, according to Wikipedia's definition, it is not a legacy system.

That is not to say that the AS/400 does not run legacy applications. As a server, it runs legacy applications written in COBOL, RPG, C, and the legacy language du jour, based on Bill Gates' definition of legacy language. Of course, Visual Basic (VB) would not be in that list, because Gates maintains the list and because VB runs on Windows. The legacy pattern cannot include Gatesware.

The thing that neither the press nor IBM nor Bill Gates highlights about the AS/400 is that it also runs the most advanced Internet applications, Unix applications, Linux applications, and even Windows applications.

Again, the AS/400 is not a legacy system, and the fact that companies do not have to scrap their applications every five years, because they continue to run on newer and newer AS/400 hardware, is an advantage, not a disadvantage, regardless of whether that pleases or annoys Mr. Gates.

If you and I can see it, why can't IBM?

Chapter 13 The Future System (FS) Project

From the Best Computer Minds of All Time

Back in the early 1970s, in the deep recesses of IBM, a number of exciting things were going on. The first that comes to mind is that the government was investigating IBM. There was concern that the U.S. government, in order to help foster competition in the computer industry, was about to break up IBM into a bunch of tiny little IBMs. Company executives knew that none of these little IBMs would be able to wield as much marketing power as one Big Blue, and there was deep concern that this would be bad for the company. Unlike Microsoft in the late 1990s and into the 21st century, IBM took this threat very seriously and devoted significant resources to defending its interests.

Another thing that was happening was that IBM's mainframe division, which, at the time, was the real champion and hero of IBM, began a top-secret project dubbed internally as *FS*, for the *Future System* project.

Part of the motivation over FS can be attributed to IBM's concern about the mounting software inventories that were accumulating in its mainframe customers' shops. Programmers were writing more and more programs every day. About every five years, IBM was changing hardware and operating systems, and this was forcing customers to rewrite programs just to stay current with IBM's new offerings. The more money the customer spent in making the transition to IBM's latest and greatest, the less money would be available to pay IBM for the latest and greatest.

Conversion Costs Too much to Afford New Computers?

IBM's thoughts focused on whether its customers' huge investment in software would be able to continually be migrated to future IBM systems, ones that IBM had yet to develop. Without customers being able to move their software investment to these new systems, IBM feared, it would be inordinately difficult for them to migrate to new computers, which would substantially reduce IBM's opportunity to sell new systems to existing customers.

In the mid 1960s, IBM had bet the whole company on the success of its System/360 family of computers. These were introduced in 1965. Company executives in the early 1970s remembered all too well that to gain the benefits of the System/360 computer family, its customers were forced to rewrite their programs in new languages. But in the mid 1960s, the program inventories were not as significant as they had become over time.

Before 1965, the IBM systems of the day were always named with numbers. For example, the commercial processing machines of the late 1950s and early 1960s were the 1401 (see Figure 13-1) and its follow-on, the 1410. The scientific machines included the 1620 (see Figure 13-2) and the 1710. These all used very primitive programming languages, with names such as Symbolic Programming System (SPS) for the scientific machines and Autocoder for the commercial boxes. To help its customers move to the faster System/360 computing system, IBM built an emulation facility so that this old code could run on the new boxes. Unfortunately, the emulation gobbled up enough resources to translate the old code during the emulation process that the new machines, when running the old programs, were not substantially faster than the old machines had been.

Figure 13-1 Huge IBM 1401 Business Mainframe Computer – CPU

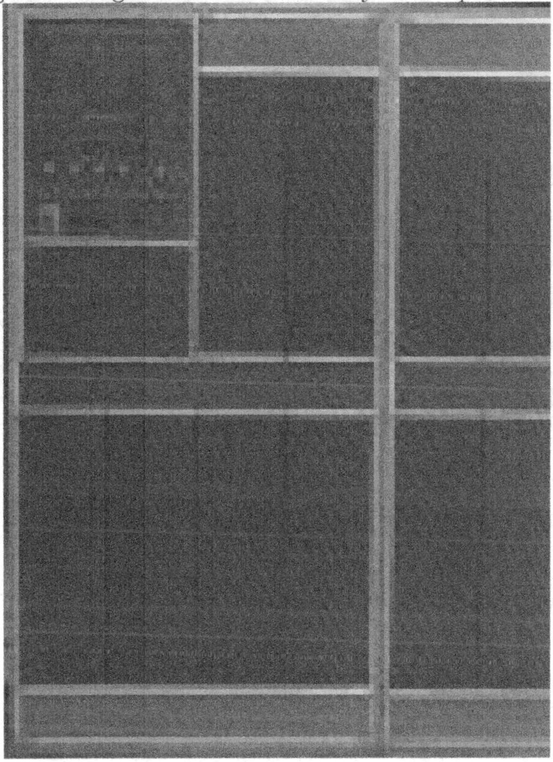

Figure 13-2: IBM 1620 at Computer Museum, Billings, MT – G. Mohanco at Console

The 1965 Rewrite

IBM's overriding recommendation for System/360 (see Figure 13-3), therefore, was for its customers to rewrite their applications to take advantage of the new machine. This was a very expensive undertaking. To help minimize future changes, IBM recommended writing programs in higher-level languages, such as the newly introduced COBOL language.

Theoretically, these high-level language programs would then be able to be ported to subsequent machines without the same difficulty as prevalent machine-oriented languages, such as the Symbolic Programming System (SPS) and Autocoder. However, COBOL suffered from some of the same disadvantages of the emulation software. COBOL programs ran slower than the lower-level languages, such as Autocoder, which had preceded it.

Figure 13-3 IBM System/360 Circa 1965 (Unknown Model)

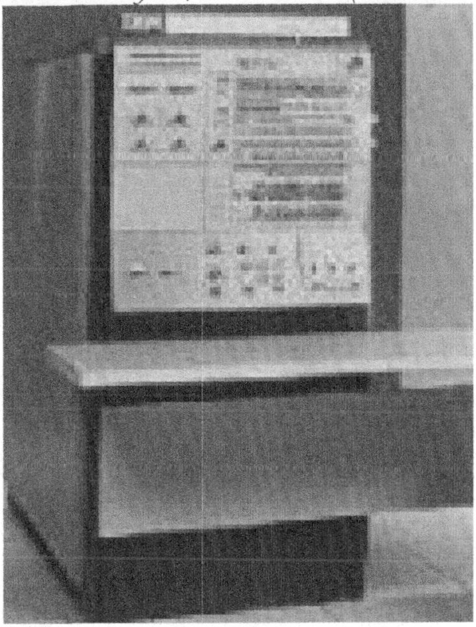

When IBM introduced the System/370 in 1970, the company touted the fact that programs did not have to be rewritten to move to the new iron. It was reasonably easy for a mainframe System/360 shop that was out of gas to choose to move to the System/370 (see Figure 13-4). The System/370 was not a radical departure in computing, and was in fact very similar to the System/360 line. Nonetheless, IBM was very concerned about what subsequent systems would look like and whether they would handle current programs while allowing customers to use all of the new bells and whistles.

There were a number of technology breakthroughs that were imminent, and IBM wanted its customers to be able to benefit from these without spending tons of money on program conversions. The company was planning for the next computer science revolution to be delivered as an IBM solution. High tech facilities such as database, data communications, and interactive computing were just around the corner. The future system would have to handle both the current software inventory, as well as these new capabilities.

Figure 13-4 IBM System/370 Model 125 Circa 1972

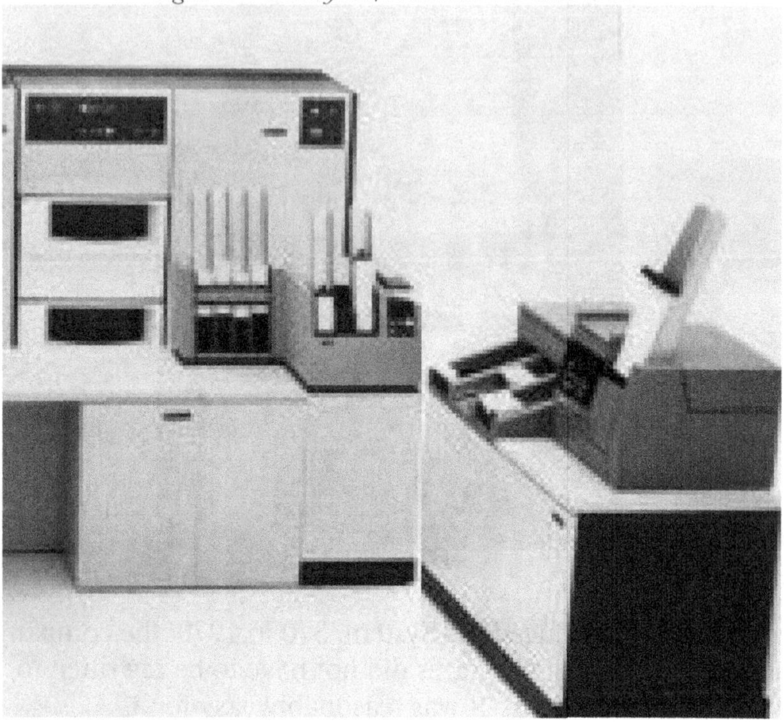

Design the Best Computer Possible

Hoping to plan the future, rather than have it plopped upon them, IBM gave its FS project team a mission to design the finest computer architecture possible, given all of the advances that were known and on the horizon, as well as those further off. IBM had a long list of features that were going to become available, such as bubble memory, and any new system would have to be able to seamlessly accomplish adding such advanced hardware to the mix.

This elite assemblage, though mostly a mainframe project team, included a few token representatives from other IBM divisions. One of the represented divisions, the IBM lab at Rochester, Minnesota, made small, reasonably inexpensive business systems (System/3). Speculation is that Rochester people were invited out of courtesy, not necessarily as potential contributors. The machines from Rochester at the time of the formation of the FS group were so small that nobody really thought that any of the FS designs would be usable in a Rochester product.

The group had at their disposal the finest computer scientists from both inside and outside of IBM. Moreover, they had access to all of the requests for additional functions and enhancements to all of the existing products. They had the full customer wish list. They knew where technology was heading. They knew the time frames. They were the most capable and the best equipped assemblage of computer designers ever formed in IBM. They were the cream of the crop, and their output was expected to be the future blueprint for advanced computing for all IBM mainframe products.

IBM invested substantial time and money in this advanced project, and was more than hoping for a big payoff. The company expected it. When the committee finished its work in the mid-1970s, it had designed the finest computer of all time. Integration of hardware and software was the cornerstone of the project. It was so complete that it was to take IBM's computing plan out at least another 20 or 30 years. It represented all that IBM knew about computing. A system built to this architecture would be splendid indeed.

Seeking Approval to Build the Best System Ever

Since the project had such high-level attention in IBM, at a certain point in the cycle, the FS committee had to present its findings and recommendations to the IBM Corporate Management Committee. If it did not get past this committee, it would no longer be funded and, as a matter of course, no systems would be developed using these specifications. The meeting with IBM's executives was crucial, as it would shape the color of IBM computing for decades to come.

As the presentation unfolded, IBM's executives were surely impressed by the excellent work that had gone into the project, as well as the ultimate capabilities of any product line that might be built using this design. But there was a dark cloud looming for the FS team.

Because this architecture was so special, it was also substantially different from any machine that had ever been built. To move to this new architecture, the presenters acknowledged that many customer programs and procedure job streams would have to be completely redone. This of course would require a substantial amount of customer reprogramming and would add a substantial additional cost for any IBM customers moving to this new architecture.

This cost was viewed by IBM's management as an impediment to the possibility of selling a system based on this architecture. Not only would the customer have to afford the new IBM system, but also the customer would have to invest an even greater amount to get the programming inventory converted to operate within the new architecture.

The IBM Corporate Management Committee viewed the customer work required as a yeoman task. By adding this effort as a prerequisite to moving to the new technology, IBM executives were concerned that many customers would not be able to afford the whole tab and perhaps would therefore be unwilling to make the change? Then what?

Many of the IBM executives had lived through the System/360 experience, in which IBM had bet the company, and could have lost it all while forcing its customers to scrap all their programs. They had sworn to IBM's larger customers never to do this again. After the FS presentation, they were no less steadfast in their resolve to maintain an evolutionary, not a revolutionary course.

The FS Answer Is History

IBM's executives were not prepared to annoy their customer set, and they were certainly not prepared to bet the company again, no matter how significant the notion was at hand. And so this spectacular FS effort of multiple IBM divisions would never get to bc IBM's mainframe architecture of the future. IBM gave the team a clear "no!" and broke up the group and sent them on their way. Countless millions of dollars were wasted in this failed effort to change the face of IBM technology forever and for better.

Chapter 14 The Pacific Project

Moving On

Besides the Future System project and the government's big antitrust case against IBM, there were lots of other exciting things going on within IBM in the 1970s. The company had hoped to use FS to help position its mainframe product line for the future, but from reading Chapter 13 you already have learned the outcome of that effort. IBM executive management forced the mainframe division to drop the project.

With or without FS, IBM was not about to sit idly by and let the U.S. government dismantle the company without a fight. Big Blue knew that it had to take action to position itself for the future, independent of efforts such as FS, to help shape its product lines. One of IBM's most significant choices of action for this was a reorganization of the company. Though a good part of the General Systems Division (GSD) reorganization had already occurred in 1969, it was hard not to notice the coup de gras when it occurred in 1975.

Building a Company to Be Broken

At this time, IBM boldly reorganized to be able to function in the future under the looming threat of the Justice Department's dissolution efforts. The biggest action that IBM commenced was its completion of GSD as a fully functional company within IBM. This was a big deal for many reasons. Unlike the addition of plants and products and people and the creation of new divisions or special purpose companies within the company, the formation of

GSD was much different, and its real purpose was unlike any other, ever, within IBM.

The General Systems Division of IBM was established in just about every way as an entire, self-contained company within IBM. By 1975, GSD, as it was called, was missing nothing that it needed to exist outside of the IBM womb. IBM gave the division all the pieces necessary to operate independently. For example, the new division had its own development lab and a manufacturing plant in Rochester, Minnesota.

It had its own research and development budget. It had its own marketing department and its own advertising budget. It even had its own independent sales force, which operated from the same branch offices as the Data Processing Division (mainframe) sales team. In 1975, along with a number of other small-systems engineers and marketing representatives," I was assigned to the General Systems Division.

Unlike the Data Processing Division (DPD) of IBM, the former one and only direct computer sales force in IBM where I had previously worked, the products that GSD sold were mostly built and marketed by GSD.

DPD was just a sales organization. It sold the products produced by IBM's other plants, such as the Systems Products Division (SPD). Of course, there were a few products that were made outside of GSD in other parts of IBM that were also in the GSD salesperson's kit. These included common devices for systems, such as tape drives, disk drives, and CRT/terminals and printers.

Why would a company create a new division that could operate autonomously within its own borders? The fact is that IBM had not forgotten the antitrust case; it was absolutely preoccupied by it. Thus, many of IBM's actions during this period were done with thinking that demonstrated that the U.S. government was to be feared more than the competition. As a preemptive action to a required bust up, with GSD, IBM pre-positioned the wholly contained company as a ready spin-off in case the government was successful in its antitrust efforts. Rather than risking the company being busted into parts that together might not equal a whole company, IBM was resolute in its contingency plan to bring two strong IBM's to bear in the computer industry. Each IBM would have the plant, the people, and the wherewithal to do well.

The Need for a Fighting Product

The big computer product for GSD back in 1975 was the System/3 Model 15D. It was the top-of-the-line small business system. GSD executives, headquartered in Atlanta, did not need much coaching to understand that the System/3, originally announced in 1969, was on its last legs and needed to be replaced with a machine that could win in the marketplace, even if the competition was the IBM company itself, with its smaller mainframe product line.

By 1975, the System/3 was tired and slow, compared with the competition, and offered no technology advances of any consequence in the marketplace. The system was well out of its heyday, and it was not long until it would be blown away by competing minicomputers and small mainframes. GSD had to act quickly. It needed a follow-on replacement product for the System/3.

As the GSD executives looked at IBM, the mother company, they saw many advances in technology being made ready for their appearance within the mainframe line of computers. They understood that, to compete against DEC and Hewlett-Packard, Wang, Data General, and others, they needed these capabilities for their follow-on product line. They were concerned not only about the real competition but also about whether the division, if released to operate on its own, would need the technology to compete directly against the IBM mainframe line.

From my employment and understanding of IBM history, I have never known anybody who analyzed the internals of the company and did not conclude that the mainframe executives ruled the company with an iron hand. The belief was, if it was not good for mainframes, it was not good for IBM. This fact was not lost on the little development lab in Rochester or the division president in Atlanta.

They knew that any system they came up with had to be substantially less powerful in terms of processing capability than any mainframe in the product line. If not, mainframe IBM would never let it see the light of day.

Mainframe IBM Brought the Constraints

Mainframe IBM was not interested in creating a cheap little computer that could run like a mainframe and give mainframe customers an alternative to giving IBM lots of money for mainframe computers each and every year. Some would say that they were not interested in "eating their children," though I find that term obnoxious. One of the ways the mainframers kept Rochester in line was by giving them dollar ceilings. For example, in the System/3's early days, the dollar ceiling was about $3,000 per month. Rochester could not build a system that would rent for more than $3,000 per month.

At the time, IBM was mostly in the computer rental business. It was a great business. Year after year, once a system was placed, IBM would reap the rental income. The only expense absorbed by the rental was maintenance, so it was a very lucrative business for IBM. (In Chapter 38, I let you in on the secret cash that IBM was bringing in during the John Opel years to make it seem like the company was doing better than it was.)

There was no lid placed on the architecture or the components, just the overall price to the customer. A generous IBM profit was included in the rental, so you can bet that the $3,000 was not all technology. Rochester was free to develop as sophisticated a system as possible for the money. It kicked off the *Pacific Project* to do just that.

The Pacific Plan Unfolds

As Rochester put its design team together to develop the System/3 follow-on, it included Dr. Frank Soltis and a small contingent that had represented Rochester in the defunct Future System project. As it turned out, these guys had taken lots of notes about FS, and were bright and creative. So it was no surprise that the Rochester Lab, the development arm for GSD, took a good chunk of FS project output, dusted it off, and used it as a starting point for their new computer design.

IBM's mainframe customers had been writing code for its systems since the 1950s and supposedly had massive numbers of programs. But GSD executives could argue that GSD's customers had only been writing code for their systems since the early 1970s, when the System/3s first became available. Therefore, it could be argued in the mid-1970s that the System/3 customer's average code inventory was not substantial, if it were necessary to abandon it for the new FS-based architecture that the lab was preparing to introduce.

Moreover, the GSD plan would include migration programs to help move customer-written code to the new system from the System/3 as painlessly as possible. Thus, the General Systems Division would ultimately build its system based on the high technology results of the FS project, as well as the innovative hardware designs brought by Dr. Frank Soltis and his numerous Rochester cohorts.

Giving the Small System a Big Heart and Big Paws

If you were a GSD executive, and you were aware of the inroads being made by the government in the antitrust case, in the beginning of the lawsuit, you would have had to make sure that your new system architecture was scalable. One of the very first competitors that GSD would face if IBM were split would be the old IBM minus GSD. The next system choice, therefore, for GSD was very critical, since it would be the system that it would use to compete against IBM. However, with mainframe IBM keeping the performance and capacity to a minimum, the first processor used with the system could not appear to be threatening to the mainframe business.

Of course, there was no resolution to the antitrust case, and IBM remained whole. The government eventually dropped the case in 1982. So the biggest problems, which IBM GSD actually experienced in 1978, when it announced the System/38 as a big part of the embodiment of FS, was getting all of the whiz-bang function to work and getting the mainframe guys off their backs.

Ever concerned that some other division was going to outclass them, the mainframers used their power to keep all systems other than mainframes down. GSD's requirement was to be a good corporate citizen and not make too much power available to its customers. Mainframe IBM was watching.

Of course, GSD also had to make sure that any new system was an acceptable percentage faster than the System/3 computers that its customers were using; otherwise it would not sell. The System/3 Model 15D was at the top of the list. The System/38 would have to provide superior price/performance compared with the Model 15D.

When you look at all the work that IBM Rochester did in the Pacific Project to bring the System/38 to life, it's a wonder that it ever got announced and out the door. Rochester had no real experience in such a large-scale endeavor. In fact, the scientists and engineers did not know they could not do the job, so they just went ahead and did it! They built 48-bit hardware and a 128-bit software machine interface with the major bells and whistles brought from the FS design and from Dr. Frank Soltis' magnificent mind. To top off the challenges, the Rochester engineers and developers had to make it all work on a small scale. Mainframe IBM had decreed that it had to be built on a resource-deprived hardware box.

What Did Businesses Want?

In the mid-1970's, just like today, many businesses were crying out for more functions in their applications, more applications, and more access to informational byproducts of applications. But there was not the plethora of software packages that are available today. So when businesses asked for such changes, their IT shop was the only place that business applications could be changed.

In the 1970s, instead of getting results when they went for services, knowledge workers were met with increasing organizational constraints. Often there was no budget for additional IT work, and the department had no way of paying for the work itself. Yet the computer-emboldened report and information users of the organization demanded more and more timely and accurate information.

Unfortunately, in many cases, the existing IT staff did not have enough time or resources to satisfy any of their requests. In many ways it seemed hopeless for a business trapped within its own budgetary constraints. There was not much anybody could do but hope that one day IT would get to the problem at hand. These were tough days, and no system existed that was capable of changing the situation.

What Type of Computer Functions Solve the Problems?

Say you were a computer vendor, such as IBM Rochester, and you understood the frustrations of the day. There is no doubt that if you could build a system that could address these frustrations and help bring management information from the disk drives to the workstation or the printer, you would have a system that would be a winner.

It would have to be a new system, designed specifically for business needs. If you could, you would address this programming and operations dilemma through new and integrated technology. Any computer company wanting to solve this real problem would have to create a totally new solution that would have to meet a number of key objectives.

A new system would have to be:

(1) Easy to implement new applications
(2) Easy to modify or maintain existing applications
(3) Easy to access stored information
(4) Easy to secure data
(5) Easy to grow the system in a non-disruptive fashion
(6) Easy to afford with better performance

Though the first five points in the list would provide the major benefits that should enable a business to find enough savings to justify the system, because of the ever decreasing costs of hardware, for the system to be salable, you would have to provide all of its capabilities at an even lower price, and you would have to supply better performance than any existing system. That is clearly a tall order.

The six points above address the people-productivity side of computing. It is a simple generic laundry list of function and facility for a new computer system to help provide the computing solutions as needed. The problem, of course, was that a system had never been built that addressed the people side of computing. But if it could, maybe, just maybe, it would help reduce the prohibitive and spiraling cost of program maintenance and development.

Maybe businesses would be able to migrate to the new system with major productivity enhancements and without major issues. Maybe they could grow over time in a non-disruptive fashion to faster models with even more productivity features. So, it would be important to provide more capacity with virtually no issues at all, including price. Thus, the most obvious benefit that you would have to provide would be a system like none before, at an improved price performance level (6) so that your customers would believe they could afford your new offering.

Well, neither you nor I are computer manufacturers, but even to an expert, this is a tall order. Let's just say that you had scoped out the market requirements properly and believed you could deliver a machine with these attributes. You would certainly expect such a machine would be immensely successful. And you would be correct!

Building a New Machine to New and Unusual Specifications

These were IBM's six major objectives for the Pacific project. The Pacific system was to be the embodiment of integration and productivity in one new box. In IBM's System/38 Product Excellence Slides, used for my MADGIC sessions (See Chapter titled: MADGIC! MADGIC ! MADGIC!), these six objectives were the cornerstone of IBM's canned slide presentation. System/38 and AS/400 prospects were exposed to the rationale behind the system and it often became the motivation for them to place an order.

Of course, in order to accomplish these heavy objectives, as a hardware and software computer system developer, you would not be able to use many things from the past. They had already not succeeded in achieving these objectives. You would need new concepts, and would have to devise a completely new computer architecture. You could not rely on the old hardware models of the past, even if they could be made to run faster. To achieve all this function, a **new architecture** would have to provide **integrated systems functions,** which took advantage of the new machine's inherent capabilities.

Large-System Function and Small-System Ease of Use

Because your marketplace would not be General Motors or the New York Stock Exchange, but rather small and midsized companies, high schools, colleges, hospitals, etc., where there are small staffs to deal with technical issues, you would have to hide all of the complexities of the internal machine. In essence, you would have to achieve the impossible by providing **large-system performance and function** with **small-system ease of use**. If you were able to do this, your system would be unique indeed, and would meet the six goals as noted.

Before 1978, IBM designed and built the Pacific System as the fulfillment of these six requirements. Announced in 1978 as the IBM System/38, the new machine was created with a new architecture built around the notion of scalability and ease of use through integration. Not coincidentally, even today IBM will tell you that the "i" in Power i stands for integration.

The large-system functions of the System/38 were thus integrated into the firmware and the operating system to provide a small-system, simple interface to an extremely powerful box. In essence, the System/38 was announced as the first small computer in the industry that was built with an automatic transmission. That's the story in a nutshell. IBM used all of its knowledge of computing to fashion the System/38, and then 10 years later the company upped the ante with the introduction of the AS/400. Using all of the resources known to it at the time, IBM eventually delivered on all six items with its historic introduction of the System/38.

System/38 Is Still Outstanding–38 Years Later!

The special qualities of the System/38 have yet to be surpassed by new technology. Its architecture was born again in a new frame with the AS/400, and again with the Power i. Overall, the 1978 Model System/38 is still unique and good enough that no system, inside or outside of IBM, has yet caught up with it. If you add all that has happened to the AS/400 and the Power i on top of what the System/38 originally brought to its customers, the picture of a system you get is quite formidable and very impressive. Pages and pages of new function each year, with more coming from the Rochester labs, make it very difficult to succinctly describe this machine. But one thing is for sure: There is nothing as good in the marketplace or on the drawing boards as the original Pacific machine, the System/38.

So if you were to design the system with the six points as described above, it would clearly be the System/38. That's exactly what the Little Lab That Could did when it introduced the system in 1978. The good news is that you do not have to design it, because it has been available for over 25 years.

The reincarnation of the System/38, in the AS/400 and Power i, also has it all. The benefits include a product cost range of between ten thousand and several million dollars, thousands of available applications, unprecedented ease of use at the operations and programming level, beat-all development productivity tools, top-flight Internet capabilities, all integrated with machine-based security features and packaged for a no-sweat installation.

One could say with certainty that the AS/400 provides the best environment of all for application developers. With the System/38 and the AS/400, for years software developers have declared that **tough programming jobs become easy.**

For Techies Only

The rest of the topics in this chapter may be a bit too much for the casual reader. I include them at this point for those who are picking up a notion of the many special attributes of the System/38 and AS/400 boxes. Rather than beg the argument with my opinion, presenting additional superior technical aspects of the AS/400 at this point strengthens my case that the AS/400 is one of a kind and the finest computer ever built.

To truly understand the integrated nature of the AS/400, all one need do is take a look at the software layers built on a "traditional" architecture. These are found on every other computer, from IBM's mainframe and RS/6000 line to Windows, Intel, HP, and Unix boxes. Without trying to be overly technical, a number of the architecture layers are as follows:

Top Layer

- ✓ Languages
- ✓ Utilities
- ✓ Spooling

Middle Layer

- ✓ Sort
- ✓ Graphics
- ✓ Communications
- ✓ Workstation Support
- ✓ Database
- ✓ Data management
- ✓ Operating System
- ✓ Machine Interface

Lowest Layer (Machine)

- ✓ Instruction Set
- ✓ Microprogramming
- ✓ Hardware

Traditional Architectures

It is worthy to note that most of the function layers in traditional-architccture machines are completely separate from each other. On most machines they are provided by additional (add on) products and are not integrated well into the machine itself. In fact, one of the most significant disadvantages of a system with a traditional architecture is that, because the system is not integrated, you cannot count on all of the layers of function being present on every machine for the same hardware type.

Since the most essential software on these machines is purchased ala carte from multiple vendors, by definition, all functions do not always exist. Moreover, when all functions do exist, there is nothing to ensure that the layers of all machines are the same.

When you develop software in such an environment, within each layer, there may be many different-named products from which to choose. Therefore, it is difficult to select the named products whose existence your base software can depend on. Try baking bread when you are not sure all the same ingredients will be there every time. The bread can never be the same.

Since the layers in the System/38 and AS/400 architecture are provided with every machine, there are no haves or have-nots with this system. Developers have the same affinity for a well-stocked System/38 as do bakers for a well-stocked kitchen. It's in there.

From the bottom up in the layers, it is safe to say that all processing on all machines is done by **hardware**. All of the other layers help the hardware know what to do. Each lower layer makes it easier to operate at a higher layer. Depending on the machine, various instructions or groups of instructions are set in **microcode**, or as IBM now calls it, the **licensed internal code**.

The **instruction set** sits above microcode. This allows a machine to present to software a notion that it actually has instructions in hardware that are not necessarily implemented in hardware. They may actually be materialized in the microcode layer through software. One high-level machine instruction may very well cause 1,000 hardware instructions to be executed as directed by the microcode. When an instruction in the instruction set is executed, it uses the microcode (**microprogramming)** layer to translate the instruction into a sequence, which the hardware understands.

Above the instruction layer is the **operating system,** which provides the personality of the machine. On top of the operating system, most often delivered as part of the operating system, is the **data management** layer. On PCs this would be the file system that you see when you look at directories and folders. On mainframes and other ala-carte-style machines in which data management has a name, you may have to purchase a named product for this layer. Something called VSAM on mainframes falls into this category.

The next layer, which is optional on other systems, is the database. PC Servers and Unix boxes and mainframes have a database only if you buy one. Oracle, Ingress, DB2, SQL Server, etc., are names for modern day server databases. You choose the database as a separate component; therefore it cannot be integrated. The layers above the database are optional on most other systems.

A key point in this traditional architecture is that it is ala carte. This means that higher-level functions in the machine cannot depend on lower level functions being there. Even if the database layer were present on a machine, which did not care which database you used, system commands could not be built to reference any particular database in a standard way. The point is that, on such systems, the software developer (programmers) would have to work harder to make up for this

Integrated Architecture

The IBM development team who wrote the language compilers on the top of the architecture knew that with a System/38 or an AS/400, the database is a standard part, and therefore they could put hooks in the language to make it easier for a programmer to perform database functions. Otherwise, the developer would be forced to access each database in non-standard ways that would be different based on the product used. For example, RPG, COBOL, Java, and all AS/400 languages are AS/400-database aware, but no language has to worry about your using Oracle or Ingress or SQL Server as a database, since none of these products is integrated into the Pacific Machine (System/38)--or any other machine on the market, for that matter.

When an AS/400 developer issues a read to the database in a high-level language, it is issued as a read, not as a complex request to special functions. No other computer system from Microsoft or Sun or Oracle can claim the same.

Moreover, just as database, the same notion applies to all other layers. With everybody else's system, nothing is integrated, because it can't be. It's all bought separately. Consider that a PC box, when it is shipped, does not know whether it will be running Linux or Windows as its operating system. Since Oracle on Linux is different from Oracle on Windows, by definition no software integration can be integrated in the PC/Windows environment.

The message is that major components of the Pacific system have been part of its basic architecture for over 25 years. They are not add-ons and are not available ala carte. It's in there. IBM built Pacific to be integrated, and 25 years later it still is inside the AS/400. Knowing all of the pieces makes it much easier for Pacific programmers to develop new function without having to work hard and without the system having to travel through unknown layers to get the job done.

Integrated Architecture Summary

On traditional systems, you have to build the system from component parts before you start using it. You have to install tons of software before you can even use the system for anything productive. You are responsible for picking and installing the pieces you want, such as database and workstation support. You have to install those pieces and make sure that they work in your environment. The resulting puzzle often has missing pieces in all other environments and is never complete, by design. With the AS/400, whose ancestry dates back to the Pacific Project, there is ***no assembly required***, and there are never any missing pieces.

Chapter 15 The Fort Knox Project

Changing Structure

As noted in earlier chapters, the System/38 was the result of the Pacific Project. IBM announced it in October 1978 as the system for the 1980s. Of course, IBM expected the product to be ready long before 1980, but at least it was able to get the new product out the door. The first live System/38 that I saw in a customer account was shipped in November 1980.

In addition to the nagging delay in first shipment, the Pacific Project was also plagued by mainframe IBM's careful strategy of ensuring that the box was not permitted to expand quickly or to grow big (See Chapter 14, "The Pacific Project"). When first made available, for example, its total disk capacity was 384 megabytes.

This was delivered via six 64-meg internal disk drives. The System/38 had less capacity initially than the System/3 Model D, its predecessor. Many businesses that had migrated from System/3 to early System/38 technology began to outgrow these limitations shortly after installation. At first, IBM did little to address their needs. Eventually, IBM announced more disk storage capacity for the system, but for some it came too little, too late.

Note: 384 MB is lots less than the disk storage on the smallest PC today.

Fort Knox Secret Objectives

The secret plan developed by the mainframe teams in IBM had the System/38 being totally eliminated and replaced by units made on the Endicott, New York, small mainframe product line. Rumors of the death of the System/38 abounded within the IBM of the early 1980s. Mainframe IBM did not understand the System/38, but viewed it as a threat to the small mainframe products that it built, and saw no real value for the System/38 as a product.

They wanted it eliminated as soon as possible after IBM made sure it could ship the new Fort Knox box that would replace it. The mainframe contingent obviously had no clue that hardware was not what attracted System/38-loyal subjects.

Without trying to learn about the System/38, they believed that the small mainframe was its equivalent. Programmers in customer shops were attracted to the System/38 because of its overall personality and the opportunity to gain major productivity improvements both in IT and in the business as a whole. Such productivity could not be expected in a small mainframe environment, but mainframe IBM did not understand this.

As growing businesses quickly outgrew the System/38, they became angry with IBM for limiting the system. Rather than take the difficult mainframe route, companies that needed more power often did not bother looking at another IBM system. They jumped to selected systems from IBM's competition, such as DEC, WANG, HP and Data General. All of these companies were in their prime in the 1980s, just waiting for IBM System/38 defections.

Just like the attempt at eServer homogenization in 2000, which continues to this day, few executives in IBM were pleased with the company's overall small business server lineup in the early 1980s. The PC had not even become a factor as a server. At the time, IBM was selling five different boxes that addressed the same set of customers and needs. One system could do the job for sure. But which one? That was the problem! Enter corporate politics.

The Fort Knox Pre-Mix

The Rochester Lab provided two of the five systems. The Systrem/38 was the most capable architecturally, and the System/34 was the darling of the small-business set.

System/38 and System/36 from Rochester

The System/36 was already planned as a follow-on to the 1977 System/34; in fact, IBM introduced it in 1983. Though the System/36 and System/38 used the same terminals and printers, as well as a similar RPG programming language, that's where the similarities ended. The System/36 was the easiest computer of all to install and make operational. Customers loved its total ease-of-use characteristics. It was also easy to learn. In many ways, the System/36 was an extension of the old System/3; whereas the System/38 was a completely new animal.

There were many more capabilities built into the System/38 than the System/36. If you start with the notion of an integrated relational database at a time when mainframe systems were not yet using relational database, you get an impression of how advanced the System/38 was for its day. In describing the ease of use of both systems, I like to suggest that the System/36 was the easiest to learn and the easiest to use right out of the box. The System/38 and AS/400 are lots more trouble to learn, but the System/38 and AS/400 are the easiest systems to use, even easier than System/36, once you have learned them.

The IBM 43XX Small Mainframes from Endicott

IBM's mainframe Systems Products Division provided the 43XX series of mini-mainframes that were all built in Endicott, New York. Some of the specific numbers used over the years on these machines include the following:

- ✓ 4321
- ✓ 4331
- ✓ 4341
- ✓ 4361
- ✓ 4381

The Series/1 from Boca Raton

At the same time, a group that seemed to belong to nobody in the corporation, the non-PC side of the IBM Boca Raton, Florida, plant made a product called the Series/1. There was a dotted-line connection between Boca Raton and Rochester from the GSD days, in that the Series/1 was seen as a GSD box.

The Series/1 was a bona fide minicomputer in the fashion of DEC's VAX and HP's 3000 series. Unlike the HP and DEC boxes, however, the Series/1 did not have a loyal following in the manufacturing industry, because IBM made it. The technical gurus of the minicomputer era did not look favorably on IBM, and the Series/1 paid for their disaffection.

The Mainframe Distributed Mini: IBM 8100

The fifth small computer in the early 1980s lineup was a little-known box called the IBM 8100. Though this machine technically was a bona fide computer system, it was a special-purpose unit that mainframe IBM had built as an intelligent distributed terminal so that its large customers would not have to use an IBM System/36 or System/38.

In the early 1980s, the 8100 was mainframe IBM's principal distributed processing machine. However, more mainframe customers liked the System/36 and System/38 as distributed processors than mainframe-dominated IBM wanted to admit. The 8100 was never really much of anything, in terms of being a viable, fully functional computer system, but it had its own processor and hardware frame. It provided some local stand-alone processing capability, and mainframe implementers got to choose from two incompatible operating systems. They were known simply as *DPPX* and *DPCX*.

The 8100 was not such a big success. It was not innovative and did not fill a product-line gap. It should never have been built, and even after its availability, it should have been scrapped. Because it had been conceived and sponsored by mainframe IBM, it was deemed holy and untouchable. The System/36 and System/38 provided the same facility as the 8100 through software, but IBM's large-system planners wanted their own toy. They had no desire to depend on a "GSD box" for any success that they might have in distributed computing.

8100 Represented Dead Technology

Even when the 8100 was most alive; it was moribund, since IBM host-based networks were on their way out at the time, with the coming acceptance of TCP/IP, the protocol of the Internet. A small startup company, Cisco, would soon rob IBM of all of its data communications dignity because stubborn, mainframe-myopic IBM would not make the move to TCP/IP. Cisco eventually stole the whole data communications industry from IBM without even a whimper from IBM. In typical IBM fashion, Big Blue almost immediately declared Cisco a partner and sold it some token technology for a few billion dollars in order to make what IBM considered a graceful escape from the market.

Just like the PC market, mainframe IBM's pig headedness had cost it another lucrative market, telecommunications. Like Microsoft and others in the PC debacle, Cisco reaped the spoils of IBM's failure to respond to TCP/IP. In many ways, it was IBM's stubborn reliance on machines such as the 8100 with IBM proprietary communications protocols (SNA and SDLC) that helped Cisco and others win the mindshare battle for data communications supremacy.

You may not have ever heard of these Fort Knox machines, but they are all historically significant. IBM in Rochester, Minnesota, had bluffed and lied to originally get into the computer business. The 96-column, card-based System/3 was supposed to be a machine whose sole purpose was to replace aging unit record equipment. Through chicanery and clandestine activities, Rochester produced a computer instead of a Tab machine, for which it was commissioned. Because the System/3 had become a success, Rochester quickly became IBM's small business computer manufacturer, as well as the operating system developer for small business systems.

This totally aggravated the Systems Product Division personnel who made IBM's large and small mainframes for the mainframe marketing division (DPD). They had such poor marketing sniffers, they believed that they were already addressing the small business marketplace with the SPD-built System/360 Model 20, IBM's expensive mainframe-based smallest computer. The System/3 was less than half the price and provided the same function. That's how far off from a good and original marketing idea these folks were, and continue to be. Rather than permit IBM to be successful with Rochester-created wares, this hard-core group of mainframe aficionados took on a negative mission: to destroy Rochester and its products, regardless of its cost to IBM.

During the late 1970s and early 1980s, IBM was still very concerned about the Justice Department's case against it. As noted in Chapter 14, Frank Cary, IBM's chairman, saw the distinct possibility of splitting IBM along the small and big computer lines. Rochester was earmarked as the plant for the small computer division. To coordinate small system operations, IBM created a full division called GSD so that when the Justice Department wanted to settle the case, IBM would offer the split on its own terms.

GSD's product to compete against mainframe was the System/38. Rochester had announced and delivered the System/38 to be able to sustain the new GSD Company. In 1982, when the Justice Department withdrew the suit against IBM, it became obvious that there were definitely too many products in the IBM small systems stable.

To complicate any thoughts of merging the product lines was the fact that they were all substantially different from one another. With the Series/1, the System/36, and the System/38, the GSD management team owned three of these five smaller computers, and none of them was compatible.

The 8100 and the 4300 series machines were built by mainframe IBM. Always wary about what the little guys in Rochester were up to, and constantly plagued by a bad case of "not invented here" syndrome, the mainframe division kept pushing its product set lower, while trying desperately to keep a big spending cap on the Little Lab That Could. Its rationale was that by pushing the product set lower, it could take more business from Rochester, and by keeping Rochester's computers small, the mainframe would look more attractive to emerging large accounts. During the time, both parties knew there was a fight going on. The secret game was fraught with encroachment, illegal procedures, off-sides, holding, and roughing the passer. But since mainframe IBM was in control, no flags were thrown.

Five General-Purpose Computers

The whole notion of a general-purpose computer is one that can do anything. You simply put in a different program and the machine does a different thing. In a company that did real planning, rather than competing and sniping, five general-purpose computer families would not be conceived and hatched to cover one small business sector. Since these computers were truly general-purpose, though the IBM 8100 was targeted for a special purpose, there was definitely no need for five distinct families.

The one major item that IBM forgot, as it scrambled to combine all these boxes into one, was that the animals had already been released. Customers who trusted IBM were already using these machines. Each machine had at least one operating system. In fact, the mainframe had three, the 8100 had two, the Series/1 had three, and the System/36 and the System/38 had one apiece. Since program compatibility depends on the program's relationship with its operating system, the merge problem was not simply five systems that had to be accommodated; it was 10 operating systems and tons of programs built over many years for each of the operating systems. If it could be done, it would be a large project indeed.

Ironically, the problem of incompatible systems and software, which the Future System project in the early 1970s was convened to solve for the big systems division, had reared its head in spades in the little systems division (three systems and five operating systems). When you add the encroachment penalty exacted by the big systems division by building two of its own competing little systems with distinct operating systems, there was a new problem in IBM that was 10 times as bad as the problem that Future System was supposed to fix.

How could it possibly happen that a company, supposedly so well managed as IBM, could wake up one day and find itself with five competing computer lines with 10 different operating systems looking for the same customer? It is no wonder that IBM wanted to solve this. You can't blame Big Blue for wanting a solution.

It must have been embarrassing. I have not even discussed the big water-cooled, Poughkeepsie-built IBM mainframes and the PC-like IBM 5120 DataMaster computers, which were also very much alive at the time. Add to that the fact that IBM had not yet shipped its first PC Server and the company had not yet entered the RISC processor/Unix business, and it is obvious that the situation was more out of hand than even five little systems and 10 operating systems.

You Need Fort Knox to Solve That

IBM decided to invest a ton of money on studying the matter. With all the money to be spent on the project, it was understandable that IBM dubbed the project **Fort Knox**. The objective of the study was to develop a convergence strategy so that one box would emerge with the powers and capabilities of all five boxes. It was a noble goal, but the project was virtually unmanaged from the get-go.

Four separate IBM laboratories devoted some of their best scientists and engineers to the Fort Knox convergence project. Most of the work on the project was performed remotely in the home laboratories of the participants. Because the mainframe captains inside IBM expected that, as a side benefit of the project, they would be able to eliminate the System/38 and the System/36 lines with the expected capabilities of Fort Knox, Rochester was asked to devote just a token few people to the project.

There is some documented history in IBM that suggests that there were powerful people in IBM who did not expect Rochester to have a requirement for any scientists or engineers after the Fort Knox hybrid was introduced. Fort

Knox was a vehicle that mainframe IBM was using to free Big Blue from the tyranny of the "wild ducks" in Rochester.

Fort Knox Lives On Today

Ironically, the IBM homogenization marketing strategy (See chapter titled Homogenization) of recent years that had been burying the AS/400 and its elegance is a continuation of this same mainframe-first bias. It is history repeating itself. Just as the mainframe division, with Fort Knox as an excuse, tried to rid itself of IBM's Rochester Lab and Plant, the eServer homogenization that the company is sponsoring today is having the same effect. The result is a lobotomized AS/400, replaced by lowest common denominator homogenization and substantially decreased sales.

The Little Lab That Could fought off all odds in 1969 to become a computer manufacturing shop. Then, after having produced the finest IBM computer ever built, in the mid 1980s with Fort Knox, the mainframe engineering community in IBM tried to blackball the lab into oblivion. Now the same thing appears to be happening quite naturally under the darkness of the eServer umbrella chapters.

Mainframe IBM Had Specific Objectives

The mainframe engineers and scientists had to be careful. There was always the possibility that those renegades from Rochester were right on the money. AS/400 systems engineers and Rochester's customers always believed that the The Little Lab That Could, if given the chance, could do just about everything better than any other company in the computing industry, including the rest of IBM. The danger for Rochester was that such non-mainstream (non-mainframe) thinking did not play well in the mainframe-dominated halls of IBM.

Rochester did get a few sparse assignments in the Fort Knox venture, but the Rochester scientists involved knew that the project was doomed to failure. There was no real management of the project, as each lab more or less did its own thing to attempt to achieve its own objectives. It is no wonder that, as the ideas were discussed, each lab saw its product as the heartbeat component of the project. Though Fort Knox was supposed to have its own converged RISC processor, each lab's design had a different shining star.

Because the new Fort Knox processor would not run any of the programs from any of the other systems or operating systems, the team decided to build one compatible coprocessor for each of the variants to cover all of the facilities that the main converged processor could not handle. The Rochester scientists and engineers knew intrinsically that it was not going to work, and so that team spent most of its time working on the notions that they might use in a follow-up convergence of its own System/38 and System/36 lines. Not much input from Rochester was permitted in the overall Fort Knox schema.

The goals of Fort Knox were quite lofty, and with no one identifiable person historically pegged as the project head, the efforts naturally took on the characteristics of the participant systems. Instead of harmony and convergence, this structure created home-team pride and division.

As noted above, but still somewhat laughable and worthy of repeating, in order to supply the five personalities that the participants believed were necessary for the box, it was determined that personality co-processors would be required. So if it were ever built, you would buy a Fort Knox with its RISC processor, and then buy a System/38, a System/36, a Series/1, an 8100, or a 43XX co-processor if you wanted to run any of those programs This was cause for some pretty good jokes in the lab and in the field, which is where I toiled. Instead of the five one-humped camels that Fort Knox began with, the end vision became one camel with five humps.

So after four years, the best that could be done from all that work was a common hardware infrastructure (bus) developed by the Series/1 group so that all processors could use the same housing. However, the real issues of program compatibility were not addressed. The five-humped camel may very well have had just one operating system driving it, but the operating system, like the camel itself, would need 10 personalities. It would be a difficult task to keep that level of complexity from appearing in end-user form, making the machine, if it were ever built, at best, unwieldy to use.

As noted, the software compatibility issue could be solved initially, at least theoretically, by including a processor for each personality that the machine needed. So if a software package that was needed for a former System/38 happened to be written for an 8100, the 8100 processor personality would have to run the package. Theoretically, five different software packages might require all five different coprocessors. Unlike Intel 8088s and 80286s of the day, midrange processors were quite expensive in the mid 1980s. So there would certainly be a big cost penalty for IBM customers if the mix-and-match-software notion could possibly be accommodated by Fort Knox.

Fort Knox Laid to Rest

As history has recorded the big Fort Knox event, nobody would ever find out for sure if it had any value at all. After four years of work, and hundreds of million in IBM gold, Fort Knox was put to rest. It had failed, as many expected. There was no real convergence product on the drawing board to prove that the project ever existed. Oh, there were bits and pieces of usable parts all over the place in the various labs associated with the project. Some of the pieces all of the labs knew about, and some were undisclosed.

IBM's problems from this go-nowhere experience may have been able to be dismissed internally as an exploratory project that had determined that a particular course of action was not feasible. But the board of directors should have demanded a return of the many millions wasted on a project with an impossible objective.

The worst result of the Fort Knox divergence was that during all the time that Fort Knox was the anointed future, IBM's small system future was not being planned. While mainframe IBM was preoccupied for four years trying to figure out how to get rid of its System/38 legacy by design, DEC, HP, WANG, and others were trying to take down all five IBM systems by outselling IBM. With no real follow-on products coming from the Fort Knox venture, IBM was in the hole compared with its competition. It would take a yeoman effort to get the small systems divisions back on track with their natural follow-on products.

Just as in Orwell's *Animal Farm*, however, some computer divisions were more equal than others. By the end of 1986, just after the collapse of Fort Knox, the Endicott plant miraculously was able to announce its successor system to the 43XX line. It sure did not take it long. The plant used a bus architecture that was developed for Fort Knox in the Series/1 division, added an I/O rack complex, and built a new, small mainframe processor, more powerful than the 43XX series. It was basically completed when Fort Knox collapsed. The processor that was built was to be the mainframe co-processor in Fort Knox. They slapped the same three IBM mainframe operating systems on the package and had their follow-on product. They called it the IBM 9370. It was completed with minimal effort, in minimal time.

Even before the AS/400 was announced, the mainframers made their second strike. At least someplace Fort Knox seemed to be paying off. They were able to converge their 8100 system onto the back of the new 9370. In March 1988,

When IBM implemented the 8100 operating system called DPPX/370 for the 9370, the 8100 as a separate machine was no longer needed. The new capabilities on the 9370 permitted it to perform all of the necessary functions of the 8100 for a reasonable price. Thus, no follow-on product was required. Fort Knox was responsible for the convergence of the two-mainframe system lines into one. Of course, it could be argued that since Fort Knox was a mainframe driven project, it is understandable that the Fort Knox entrails that were usable first happened to be mainframe vintage.

Since the Rochester lab had become a computer shop, because of clandestine activity, it had learned well. While it had no funding for the research and development of the System/38 or System/36 replacement systems, the lab persisted in moving a secret 3X convergence effort through Rochester, while being mostly excluded from the Fort Knox project. When Fort Knox failed, the lab was quickly called on to create its follow-on system. Without the clandestine meetings and theory testing that went on during Fort Knox, the Little Lab That Could would have had a more difficult time performing than if it had chosen to swim Silverlake.

Chapter 16 The Silverlake Project

The Search for the Follow-On

The failure of an important project can create the emergency atmosphere needed to ensure the success of a follow-on effort. Fort Knox was a major failure, and even though Rochester was not to blame, the funding that Fort Knox gobbled up included what would have been used for the lab's next set of products. Rochester was hurting for a follow-on machine to the System/38 and even more so, the System/36. There were several hundred thousand System/36 customers, some of which had been hanging at maximum capacity for way too long. There were only 20,000 to 50,000 System/38s. Nonetheless, the needs of all these customers had been neglected for four long years during the travails of Fort Knox, and it was about time that they reappeared on the planning charts.

The goal of Fort Knox to unify the hodgepodge of smaller IBM computers was no longer important, but the company was still looking for a computer star to put DEC and its imitators on the run. These guys were growing too fat, at the expense of IBM. During the Fort Knox fiasco, these competitors had stolen many prospects and installed accounts from IBM. The mighty IBM had noticed and was alarmed, and through Rochester it was getting poised to strike back. It would be appropriate to see IBM reenergized over Microsoft and HP and Intel, as it was against DEC and company in 1986.

The Silverlake Project Begins

With the death of Fort Knox, there were some 5,000 IBM employees in Rochester Minnesota, scientists and engineers included, who could breathe a sigh of relief that all their work would not be going to Endicott. It took little time for the realization of freedom to reach them, and the hard working people from Rochester knew what they had to do. In little time, the Silverlake Project, for the convergence of the System/38 and System/36 computer lines, was underway.

From the outside, it appeared that all of IBM was in a state of confusion after the Fort Knox bust. However, some smart people in Rochester had already been doing some work in preparation for the ultimate demise of Fort Knox and the need for a new set of products for the midrange. Many of you already know that the outcome of the Silverlake Project was the Application System/400, or AS/400.

So how did Rochester pull it off? During the off-season (the four years of Fort Knox), The Little Lab in Rochester had not stopped thinking about its future. Though no future was funded, a few clandestine projects were wrapping up, and the conclusions began to make a lot of sense. Among other things, Rochester had "discovered" that through an emulation mechanism it had built, System/36 programs could run under the control of the System/38. Though this function would never be released for the aging System/38, it would become the key difference between the System/38 and the AS/400.

Need More Powerful Processors

However, after four years of no hardware development, Rochester needed more than System/36 emulation facilities to have a successful renaissance. It needed lots more than software in order to stay alive. It needed a new processor, new packaging, new hardware architecture, as well as higher-speed, higher-capacity input/output circuitry and devices.

This is where most of the project work was going to take place. Of course, after the hardware was developed, Rochester would also have to extend the operating system to support the new system hardware.

Following the Fort Knox debacle, recognizing that there would never be funding enough for both a System/38 follow-on and a System/36 follow-on, the Lab decided, and gained the approval of Steven Schwartz, an IBM general manager, to build the combined follow-on product. Along with the okay, came about $1 billion in funding. This did not come without the lab making a few promises to IBM. Among the many promises, Rochester would take as many pieces of Fort Knox as were readily usable, including its own System/36 emulation, and the Lab would work on a follow-on product that would combine the strengths of the System/36 and the System/38.

The resulting box would not be Fort Knox, but it would accomplish the consolidation of two very important small business computer lines. Without the mainframe part of Fort Knox, Rochester knew that it could handle this convergence mission. Rochester had complete control of the project, the resources, and its own destiny to ensure that it would actually happen, and that it would happen right.

A big plus was that there were no mainframe folks on the design committees whose agenda was for Endicott to assume Rochester's role in the company. IBM had been beat up so badly by DEC and company during the do-nothing years that the company now wanted to take out DEC a lot more than it wanted to take out Rochester. As you will see, however, after the DEC mission was accomplished, the same old mainframe-first pattern emerged once again.

Silverlake Goals

In Rochester, a handful of engineers and scientists, Dr. Frank Soltis among them, formed an ad hoc group and brought forth a plan for the next generation of Rochester computers.

The ground rules that the team had to work from were clear and formidable:

1. The product they designed had to be on the market within two years.
2. As much as possible were to be salvaged from the Fort Knox wreckage.
3. A proof-of-concept prototype was needed.

This was the hallmark of the Silverlake project. I lived through these times in the marketing arm of IBM as a systems engineer in the local branch sales office. Rumor after rumor was flowing out of Rochester at the time. It seemed that IBM had lifted the cloak of silence from the plant to help stop the erosion of clients from the System/36 and the System/38.

Promises, Promises

Rochester had promised Steve Schwartz and the rest of IBM that it could deliver a new system in record time. To help get the job done, IBM went through the Fort Knox shopping cart and found a few items that could help. Among them was something called the zero insertion force (ZIF) packaging cages that permitted solid logic cards to be more reliable and easier to insert and remove.

The cage, and thus the logic cards, had contacts on three of four sides. This was the same rack and cage technology that was used in the 9370, direct from the vault of Fort Knox, and was developed for Fort Knox by the Series/1 Lab in Boca Raton, Florida.

There was always somebody who wanted to give Fort Knox the appearance of having been a project with some merit. Powerful players in IBM with their Fort Knox t-shirts and leftover mentality imposed their will on the Rochester lab. Of course, to get its systems approved, the lab acquiesced.

As I recall, the early AS/400 units shipped to customers had some hardware issues related to the ZIF technology. They were very sensitive and created downtime issues on early shipments. Eventually, this was corrected and the Systems Product Division (SPD) bus, developed by the Series/1 lab, stayed with the AS/400 until just a few years ago.

A Project Full of Lesser Heroes

With a number of heroes working many long shifts per week, Rochester was able to complete the hardware and the software for the new system in little more than two years. As noted, a follow-on system change was always a big project, typically completed in the five-year range. Even though this was a Rochester endeavor--and to some in IBM, Rochester was the competition--kudos were bestowed on the lab from all parts of IBM for bringing in this project in record time.

At the time, at $1 billion in funding, it was the most expensive computer development project ever undertaken by Rochester, but the goals were lofty. The typical time from funding to product announcement in IBM had been five years.

The two-year time frame was dramatically shorter than normal. So there was a high degree of risk with the project. However, unlike the Pacific (System/38) project that was an exercise in one-of-a-kind, never-been-done-before computing, the Silverlake project was an extension of an existing architecture. Therefore, all of the extremely creative foundation work had already been done with the introduction of the System/38.

AS/400: An Instant Success

In June 1988, two months later than promised, the AS/400 family of computers was announced. As I have said several times in this book, I had the personal pleasure of presenting the announcement in the IBM Scranton location. Our announcement was held at Marywood University's Center for the Performing Arts. It was a beautiful setting. Hundreds of IBM field managers, marketing representatives, and systems engineers from across the world presented the good news of the AS/400 to several million people in just that one day. IBM was very serious about the AS/400 becoming an overnight success. It did. However, I would bet IBM has not invested as much in AS/400 promotion as it did in only that one day. It's amazing how successful a company can make something when it intends to.

The AS/400 quickly became one of the most popular computer product lines ever introduced. It remains a major source of profitability for IBM today. The Silverlake project was highly ambitious, but the lab had placed strict controls in place to keep its scope from spinning out of control. Instead of everything being invented from the ground up, key building blocks were taken from anywhere they were available, including the completed parts of the Fort Knox project, as well as from the two products being replaced: the System/36 and the System/38 minicomputers.

Nothing about Silverlake (which by announcement day was called Olympic), looked like the System/36 or the System/38. It was a rack-mounted unit compared with the two console type systems that it had replaced. It had the same physical appearance as a 9370, because it used the same racks and cages, but internally it was completely different.

It really did not matter that there were no big functional announcements with the system. It was substantially faster and had substantially more capacity than both the System/36 and the System/38. Industry watchers were able to observe the big thumb of mainframe IBM ease off the Rochester lab for this brief period, as it was able to announce and deliver a powerful hardware solution that was about to knock the socks off the competition.

Note: Projects in IBM are given interesting code names at their inception. *Fort Knox*, *NorthStar*, and *Silverlake* are several examples. It was so important for IBM to prevent the erosion of System/38 and System/36 accounts from IBM that the company was leaking internally facts about the project and everybody knew it was Silverlake. IBM's field sales force was leaking externally to its customers that something good was on its way. Silverlake was so over-hyped as it approached reality that the company changed the project name to "Olympic" before the product that would emerge from the project was ready for announcement.

Because all of the hardware was being replaced, major software enhancements were pushed off until after the basic system was operational. You've got to credit Rochester with doing what it had to do to get a definitely new system out on the market on time, with lots of hoopla. There were few who did not notice that IBM was in business big time with its new AS/400. It was a combination of Tom Furey's (Rochester lab director at the time) great leadership in the lab, a tight schedule, rigid scope control, extensive reuse of Fort Knox and other existing technology, and an exceptionally motivated project team. Silverlake remains one of the great success stories within the IT industry.

Silverlake is also a great testimonial to the Rochester laboratory and what it could actually do if IBM were willing to free it from the constraints of bondage designed to benefit the mainframe. Just 12 years after the release of Silverlake as the AS/400, however, mainframe IBM again decided that it was going to control the destiny of its most threatening, competing server line in the company. IBM blended the AS/400 in with all its other servers under the eServer umbrella.

The mainframe and the AS/400 are now the only proprietary server lines left in IBM. IBM invented both, and both machines use all-IBM technology. Neither platform needs Intel for a processor or Microsoft for an operating system.

If these two groups, the makers of the most desirable and most powerful and reliable computers ever built, could somehow make peace and convince IBM that both have a major role in the company's success, it would go a long way toward ensuring the survival of the AS/400, and could also make IBM stock a good buy once again.

Chapter 17 The Rebranding of the AS/400 As the iSeries (then Power i)

AS/400e Becomes eServer iSeries

In 1997, IBM renamed its then new line of AS/400 Model 6XX's as the "AS/400e series." This subtle renaming was an ominous forewarning of what was to come in October 2000. However, in 1997, it was a no-fanfare event, and IBM did not need to change much to support the new name, since the AS/400 part was still going to be the AS/400.

The 1997 rebranding was apparently done by Rochester itself, while it had some control over its own destiny and before the savages from corporate IBM took control of the product line. The intention was to highlight a new model line at the time as highly scalable, secure servers for e-business. Lou Gerstner had coined the term e-business for IBM, and it was politically correct to pay e-homage to the e-chief. *InformationWeek* gave IBM kudos for its announcement and predicted that the company would complement the AS/400e series rollout with the most aggressive marketing campaign in the history of the AS/400 Division, one that could cost a "cool $100 million."

Note Anybody writing about IBM's naming of products and/or its own divisions has a difficult time keeping up with the many changes. As of mid March, 2004, when the IBM Company company merged its Components Group into the ServerGroup, a new division was formed called STG. Interestingly enough the new STG has a real name, the "System Technology Division." This is a big division and it includes Servers, Storage, and Components (chips). The Power i (AS/400) organization was then formally known as the IBM eServer Power i Group under the STG Division. Now with the i5, it's changing again. For purposes of this book, I refer to the i5 Group as the AS/400 division, since I am most familiar with this nomenclature,

and if I changed all references to Power i, you could bet that a new group would pop up as quickly as we settled in with the Power i name. This whole book is about the AS/400 so we'll stay with that naming convention to avoid confusion.

When the big whigs at IBM heard about the "cool hundred million" in advertising that InformationWeek had predicted, they had to do some spinning to get out of it. If Rochester planned to spend a renegade cool hundred million to rescue its AS/400e from IBM, the mainframe-dominated IBM was going to see that that did not happen.

In the late 1990's, News/400 (now Power i News) was privy to a non-disclosure revealing of the particulars of the newest AS/400e at the time. At the meeting, the representatives were told clearly that IBM did plan a strong marketing push for the new line, but it was highly unlikely that Rochester was going to be able to spend $100 million on the effort. Hey, it might have been successful.

Poor AS/400 Marketing Becomes No Marketing

For a few years at this time, IBM's AS/400 customers had been getting annoyed at the poor marketing the company was doing for AS/400. The AS/400 name never meant anything by itself, and most would agree it would be good to give the product a name that would fit the times.

Most guys like me felt that the little "e" in AS/400e was just not enough. I thought that the AS/400 should be renamed *The IBM Business System.* Just like Windows describes what it is in its name, I felt that *The IBM Business System* would do the platform justice and call it what it is. Including the "IBM" would show that the AS/400 was the business system of choice in the IBM Company and would let the other brands keep their identities: IBM mainframe, IBM Unix box, and IBM PC Server. Why not call things what they actually are?

Rochester humored AS/400 customers looking for something from IBM. They leaked that there was a big rebranding coming and that it would be what everyone was looking for. The company referred to it as Mach1. It was going to change all the names of all IBM's servers big time and for the better. I figured that my suggestion of *The IBM Business System* had already made it to Madison Avenue. I learned shortly that I was wrong--way wrong.

The eServers Are Announced

In October 2000, the long-rumored and much debated rebranding of IBM's disparate server lines, known under the code-name "*Mach1*," was announced. From that day on, new AS/400s, as well as those announced earlier in 2000, would be christened as eServer Power i 400. There would be no "IBM Business System," ever. AS/400 customers were assured that IBM cared about their beloved AS/400 machine, because they kept the venerable "*400*" in the name. Thank you, IBM, for small favors.

However, the 400 name added to eServer Power i was cumbersome even for those who liked the vestigial "400" moniker. In customer circles, where reference to the eServer Power i 400 is needed, the old name AS/400 continues to be used. When the new name is appropriate to use, the new name is always shortened to the Power i. The "400" part of Power i is gone, but the name "AS/400" persists for customers as the product that IBM stubbornly calls the Power i.

In essence, IBM created an umbrella brand called eServer and pushed all of its server products under the umbrella so they could not be individually recognized or differentiated. IBM was sick of people talking about its diverse (read: incompatible) product line and--whoosh! --with a stroke of the wand and some true marketing genius, IBM was able to call all of its server products eServers. The fact that none of the servers under the umbrella is compatible in any way did not seem to faze IBM. As with most IBM projects, it was declared a success and the managers who brought it forth were heralded for their marketing insights.

No server was permitted to keep its former identity. The lineup that IBM presented as eServers were delivered as four separate series of servers, under one big eServer umbrella. Many IBM customers still get the "z" and the "x" series mixed up; but after a few more years, I am sure it will become clearer.

Soon, there may not even be an explanation of the series letters necessary to gain meaning about the underlying computer systems. Without whining about IBM's poor marketing at this point, the new lineup in alphabetic order is as follows:

New Name	Old Name	Means
Power i	AS/400	IBM Business System
pSeries	RS/6000	IBM Unix box
xSeries	Netfinity	IBM PC Server
zSeries	System/390	IBM Mainframe

How to Speak the eServer Language

So now, when somebody wants to know about IBM's Unix box, they are told that it is the pSeries, for "performance." When the prospect flinches, IBM has to tell the prospect that it was once known as the RS/6000, since nobody has ever heard of the pSeries.

When somebody wants to know about IBM's mainframe, they are told that it is the zSeries, for "zero" down time. When the prospect flinches, IBM has to tell the prospect that it was once known as the System/390, since nobody ever heard of the zSeries.

When somebody wants to know about IBM's PC Server, they are told that it is the xSeries, for "excellence." Once the prospect flinches, IBM has to explain that it was once known as the Netfinity, since nobody has ever heard of the xSeries. In fact, the prospect would probably flinch at the name Netfinity, too, so IBM has to say that it was once known as an IBM PC server, since nobody has heard of an xSeries or a Netfinity.

When somebody wants to know about IBM's business system, since IBM stopped acknowledging in any way that the AS/400 is IBM's business system, IBM tells them that any of the systems under the umbrella will fit the bill, starting with the xSeries and ending with the Power i, if IBM ever gets to "i."

After all, IBM seems to believe that all of its servers have similar capabilities regarding business applications. However, the last system in the IBM care line is the Power i, even though "i" comes before "p," "x," and "z."

The rebranding has created a big problem for the AS/400, which is why most AS/400 fans refuse to call the system the Power i. The jury is still out on whether i5 catches on.

Somehow in the euphoria of the Year 2000 rebranding and the positioning of all systems as e-business capable, IBM no longer permits the AS/400 to be highlighted as the small or midsized business system, since all eServers are business systems. Therefore, there is no explanation for what an AS/400 might be, and that's why it is no longer called by name. Nobody knows its name.

Chapter 18 The On-Demand Computing Project

I Can't Get Any More Power, Captain

Imagine a day when your company's order entry system can no longer keep up with the plethora of transactions that keep coming its way. Of course, extra demand for order entry is good for business, but not if you're going to lose precious sales, and perhaps even lose customers, because you cannot process all the orders.

Depending on your business, if you can't do the order job, customer loyalty may be only enough for your customer to give your company just one more try. However, if trying to reach you, to give you an order will impact your customers' productivity, their next move will likely be finding another company that can do the job. That's business. It's nothing personal.

Now, that's not a good thing for your business. IBM would like to capitalize on a businessperson's perspective, as to how much poor service may cost in terms of company viability. IBM is clearly a leader in providing solutions for this problem today. The solution was once simple, yet time consuming and expensive. You would upgrade your system.

With an adequately fast order entry system, customer orders are never held up. The upgrade could be as simple as bringing in one more Windows server, or as complex as rebuilding the underlying network or adding segments for the additional order takers if necessary. If you are running on a large, older model AS/400, the solution may involve a major, costly upgrade to the system. Simple, yes, but there would be work involved, and there might be some planned down time along the way.

Handle the Binge Periods

What if the ordering phenomenon you are experiencing is a one-time binge? What if it goes away as quickly as it came, and after you upgrade you find yourself with 10 times more capacity than you need to get your job done? Well, that may be an ideal situation for IT, since it would give a few years of constraint-free computing, but it is not necessarily a good thing for the business.

The plain business fact is that the cost of anything in excess of what is needed may have a negative affect on a company's ability to compete. So 10 times too big is way too big.

There is the possibility of good news on the horizon, according to IBM. An emerging technology set in the IT industry is bursting forth to help companies that find themselves in this proverbial computing pinch. It is sometimes called on-demand computing. Another name for it is utility computing.

The idea is easy to explain. Just as you don't generate your own electricity or store your own gasoline or pump your own natural gas or operate phone-switching circuitry, on-demand computing says you don't have to operate a major IT shop to plug into IT capabilities.

Just as you request electricity, the idea with utility computing is that you would plug your local computer infrastructure to the "compute on-demand" outlet in your home or business. When you need more order entry, you just draw more. The meter runs, and periodically you get a bill. Nothing could be simpler, if you buy the industry's arguments.

Not for my money--not yet, at least. The full notion of on-demand computing as a solution to paying for the peak level of computer and software capacity that may be needed at times will not reach us, however, until significant new technologies are made available. That is not to say that your local compute-on-demand utility company is not gearing up to handle your needs as we speak.

As an aside, you may recall from Chapter 7 that Otto Robinson, Steven Jobs, and Bill Gates used AS/400 systems to be able to respond to their business needs so they could maintain competitive advantage. Though I have never met Steve Jobs, I would bet he would agree with Otto Robinson and Bill Gates that it really does matter what kind of facility the utility computing company passes down its computing umbilical cord.

Who Are the Compute On Demand People?

On May 5, 2003, in the "Today's Top News" section, the network staff at *Network World* wrote the following:

> **"Computer Associates, HP, IBM, Microsoft and others are making big promises with new systems aimed at helping datacenter customers more effectively cut costs, reduce complexity and control resources--all with less human intervention. While the potential for such self-managing systems--typically referred to as utility computing--is appealing, reality and history suggest the technology has a long way to go before users reap any significant benefits.**
>
> **"HP is expected this week to flesh out its plans for utility computing, whereby customers can build networks that dynamically respond to changing conditions and ensure that business applications get the network, server and storage capacity they need on demand. Specifically, the vendor is expected to announce new virtualization tools for pooling disparate data center resources, building on its Adaptive Infrastructure Platform announced in November.**
>
> **"CA, IBM and Sun (with its N1 family of products) recently have unveiled their own utility computing products. Likewise, Microsoft announced Dynamic Systems Initiative (DSI), its multiyear plan to create a self-**

managing Windows environment that exploits XML-based technology, built into applications, operating systems and management tools."

It is easy to be for and against these initiatives. Why would a company not want to have plug-in computing? I certainly would not be one who would lead with the fact that this notion cannot become reality for IT shops. If CA (Computer Associates), HP, Microsoft, IBM, and Sun think that a new computing model is needed, one thing is for sure: There is a business opportunity in it for them. If they get you thinking that way, the business model may become a reality. However, over the more than 30 years that I have been in this industry, I have never seen anything worthwhile happen overnight.

First of all, let's take one of the last great notions in computing, the Internet. The old information superhighway still has a number of bumps, and companies are reluctant to stretch all of their own highways onto the superhighway, for fear that errant drivers will mow them down, or the Midnight Corporation will have free access to their wares. The Internet has been dotcom-ing for well over 10 years now, and to say it is kink-free would be a gross overstatement.

AS/400 Participation in Utility Computing

Before the Internet, the very same computer moguls told us that client/server would one day rule the world. Well, IBM was not as heavily involved as it should have been during the client/server revolution, and the AS/400 was actually missing from the foray. IBM kept it missing in action, believing that it had the bases covered with Unix and Windows. In its early days, some of you may remember, Rochester did not permit the AS/400 to have even simple file and print serving.

Will IBM keep the AS/400 from being a utility computing server, just as it was not a client/server or Internet server until the company changed CEOs? Eventually, once Gerstner arrived, IBM got concerned that client/server might actually rule the world, and that IBM would not have the right players as rulers.

In react mode, the company began to retrofit the technology on its AS/400 and mainframe servers. But it was so late in the game that Larry Ellison, billionaire CEO from Oracle (thanks to IBM), declared that client/server as an effective computing model was dead. IBM did not hear Ellison's message. While the rest of the industry focused on the Internet, IBM was building its AS/400 client/server repertoire.

Note: Larry Ellison history: The late Tedd Codd (died April 18, 2003) was an IBM researcher for many years before breaking away and forming the Relational Institute, a database think tank. While with IBM, Codd was the first to describe relational database, and is universally recognized as its originator. He wrote a number of research papers in the late 1960s and in the 1970s. His work was held to high acclaim in academic circles across the world.

His major paper, "A Relational Model of Data for Large Shared Data Banks," was presented to the Association for Computing Machinery (ACM) became the model for all relational databases. Ironically, Tedd Codd is one of Larry Ellison's favorite authors. Ellison, one of the few computer moguls who did not make his billions in the PC industry, is an entrepreneur who has never let any grass grow under his feet.

While IBM was lamenting Codd's relational thesis, because it might affect the profits of IBM's mainframe hierarchical database, the Information Management System (IMS), Larry Ellison was taking Codd's initial ideas, and many other ideas from papers written by IBMers working on the internal System "R" IBM relational database development project, and his company used them to beat IBM to market on relational database. Ellison's company grew to become Oracle, the largest database company in the world.

If you are looking for some additional dividends that IBM stockholders have been deprived of, look no further than the $10 billion plus relational database marketplace that IBM invented and then tried to forget.

Just like with the AS/400, the mainframe captains of IBM were annoyed that Codd was making all this noise about a database model that was not in the IBM truck to sell. Codd was viewed as being anti-IBM by a number of IBMers, as he debated industry leaders on the merits of relational versus the standards that were being developed in other areas.

His work did not go unnoticed by the Rochester lab, which snatched the relational concept and built the first relational engine into the 1978 model System/38. Oracle brought out its first database product in 1979 and got credit for having the first relational database implementation. IBM announced Structured Query language/Data System (SQL/DS) its first mainframe relational database in 1980, the same year the System/38 was first shipped.

SQL/DS came with SQL, and thus IBM billed it as the company's first relational database. It was a number of years before Database/2 (DB2) the big mainframe relational database became available for IBM's water-cooled mainframe systems. Rochester's System/38 was way ahead of the curve but got no credit in IBM as a relational database.

There is a lot of similarity between IBM's acceptance of Codd's database thesis and the AS/400. IBM lost the database marketplace to Oracle long ago and is trying to win it back. If Oracle had never become successful, IBM would never have introduced relational database products of its own while its hierarchical products, IMS and Data Language/ 1 (DL/1) were still selling.

Because there is no AS/400 clone, nobody will be able to snatch the AS/400 marketplace from IBM to show it has value, and IBM will not find value in the AS/400 until its market is threatened from the outside. One might conclude that IBM would be happy if the AS/400 brand of technology would just go away, as relational database would have without Larry Ellison.

Ellison Was Right

Ellison was right. By the time IBM finished its client/server retrofitting, the revolution was over, and we were all onto the

Internet. Billions of dollars were lost as companies tried to force-fit their long-running traditional applications through the client/server model. Finally, the industry realized it was fruitless. Ellison boldly announced that the idea was unreal and it was dead.

Companies needed many times the developers and support people to keep the client machines refreshed with the latest and greatest code releases. Logic doomed full client/server to failure right from the beginning. Ellison and company bought the nails needed to close it up as a viable, affordable technology. Still, some have not gotten the message.

The Internet was right there to take over. As IBM's Lou Gerstner declared in 1994, this model is server-centric. In other words, Internet computing requires very powerful servers and universal clients (browsers). With IBM as the builder of the most powerful computers in the world, the company merely needed to begin to call its "systems" servers.

The universal client became the browser and thus, with a browser on every machine that's been built in the last 10 years, the Internet model worked fine. Unfortunately, the browser wars between Microsoft and Netscape, and the dogfights on the underlying technology, have not delivered true universality at the client, but it is not too bad at all, compared with everything else in the IT industry.

Don't Bring That in Here!

In fact, instead of bringing the IT world together whereas client server had brought it apart, the Internet further divided the camps. For the most part, the universal client is used only on the Internet. Green screen prevails indoors. Companies have found one reason or another to keep terminals and terminal emulators of the "telnet" variety in action for their in-house activities.

Thus, any technology that is to be exported from in-house to the Internet, requires a major facelift and a big IT project and big IT funding. This then results in more applications that have to be maintained on two different computing platforms – "Indoors" and Internet.

Which form of computing will on-demand take? Will the notion of the universal client come back into play here or will there have to be different outlets in the wall for 3270 terminals, 5250 terminals, LAN based devices, DEC VT100 telnet, terminal emulators or browsers.

You can bet that your friendly compute-on-demand company will have a recommended approach, which may be for you to continue as you currently operate. But you can see the problem. If companies have not been unable to adapt the universal client to in-house operations in the last 10 years, how long will it take to conform to the rigors of on-demand computing once the technology is available for a dry run?

No Competition If All Vendors the Same

Now, go ahead and add up the number of players in this new potential market place. IBM alone is investing $10 billion into this model. With so many players trying to gain the market and differentiate their products as best, in its current iteration, utility-computing plans have to focus on a single vendor. Competing vendors do not create sameness as a differentiating factor; they create difference. There are no standards in this area and that promises the most adventurous takers a nightmare of integration issues.

> **"The concept, the approach, and the reason for doing utility computing make a lot of sense. But getting customers to change their thought processes and how they buy equipment is not something that you just turn the light on and it comes,"**

So, says Jamie Gruener, a senior analyst with The Yankee Group. You are right, Jamie. More than likely, the first companies inclined to make the move are those that have proven after years of frustration that client server is not a sustainable computing model. Their systems are probably so out of shape that they would welcome any change. Ironically, a client-centric model is probably the worst candidate for universal utility computing.

Is Anybody Right for Utility Computing?

My perspective is that on-demand computing as a utility model is many years away. However, it is lots closer in those shops that have broken away from homegrown code and have invested in one of the many industry-standard application packages.

To the extent that package vendors such as CA control their client set, these types of customers for this type of packaged application are the ideal candidates. The more "same" that different clients can become, the more likely a form of utility computing can be used in their organizations

Freedom and utility computing are definitely at odds with each other. The notion of computing freedom will interfere with the notion of utility computing and will make any transition that more challenging. IT staffs are not necessarily motivated to absorb the kind of culture shock that the model will present.

Utility computing will force data centers to eliminate any facet of unique operations. For example, the database staff would have to implement using the same tools and processes as the application development team. All of this would have to fall in line with the server department, which, by definition and even more so with the utility model, would have to be in synch with the network administrators and so on and so on.

Can Harmony Be Dictated?

The base problem is that IT staff in one organization does not necessarily work the same as in another organization. These fundamental differences will create major integration issues for utility computing vendors. The differences are far greater than the similarities. Even within the same technology house, the disparate elements are often permitted autonomy. It is common to have groups isolated from one another.

For example, the applications group does not necessarily care about the network bandwidth required for its new implementations, and the group often does not even talk to the infrastructure group. Considering that companies already know that cooperation helps solutions and yet they still cannot get their internal staffs to work in harmony, one would wonder how changing all applications and taking portions of them outside would help that situation?

There is, of course, the "they can do it better than we can" mentality. Many more companies, some very large, have declared their IT staffs to be inept after years of investing millions and even billions into applications and infrastructure. They have given up the ghost and have signed up with IBM or with EDS or Perot Systems or others to take over their IT operations. In nine years, for example, IBM's revenue in its Global Services unit has climbed from $4 billion to over $40 billion.

For those IT shops that are naturals to give it up, IBM Global Services would be happy to take it on. They'd be happy to design the outlet in the wall. But, for those shops that aren't ready to give it all up, the utility computing model ultimately offers some hope that future expansion can be accomplished in an orderly fashion. It may be fortuitous for IBM that the blue trucks that come to your door with "IBM Utility Computing" written on them will be run by IBM Global

Services. Hey if the utility model doesn't work, IBM's Global Services unit can take over the whole thing.

If you are IBM Global Services, that's a great model. In this model, IBM gets more full outsourcing deals while the utility computing notion is being tweaked. Even if utility computing never works, it is certainly a great marketing ploy for a services oriented company with all blue trucks to get its foot in the outsourcing door. I am not suggesting that is IBM's goal but the company is surely positioned well in a win-win game. Both wins in this instance would be on the IBM side of the ledger, regardless of whether the customer or the customer IT shop comes out ahead.

IT directors who are looking for every way to help the company struggle in these trying times see the notion of utility computing as promising for a more efficient future for both the company and the IT organization. Today, in order to handle peak demand (such as during heavy retail seasons, when transactions skyrocket), many companies over-commit their computing resources, hoping to ride out the crunch period.

This is risky, but there have not been many better ways to handle excess demand than over-commitment or overbuying. Since most IT shops are running pretty lean in recent times, there is the idea that anything that can help the IT staff to provide a better quality of service is worth examining. That's why utility computing is getting a hard look.

What Happens Once Utility Computing Is Adopted?

The answer depends on what the utility is providing. Simple applications such as e-mail and Web hosting can be done most readily using a simple utility model over the Internet. Yet, ironically, most midsized and large companies with IT staffs do these things in-house. If the objective is to take the bread and butter applications outside of the organization and add to them once moved to a service provider, then what you have is an outsourcing deal, followed by a utility deal, as usage increases. Such things are not so easy to pull off.

The most complex notion would be if the existing infrastructure, programs, and procedures stayed and the utility augmented the pieces that needed a boost. That would be a major task indeed. Nothing is impossible with a services company, because everything has a price. However, high integration costs in this some here, some there, partial utility computing model may be impossible to endure. As the "man in the white hat," a services company is uniquely and appropriately equipped to make sense of such conditions and to handle such business opportunities.

Because of the substantial integration costs in the partial utility computing model, the least expensive option for the company may be to outsource it all, and have the utility computing performed at the service vendor's site. Once integration costs are considered, the business will be forced to take a hard look at giving up its own IT shop or a substantial portion thereof.

So, for the foreseeable future--and I regret to suggest this--integration costs are not going to be affordable. Thus, utility computing has all the makings of a modern bait-and-switch gimmick to get companies to outsource IT operations. Because the fallback will be used more often than the lead offering, you can bet that no utility computing company will be without a well-oiled outsourcing offering.

Working for the Utility

So what really happens with outsourced utility computing? The whole idea is so revolutionary to the organization and to IT that there is immediately a level of chaos introduced. The IT staff soon realizes that it is a "them or us" proposition. Mental and physical human resource defections begin to occur rapidly. Since the services company knows that such chaos will be the order of the day, they typically lay a preemptive strike at the option of the company.

From an early point in the implementation process, the employees of the company become the employees of the services company. Sometimes this is good and sometimes this is bad for employees. One thing is for sure, if utility computing becomes a big thing in the future, most IT employees will be working for the utilities.

Making It All Better

With all of the complexities and uncertainties about IT and the real risk that a company may have the wrong IT software or be cursed with an inferior staff, it is no wonder that business executives want to simplify their lives by farming out this major headache. From a business perspective, IT outsourcing has many of the same advantages as utility computing. The company has somebody else assume all of its worries and life goes on happily from that day forward.

Of course, I am facetious. If life is good from the outset in these situations, it does not necessarily stay good. The big loss is the ability to leverage IT for the competitive advantage of the firm. When everything is the same, nothing is different.

Thus, there are no competitive edges. If you have no ability to implement your next dream because your "electricity" looks the same as your competitor's "electricity," when it comes from the utility plant, it's the company with a generator that has the competitive edge. If your company is the same as everybody else's, why should somebody do business with you?

Capacity Upgrade on Demand

IBM has always thought of pricing as an art. I can remember when Bo Mott, an absolute ace computer salesman in Scranton accepted a position in the IBM pricing department in Endicott. Bo was a salesman. Pricing was an art. It took a great salesman to make sure that after the accountants ensured that the price was high enough for the company to make a profit Bo got to determine how much the customer would be willing to pay and whether the price were high enough.

Bo Mott and company, the internal pricing "salesmen," figured how much the product or feature would be worth for the customer. IBM liked to charge by value, not by cost.

IBM is well known for charging different amounts for the very same hardware. Even though it would cost IBM no more, regardless of what speed, different speed machines would cost different amounts.

My first introduction to the notion of capacity upgrade on demand (CUoD) was in the 1960s, when I was a data processing major at King's College in Wilkes-Barre, Pennsylvania. The school had a 1622 Card Reader Model 1 that was capable of reading 250 cards per minute. IBM also had a 1622 Card Reader Model 2, which was capable of reading 500 cards per minute.

The IBM customer engineer for King's was the late Tom Balon. One day Tom told a bunch of students in the computing center a fascinating story about how IBM field upgrades were performed on the 1622 Card Reader.

Pay for Value

Tom noted that IBM's rental system charge was twice as much for the Model 2 as for the Model 1. That sounds reasonable until you realize that no moving parts were shipped for a Model 2 upgrade. He said the machine was field upgradeable. As I recall, he said that IBM would ship him a Model 2 upgrade that was a set of instructions telling him how to remove a part that caused the machine to run at one-half the speed. As I thought of IBM's new notion of CUoD, I realized that the company has been doing that kind of thing for a very long time.

Borrowing from the notion of utility computing, IBM's AS/400 product line now offers on demand computing. It's not like plugging the infrastructure into the wall and getting all you want, but from your company's perspective it may be even better. It sure is substantially simpler and has none of the bad staffing or software convergence points discussed above.

IBM's new midsized AS/400 models now provide six or more processors to help get all the work done. IBM's incremental cost of building another processor is not much since most of its cost comes from the R&D to design the processor and build the prototypes and the manufacturing equipment. Based on how many processors IBM expects to sell, they set the price per processor. If demand exceeds the IBM target (skimming sales strategy) the company makes a lot of money and may in fact be able to reduce the price of its processors.

In its CUoD model for the AS/400 product line, IBM ships several more processors with the system than the customer orders. The company pays only for what it orders. On smaller models, for example, three of the six processors may be inactive. IBM charges nothing for these unused processors unless they are used.

Use It When You Need It

When customers face high demand, they can turn on the additional processors one at a time to get over the crunch period. They can also turn them off when they are no longer needed. For IBM to provide this service, the company had to develop some utility computing software within their new AS/400 models. The computer itself keeps track of the hours that the extra capacity is being used and it interfaces with IBM's billing computers so that the customer gets billed for the extra computing capacity that is used, and only that which gets used.

It is a really great idea. Of course if demand increases for a protracted period of time, or the capacity is needed permanently, the customer can opt to purchase the processor and, with no down time at all, can be operating at a higher capacity than what had been originally purchased. Compared with the full utility computing notion described above, this has none of the disadvantages and IBM takes all of the risks. From my eyes, this deserves a big happy smiley face. Kudos to the AS/400 executives.

This is such a good deal for AS/400 customers that I don't know how IBM Global Services let the Little Lab That Could get away with it. At $40 billion and growing, companies in AS/400 land that choose the AS/400 approach never get to add to the IBM Global Services revenue pot. Though this is good for AS/400 customers, and for the Little Lab That Could, it is not good for Global Services.

In Chapters 19 and 20, I discuss the impact of the software division and the Global Services Division on the AS/400's survival in detail. Among other things, I demonstrate that the AS/400 server line contributes less to both the IBM software division and the IBM Global Services Division because of the nature of the machine: software integration and ease of use.

That is a double whammy for two important divisions. There is no intrinsic reason for these divisions to like the AS/400. Now, with CuOD for AS/400, IBM Global Services is again getting shut out. The revenue that could be services revenue goes to the AS/400 Division, not the division that sells utility computing. A good AS/400 deal such as this may not last long before being discovered by the rest of IBM.

With IBM having recast itself as a software and services company, it is not wise for Rochester to take money from the pockets of the two biggest divisions in the company. Just like it is not wise to fool Mother Nature, it is not wise to fool Mother IBM. Eventually, the AS/400 Division will have to pay the piper, one way or another.

Tell Somebody

Nothing sells by itself. Right now, my neighbors may be too small for on demand computing, but then again, maybe not. One thing is for sure: They know nothing about any company's plans for this new notion, and they are not about to hear about it from anybody any time soon.

More telling than that is the fact that just about nobody other than IT folks in an AS/400 shop knows about CUoD, the AS/400 innovation for non-disruptive on-site processor capacity on demand. Though corporate IBM is planning to spend $10 billion on advertising for utility computing, you can bet that none of that will occur in a way that highlights the AS/400 system.

So it is safe to say that AS/400 sales will not be impacted much by this revolutionary capacity expansion notion. As long as services and software control the advertising purse strings, excessive AS/400 sales won't get large enough to hurt them. Because of its long-term vigilance in keeping the AS/400 a manageable problem, overall CUoD may mean nothing to IBM. As long as powerful IBM Divisions can control the future of the AS/400, however, it will not benefit from many new initiatives, no matter how innovative.

Chapter 19 The Rise of the Software Division

The Reigning King of Software

Who do you think has been the world's largest software vendor right from the beginning of computer time? I mean from the 1950s, when the word software was invented. You might say Oracle, as they have been bullying their way around the industry recently, but then again, that company is just 25 years old.

You might say Microsoft, the perennial bully of all other software vendors, and the first company ever recognized as an all software company, until it started selling that darn mouse. But it, too, is just approaching its 30th year. You might also say Computer Associates or PeopleSoft, long known as mainframe and Unix software houses. They are also babies in the industry. So, if you pick any of these, you would be incorrect. The least likely candidate is the winner. Anyone who says IBM is 100 percent correct!

Only Kidding!

Well, if this paragraph were written just a few years ago, everything that I said would be true. However, Bill Gates has brought his little Microsoft Company to well over $30 billion per year in revenues. As such, Mr. Gates now leads the software pack. IBM had never counted its total software revenue separately until it formed the IBM software division as a separate division in 1996.

The software group's revenue back in the early 2000's was already a lofty $13 billion, and it has been growing rapidly since. Of course, we expect that IBM's total software revenue as reported then was substantially more than the $13 billion noted because of some software that was still tallied against hardware divisions and some that was brought in with contracts from IBM's $40 billion dollar Global Services Company. By the way, Oracle at the time was third, with about $10 billion in annual revenue. Everybody's numbers are far greater in 2016.

How Did IBM Become a Software Player?

First of all, IBM always was a software player, and from the looks of it, it will always be right up there, and may again be number one. Other than IBM and Univac in the 1950s, there was nobody else into software for a long while. IBM immediately began writing software to enhance the program development process so that more programmers could write more programs.

Their objectives were selfish, since without programmers, IBM systems would provide no value for customers. If there were no value, there would soon be no sales. Right from the beginning, IBM was a leader in computer languages, and then as operating systems became a part of the necessary action, IBM became the unquestioned best at creating operating systems software.

The Software Group Delivers

Today the software group focuses on a number of products that are said to be in the *middleware* area. It is in this middleware area that today the IBM software division makes most of its money. That is also the place where the software division invests most of its money, as noted in the below quote from IBM's software honcho, Steve Mills:

> **"We continue to invest in MVS on the mainframe and OS/400 for the Power i platform. There are investments**

we have to make in support of the hardware platforms -- the operating systems are important. But the bulk of the money goes into middleware. And that's where the growth comes from." — Steve Mills, IBM senior vice president and group executive, as quoted by *ComputerWorld.*

IBM middleware runs on all IBM platforms, and the company is investing a bundle and making a bigger bundle by selling its middleware for almost all platforms--from Windows to Sun Solaris to Unix. Products such as Domino, WebSphere Server, MQSeries, and the DB2 Universal Database are some of the hottest sellers in IBM's new software lineup.

Though IBM continues to be next to the top in total software revenue, until a few years ago, its software was traditionally managed as part of hardware marketing. This is one of many traditions that IBM CEO Lou Gerstner and his management team changed in the mid 1990's by bringing in John M. Thompson and giving him the assignment of creating a real software business within IBM. The relatively new IBM software division is involved in the creation of an integrated strategy for a highly diverse product line. Of course, in many ways it means that IBM has been rethinking how it sells software.

Industry analysts believe that IBM has the potential to become a major force in the software market, especially after the big time acquisitions of Lotus, Tivoli, Informix, and Rational Systems. In 2002 alone, IBM acquired seven additional companies, whose products and intellectual capital the company is absorbing while it continues to deploy their solutions.

Note: IBM purchased Informix for $1 Billion in 2001. Informix was a database company that competed with IBM, Sybase, and Oracle. Ironically, Informix's roots stem from the same original research of IBM's Tedd Codd as does Oracle. IBM invented relational database then let others bring it to market. Ironically, the $1 billion IBM

spent for Informix would not have been necessary if IBM had promoted its own database interests back in 1980, when Informix and Oracle and Sybase used IBM research to get their starts.

In fact, Microsoft, which today owns about 15 percent of the database market, got its own database experience from the same IBM work after it was shaped into the publicly available Ingres database originally conceived and built by Mike Stonebreaker of UC Berkeley. Later, Microsoft built its SQL Server product from its experience with Ingres. The point is that there would have been no Ingres if IBM had decided that it wanted the relational database market after it had invented it. A little vision and a little marketing could have saved a lot of money.

The restructuring of IBM into a more software-oriented company is likely to have a profound impact on the software market. Effective strategies in the software business need to be flexible as the business is constantly evolving. IBM must be careful as it absorbs software into this one division so that the prominence of the division does not impact IBM's overall reputation to its traditional hardware customers.

AS/400 Impact

It's great to know that IBM is doing so well in software. As a retired IBM person, I am encouraged that my former company believes that it is having great success in this important area. However, with three kids in college, my IBM pension is not quite enough for me to root solely for IBM. I earn my living in the AS/400 marketplace, and from my consulting eyes, IBM's software group is not helping things much in this space. In fact, the AS/400 community could easily conclude that it would be better off without IBM's software group. Without better inter-divisional cooperation, they see software group contributing negatively to the AS/400 platform's ability to survive over the long term.

Searching for an appropriate single letter to describe the AS/400 during the rebranding days of the year 2000 (see Chapter 17, "The Rebranding of the AS/400 as the Power i),

Big Blue appropriately chose the letter "i" for *integrated.* So, for almost four years, IBM has been calling the AS/400 the "Power i," though the company was not been able to get its customers to do the same. Even now the box is known as the "i5." The letter "i" is appropriate because the AS/400 has a history of being an "integrated" hardware and software platform. If there is any system in IBM whose claim to fame is "integrated," it is the AS/400.

And the Software Division Is?

So to put integrated in perspective again, let's take another look at the purpose of any software unit, including the IBM software division. It is without question to sell stand-alone, "add-on" software that is not integrated and shipped with the hardware.

What is the purpose of an integrated platform? It is to integrate software functions into the machine itself to make the machine as seamless, as complete, and as easy to work with as possible. Included in the functions that are integrated are middleware and other software. These are the IBM software division's major revenue source.

To be clear of what I am saying let me say it differently. If a customer chooses an AS/400, the software that IBM integrates into the AS/400 is software that the IBM software division does not get to sell. Thus, it follows that the software division would not look at the AS/400 as a revenue friendly box. To the extent that a software division has any say in AS/400 marketing, "integrated" would not be in its marketing message. Free, integrated function is anathema to anything that sells piece parts software.

This is an internal IBM problem. IBM can solve this. IBM' corporate management team is the problem here. To have harmony in the divisions, IBM must make it worthwhile for its software division to play ball with the AS/400. It cannot be dictated. So, the integrated pieces that sit within the OS/400 realm need to be priced so that for each OS/400 that is shipped, the software division receives enough revenue to make it want AS/400s to survive.

And, for its part, the software division must offer funding for certain AS/400 development efforts. No, it's not that simple. But, that sure would be a start. The biggest problem that I see is that if the AS/400 does not get the revenue for its work, then it may not be inclined to work for the benefit of the software division and the AS/400 might fall apart from the inside. If IBM can overcome its bureaucracy, however, there is room for both software and AS/400 servers.

Middleware offerings are said to be the area in which the software group is destined to excel. In the Microsoft area, as well as in the Unix area, for example, substantial middleware is necessary to provide a tie in between essential elements of an application solution and the operating system.

With an integrated system, such middleware is not needed and not desired. The biggest risk to the AS/400 would be if the software division were permitted to impose its dictates on the AS/400 division. The risk is that a plethora of piece parts middleware solutions for the AS/400 would make it a non-integrated platform.

It is up to IBM management to permit each division to do what it needs to do when there is conflict, but IBM's leaders must encourage the AS/400 division to be successful by charting its own course, not a course has advantages only for the software division.

> **Hint: <u>What is middleware?</u> Middleware is software that connects two otherwise separate applications or products. It serves as the glue between two applications. Middleware is sometimes called plumbing because it connects two sides of an application and passes data between them**

Ala Carte Software

Ala carte system software has been a mainstay of the mainframe for many years and IBM has made lots of money on middleware such as VSAM, CICS, and DB2. These features were all given names because named products can be sold. In the mainframe area, there have always been features, such as these that you would have to buy to build a more complete operating system. These products were all separately orderable, separately installable, and separately maintainable as optional pieces of an operating system that was shipped incomplete. That was the IBM mainframe way! The mainframe continues to be the ideal spot to sell software division products, but the Unix and Windows platforms are similar enough that the same model works.

With an AS/400, the integrated system, essential elements are included within the operating system itself and are part and parcel of the overall computer system experience. In the integrated model, the powerful IBM software division gets less revenue. This is great if you are a customer but not great if you want to sell software. This cannot be the software division's preferred model!

Is Software Piece Parts?

To understand the natural lack of affinity between the IBM software division and the AS/400 Division, imagine a company or division or group, that makes its living by selling piece parts working with a division whose integration mission is to show no piece parts, but instead have all function and facility as part of one integrated product offering. It's a marriage that could never happen naturally, and if it were forced, the fights would reach epoch proportions. The conflicts may already be at that level.

You might ask yourself, how could the software division hurt the AS/400 Division? Remember Steve Mills' quote from above, in which he said the bulk of IBM's software development dollars are not going into operating systems (such as OS/400, the lifeblood of the AS/400), but rather to funding middleware products that can be sold on all platforms? Reading between the lines, one could conclude that more functions are not about to be integrated into operating systems. Again, corporate IBM cannot permit that to happen or IBM will dismantle its AS/400's integrated character one piece part at a time.

Can the AS/400 Division Make the Software Grade?

Obviously, IBM cannot tell Sun or HP or Dell that they must sell X number of licenses for the latest middleware product, such as for example, the IBM WebSphere Server, an item proudly sold ala-carte as a piece part by the software division. However, IBM can certainly add a heavy burden to Al Zollar's woes as head of the AS/400 Division if he does not sell his quota of the software division's WebSphere server product.

Can you see this talk in IBM's back room?

> **"What was that, Mr General Manager, your AS/400 system is integrated? Tell someone who cares. The software division says that you should sell X number of copies of WebSphere Advanced Server per year. We can arrange to have somebody else in your parking spot as early as next week if you don't understand how important selling software is."**
>
> **"Sorry, Mr.GM, as long as the numbers are there, you can keep the job. We thought you knew."**

So what happens if the AS/400 GM, position held by Al Zollar does not make its software numbers? What if the AS/400 division can't sell WebSphere or the piece parts solution du jour? Does anybody care if the GM is ousted?

I care. I care because the AS/400 GM decides or should decide from day to day how much "i" there is in Power i (AS/400 –i5). He's the boss. If the GM thinks that the more "i" that he puts into the AS/400, the less likely his kids will be attending school in Minnesota next year, the more pressure there is for the AS/400 to lose more and more integration. At the same time, the software company is more likely to pick up more and more revenue from AS/400 piece parts. The AS/400 GM cannot let that happen even if it costs his job. Yet, that is a natural threat of a relationship that is not symbiotic.

The software group is structured naturally to be a foe of the AS/400 division no matter how much folks like me would like to think otherwise. Steve Mills, the IBM software division's senior executive is motivated to care more about the bottom line for software than the little "i" in Power i and i5. You can bet your piece parts on that. IBM corporate management must effectively address this

The whole focus of this book is to help the AS/400 be successful again. It is IBM's best new account vehicle. IBM has a long way to go but I am encouraged that the software group is beginning to keep its power in check. I have seen major efforts on the part of the two divisions to cooperate and get it right for IBM customers. I do not know yet, whether that is because the division chiefs have found common interests or because IBM's top manangement team has chosen to assure the company's success by being more actively involved. In either case, it makes the future more promising for the AS/400 and for IBM.

I am about to show a demo case of how the software division once laid a big sting on the AS/400 division in terms of integration and in terms of delaying essential function. After we discuss this real example, that I personally experienced, we'll turn our attention in the next chapter to the IBM Global Services Division that is now run by John Joyce, who took over the reins in early May 2004 from IBM Senior Vice

President Doug Elix. Joyce had been IBM's chief financial officer since November 1999. Elix, the former services chief was promoted to IBM's top sales position after Mike Lawrie, the company's former top sales executive left Big Blue to become CEO at Siebel Systems, a maker of top flight customer relationship management (CRM) software solutions.

In the next chapter, I'll show you how there are also issues that prevent John Joyce's Services group from being a die-hard AS/400 fan. For now, let's see how the software division derailed a historic groundbreaking multi-multi-million dollar set of AS/400 development tools created by IBM Toronto. Again I give this example, to show how IBM's top management must act as the referee to give all its divisions a fighting chance.

Software Group Hurts AS/400 with Cancelled WebSphere

The newcomer software division, formed in 1996 now represents almost one-sixth of IBM's total annual revenue. In 2003, IBM Global Services began to account for more than one-half of IBM's total revenue. Together, then, software and services numbers are approaching two-thirds of IBM's revenue. Having two-thirds of the revenue sources of IBM feeling that your style of computing (integrated and pain free) does not help their goals is not an indicator of a prosperous future.

Software Division: Integrated Is Not Good

In 1978, when the System/38 was announced, just about anything important that needed to be in the system was included. However, new software technologies emerged over the years that could not have been incorporated into the base System/38 in 1978. To be sure that these items made it out the door, IBM announced the functions as individual software products to provide additional revenue streams to help pay for new development. However, when an item appeared so important that it was essential to the "i" in the machine, IBM would take on the effort and dutifully build it in or at least integrate the product so that it appeared to have been built with the original System/38. Two examples of this with the AS/400 product are the 1994 rewrite and integration of the TCP/IP (Internet Protocol) stacks, and the integration of the Apache Web Server.

The biggest problem that the AS/400 division has right now with the software division is that Mills' group has the corporate software mission and this can inhibit Zollar's group from integrating essential software. In a business that likes to sell what is on the truck, the AS/400 division has the unenviable job of trying to convince IBM that it should build again function that is already available and for sale on another division's truck.

A great example of this dilemma is the WebSphere server product set. If this product did not have a name and if it were not big in IBM, it would merely be looked on as a servlet server. A servlet server is little more than a bolt on to a free Web server that is a bolt-on to the operating system. Its job is to provide the dynamic portion of Web pages while the Web server provides the pretty stuff. If servlet serving seems like something that a modern day operating system should have built-in, you've got the first problem right on the mark. Of course dynamic Web serving should be part of an integrated operating system.

The second problem for the AS/400 division is that a separate division, disinterested in the AS/400 machine's future opportunities has the ability to deny the AS/400 division the right to develop products that fit its marketplace. A major example of this was the software group's denying the AS/400 its opportunity for a head start in Web development tools.

IBM thought that it had done such a good job of making the AS/400 system a programmer's dream in 1988, that after that date, it did little to keep the system up to date in terms of development tools. In May 2000, over 10 years late, IBM's Toronto Laboratories, originally an affiliate of the Rochester labs in charge of programmer tools, and now a part of the new IBM Software Division, created a product plan that would finally bring the AS/400 development product line up to date in client/server, as well as Internet development, tools. They called their offering the WebSphere Development Tools and made a partial installment available in October 2000.

By May 2001, with a new version of the AS/400 operating system, IBM delivered the whole banana. Along with the October tools that included a Visual RPG language and a GUI development tool called CODE, IBM introduced WebFacing. This new tool enabled a regular AS/400 developer who knew nothing about the Internet to put a new face on applications without having to rewrite any part of them. Once run through WebFacing, the applications were beautified and could be called through any Web browser. At the same time, Toronto integrated all of the tools in one package so that there would no longer be development haves and have-nots. For existing AS/400 customers, the whole deal was free. This had prospects to be the shot in the arm that AS/400 shops needed in order to get their applications out to the Web.

There was one catch, however. Toronto had built the WebFacing and the Internet tooling to interface with a free software division product called the WebSphere Application Server (WAS) Standard Edition. IBM's Toronto team emphasized that the whole thing was free for existing customers. IBM was finally serious about bringing the AS/400 developers to the Web. Shortly after May 2001, all the development work was completed and IBM released the product. The press received it very well and it looked like it was just the ticket to move Internet development from the back alleys right onto the AS/400 platform itself.

Software Group Rains on the Parade

IBM Toronto was selling this solution to all of its customers. This Lab had finally acknowledged that Java was not working for AS/400 aficionados who wanted to use their traditional languages for the Internet (see Java in Chapter 26). Within a month of this announcement, the software division lobbed a grenade at Toronto's efforts and blew the software tools deal apart. They canceled the WebSphere Standard Edition product upon which the multi-multi-million-dollar tools were based. They eliminated the free servlet server. The Toronto labs millions were wasted and the modernization effort for AS/400 Internet developers ended before it began.

Just recently, with a fee "express" offering with i5/OS, IBM hopes to have solved the problem. After several years of stagnation caused by what appeared to be mean spirited action by IBM's Software Group, Toronto has another chance to make AS/400 Interent development a reality.

Besides its negative impact on developers, it made IBM's top management look like they were unaware that this was happening. Millions were spent on nothing. This is indicative of the big problems IBM has been having in its management structure and its management. (see Chapter 38, "Time for New Management at IBM?").

The most surprising part of the WebSphere debacle is that corporate IBM management let the decision stand for two years while their Windows and Unix antagonists besieged AS/400 developers. This devastating delay suggests that perhaps an IBM management sickness or structure sickness has never been diagnosed properly. From what I observed, no heads rolled inside of IBM for this wasted effort. That IBM's customers did not openly revolt is unfortunate. This can be attributed only to IBM's failure in the first place to tell its AS/400 constituency that it had solved the Web development problem. Most AS/400 customers had never gotten the message that they were free to develop on the Internet before the software division shut the cell door tight again.

During the two years of inaction, the software division offered a cacophony of new packaging wrinkles trying to get the AS/400 shops to bite. For example, they first offered WebSphere Advanced Version for $12,000, and hen lowered it to $8,000.

This was followed by other actions. None of my customers thought that paying for something that should be free was a good deal for them. Unfortunately during this period, most developers just continued to ignore the AS/400 for Web development. Meanwhile the clock on Internet application development was ticking, yet few AS/400 Internet applications were being built.

Eventually, somebody in Rochester got upset enough to announce that a free open source competitor to WebSphere called Tomcat would be made available for easy installation with the AS/400. This appeared to be a direct missile fired from Rochester at the software division, since the WebSphere server was the company's strategic product. Tomcat was a free, competitive product sponsored by Apache Software Foundation. IBM's AS/400 customers became even more confused.

Almost immediately, as if Big Blue software had fired back instantaneously through IBM's top management, Rochester announced that Tomcat was not a strategic product, even before it was made available. They said that a better IBM product would be coming. A viable and current-level Tomcat, integrated by IBM into the AS/400 operating system, never emerged. Again, so few AS/400 developers were watching that it almost went unnoticed.

The software group had obviously won the battle. It reminded Rochester that WebSphere, not Tomcat, is IBM's strategic servlet server. It demonstrated to the AS/400 community that the software division was not its friend. When Tomcat finally was released, IBM had ensured that the product was "poor performing" and back level in function so as to intimidate its AS/400 customers from giving it a try. One might conclude that IBM released Tomcat after it had become non-strategic only to save face.

Note: IBM systems implementers learned a long time ago that if IBM no longer thinks something is strategic, it costs more to use the product even if it is free. So the company's attempts to appease with non-strategic half-solutions were universally rebuffed by the intelligent AS/400 customer set.

IBMers Were Good Soldiers

During the WebSphere two-year waiting period, I spoke with Bill Rapp, IBM's Internet Architect for Power i, about the problem. He had written the foreword for one of my earlier WebSphere books. I also spoke with Dave Slater, IBM's director of worldwide marketing for the new development tools. Dave had written the foreword for my first book on the WebSphere tools. Both of these gentlemen were very positive about a very negative thing. During the two years of no action, I got the feeling that IBM was under a WebSphere gag order. The whole situation made me want to gag.

More than anybody at the time, I was upset because I had just invested my time writing books about free products that nobody could afford now because IBM had priced the product set too high. IBM should give both Rapp and Slater big bonuses because they were such good IBM soldiers during the ordeal. If I were still with IBM and part of this debacle, I would have been fired for sure. To anybody watching from the sidelines, it was a circus at its best. Moe, Larry, Cheese.

Because IBM promised to maintain better interfaces for WebSphere than Tomcat, and the company eventually delivered an Express version of WebSphere for much less money, most AS/400 customers rejected Tomcat because it would be a full piece-part implementation where IBM promised with Express to make WebSphere easier to install and to support it.

From 10,000 feet, it appeared that the software group wanted AS/400 customers to buy WebSphere for the AS/400, not receive it for free. It did not want AS/400 customers to get WebSphere or any servlet server for free since it would not help the software division's revenue stream. And above all, because it would receive no revenue, the software division did not want an unnamed servlet server integrated into the AS/400.

Who's Got Power?

Of course, servlet serving, just like Web serving, should be integrated into the AS/400 operating system (OS/400), and it should be free. If the software group were not in control, Rochester or Toronto would have built a free servlet server for AS/400. But because of WebSphere's existence, they were prohibited from doing so. The IBM software division was able to kill a multi-million-dollar Toronto development effort within a month of its announcement. That shows you who has the power in the corporation. Hopefully, as i5 takes off and IBM begins to concentrate on server revenue in the future, and after Al Zollar gets a few more Rochester years under his belt, even this may change for the better.

Hope on the Horizon

For a year or more after it was announced, WebSphere Express was a chargeable item for installed AS/400 accounts. Its exacted toll wound up in the coffers of the software division. It looked like it would never be covered under the "i" blanket of Power i or AS/400. Servlet serving was not about to be integrated. Too bad for the AS/400.

> **Note: From April 2003, when the non-integrated WebSphere Express for Power i became available for just $2,000, until May 4, 2004, IBM developers finally had a clear strategic direction from IBM Rochester about how to develop Web applications. Though it cost $2,000 and it was not integrated, the combination of the WebSphere Development Studio product #5722-WDS, the WebSphere Development Studio client (WDSc) product, and the WebSphere Express Server, product number 5722-IWE, finally gave AS/400 developers what they needed to get the job done.**

When you're wrong, you've got to admit it or you lose credibility quickly. Right now, after the May 4, 2004 announcements, I am ready to conclude that I may be wrong about the software division. My friends in IBM tell me that Al Zollar worked out the deal with Steve Mills to include WebSphere Express with every refresh of the OS/400 operating system, renamed to i5/OS in May 2004 to match the new eServer i5 models.

Even before it was free of charge (as it should be), IBM's Rochester team were building integration facilities into WebSphere Express using the Administrative Graphical User Interface (Admin GUI) facility of the integrated Apache server. So, just like we consider Apache integrated in the AS/400, AS/400 finally has an integrated dynamic servlet server. Let's hope cooperation continues.

That's good news. The best news is that AS/400 division and software division are finding common success points. That means there is lots of hope on the horizon.

Chapter 20 Gerstner's Baby: IBM Global Services

IBM Is a Services Company

Back in 1956, the U.S. Justice Department encouraged IBM to sign a Consent Decree under which IBM agreed to play nice. Before this time, the company's marketing force was very aggressive and would do just about anything for a sale. In many ways the IBM of the 1950s was very much a predator, as Microsoft is today. One only needs to look back at Microsoft's trail of dead software companies to get an idea of what the word predator really means.

IBM would do what it could to ensure that a big sale did not end up in the wrong hands. IBM's definition of the wrong hands was not necessarily the same as yours or mine would be. The wrong hands, from IBM's perspective, were those attached to any person not employed by, or otherwise operating on behalf of or for the benefit of, the IBM Corporation. As one would expect, IBM's competitors were all cursed with a set of "wrong hands."

Before the consent decree, IBM salesmen were free to disparage competition or to announce new products that were not even on the drawing board in order to stop a competitor from being successful, even if IBM had nothing to offer at the time. Making IBM play nice was essential for any fairness to rule in the new computer industry. In the mid 1950s, for the most part IBM was the computer industry, but the notion also included IBM's massive card tabulating business.

IBM was a master of using its early Services Group to capture the computer business of companies that chose not to buy their own equipment. To have the competitive edge, the IBM hardware divisions would sell or rent equipment to its Services Group at a substantial discount. Nobody could compete against IBM in hardware or in services. It just was not a level field. Big Blue dominated both services and computer rentals in the 1950s.

I'll Be Good!

As part of the consent decree with the government, IBM promised to excise the services people from company, and it created a wholly owned subsidiary, called Service Bureau Corporation, to run its services business. As services played less and less of a role in IBM mainline thinking, and as the government instituted a formal antitrust suit, at some time in the 1970s IBM sold the Service Bureau Corporation to Control Data Corporation, and other than hardware maintenance, it basically withdrew from the services marketplace. The company felt its resources, capital, and energies could be used better elsewhere.

Though IBM had just become successful in computers, the 1956 settlement had to do with its monopoly of the big punched card units of the 1940s. IBM thought it was adhering to the spirit of the consent decree, but many in the industry, primarily IBM's competitors, still did not trust that IBM was playing fairly. Its success with System/360 in the mid-1960s created a lot of jealousy in the industry, and the government once again began to pry into IBM's affairs.

On January 17, 1969, just five months before I began my career with IBM, the Justice Department filed its complaint for *United States v. IBM.* It was filed in the U.S. District Court, Southern District of New York. The Justice suit alleged that IBM had violated Section 2 of the Sherman Act by monopolizing or attempting to monopolize the general-purpose electronic digital computer system market, specifically computers designed primarily for business.

Records of the case against IBM can be found at the Hagley Museum and Library, http://www.hagley.lib.de.us/1980.htm#bioghist. It is most interesting reading.

There were a number of charges filed against IBM. The government contended that IBM planned to and did eliminate emerging competition that threatened the erosion of its monopoly power by devising and executing business strategies, which were not illegal, but which did not provide users with a better price, a better product, or a better service. Specifically, it was alleged that IBM had hindered the development of service and peripherals competitors by maintaining a single price policy for its machines, software, and support services (bundling); the company had granted discounts for universities and other educational institutions, and by so doing, the government claimed, IBM had influenced those places to select IBM computers; and that IBM had introduced under-priced models knowing that they could not be produced on time, and that it did so to prevent the placement of competitors' machines.

For example, IBM had prematurely announced new systems, such as System/360, claiming that it was a superior product and that its introduction was imminent, when, in fact it was many months from completion.

The trial began May 19, 1975, and spanned a period of over six years. On January 8, 1982, after thousands of hours of testimony (testimony of over 950 witnesses--87 in court, the remainder by deposition), and the submission of tens of thousands of exhibits, the case was withdrawn by William F. Baxter, Assistant Attorney General in charge of the Antitrust Division in the Department of Justice. Baxter signed what was called a **stipulation of dismissal,** stating that the government's charges were without merit. As a point of controversy, it was later discovered that Baxter had failed to disclose that he had been retained as a consultant to a West Coast law firm defending IBM in private antitrust cases.

Baxter had reviewed the case and met with both sides in 1981. His reasoning for dismissing the case was that the Antitrust Division's view regarding Section 2 violations had evolved since the commencement of the suit. The government was backing off antitrust actions during the new Reagan Administration. Baxter believed that the cost of continuation would be too high and that the government was unlikely to win the case. Baxter maintained that IBM had achieved its large market share legally without resorting to predatory practices, and that Section 2 could not be filed against a company because of its success.

Unbundling

On June 23, 1969, IBM announced unbundling as part of its answer to the Justice Department's allegations. This also happens to be the day I joined IBM. IBM wanted to win in the marketplace, but unlike Microsoft, it had a deep fear of the power of the Justice Department to hurt the company. Ironically, as part of the unbundling, IBM was back into the services business.

At the time, IBM used field software technicians, known as systems engineers, to help customers implement systems on new IBM hardware. If a customer needed a bunch of programs written to close the deal, for no charge IBM would send in a systems engineer to make sure that the customer was happy. I began my career as an IBM systems engineer at the exact time that IBM declared that the role of the systems engineer would be changing dramatically.

IBM set rates for basic, intermediate, and complex programming jobs from $22 to $66, as I recall. No customer would be permitted to receive free services from IBM after

June 23, 1969, unless the customer signed an agreement that all of the mutually planned support would end on December 31, 1969.

The Branch Office Effect

I can recall how boring it was in my new job in 1969. In the Utica, New York, office, where I worked, SEs had become accustomed to working 50 or 60 hour weeks for Big Blue as needed to ensure new installation success. Because of the continual excess hours, SEs freely went about their business, personal or otherwise, during the day, in or out of the office. Nobody punched in, and nobody seemed to care where you were, as long as you brought in results, as determined by your manager. After the unbundling, SEs in Utica and in most branches in the country came under scrutiny. Under the new IBM, we were billable assets. No one was permitted to leave the office unless he was working on a contract for a customer. It was terrible. Nobody in the IBM local offices liked it, and it was nothing like the job I had signed up for.

Without systems engineer's in the accounts drumming up new uses for the technology, many customers did not move as quickly to order new IBM products. Nobody was available to describe new features of products or new hardware offerings other than the semi-technical sales people, who many customers did not trust. IBM's business began to decline. Buck Rogers, the IBM Data Processing Division (DPD) president, who made the unbundling decision, was sent to the back woods in IBM for the rest of his career, and IBM began to pretend that unbundling never happened.

It Could Have Hurt!

There were SEs and systems engineering managers who were severely castigated because they were helping customers for free, and the word of this traveled swiftly among the ranks. SEs would no longer visit customer accounts, fearing that there might be a perception that they were giving services away. Local managers dealt with this mostly one on one, and when the big IBM managers came in to talk to us, they soon began to say, "I don't want to hear about unbundling."

The modus operandi became simple: If a customer were willing to pay, a marketing rep would sell a contract. If the customer were not willing to pay, the office commissioned a systems engineer to get whatever work needed to be done, completed by the time the system arrived. It was almost business as usual, but nobody admitted it.

By the time Lou Gerstner arrived, on April Fools' Day 1993, IBM was collecting a nice $4 billion per year informally through its unorganized services business. This included hardware maintenance. IBM was a $65 billion company when Lou Gerstner took the helm. So $61 billion came from sources other than services.

Gerstner saw great promise in services and mobilized a separate services group within IBM that eventually became known as IBM Global Services. With 2003 revenues over $40 billion, IBM Global Services contributes over half of IBM's $80 billion revenue stream. With software contributing $13 billion, the parts of IBM that kicked in $61 billion in 1992 now pony up less than half of that

Lou Made IBM a Services Company

Gerstner saved IBM from itself in many ways. The IBM that was hardware shrunk by one half, and the IBM that was services grew to be almost the size of the whole IBM that was in place when Gerstner took office. Where would IBM have been without Gerstner? Really! John Joyce, IBM's CFO at the time and now the head of IBM Global Services, explains the shift in these words:

"IBM has spent the past year rebalancing its operations around what it sees as the IT industry's 'profit opportunity' shift toward software and services."

On June 24, 2002, ComputerWorld reported that IBM's stock had been reclassified on the FTSE All World Index as a software and services company rather than as a hardware company.

When asked about the change, an IBM's spokesman noted that the change was appropriate because a majority of its revenue was coming from its software and services businesses, rather than from its hardware business, which had historically provided the majority of IBM's revenue.

The division that did not exist in 1993, IBM's Global Services Division, has brought in more revenue than the hardware division since the second quarter of 2001. The FTSE All World Index Series is a family of broad-based global indices that includes 49 countries and about 2,400 stocks. The FTSE is a trademark of the Financial Times Ltd. and the London Times. The shift in IBM to services is no longer subtle; IBM thinks of itself as a services company rather than a hardware company. With more than half of its revenue coming from services, it is easy to understand the change of perspective.

It is important to get the picture of how big the IBM Global Services Division is at $40 billion plus compared with the relatively dwarfy AS/400 division, at about $8 billion if IBM is lucky. John Joyce's Global Services Division wields great power in IBM, while Al Zollar's AS/400 division is not seen as one of his major contributors, and therefore, perhaps not one of his favorites.

AS/400 and Services

Why would John Joyce care about the AS/400 Division? In a word, money! Joyce as Doug Elix, his immediate predecessor does not yet get much revenue from the AS/400 part of the IBM hardware house. When you run a group whose mission is to provide the assembly necessary after hardware shipment, an integrated server cannot be your favorite product. On the other hand, Joyce has got to be pleased with the "assembly required" nature of the IBM software business because they sell software that is not integrated with AS/400. The less integrated the AS/400 can become, the more assembly John Joyce's team can provide, for a fee, in a given situation.

Mary Lou Roberts is an industry reporter for Power i Network. On August 28, 2003, she wrote an insightful piece that was published by the network. She starts her piece by noting the constant lamentations by what she calls Power i lovers. I am sure this refers to AS/400 loyalists who are probably customers. She talks about why they love their platform and how they cannot understand why IBM can't see that it deserves its proper share of advertising and other promotions, such as being proposed naturally as a system solution by IBM Global Services.

My friend Carmen Pascucci, a former IBM Global Services guy himself, tells me that there is nothing in the IBM Global Services playbook that suggests that the AS/400 should not be included in its bids. He acknowledges that Windows and Unix are hot, and that even his first love, the mainframe, is sometimes neglected. Carmen did not use the word "hot" with the AS/400, but he has not seen anything indicating that the services division is anti-AS/400.

Yet Mary Lou Roberts has an insider at IBM Global Services who is convinced that Carmen has not seen the whole picture and that IBM Global Services overtly and purposely ignores the AS/400 in its proposals. Mary Lou Roberts' piece is called "Is the Power i too Good to Market?" Her conclusion, after referencing the inside source, is that it most certainly is too good to market, and that's why IBM Global Services and the company in general do not market it. One would think that all inside promotional material for the AS/400 should be marketed with the following warning:

> **"Warning: Sell this box at your own risk, but be advised that the integrated nature of this machine will inevitably cause you to earn less revenue for IBM from services. There will be nothing that you will be able to do about it. Furthermore, your customer will be lost forever, as it will never go back to piece parts solutions. Caution! Caution! Caution! Sell at your own peril."**

Mary Lou Roberts captures the IBM insider's concerns as follows:

> **" '…it just wouldn't make sense to push the Power i. IBM—historic home of the big iron—is all about services these days. In fact, of IBM's 315,000 or so employees, 173,000 work in Global Services, according to Sound View Technology Group.'**
>
> **'The Power i is such a good machine that it doesn't sell services,' the IBM insider believes. 'Plus, most of the IBM software you'd want or need already comes packaged with the box. If IBM really marketed it, everyone would buy it. … But then IBM wouldn't sell services, software, and reliability/backup. As it is, the customer is the best marketing the platform has.' "**

Well, there you have it; another big moose division may be lined up against the AS/400. Is it possible that the AS/400 can survive IBM and all of its internal bullies?

It sure can if IBM corporate management does its job right! There is lots of services revenue available in AS/400 shops. It just may not be in building piece parts into a whole system. AS/400 shops are solutions oriented. AS/400 should be the king of the SMB marketplace. If this were so, there would be lots of IBM services opportunities in taking AS/400 customers onto the Web-- using portals and content management products and things that today AS/400 shops can only dream about. So, there is lots of money besides systems assembly activities that IBM's services division can gain if it pays attention to AS/400 needs.

Because I am very positive on the AS/400, especially in light of the May 4, 2004 product announcements, I am going to end this chapter on a positive and humorous note. I have a quote from an AS/400 CIO of a billion-dollar wholesale distributor (whose name is withheld by request). The CIO expresses some grassroots sentiments about why he finds the AS/400 as the only platform that he can use, regardless of its positive or negative impact on IBM's bottom line:

"I can tell you why I insist on working with an AS/400, and would probably look elsewhere for employment if the company insisted on changing platforms. I'd be happy to tell you my reasons. I don't really care about the AS/400 technology. I work for cheap bastards who won't hire anybody, and I don't want to come in nights and weekends because the system crashed."

Services and AS/400 Servers:

IBM has always had a love affair with services. However, the company got its hands slapped early on for using services and "time sharing" as monopolistic competitive weapons. As an outsider, Lou Gerstner brought in a completely new perspective to the job. Lou saw the poor shape the hardware divisions were in and the impact that the PC companies and the Unix companies were having on IBM revenue. So, instead of trying to understand all he could about hardware to sustain IBM revenues, he bolstered the company by aggressively going after a new breed of business, services of any kind. If there is one reason why Gerstner was able to turn the company around, it was his lack of attention to the traditional revenue sources and his focus on the services opportunity.

It is safe to say that IBM would not be a company today without Gerstner's immediate actions that rescued it from record losses approaching $10 billion in one year. Understandably, Gerstner had energy for just one great trip. While he was "Mr. Services," his hardware lieutenants were not empowered co-CEOs and thus were unable to rescue the traditional side of the business as Gerstner was bolstering services and software revenue.

Unfortunately, as Gerstner was bolstering the services opportunities and IBM Global Services Division gained more prominence by bringing in substantially increased revenue per year, the amount of time and dollars the company made available for promoting the AS/400 was substantially reduced. A machine that is self installing, self monitoring, self adjusting, easy to develop applications, easy to upgrade, easy to change software releases, easy to apply fixes, whose owners can just let it alone in the corner or behind a brick wall, did not appear to be the kind of machine that a services company would want to highlight. It's that simple.

But, as previously noted, and as IBM Global Services is finding out, there are lots of customizing and tailoring opportunities in AS/400 shops. Considering that most AS/400 shops use Windows or Unix servers for their Web work and for email, there is a tremendous opportunity with AIX and Linux and Windows on the new i5 Server to keep IBM services folks busy for a long time to come. Additionally and even better, there is a great services opportunity in moving Web applications from Windows and Unix onto OS/400 (i5/OS). Now, you're talking!

traditional side of the business, Gemstone was bolstering services and software revenue.

[illegible]

Chapter 21 The Cost of AS/400 Ownership

Not Yet a Million Sold

IBM anticipates selling about 50,000 AS/400s each and every year. Recently the number has been as high as 90,000 and perhaps even more recently as low as 30,000 units. With less than 100,000 units per year, one can see that the AS/400 is far from a commodity, and thus many of its unique parts are not acquired or built at a commodity price. So, quite naturally, the AS/400 costs somewhat more for IBM to build than if the quantity shipped were more like one million units per year. However, it is also true that IBM, to replace one-of-a-kind parts, is using more and more commodity parts. So the system's overall cost is coming down.

AS/400 customers know intrinsically that the money they pay for their system is well worth the price. They don't worry about the system becoming locked up and having to be re-booted and, unlike Windows units, they don't have to worry about the machine being down for almost three weeks of every year. Moreover, because it is a multi-user server machine, AS/400 IT staffs do their support thing to just one machine and do not have to worry about a "farm" of hundreds or thousands of independent PCs to accomplish the company's business processing mission.

If It Costs More, Doesn't It Cost More?

IBM has had a hard time over the years selling the industry on why the same hardware costs more in an AS/400 than any other machine. Over time, with the help of various industry consultants IBM has been able to formally quantify some of the value of its AS/400 using a technique known as the *total cost of ownership*. The moral is that all of the things that you must pay for in a non-AS/400 solution are part of the total cost of computing and the things you get that you don't have to pay for with an AS/400 should be considered in the formula.

Before getting into the specifics of what this is all about, let's look at something that has become very familiar to many of us over the last 20 years: the proliferation of PCs in business and the costs that are incurred in various areas of the company when PCs are deployed. This will form a basis from which to calculate the total cost of computing.

PCs Cost a Buzillion Per Year

There are numerous issues that all cost money when companies must deal with PC networks and PC servers. Some are easy to spot while others may be invisible until they take their toll. Let's take a look at some of the common PC issues in many corporate offices today.

Independent Islands of Office Computing

Each PC is an island. Each user in an office believes that the PC on his desk is his to use as he sees fit. Though certain office suites may be installed on each PC, many PC staffs do not cripple (lock down) the users' ability to modify and customize the application to their own pleasure. This freedom creates anarchy for the organization in that after awhile, no two systems are the same. It may be a boon for individual creativity and specialization for the individual user but it is anathema to comprehensive, coordinated technical support **when** the PC begins to act funny. The support staff must research each individual PC when a down situation arises because there is a lack of common software and common components. This causes extended downtime. Extended downtime costs the company in at least two ways:

1. More support resource is used to fix the problem
2. The user, whose PC is being worked on, is out of business for a longer down time.

Since the company pays for this wasted effort, its effect on the cost of computing is amplified.

Recovering Corporate Data Assets

There are always problems with PC networks. It is axiomatic that a network creates problems. A manager who denies that the installation has any problems either is the exception to the average or has a consulting company fixing his problems. Things break and there is a higher propensity for them to break when PCs and PC servers are networked together.

Hardware breaks, software crashes, viruses infect, and data become corrupted. Each organization must have a tried and tested plan for backup and recovery or such problems become nightmares. The PC Network that is built on the cheap often has no plan for down time or recovery. It is even a problem in many installations to suggest that a particular somebody is responsible for daily backups. It is an even bigger problem to require recovery procedures. And, how do you test the recovery procedures if they do exist? There are lots of issues in recovery such as locating the original installation applications and the operating systems. If there is no real plan, the CDs for these applications may not be in a secure location? Then after all is said and done, when the machine does go down, who gets to re-install everything and who gets to recover the corrupted data? The gentle recovery plan in most PC shops includes no names.

The less likely a system or network is going to suffer from these situations, the less it costs the company. If a PC server based network is the system of choice then the firm can no doubt expect to save money on hardware and perhaps on software compared to an AS/400 solution. However, the cost of recovery and even worse, the inability to recover and operate effectively adds substantially to the overall cost of ownership.

The Network Impact

When a company has standalone PCs and it chooses to network them all at once, it's got a better chance of creating a reasonably reliable "error-free" company network than if the network is homegrown piecemeal, one system at a time. Yet many networks start with several units and are expanded by need, not by plan. It doesn't take too long for a company to realize that it needs a person to take care of day-to-day network operations and there are often issues when the responsible party is out of the office. Companies need emergency plans in case the network crashes or the manager suddenly cannot do the job.

Since the data needed for daily operations is often not on the user's PC, the network is needed to get to the proper server and the proper printer for the job. Having the network up is just as important as the backup and recovery procedure for applications and data. What happens when network components or strategic server PCs go down? The company must have hardware maintenance agreement for both the PCs and the network. If the typical response for service is measured in days, there is a definite cost of not being able to do business as well as having idle personnel.

The PC impact

A PC is not a PC is not a PC. You may have heard the old adage that you get what you pay for. When you are adding up the costs of computing, there's another adage you should keep in mind. The lower the price of the PC, the less reliable the unit and service will be. If you find a bunch of el-cheapo white boxes from the guy down the street, you may be a temporary hero in the organization but your day in the sun will be short lived. And the clouds will come!

The total cost of ownership of a PC is inversely proportional to its cost. The majority of inexpensive PCs are cheap PCs. The costs come when the machine fails or applications fail and you are looking for the CDs that are supposed to help you recover, but there are none or they are incomplete. Try looking for device drivers for your PCs when they are not supplied on removable media such as CDs.

The options are few when you don't have what you need. You must ask yourself if your company can afford to buy new hardware, wait to get it in and have it installed for each PC that needs recovery? If you can afford the costs, the next question is whether there is a company nearby or a person nearby that you can count on to perform the needed installation / recovery tasks in a timely fashion. Sometimes there is and sometimes there is not.

Downtime Impact

We have introduced the notion of downtime in a number of the areas already discussed. It is a critical factor in the success of a PC server based network. You must be able to handle downtime by plan or your business will suffer and it will cost you more than you'd ever want or expect to pay.

When PCs fail, your users are forced to work at a lowered level of efficiency and their effectiveness is also reduced. Their expected work products drop in direct proportion to the degree they need a computer to get their jobs done. Downtime on the network or on any required network resource such as a printer, fax server or Internet connection can create a critical business situation.

The AS/400 Solves Most PC Problems

Though none of the above scenarios can be viewed as positive, if the system or network provides no value, then the cost of downtime can be minimal. This is not a joke. There are many companies who get sub par information and processing assistance from their own PC network because it is also easier to buy inferior software or simply use spreadsheets for many business functions.

All companies who use computers effectively, however, have what are called mission critical business applications and these applications must be run on a stable and reliable platform such as an AS/400. When a company does a careful evaluation of all the costs involved in computing, including downtime and recovery, the total cost of ownership is much higher for a PC when used for serious network application serving than when using an AS/400 as the main system.

Even in organizations in which PCs are the principle desktop machines, those who carefully evaluate their mission critical needs trust them to an AS/400 rather than risk disaster with a PC solution. The AS/400 midrange server has a 99.9% reliability rating for uptime and it serves to lower the total cost of ownership (TCO) over the course of its use.

When an AS/400 is used, the data and programs are secure and continually available to the users. The AS/400's unprecedented reliability addresses the one major single point of failure. Of course, even with an AS/400, disaster recovery plans need to be prepared and tested and updated, but the chances of needing the plans are substantially reduced as is the overall cost of doing business.

The Irony of Being Good

Nobody in the industry questions that the AS/400 provides the lowest cost of ownership. The question is "What does this fact do to IBM's bottom line?" I wrote this book because IBM does not really try to sell AS/400 boxes. So, the lowest TCO means nothing to IBM's bottom line since AS/400 revenue will not increase because of a lower TCO. The IBM Company keeps all the reasons to buy an AS/400, including TCO a secret from potential new customers.

TCO is just another one of those reasons why a prospect would want an AS/400 if the prospect knew it existed. Of course there are those who believe that IBM has intentionally or unintentionally eliminated most of the ways a prospect would ever learn about TCO or any other aspect of the AS/400 value proposition. Once the AS/400 became well hidden under the eServer umbrella, it was virtually removed from IBM's corporate playbook..

It is appropriate that I repeat that IBM is a services and software company and secondly a hardware company. Another look at the revenue numbers discussed in Chapters 19 and 20, points out clearly that services and software contribute more than 2/3 of IBM's revenue. As ¼ of a hardware lineup with declining revenue numbers, the AS/400 means less and less to IBM each year. Because it does not help the software division and services division achieve their revenue targets, from their perspective, and they are the breadwinners, it would be OK if the AS/400 disappeared.

When an AS/400 is sold, the software division sells less software. So, in a heartbeat the software division would vote against the AS/400. Without all the software division products to integrate in the customers shop, the services division sees less services revenue each time an AS/400 is sold. Though there is less customer cost, those costs are revenue to the services company. So IBM's services unit gets shortchanged when a reliable, automatic transmission-driven machine such as an AS/400 is sold compared with any other IBM server. Under these circumstances, why would a company, such as IBM that publicly refers to itself as a services and software organization want to sell an AS/400?

Good point. So, we conclude that for the good of IBM, not the customer, IBM does not want to sell AS/400s. It's plain and simple and it is logical. If the company did want to sell AS/400s, it would surely figure out how. The thing that keeps the AS/400 alive in IBM is not TCO advantages, no matter how good they are for IBM's customers. It is that its minimal sales do not substantially affect the golden opportunities of the software division and services division.

If AS/400 sales were up, it would quickly become a services and software revenue deterrent and somebody again would be trying to eliminate it—regardless of the customer impact. We can easily see why either of these divisions, which can and do recommend hardware, would not see any need to propose an AS/400 in any circumstance.

With IBM's other servers, the IBM Company gets its fair share and perhaps even more of a share of the other costs from the TCO formula. These are the costs that AS/400 customers do not expend when they own an AS/400. As long as PC s (any vendors), and Unix/Linux boxes, and mainframes are available for IBM to sell, it makes business sense that there will be no big push to promote the AS/400. In other words, because its impact can be minimized and IBM chooses to minimize its impact, the software and services divisions have no big reason to push for its elimination. As much as any of the other reasons, that is why the AS/400 is permitted to remain alive.

As long as software intensive and services intensive servers are being sold, the software division and the services division will do well enough. If a competitor were getting those extra services and software dollars instead of IBM, the company would be selling its integrated AS/400 solution. But IBM is getting rich on software and services and therefore it is okay. Because both the software division and the services division saved IBM during the Gerstner years, nobody in IBM is looking to minimize these two stalwarts by promoting an integrated approach to computing.

The cost of ownership would certainly increase if IBM discontinued the box from the product line. The company's biggest problem in eliminating the AS/400 is that Big Blue would not want to deal with the PR nightmare that would come with shutting down AS/400 style computing too abruptly.

IBM wants even its AS/400 customers to like the company so they continue to choose IBM solutions over the long term, even if there is no AS/400 solution in the future. Eliminating the AS/400 abruptly would be a PR disaster indeed. But, evolving the AS/400 and OS/400 in a manner that keeps it lacking essentials to the point that it eventually becomes irrelevant is certainly a viable option for a software and services company.

Chapter 22 Marketing 101

University Marketing for the Masses

Marketing is a broad term that is often mistaken for sales or advertising. It is much more than that. It seems to me that the AS/400 faithful have a very good notion as to the term marketing, and that their continual pressure for IBM from 1990-on to today—to do some marketing—comes from knowledge and not a lack thereof.

Of course, promotion is a big part of the marketing game and it certainly is the most obvious area in which IBM has performed far less than satisfactorily according to its AS/400 customers. When customers know what needs to be done marketing wise and top executives refuse to do what is needed, the result is a company that cannot sustain a $100 billion annual sales level. In order to succeed in marketing, you have to try.

Dean Asmussen of Enterprise Systems Consulting offers his own version of why IBM needs to advertise and why the continuing threat of Microsoft Windows is one of the big reasons why:

> **"I'd prefer to see press coverage in the publications that bosses read. The people up top don't know what runs their business, but they will read an article on Windows Servers and how great they are and say, 'Well, we've got to replace everything that we've got with those."**
> **Article Feedback Power i News, August, 1, 1998**

Dean is absolutely right. But it's not just advertising. The whole marketing picture has been messed up inside of IBM, and the customer focus that is a hallmark of all marketing organizations is among the major missing pieces.

Monopolies Need No Marketing?

In this chapter, I present a short lesson in marketing, so that we are all on the same marketing page when we hit the late Al Barsa's favorite chapter, "It's the Marketing, IBM." There was a time that nobody had to remind IBM of its marketing duties with any of its products. The company executed on all four marketing cylinders, and it was continually at the top of its game. For IBM to become #1 again, marketing using the four p's will be necessary.

IBM for years was universally recognized as the best marketing company in the world. In retrospect, a better evaluation of IBM's history during its successful years might very well prove that the company was just the best computer monopoly in the world, and marketing did not really matter for a company with such big monopoly power.

Without warning, a real marketer and a real entrepreneur, who was also a cutthroat business person—Bill Gates, changed all that for IBM. Yes, Gates, though retired is still the face of Microsoft and Windows. He created a monopoly in his own software business, but he created the software business and his own monopoly single-handedly.

Bill Gatess, for all of his cunning, is a terrific marketer, and he beat IBM hands down in what the world once thought was IBM's best game--marketing. You've just got to love Mr. Gates for taking on the big and the small, overcoming all odds, and prevailing big time. Winning in the trenches is very important to Mr. Gates, and he never lost a battle easily. When Gates lost, you could expect him to be backlike the spider time and time again, until he succeeded.

Since the Watsons left IBM, there has been no character within the company who could compare with the likes of Bill Gates. IBM has paid a high price for that. IBM would have been far better off over the years to have copied Gates' marketing strategy while he was helping the PC industry copy IBM's product ideas to the ultimate exclusion of IBM in the PC marketplace.

Marketing Is Obvious If You Pay Attention

Before I taught my first college class on computers, I was teaching marketing management at College Misericordia in Dallas, Pennsylvania. I was just 29 years old, and I worked for the "finest marketing organization in the world," IBM. My M.B.A. and business background, along with my IBM experience, had convinced me that I understood marketing well enough to teach it. Lots of years have passed since then, but I am still happy about a lot of things and thankfully in good health.

Long before a student gets to take a course such as marketing management, he must progress through a number of introductory courses. The simple principles that I expected my students to understand when they came into my classroom seem to have been lost in the IBM corporate marketing department. We are going to explore these principles as well as the notion of branding in the remaining pages of this chapter.

The marketing books have changed and the prevailing authors have changed but the guiding marketing principles have not changed since I had the pleasure of being a marketing instructor.

The two books that I will refer to in this chapter are required texts for the marketing emphasis area in the business program at Marywood University. I had the pleasure to serve Marywood as a faculty member in IT on the undergraduate and graduate level. I taught IT courses at Marywood as well as Operational Management. These books that will be cited are as follows:

Marketing Concepts and Strategies, by William M. Pride and O.C. Ferrell, Houghton Mifflin Publisher.

Marketing Management Knowledge and Skills, by J. Paul Peter and James H. Donnelly, Jr., McGraw Hill Irwin Publisher

Marketing 101

From Pride and Ferrell:

> **We define marketing as the process of creating, distributing, promoting, and pricing goods, services, and ideas to facilitate satisfying exchange relationships with customers in dynamic environments. (p.4)**

In the most basic introductory course in marketing, there are four do-or-die principles (the four P's) of marketing, as listed as follows:

- ✓ Product
- ✓ Price
- ✓ Promotion
- ✓ Place (Distribution)

It is my humble opinion that IBM hits partially on just one marketing cylinder with its AS/400 offering. Having said that, I also believe that nobody (customers especially) would have been bugging IBM for years about its failures in marketing in the other three areas if the AS/400 product itself were not so special.

Customers are a very important part of the marketing mix, considering that a company exists only in that it can satisfy its customers' demands for products and/or services. In once sentence, Pride and Ferrell say it all:

"Customers are the focal point of all marketing activities." (p.4):

Most first year marketing students believe that marketing and sales are the same thing. More astute students include advertising in their notion. IBM may have contributed to this misperception in its early days as it referred to its sales force as marketing representatives as opposed to salesmen. Let me tell you this. I knew many of them. IBM's marketing representatives were great salesmen (sales persons, in today's vernacular). However, they did not work for the marketing department of IBM; they worked in the sales office

Pride and Ferrell sum up the necessary ingredients and the rationale for marketing and help the marketing student understand that, as important as the four P's may be, the customer relationship is the driving force behind the success of all truly marketing-oriented companies.

> **"The essence of marketing is to develop satisfying exchanges from which both customers and marketers benefit. The customer expects to gain a reward or benefit in excess of the costs incurred in a marketing transaction. The marketer expects to gain something of value in return, generally the price charged for the product. Through buyer-seller interaction, a customer develops expectations about the sellers' future behavior. To fulfill these expectations, the marketer must deliver on promises made. Over time, the interaction results in interdependencies between the two parties."**

Repeat Business Comes From Trust

There is no question that IBM's Power i business today depends on repeat purchases from satisfied customers, most of whom feel they have a definite dependency on the AS/400 product line. Like all other types of customers for all other companies, IBM's AS/400 customer expectations revolve around solid products, good value, and dependable service. However, because of the major investment that a computer customer makes in a particular hardware platform, AS/400 customers expect that IBM will continue to enhance the AS/400 so that it continues to be relevant to their businesses. They also expect that IBM will continue to market the AS/400 so that they do not end up being one of just a few customers who use the platform. From the nineties on, IBM AS/400 customers have had a deep fear that IBM did not care about their needs. They observed IBM highlighting its other server lines but not the AS/400 line. The fear for thee customers was that if sales slacked off, this would prompt IBM to end the life of their trusty AS/400 as an IBM product. These are real customer concerns, and IBM for years did little to allay these fears.

Pride and Ferrell discuss the simple motivations for protecting positive customer relationships and maintaining an atmosphere of trust:

> **"Marketing activities should attempt to create and maintain satisfying exchange relationships. To maintain an exchange relationship, buyers must be satisfied with the obtained good, service, or idea and sellers must be satisfied with the financial reward or something else of value received. A dissatisfied customer who lacks trust in the relationship often searches instead for alternative organizations or products." (p.10)**

In this book, you have the opportunity to learn about many aspects of IBM that are positive and many that are not as positive. IBM's history indicates that the company is willing to spend hundreds of millions of dollars, if not billions, on internal projects for internal rewards, regardless of customer impact.

The Fort Knox project is one of them that had the potential to eliminate a whole class of customers from IBM to please the mainframe faction within the organization. The Fort Knox II project, outlined in the concluding chapters, is more of the same. Instead of adhering to customer relationship principles and fostering a trusting relationship, IBM has created an aura of mistrust among its customers, either by error or by design.

How IBM views its product set and how its customers view IBM is at the heart of the trust issue. The whole idea of a book titled *Can the AS/400 Survive IBM,* which I wrote in 2005 was about the IBM and AS/400 customer-trust relationship. In this regard, even with the Power I units, IBM is not doing too well.

Now, let's continue our marketing 101 topics and look at all aspects of the AS/400 marketing mix, starting with product (including product branding) and moving through the rest of the four P's.

Product

The AS/400 system was not the only product that the AS/400 division sold when it sold things. But it is the only one we care about in this book. Those products that are not integrated within the box have their own marketing plan. For example, Power i Access is a separately "marketed" software product; whereas DB2 is integrated and sold in the AS/400's integrated operating system packaging. IBM I, the new OS name is a separately orderable product for Power i.

How many products makes up the AS/400 machine itself? It is more than just the one machine; that is for sure. Well, you would have to dig out all the models that are being sold at any particular time to answer that question properly. Each AS/400 model package, now called Power I, is a separate product unto itself. Each has features and costs that are different from other models, and thus each model needs to be differentiated by its particular features in order to be sold properly.

IBM does not use advertising to do this. The company uses sales affiliates known as business partners, which serve as

IBM's direct sales force. That is one of the major flaws in IBM's new marketing plan. See Chapter 1 and the follow-on chapters which discuss a better plan.

When IBM tries to lump all the features of the AS/400 together, it creates a message that probably does not exist in any one AS/400 model of today. In essence, when the company has in the past advertised the AS/400, it has done a little homogenizing of all the AS/400 models to present the salient features that can be digested in a brochure or a Web ad or an ad in a trade press magazine.

IBM also holds sporadic marketing seminars for its existing customers, as well as Web-a-thons. There is little if any TV advertising for the product set, and thus the description of products, because of the different models, has always been difficult for IBM to present in a consistent, coherent image. In fact, it can be argued that IBM efforts have been so poor in this regard that it is a fair shot to wonder if IBM really knowshow to highlight its finest system.

As an example close to home, Betty Carpenter, who retired from Pagnotti Enterprises in Wilkes-Barre several years ago, had her perspectives on IBM well documented in Chapter 23. Betty was never happy about the company's most revent AS/400 messages—mostly because there were no messages that she could show her boss.

Betty does not like IBM pushing the notion of the multiplatform, multi-operating system with Linux and logical partitioning and other highly advanced and complicated capabilities. From Betty's perception, these do not apply to her business. They do not apply to pagnotti Enterprises. At least Betty has not been convinced by IBM that they apply. And that's the point. She always hoped that IBM would talk to her so that she could tell IBM what they ought to be telling her boss.

Betty and others are not happy that IBM's message is never to educate. It is to sell something but the something is non-descript. IBM has an arrogant streak and so it feels it does not have to explain the newest and wonderfully advanced concepts of the AS/400 even for long-term customers such as Pagnotti Enterprises.

IBM figures its AS/400 customer set must already know about such concepts for their availability to make any sense. In the past IBM would explain the concept and then tell the customer why it is worthwhile. IBM no longer has the time to eductate its customers about IBM products.

The sales prospect is supposed to already understand the features and the IBM spokesperson assumes that the audience already understands new facilities that are being made availableon the newly enhanced AS/400 / Power I line. The customer, without any help from IBM marketing is supposed to already know why the new capabilities pertain to their respective companies. IBM misses the mark in this presumption for many of its customers. Thank you IBM for thinking all of your customers already know the concepts but sorry, we don't!

Traditional AS/400 customers do not see the product in the same way IBM sees it. Over the last twenty years, for example, the AS/400 changed names multiple times and during those changes, the machine has become a mainframe capable machine. In fact, IBM executives now openly refer to it as the "mainframe for the masses."

Tremendous new capabilities such as logical partitioning, full Linux support, IBM Unix via AIX, and built-in Windows processors had become part of the AS/400 landscape almost twnty years ago. However, none of these "new" facilities were why an AS/400 customer chose to be an AS/400 customer.

For its own reasons, IBM distorted the presentation of the AS/400 product to highlight those foreign capabilities for reasons that are not generally understood by AS/400 customers. Moreover, a 2005 marketing theme of the "mainframe for the masses" did not play well for small companies looking for a nice, easy to use, reliable business computer system. They had rejected the notion of the mainframe many times in the past.

Thus, there has been plenty of fallout because of the perception of increased complexity in the AS/400 product, rather than the notion of increased capability. AS/400 customers and those of us in the support channel think that IBM must address this by helping its traditional customers understand that there is still value in the box that they have adopted to run their business.

Smaller prospects have their favorite features and larger prospects have theirs. So, as IBM hopefully introduces smaller and more affordable AS/400s over time, based on the new Power chips that the company has been building for Sony's PlayStation and/or or Apple's powerful computers, the new appearance of complexity must go. It must be removed at the product level and a friendly product image must be portrayed.

Branding

It would be inappropriate to suggest that we can exit the Product area without discussing branding. IBM now knows the AS/400 as the Power i. An indicator as to how effective this new brand is comes right from IBM's AS/400 customer set. The customer base still refers to the box as the AS/400. You don't have to know anything about branding to know that IBM has a big problem there. Its customers simply have not accepted its new brand name for the AS/400. The topic of AS/400 rebranding is fully covered in Chapters from 17 to 24, and in-between.

Pride and Ferrell, our marketing gurus, offer great counsel to the IBM marketing organization in their branding efforts, if only IBM would listen: What is a brand?

> **"A brand is a name, term, design, symbol, or any other feature that identifies one seller's good or service and distinguishes it from that of other sellers. A brand name is the part of the brand that can be spoken." (p. 316)**

One of the major customer complaints about IBM's AS/400 branding is that the company now uses the term eServer to homogenize all of its major computer products under one brand name. The name has no meaning unto itself and tends to homogenize more than differentiate or "distinguish" the AS/400 from other computers, either inside or outside of IBM.

Since AS/400 customers believe their machine is unique, this naturally irritates them, and they find little positive logic in IBM's theme. A brand name, according to Pride and Ferrell, should distinguish a brand to help differentiate it from other brands. IBM is already an effective brand. AS/400 customers believe that the eServer brand that IBM was trying to promote in the mid 2000 era confused AS/400 customers more than it helped to differentiate, distinguishe, or highlight the product.

Why IBM chose to spend so much marketing dollars on a rebranding that merely noted that the AS/400 was an IBM eServer was a big puzzle to many. The IBM name would have been a far better brand than the unknown brand eServer.

Having the IBM name in your product's arsenal and creating a new name to describe products already known by your major brand is at best unnecessary and at worst confusing and at the bottom line was not smart. The fact is that IBM was already the third most well known brand in the whole world. The eServer name in which IBM wanted to lump the AS/400 was not on anybody's top brand list.

See the chart in Figure 22-1 to get a feel for how much the IBM brand is worth. Also notice Coca Cola is at the top of the list. Many of you remember a few years ago that Coke decided to change the taste of its product, and its customers rebelled against the company's toying with the revered old-time formula. As Coke realized what it had done, it quickly brought back the old formula and regained its positive image as "Classic Coke." If IBM were only so smart!

While you are peeking at the chart, notice which brand was is number 2 when the study was taken. That is not by accident.

Figure 22-1 Six Top Brand Names In the World

Rank	Brand	Brand Value ($Billions)
1	Coca-Cola	70.45
2	Microsoft	65.17
3.	IBM	51.77
4.	GE	42.34
5	Intel	31.11
6.	Nokia	29.44

Source "The Global Brand Scoreboard," Aug. 4, 2003

Under the category of types of branding, Pride and Ferrell offer a number of approaches to branding products. One is individual branding and these distinguished researchers note that

> **"individual branding… is a policy of naming each product differently." (p. 306)**

Yet, the eServer brand does not name each product differently and in fact puts one name on multiple products. The IBM eServer Power i does not highlight the differences of the AS/400 from the pSeries, the xSeries, the zSeries, or even IBM's competitors. Therefore, the IBM homogenization branding strategy is a clear loser. Pride and Ferrell continue this quote:

> **"Family branding is a policy of naming ... all of a firm's products... with the same name or at least part of the name: 'Kellogg's Corn Flakes, Kellogg's Rice Crispies' " (p. 307)**

Names such as the System/360 and the System/3 do the trick much better than those under the "goofy" IBM eServer umbrella. The two referenced products, System/360 and System/3, were families of computers. Just as Corn Flakes and Rice Crispies are different from each other and fit nicely in their own family brand, System/360 and System/3 are different from each other, and in their day they fit very nicely in IBM's product mix as different products clearly defined for different markets.

If Kellogg's wanted to create a mid-level brand such as eServer, perhaps it would come up with a great brand name like HealthyGrain. Now, let's see how the new brand fits the products. Kellogg's HealthyGrain Corn Flakes and Kellogg's HealthyGrain Rice Crispies are not very crisp and to the point. In fact both full names are kind of flaky. You'd be starving by the time you got the name out of your mouth. Who cares about HealthyGrain when the product is Kellogg's?

You and I already know that Kellogg's means good grain cereal. By the same logic, who cares about eServer with IBM? You and I know IBM means the finest computers in the industry. IBM already means great computers, just like Kellogg's already means great cereals. A mid-level brand is superfluous.

To summarize some basic branding principles, let's go back to Pride and Ferrell:

Selecting a Brand Name: (p. 303)

"First, the name should be easy for customers... to say, spell, and recall. Short, one-syllable names such as Cheer often satisfy this requirement.

"Second, the brand name should indicate the product's major benefits and if possible, should suggest in a positive way that product's uses and special characteristics; negative and offensive references should be avoided. For example, the brand names of such household cleaning products as Ajax dishwashing liquid, Vanish toilet bowl cleaner, Formula 409 multipurpose cleaner, Cascade dishwasher detergent, and Wisk laundry detergent connote strength and effectiveness.

"Third, to set it apart from competing brands, the brand should be distinctive. If a marketer intends to use a brand for a product line, that brand must be compatible with all products in the line.

"Finally, a brand should be designed so that it can be used and recognized in all types of media. Finding the right brand name has already become a challenging task because many obvious product names have already been used."

I would suggest that, according to Pride and Ferrell's principles, IBM's AS/400 eServer branding is well off base. In fact, I would offer that HealthyGrain is a better mid-level brand than eServer because it is intuitive for all. Yet it is superfluous.

eServer is such an obvious poor choice that IBM's AS/400 customers became annoyed at IBM and held the Company accountable for the lack of respect that the AS/400 commanded in the marketplace. IBM customers blamed IBM's poor branding.

Peter and Donnelly in their marketing management text offer their own "brand" of sound advice for brand equity:

"For some organizations, the primary focus of strategy development is placed on brand building, developing and nurturing activities. Factors that tend to increase the strength of a brand include: (1) Product quality – when

> **products do what they do very well (e.g., Windex and Easy Off [AS/400]); (2) Consistent advertising and other marketing communications in which brands tell their story often and well (e.g., Pepsi and Visa); (3) distribution intensity whereby customers see the brand wherever they shop (e.g., Marlboro); and (4) brand personality where the brand stands for something (e.g., Disney). The strength of the Coca-Cola brand, for example, is widely attributed to its universal availability, universal awareness, and trademark protection, which came as a result of strategic actions taken by the parent organization.**
>
> **"Thc brand name is perhaps the single most important element on the package, serving as a unique identifier." (p. 88)**

With regard to the AS/400, it is undisputed that IBM is blessed with a special product that does its job very well, compared with all other computers. Yet IBM fails in the brand advertising and has in fact removed the most important name ever given to the brand, AS/400. IBM does not tell the AS/400 story often and when it does, it is a distortion of what customers think. Though Intel and Windows are everywhere, the AS/400 is not visible for the computer purchaser at the time they are ready to purchase. It is a non-player, though competitors such as Intel and Windows are ever present.

Finally, the AS/400 as a name was always a poor name itself, but substantially better than eServer Power i 400. IBM has done its best to keep its AS/400 and Power i brands weak while competitive brands, such as Windows have gained phenomenal strength, making Microsoft the second highest company in terms of brand awareness (Figure 22-1). It is clearly time for IBM to return to marketing basics.

Pricc

The AS/400 overall is over-priced big time. There are two basic pricing strategies that companies use to sell products. A skimming strategy is used when a new product is out and the company wants to recoup its R&D quickly. This is often the first strategy for a product. As the product, such as a flat panel TV is accepted and more and more R&D is recouped, the company may lower prices and revert to a penetration strategy. In this approach, the price is continually lowered to be affordable so that more and more people can buy the product.

Because there is no competition per se for an AS/400, IBM's strategy is both penetration and skimming. IBM limits the marketplace for the system and provides extra "value" in the box. The company then hopes that the value is recognized and it is not a deterrent to purchases. IBM often uses the total cost of ownership examples to prove that the AS/400's cost to purchase is more than made up by its reliability and its ease of deployment.

There is a big problem today with the perceived value of the price of AS/400 interactive computing. This is covered in detail in Chapter 25, "The Dead Goose That Once Laid Golden Eggs." In a nutshell IBM charges its loyal and traditional AS/400 customers substantially more for the very same machine than it does a Windows user who does not need the AS/400-specific facilities.

This is a sore point with AS/400 loyalists, who today represent the bulk of the platform's customers. IBM had better get this one straight before too long or it may suffer a backlash from a customer set that thinks they are being ripped off. In other words, there is potential future market loss due to IBM's pricing.

Place

We'll look at place before promotion. Place is often called distribution, but the "d" in distribution ruins the notion of the four P's. Place simply means where you sell the product. In the tavern business for example, marketers joke that there are three marketing criteria for that type of business.

These are location, location, and location. I think that IBM has a problem with "place." Let me just say that if I wanted to buy an AS/400, because I've worked in the industry I know that I would have to call an IBM business partner. However, my neighbors and yours would not know that. As long as IBM does not make it easy for prospects to contact the company to buy a product, prospects will not contact the company, and IBM will not get the business.

Promotion

This is the area in which most people see the notion of marketing. This area is responsible for attracting customers. Whether it is through a direct sales force or the Web, somebody must generate business and somebody must close business.

AS/400 customers think they would be better off if ordinary citizens knew what an AS/400 is so IBM's promotion problem includes its customer's perception of how well they try to sell the box as well as the promotion necessary to sell thc box.

If ordinary citizens knew, then that would mean that my neighbors and everybody else would know about the product. In a "knowing world," it would also mean that AS/400 professionals would have an easier time defending the box against attack.

If people knew about it, they might even buy it. That is the primary reason why AS/400 customers want IBM to advertise. Without IBM's help, its customers do not think they can sustain the AS/400 identity battles in their own organizations.

Another reason is that as more people know about the AS/400, and they begin to believe in its reliability and ease of use, the more will want it. It's got phenomenal potential if somebody smart were to highlight the AS/400 to the public using common sense terms that everybody is able to understand. It would not take long before AS/400 sales would increase. Then eventually, despite Al Zollar's opinion to the contrary, Windows could become a target, and the AS/400 could prevail.

Problems on the Home Front

Rochester, the home of the AS/400 was never a recognized powerful IBM Division, and therefore Al Zollar, the AS/400 GM, did not have enough corporate power. As noted, the software and services divisions grew larger than the AS/400 now the Power i product set in the last few years.

Neither of these two "divisions" were in line to help the AS/400 in any way. That is what the marketing textbooks would call a big IBM marketing problem. It is a promotion problem because the AS/400 cannot be promoted when more powerful divisions in IBM had a vested interest in their unit being their favorite server.

The dark side of probability shows a potential future in which IBM chooses not to sell AS/400s even though it can. Software and Services (chapters 19 and 20) now rule the revenue day at IBM. Since IBM's survival depends more on it being a software and services company more than a hardware company, it is key that the software and services divisions see value and revenue opportunity in backing the AS/400 platform.

IBM inadvertently leaks little pieces of its possible new corporate strategies from time to time. Mike Odierna, when he held the position of IBM Worldwide AS/400 eBusiness Segment Manager minced no words as he gave the logical reason for the AS/400's market perception problem. From Mike's vantage point it's actually not a problem; it was the IBM plan!

"The IBM Corporation, I think now more than ever, is focusing on being platform-neutral. With IBM services growing fast, it appears the company simply isn't interested in putting the majority of its eggs in the AS/400e basket either--especially since the system is so user-friendly."
Article Feedback Power i News, August, 1, 1998

Some Inventions Never Make It

Many of us can recall their parents or uncles or aunts talking about the mystery inventors of the past. We've all heard of the advanced carburetors that could give 100 miles per gallon. There are stories of the big auto companies buying up those ideas and paying off those people so that that technology was never released. There are stories today that the medical community already has a cure for cancer but they are holding it back for more profits in the future.

Can this be what IBM is doing with its AS/400? Is the AS/400 like a great carburetor that will cause a problem in oil sales? IBM's AS/400 can make life easier for all businesses. However if IBM can make 10 times as much profit selling software and services on somebody else's difficult-to-use box, the plan just may be to let the AS/400 die the same death as the advanced carburetor.

It is possible that IBM knows exactly what it is doing and that its purpose is exactly what we think its greatest fear is. Now that's a sobering thought.

Customer and Business Partner Marketing Opinions

In June 2003, IBM went to its business partners in a council forum to get some advice on marketing. For IBM to do this, there had to be some big reasons. I certainly do not want to downplay this initiative, but knowing IBM, I would bet the purpose was for IBM's marketing lieutenants to feed the partners some good pitch and offer them something for their businesses.

In return, IBM was looking for some good marketing press from this elite group of business partners. If they would only say that IBM's marketing is right on, IBM could use their words to defend itself against its ruthless customers' attacks. IBM's AS/400 customers in particular are so disappointed by IBM's inept marketing that they take every opportunity to blast the company.

To get them to say, "See, IBM business partners think we are good in marketing" must be a major silent objective of the council. It is a gimmick, and nothing more. It's like wining and dining the foxes so that they will praise the effectiveness of the hole-ridden fences around the hen house. IBM is using co-marketing and co-funding and programs to optimize everyone's resources–including IBM's.

So for business partners, there was a little IBM cash on the table to help buy some good will. (I'm sure it was not much, but it was much better than nothing.) There was also an opportunity to get some marketing training from IBM that might help the partners' business planning and execution.

For IBM's benefit, after treating these folks nicely for months, it was natural to believe that maybe these business partners would have something nice to say about IBM's marketing efforts. But even if they yelled it at the rooftops, it would not repair the fence around the hen house, and it would not help Power i marketing.

I am not suggesting that this is all bad, but from my vantage point, IBM's motivations were always suspect. Moreover, this was not an AS/400 thing. It was an overall IBM server group overture, so I saw little hope for AS/400 regardless of the makeup of this council.

If IBM and its Business Partners weree more in harmony that would help the IBM executives and perhaps the Business Partners, but it would surely not help AS/400 customers. The fact that the topic is marketing, and that is admitting something itself, left the community with some small hope.

What takes away some of that hope is that IBM never believed that it needed an AS/400 or an all-IBM marketing customer council, per se, however, because COMMON (the AS/400 users group) and SHARE (the mainframe users group) provided that for the company twice a year. IBM chose not to listen to COMMON, which had given Bog Blue a clear directive to advertise the AS/400. IBM apparently was not empowered to act. It would have been good to formalize a feedback mechanism into all such councils.

However, there was always the risk of IBM brainwashing through the wine and dine mechanism. My point is that there already was a theoretical dialogue between IBM and its customers. Again, the IBM people who heard the COMMON message either did nothing with it or are overruled at a higher level. Then again, maybe they were at the conference to have some fun, not to make IBM a better company.

The Four P's

So there you have the four P's of marketing and a slight report card of IBM's prowess in these areas with its AS/400. The grades are not very good, I am afraid, because IBM does not study well enough and does not concentrate, and it does not focus on its hardware market opportunities.

The Bottom Line

As I reviewed my marketing books looking for the one profound thing to say about IBM's marketing management, no matter where I turned, I found the best authors available to colleges and universities today, such as Peter and Donnelly, Pride and Ferrell, spelling out the things a company should and should not do. Listening to customers if not delighting customers seemed to be a common theme of the most successful, real-life examples.

While the top-flight marketers suggest that companies be customer driven to ensure a ready market for goods and services, IBM suggests that it already is market driven. Yet when you see the company in action, it seems to be strategy driven.

Microsoft is checked by IBM's Linux card, especially if Linux desktop takes off. Only IBM checks Intel. Can this be the strategy IBM is playing? Everything else sure seems to be lost in its dust.

Big Blue had been investing less in everything else except services and software, and some statistics indicated that 65 percent of the IT services number was going offshore, and the word on the street is that the "O" word (outsourcing) cannot be discussed by mere mortals unless IBM's thought police are involved in the act.

IBM as a company for the last thirty years has definitely been an enigma. The company has not been able to structure itself so that it could sell out all its products and take all the business it could from the marketplace.

Instead, in the hardware marketplace, IBM tried to make its diverse system products all appear to be the same rather than to sell them. This could not work because the products were not not the same. It did not matter if IBM called four different products "eServers" or "SameProducts." All four products weree different, and IBM lost a lotof marketing dollars trying to tell its customers they were the same. .

On August 14, 2002, Greg Youngren, senior partner at A+ Midrange Support Wizard, LLC, offered his thoughts on the IBM marketing dilemma:

A FLAGGING FLAGSHIP

"I'm sure that [IBM] is feeling pressure from HP and Sun Corporations. But [it's] disappointing if IBM is slacking in keeping one of their [flagship] systems--Power i--in front of its competitors."

I am convinced that there is no textbook marketing model for IBM. But the "let's pretend that we're something that we're not" product model has not worked. Whatever hardware business IBM is getting comes from natural occurrences, not from selling or from anybody being inspired to buy IBM, an eServer, or even a SameProduct.

IBM no longer seems to know how to get customers in the door (and there are very few doors available), and the company has forgotten how to close customers when they happen to wander in. Whatever product marketing game IBM is playing, the company is losing.

The biggest improvement that IBM can make is to admit that it has failed in marketing and start over. Once company executives admit that, they can work on the next priority, which is to stop the bleeding. Marketing in IBM is so far off the mark that the company needs to re invent its marketing department – whatever that means.

I would recommend having the marketing managers stop whatever it is they are doing because it is not helping. They need to sit down for a few weeks with Marketing 101 books and Marketing Management books and Harvard Business Review Cases and they need formal classroom oriented modern marketing training with real industry leading marketing professors and/or professionals. Then they need some trustworthy marketing consultants to help the company get the customer-focus and market-driven image back to where it should be.

In summary, my analysis from the academic side suggests that it is high time for IBM to go back to marketing school. Something is definitely missing.

Chapter 23 It's the Marketing, IBM!

The Mindshare Battle

The late Al Barso Jr. would scream at the top of his lungs at IBM's semiannual COMMON users group convention that: "It's the marketing, IBM.' Why would technogeeks such as Al Barsa not tell IBM what to do to make its producet line technically fit its customer set? Why would a great guru such as Al scream about IBM's marketing?

Well, that answer is simple. Neither Al, nor I, nor many IBM AS/400 experts or customers believed that IBM cared about what we thought. Many of us believed that IBM did not believe in the AS/400 product line appropriately enough to market the line appropriately.

It is easy to poke holes at anything today from what a person wears to what they drive to where they live. Unless you are already an AS/400 advocate or an IBM AS/400 customer, you have no need to be concerned about how IBM chooses to market its products or whether it endorses a particular machine or operates contrary to your beliefs.

But I regret that I cannot suggest that the same applies if your livelihood or reputation relies on what IBM freely admitted in the past was the best system it had ever produced. What happened to further endorsements, IBM?

> **"From a public awareness perspective, today's Power i [renamed from AS/400] has less public mindshare than the AS/400 or the System/38 ever had. The Power i, despite its low cost of ownership, is the system that aspiring IT professionals vow to remove, because from their perceptive it is irrelevant. They don't know it and they don't understand it, so they want to do away with it."**

Al Barsa, Barsa Consulting, www.barsaconsulting.com
October 24, 2003

Words from the Master

This quote is so chilling that I included on one of my covers. Al Barsa in his prime was the recognized world master of the AS/400. Unlike me, Al is untainted from having ever worked for IBM. Yet, like me, he cared as much about the AS/400 and its loyal constituency as anybody. While you are digesting what this chapter is all about, please take Al's comments prior to his death as they are intended.

If IBM chooses not tell the new IT professionals that it has a machine upon which they can build a fine career, and the message is not clear and irrefutable, why would anybody, on his or her own, conclude that the land of the AS/400 is a land offering promise?

I begin with a quote from Al Barsa because, more than any person who once lived in the AS/400 community, Al fought IBM every chance he could to convince the company that it should market the AS/400 properly. This book and this chapter is replete with examples of how IBM doggedly refused to support the best product that the company had ever produced.

It's not Al's fault; he's a brave departed soul. You'd be surprised how many top-name AS/400 "experts" that I contacted, who would not contribute to this work for fear of retribution from IBM. Al Barsa was a true and fearless leader. Thank you, Al. RIP

I still think too much of IBM to believe that there will be retribution for me or for anybody who contributed to this work. I would have been pleased to give IBM my recommendations in another forum, if one had been open to me. For as much as some in IBM may not be happy with this book, as it pushes them to be successful, I hope that IBM will understand that this message is intended to prompt the company to take action and make the right decisions for the future. IBM can be # 1 again. But, it must first decide tobe #1.

AS/400 for the Masses

This chapter is about what is going on in IBM with its most special system, the AS/400. Unlike a yo-yo or a top or a water gun, the average person on the street cannot make an AS/400 work. Moreover, the average person has no clue about how internally powerful and elegant an AS/400 computer may be.

However, with a little bit of knowledge, anybody can learn enough to appreciate the wonders of the machine without knowing how to use it. This book explores some of the reasons why IBM refuses to discuss its AS/400 computer with the public in any meaningful way.

> **"Most people are not truly aware of what the AS/400 is (general population, business owners, business executives, colleges, school corporations, and IS personnel). Many people who are aware of the AS/400 have absolutely no clue as to what it is and can do. This is a great weapon for competing vendors, and they use it. They say: 'The AS/400 is proprietary' or 'The AS/400 is expensive' or 'The AS/400 is a dead platform.' Each one of these statements is essentially false, but most people can't refute it. And lately the silence that is coming from Armonk [IBM HQ in New York] on the AS/400 just helps fuel this kind of talk."**
> **Michael Crump, Ball-Foster Glass Container Corporation, Article Feedback Power i News, August, 1, 1998**

> **"Within IS departments, you often have different factions. You've got your networking people, AS/400 people, RS/6000 people, different platforms, and then you have upper management, who don't know much about the AS/400, and they think of it as old and being replaced. It's old green-screen stuff. You end up having to defend it as not old technology."**
> **Kathleen Kostuck, Independent AS/400 Consultant, Article Feedback Power i News, August, 1, 1998**

Where's the Chicken?

The only time Betty Carpenter of Pagnotti Enterprises in Wilkes-Barre sees IBM promoting the AS/400 is when she gets an e-mail from her business partner or hears about the contents of a technical seminar from a friend or business associate. And Betty is an IBM AS/400 customer. She never hears about the AS/400 on television or in other regular-people media, nor does her boss, Ken Weaver, the CFO of Pagnotti Enterprises.

Ken questions why Pagnotti has an old AS/400 and why they can't just move to something modern, like Windows. Since no one at IBM seems to care, both Betty and Ken are beginning to question why they have an AS/400 running the company's mining and insurance businesses.

Like many AS/400 shops that are not looking for a mainframe, Betty is not impressed with the few communications she receives from IBM's business partners about her AS/400 and prospects for upgrading from their Model 720. She resents all the push about Linux and logical partitions and wonders why IBM has nothing to offer her. Betty sums up her feelings this way:

> **"They [IBM] have taken a simple notion and made it complicated. They have tried to make caviar, when all most of us want is good old reliable chicken: keeps clucking and doesn't stink."**

Pagnotti is evaluating its next system. I serve as the company's computer consultant. Recently, I asked Betty to listen in to an IBM Webcast that I thought might help her get up-to-date with what IBM is talking about. Again, IBM had the wrong message for Pagnotti:

> **"I started to listen, until I got disgusted. All they seem to care about is multi-platform--Unix, Linux, etc. That's not us."**

Some people like, and perhaps need, the more complex aspects of computing, such as Linux and logical partitioning, that have recently come to the AS/400. For some, the innate personality of the AS/400 is not enough. So among the ranks, AS/400 customers actually do have different needs.

Give Us Some Cake!

From the mid-1990s, when IBM developed its love affair with Sun Microsystems' Java language and programming environment, many AS/400 customers were put off by IBM's suggestion that they should switch from the RPG language and move to Java (a low-level language).

IBM spent tons of R&D dollars building the AS/400 server into the finest Java platform in the industry, but the bulk of IBM's AS/400 customers want nothing to do with it (see Chapter 26). Now that IBM has a wonderful Java built into the AS/400 system, the company does not sell the AS/400 to the general Java community. Instead they try to sell Java to the AS/400 community.

People like Betty Carpenter see IBM trying to force its AS/400 developers to become Java gurus in order to work with the Internet or ultimately to survive in the industry. Betty says, "No way."

Jon Paris is a former Toronto IBMer and noted speaker at COMMON. He is now with HAL North America. Jon's comments below help point out the craziness of IBM's marketing activities with Java.

> **"Rochester [IBM Lab] is spending 95 percent of its resources to please the 5 percent of its customers who use Java. And it's spending the other 5 percent of its resources**

to please 95 percent of its customers, because 95 percent of its customers depend on RPG."
Jon Paris, RPG guru, HAL North America

The IBM Rebranding of AS/400

IBM changed the name of the AS/400 in October 2000 to help tame it and to make it behave better when in mixed company. Mixed company, in this reference, pertains to IBM's other servers. IBM behaves as if it has no interest in the superior AS/400 getting a leg-up on its other, less-capable server units (see Chapter 17, "The Rebranding of the AS/400 As the Power i"). Most AS/400 customers, who still care, are absolutely upset by IBM's rebranding and its attempts to mask the wonders of the AS/400 platform. But the marketing emasculation of the AS/400 started long before the year 2000. The rebranding did not cause customers to complain about IBM's marketing. The rebranding showed that IBM was minimizing the AS/400's role as an IBM mainline server. IBM had been hearing its customers' complaints about its poor marketing for many years the rebranding signaled that it was not about to mend its ways.

I find myself from time to time being befuddled at IBM's lack of response to all this. So I ask myself wake-up questions and I answer them. Is the marketing of the AS/400 done poorly? My answer to that is "absolutely, if at all!" I ask, "Is IBM going to change it?" Again I answer myself in the negative: "I sure don't think so." In fact, I would argue that IBM is pleased just the way it is.

It does not take much to prove that IBM has been ineffective in marketing the AS/400. The big question is whether the poor performance is intentional. Is IBM ineffective by design or by incompetence? To keep getting a better perspective on the answer to this question, let's look at one of IBM's ads that helped spur a negative reaction in the AS/400 community. This is a print ad that Big Blue was using in its June 1999 campaign:

> **"What if there was a box . . . a magic box. A box that contained all the answers to all the questions you've ever had . . . There is such a box . . . A magic box. It's called a server. . . ."**

Wow! I can tell you this: My neighbors were not running over to my house that day asking what that ad was all about. The ad, when seen by the AS/400 community, is read differently:

> **"What if there was a box, a tragic box, a box in which you could bury your product's uniqueness among a sea of conformity? There is such a box. It's called a coffin. And this campaign is driving the nail in the lid."**

These are the words of Neil Palmer, an AS/400 technical specialist at DPS Canada Limited, as repeated in the halls after a COMMON session in San Antonio, in the fall of 1999, as reported by *Power i News*. Neil said it well, but the frustrations of IBM customers persist after all these years.

> **Note: COMMON is an AS/400 users group. Twice a year, many AS/400 professionals from across the world pack their bags and head to a conference sponsored by COMMON. At the conference, they hear the best speakers that IBM has to offer, expounding on the AS/400 for a full business week. It is well worth the trip. IBM also hosts a "sound off session," in which COMMON members tell IBM what is wrong and what is right. For years customers have been telling IBM to advertise on television, but the message falls on deaf ears.**

Palmer's is typical of an AS/400 user's reaction to IBM's June 1999 plan to ignore the major differentiating points within its different product lines, and to mush all of its server computers together in one big server stew. If that doesn't sound like a plan to sell anything, maybe it wasn't intended to sell anything. However, that was the IBM campaign in

1999. The AS/400 was not even mentioned in the ad, just a magic box.

Customers Should Decide the Product Mix

If your company felt that it had too many products, could it, by decree, begin to fill orders and ship whatever size and color widgets happened to be in the top of the bin? Could your company simply decide not to sell ***product A*** even if your customers demanded it? Would it get away with shipping ***product B*** when ***product A*** was ordered? Could your company get away with telling its customers all about the generic properties of an ***xWidget*** and expect that its customers would know enough to order the ***wSeries*** rather than the ***bSeries xWidget?*** Of course not. Your company could not get away with that type of strategy. It would take them out of business. It's common sense that your company would not even try such a strategy. Yet IBM is doing the exact thing.

A blender marketing mantra cannot work for any company for any length of time, unless the product it sells is supposed to be blended. Even the folks in Pleasantville revolted when they learned the truth about black and white. Though an interesting thought, it is unlikely that the world would engage in a love affair with your company and the world would be completely non-discriminatory in its choice of your products--as long as you were selling them. Do you think you would hear your customers ever telling you, "Ship whatever you like; we'll take it. We love your company?"

IBM's limited AS/400 promotional campaigns over the years appear to be directed to sell nobody anything and tell nobody anything about anything, hoping that anybody who might be interested would just buy what they wanted from the items available on the IBM truck. Is it any wonder that IBM's customers who root for the AS/400 product more than IBM itself are frustrated at IBM's actions (mostly inactions) so far.

> **"It's fair to say that AS/400 marketing has never been fabulous--the best effort may have been 10 years ago, when IBM launched the system with *M*A*S*H* TV commercials--but at the San Antonio COMMON IBM user conference, last September, dissatisfaction peaked. There, particularly during COMMON's AS/400 sound-off session, prominent AS/400 industry players exploded in barely controlled anger--or frustration, at its least--leveled directly at the AS/400 division. The message was clear: In an industry where more and more IT decisions are governed by mindshare than technology, the AS/400 is in a position to lose out--either market the AS/400, or the platform will die under the steamrolling market presence of Windows NT."**
> **Chris Miller, Web editor for NEWS/400, Article Feedback Power i News, August, 1, 1998**

Chris, is it possible that IBM's goal is for the AS/400 to lose out in the marketplace? Does that make any sense at all? Are IBM's actions spawned from design or from incompetence?

> **"From what I understand, it's probably more a case of IBM corporate policy. IBM seems to advertise IBM instead of advertising its products. It's like GM throwing an ad out there that says, 'Hey, we've got some great cars, come out and buy one' without telling you what they've got. [A customer asks] 'What do I want? A Cadillac? A pickup truck?' And they say, 'Aw, it doesn't matter, come and talk to us.' People want to hear a bit more than that before they go out and look into a server. It's hard for most people to find that information."**
> **Neil Palmer, NxTrend Technology, Canada, Article Feedback Power i News, August, 1, 1998**

Neil, what if it really doesn't matter to IBM if you buy AS/400 hardware or other IBM hardware? Are IBM's actions spawned from design or from incompetence?

> **"I'm very surprised that since the AS/400 users are the most satisfied, fanatical about the platform, that they haven't taken it upon themselves more to write to non-AS/400 magazine editors. I agree that IBM needs to do something, but another question we should ask each other**

is, 'What have you done today?' There's something we can do to impress those people."
John Carr, EdgeTech, Article Feedback Power i News, August, 1, 1998

What if IBM really does not want to reach these people, John? Are IBM's actions spawned from design or from incompetence?

Power i News and Power iNetwork.com, formerly News/400 does a great job in keeping the AS/400 public informed, and they don't shy away from a fight. It's interesting to note that the above complaints were lodged against IBM way back on August 1, 1998. Chances are this long lasting marketing problem is a problem that IBM has chosen not to solve. My vote is the answer to the question is "from design." Perhaps to IBM it is not a problem at all.

Wouldn't It Be Nice?

I was going to begin this chapter by talking about what I would do if I had a nice business like IBM's and my customers were complaining about my marketing. Actually, I do have a nice business. In fact I have a couple of nice businesses. I have my consulting practice, Kelly Consulting, and then, along with Joe McDonald, I have a little publishing operation called Lets Go Publish!

Though I feel my customers, at least in the consulting practice, love my little company and the services that I provide, I see nothing like the rabid affair that AS/400 customers have with their AS/400 machines. There probably are lots of us out here that would love to have a product or service that our customers want at the same level of intensity as they want their AS/400. I want my "Mapo!" And that's about it.

AS/400 Marketing Is MIA

For the last 10 years, IBM has done less and less to promote its AS/400 product in any way that a company really wanting to sell a product would do. That's a fact. Instead, other than its ThinkPad ads sponsored by a division that is in the red year after year, I cannot recall seeing an ad for any specific IBM product in the general media.

Sure, the company advertises the AS/400 some times in the AS/400-only publications. But that is strictly preaching to a choir. Occasionally, in *Information Week* or *Computerworld* magazines, there may be something, but over the last 10 years, especially since the magic box campaign, followed by the eServer homogenization of 2000, there has been no din at all in AS/400 product advertising. In fact, there has not been even a peep!

The eServer umbrella name in which IBM has its AS/400 hidden is a corporate euphemism for "love IBM." Since eServer is not a product, it represents IBM. When I see an eServer ad on television, I think, they want me to love IBM. My neighbors, the folks to whom this book is dedicated, are my barometer as to whether the AS/400 message is sneaking out from under the umbrella. After four years of eServer, and several years of pre-homogenization, my neighbors are no more enlightened. They remain unimpressed.

Michael Crump of Ball Foster Glass Container Corporation has a similar opinion on IBM's advertising. This is what Michael has to say:

> **"While I understand IBM's approach on how it is marketing the company as opposed to the products, it also causes problems. IBM is making inroads into Internet awareness with its current ads, but this is done at the sake of the AS/400, which has the least to gain from this approach. I call it 'product blanding' . . . it will probably help minimize product cannibalism [among IBM products], but, in light of the NT [Windows] hype, the AS/400 will suffer the most from it."**
> **Article Feedback Power i News, August, 1, 1998**

So one of the things wrong is that the advertising message is messed up, at least if you are an AS/400 watcher and you want the product to succeed. Occasionally, from under the eServer umbrella, on TV, IBM will mention the name xSeries [PC Server]. My neighbors tell me that when they see IBM's ads, they think they are for somebody else, because they know they are not for them. Puzzled at times by what the message is, my neighbors ask me what product IBM is trying to sell, and how would they know if it applied to them.

That says it all. Even if the Power i, which had been IBM's under-umbrella name for the AS/400 til IBM changed it to I5, were to be mentioned in these ads, it is the mythical eServer umbrella, representing all IBM servers, not a specific product, that consumers are left with after taking in the entire ad. Any product message, xSeries or AS/400 or anything, does not make it to REM sleep. Thus, it's just bad advertising at best.

I know of no computer person and certainly no AS/400 person who is asking IBM to advertise so that the name IBM and its umbrella name for hardware, eServer, can be better known. Nobody is asking for IBM company awareness advertising. IBM is already the third most popular brand of all time. The AS/400 and the mainframe community have a right to ask IBM to do more product advertising. After six years of magic boxes and eServer umbrellas, and small planets, the verdict is long in. In language my children would understand: "It stinks!"

To please many others, and me too, IBM has to take a hard look at firing its Madison Avenue advisors if the company hopes to continue selling hardware. I hope IBM hears me plain on this one. The ads stink. The eServer marketing campaign stinks. But the biggest indictment comes from IBM committing the biggest marketing sin. IBM no longer listens to the pleas of its customers. If Donald Trump were running IBM marketing today, he'd get to use those two words that many have heard him use in The Apprentice. My suggestion would be for "The Donald" to direct those now famous words against the lead IBM marketing dog and the "idealess" Madison Avenue money takers.

Customers Deserve Something

IBM's loyal AS/400 customers spend about $8 billion to $10 billion per year on AS/400s and related products. These customers have asked IBM for way more than six years, and closer to 10, to unravel the cloak of secrecy from its AS/400 and reveal it to the general public in the best way possible. AS/400 customers are vocal in this demand. In forums, conferences, e-mails, and in private conferences with company executives, they relate negative impressions of IBM's advertising at every opportunity.

After this long, many have begun to think that IBM is too dumb to get the message. I don't think that is true. IBM cannot miss their message. In fact, I think that IBM has gotten the message, loud and clear. I think that IBM thinks that its AS/400 customers are too dumb to get its message. Here is the message I see IBM sending:

> **"IBM as a company has no special love for the AS/400. Get used to it. There will be no advertising."**

Maybe there is more to the IBM message:

> **"Hey, AS/400 customers, it's just a product, not a love affair. And if you are in love with our product, get a life. It's our product, not yours. And we have to take care of all our products, not just the one you are in love with."**

A Microsoft Plot?

In many ways what is happening to the AS/400 is surreal. It is as if Microsoft has placed a pod from the movie *Invasion of the Body Snatchers* next to every decision maker in IBM who, left to his own devices, might be able to make a good decision about advertising. I can see a remake of the movie about 10 years from now, when the letters IBM mean "I Be Microsoft." By then the pods should have complete control of IBM, and it couldn't be any better for the competition if Bill Gates had written the script himself.

Not Even a Bone

One would think that after about 10 years of begging, IBM would throw a little bone its AS/400 customers' way. Why would IBM not run a couple ads that mention AS/400 just to get the crowd to shut up? From my vantage point, the TV ads for the eServer xSeries don't help the situation at all, since my neighbors don't understand them.

A bright marketer would at least put out a few token ads to please its AS/400 customers. At least the company would be showing its customers that it cares about what they say. The current approach of arguing with the customer requests is not just bad marketing and advertising; it's also bad customer relations.

Al Said It Would Be Like This

My perspective about the person at the top is that the person at the top takes the hit. The little guys underneath the person at the top should only take a hit if the top gun takes a much bigger hit. I heard Buell Duncan, recent past AS/400 division general manager, speak, and I always believed that he tried to do what was right for the AS/400 and the AS/400 community.

I heard Duncan's predecessor, Tom Jarosh, speak and he too had a positive energy about the AS/400. With both of these gentlemen, I always felt that somebody with immense corporate power always inhibited them from carrying out their plans of doing what was right.

I have never met Al Zollar, chief of the AS/400 division in 2004. People who I know who know Al Zollar rell me that he works hard for the AS/400 community but he, like his predecessors is constrained by his superiors of being able to have much of an impact. I am concerned that even if Al Zollar is permitted to spend precious time on behalf of AS/400 customers, he is not in control of the budget dollars to effect much change..

My purpose in the material that proceeds from now to the end of the chapter is to highlight a situation in which Mr. Zollar was a principle participant and he did not soothe the concerns of the AS/400 masses. Just like me, the AS/400 masses want positive action, not the run around.

As you will see in the dialog, Mr. Zollar's defense of his positions is not convincing. Please know that it is not my intention to personally attack Al Zollar. I don't even know him. Unfortunately, as the General Manager of the AS/400 division, Mr. Zollar is the one with the mission to stand up and take the customer heat

Perhaps there is nobody in IBM who can promote the AS/400 insidc of the company and gain top managements concurrence. For IBM to be successful in hardware, that has got to change.

Al Zollar Says "No TV Ads"

At the September 10, 2003, COMMON Conference in San Antonio, Kate Evans Corrcia, a senior news editor for Search400.com took lots of notes at the meeting, and a good part of what follows regarding Al Zollar and Cecelia Maresse (IBM Power i marketing manager) comes from information that I picked up by reading Kate's write-up in Search400.com. Fccl free to take a run out to Search400.com to get her full article. It's nicely done.

Negative Press Coverage

IBM's lack of fair treatment for the AS/400 in advertising and overall marketing is receiving a lot of press coverage. IBM's AS/400 customers are quite concerned about IBM's willingness to stand by its products for the duration and the press is covering this regularly. Though the AS/400 as the object of this concern is gaining notoriety for IBM's lack of a marketing strategy for the box, this is all negative press coverage and overall, it is a black eye for IBM.

It's bad for IBM and it's bad for AS/400 customers. It makes the AS/400 loyalist feel alone without the benefit of a sponsor such as IBM who should care, but seems indifferent to customer concerns. It's a lot like unrequited love. Reading about IBM customers complaining about how IBM is treating or not treating them cannot do any good for IBM in attracting new customers. In frustration, sometimes I ask myself, "So why don't they fix it?"

Each year, twice a year the premiere AS/400 Users Group holds its annual technical conference. In fall 2003, the U.S. Conference was in Orlando. Al Zollar, the head of the AS/400 division in IBM, who is trying to earn his AS/400 stripes from this person's perspective, offered his views to AS/400 customers on AS/400 television advertising and the lack thereof. Kate Evans-Correia was in the Hall with Al Zollar that day.

Her opening paragraphs are quite telling about Mr. Zollar's message:

> **"If you're hoping to someday see an Power i ad during the Super Bowl, get over it. In fact, squash any hopes you have about seeing an Power i TV ad anywhere, anytime. "It's not that IBM's Power i general manager, Al Zollar, is opposed to TV advertising; it's just that he doesn't believe it's where Big Blue's marketing dollars would be best spent--at least not for the Power i."**

Poor AS/400 Marketing Takes Center Stage

Evans- Correia noted that Power i poor marketing took center stage again at the COMMON Conference as it has for the past six years or more that I can remember. IBM executives were pummeled with complaints about the company's poor AS/400 marketing. Al Zollar may very well get it, but he appears constrained by the same type of thinking in IBM that decided that Fort Knox was a good deal for the company.

It has become common knowledge that IBM's corporate marketing department has decided that none of its IBM-made eServers will be advertised on TV. That factoid does nothing to ameliorate the concerns of AS/400 stalwarts that IBM is not highlighting their favorite product. Additionally, if you are the head of the AS/400 division, it gives you no wiggle room when your customers are nailing you to the wall in a public meeting at COMMON.

If I were Al Zollar at COMMON's Sound-Off, I would be hoping for time to fly because there was nothing that could be said to the AS/400 crowd to make them feel like they were about to get any help from IBM. Of course, he could have lied but he's a better man than that. He had to know that AS/400 customers, whose jobs IBM's decisions affect, would be going back to AS/400 shops in which there is continual bickering with the Windows contingent about whether the AS/400 is worth its salt. Unfortunately, he was not able to give them much help.

PC "gurus" are often preoccupied with dancing bears and spinning globes, but when these arduous tasks are completed, they find time to tell their company executives, and whoever will listen, about how the company should be using Windows or Unix to run its business. IBM's public silence about the AS/400 as a fine business server helps give the small-time PC guy's talk much more weight in an organization than it should have. That's why AS/400 customers at Sound-Off hoped that IBM would change its mind and that Mr. Zollar would be able to tell them that things were going to get better. That message never came.

From one source or another, insiders and outsiders are pounding IBM executives about its "legacy" AS/400. AS/400 IT staffs are very annoyed at IBM because they have to handle all the heat themselves.

For close to 10 years, IBM has floundered in its message and consistently refused to advertise on TV to help its customers fight its battle. Many AS/400 shops are concerned that they are ultimately going to lose the war as their company makes a decision, stupid though it may be, to switch to a more popular non-AS/400 platform, such as Windows or Unix, or more than likely, the current darling, Linux.

How About Some Help, Al?

Al Zollar does understand that these friends of IBM and the AS/400 need his help. They are crying for help. He hears them. They are telling IBM through Zollar that they need help N-O-W. Unfortunately, at this COMMON his message was not too consoling. After more than six years of begging for TV advertising Mr. Zollar was forced to hem and haw about giving AS/400 professionals what they have been and continue to ask for. They feel they need help with their executives through living room, emotional advertising. IBM's corporate advertising power brokers apparently have given the AS/400 division no wiggle room with advertising and that message was very clear.

Microsoft gets CEOs and the rest of us in the living room. Because of that, most regular human beings think more highly of Microsoft as a computer company than they do of IBM. By the time your company executives get to the boardroom, their decisions are often made from information that they picked up in sources such as living room advertising.

Besides, it's been a long time since IBM had a sales force able to come face to face with a real customer on the customer's premises. So, with no one-on-one and no one-on-many customer meetings -- as a marketing strategy, IBM today hooks few new AS/400 customers. Whether in the living room or in the boardroom, IBM marketing is in absentia. It doesn't get the business because it's not there asking for it.

Why Isn't IBM Advertising the AS/400 on TV?

Evans-Correia's perspective is that after getting the question squarely in his face, Zollar wasn't about to buckle under the pressure. He was obviously more concerned about not giving hope to the beleaguered AS/400 masses than telling them that he was not permitted to offer any. After six years of no action, Zollar tried this one on the group:

> **"We are not going to invest in TV until we can prove it sells."**

Hey, what exactly does that mean? IBM is going to wait until it proves that by not advertising, it can find out whether advertising sells. Maybe it meant that IBM would do test marketing? No, it means that Mr. Zollar has not been given any advertising dollars and it looks like he will not be given any advertising dollars. But, he could not really say that.

It's really too bad that IBM will not advertise its "z," "p," or "i" Series machines. Surely it is that IBM strategy that makes IT major after IT major turn away from IBM's best servers. No wonder more and more companies think that IBM is not for them. One would think that if IBM is not going to tell America and the world how great its products are, few on their own will conclude that they have any merit at all.

With no choice and no relief available for the crowd, Mr. Zollar shared with the masses that he was very aware of the image the Power i has among the general populous, but he insisted that advertising the Power i on TV would not change the server's image. IBM's eServer corporate advertising contingent ruled the day.

Even if Al Zollar heard Al Barsa's famous diatribe to Tom Jarosh of four years ago, he would still have been powerless in this setting while representing IBM's corporate advertising curmudgeons. AS/400 COMMON folks may remember how Al Barsa pulled no punches as he let Tom Jarosh, Zollar's predecessor once removed, know how most of his AS/400 customers felt about IBM's advertising.

> **"Every executive in the United States knows what Archer Daniels Midland does. And Archer Daniels Midland sold $12.8 billion last year, although I would bet you that 90 percent of those business executives have never done anything more on a farm than just visit. Yet AS/400 and its drag-along business is $16 billion, and no one has ever heard of it. The AS/400 absolutely needs large-scale advertising . . . the AS/400 has got to be on television."**
> **Al Barsa, Barsa Consulting, www.barsaconsulting.com,**
> **Article Feedback Power i News, August, 1, 1998**

Zollar did his best to calm down the crowd at COMMON but he did not have the right message. In fairness to Zollar, I don't think there was anything that he was able to do. Big IBM again was the culprit.

While COMMON users pointed out to Zollar that they felt that Microsoft Windows products are pushing the Power i into oblivion, Zollar again tried to deflect the bullets. He shared that IBM is not going to declare war on Windows. He suggested that such a task is futile.

What I got out of that is that IBM thinks fighting Microsoft is futile. He added that nobody is going to be able to best Windows in terms of user base and general popularity, and then said:

> **"There's no amount of money that's going to make that happen."**

That certainly is the IBM marketing campaign that I have been watching since Bill Gates stole the whole PC business from IBM. Why IBM chooses to never put up a good fight to get it back is always a puzzle to me. If Bill Gates thought the way IBM thinks, Microsoft Internet Explorer would never have taken on Netscape and Windows NT Server would never have taken on Novell. In both instances, Microsoft was a dark horse but still chose to engage and win. The defeatist attitude from the top of IBM surely reflects the lack of marketing actions that AS/400 users observe and lament. Al Zollar may be perceived as part of the AS/400 problem, but sending an unarmed man to fight Microsoft is not Al's fault, it's IBM's. The company just doesn't get it.

This IBM message would be the last thing I would want to deliver at a COMMON Conference. It might have helped Al Zollar to be transparent but he was bigger than that. Maybe with the May 4, 2000 announcements the AS/400 will get a little boost and maybe the IBM corporate advertising team will have a new mission or maybe they will be replaced. Folks who know Mr. Zollar have shared with me that he is a good guy and that because of him; functions like WebSphere will be able to be integrated into the new I5 server. If the AS/400 becomes stronger, perhaps Al Zollar will be in a better position to bring advertising gifts or stories the next time he gets to visit COMMON.

Can you imagine Bill Gates taking IBM on and winning, and now IBM's AS/400 general manager is put in a position in which he must pay homage to the corporate advertising masters by suggesting that taking on Bill Gates' little company would be futile? "Nobody is going to be able to best Windows." That's great, IBM. So what does IBM do now? Roll over?

IBM sure thinks it knows best. In the next part of the discussion, Mr. Zollar noted that it "is not an intergalactic battle!"

The fact is that the IBM / Microsoft foray is not a battle at all because IBM corporate does not permit the company to fight. As always, when facing Bill Gates, Big Blue is unarmed and waving a white flag. This time, IBM had all the guns locked up. Winding up his session, Mr. Zollar then requested input from the group as he asked:

> **"Are there as many people buying Power i as Windows? No. But that doesn't mean [the Power i] is not going to be successful."**

As you can see, he answered his own question. Zollar's arguments, summed up, mean that AS/400 customers should not expect advertising from IBM because IBM thinks the AS/400 is as successful as it wants it to be at this point of its life.

Unfortunately, IBM gave Mr. Zollar no rope in being able to help the AS/400 customer set with IBM's AS/400 market perception problem. Doing that for the COMMON crowd was clearly beyond his granted powers. Suggesting the AS/400 is going to be successful under all circumstances was the best he was able to do.

I don't mean to be disrespectful to Al Zollar, or to anybody in IBM, but like most AS/400 loyalists, I am very annoyed. Every day I am one of those people asking for IBM to listen so that the AS/400 can survive.

Even when I was with the company, IBM would claim that it has empowered all of its employees to do their jobs effectively. From my eyes, IBM has set up the AS/400 GM job with inadequate power. The AS/400 GM cannot make the AS/400 successful since he is not empowered (budget-wise) to do so. That sums up IBM's COMMON experience. Hopefully, IBM will do better next time and the time after.

An AS/400 Marketing Department

Eventually at the COMMON conference, a lady with a sense of humor from the IBM team came to speak. Cecelia Maresse is vice president of Power i marketing. She also tried to defuse the agitated crowd by noting that IBM planned to look deeper into the TV market but needed to take its time testing the waters, promoting the eServer brand itself, before the Power i in particular.

I know that the IBM executives at COMMON were all bright but they had an impossible mission -- trying to defend its marketing. Until I knew what Cecelia Maresse's title was, I did not think that IBM had a marketing department for the Power i worthy of a vice presidential slot. Again, that is not a personal shot at Ms Maresse. I see no IBM marketing that helps the product in a meaningful way.

After noting that IBM had to take its time with the company-specific server ads, Maresse expanded her statements:

> **"We're just starting our television advertising…for now, we have no Power i plans. We're going to see what this [current TV ads] tells us."**

Maresse, like Al Zollar, is just doing her job. But it sure would be nice to find somebody who has the power to make a real decision in IBM. Maresse's words, though honestly spoken, did not warm me up at all, and they offered little consolation to the crowd at COMMON. In my mind, I kept hearing the words of Paul Simon:

> **"Cecelia, you're breaking my heart.**
> **You're shaking my confidence daily.**
> **Oh, Cecelia, I'm down on my knees.**
> **I'm begging you please to go home."**

You might as well go back to Rochester, because you do not have the power or the budget to help. The eServer has been out for four years or so now, and I have been watching the silly eServer ads for that long, wondering when I was going to hear the word Power i. Not once! The ads are not working for the Power i; that is for sure, because there are none!

I sometimes have bad dreams about waking in a cold sweat and finding myself in a very embarrassing, un-winnable situation. I transferred my dream fear to the plight of Maresse at COMMON. How would you like to be on the panel of a meeting in which the theme is, "It's the marketing, IBM," and you look down at your name tag and you notice that you hold the title *Vice President for Power i Marketing.* Wow!

Though not permitted to bear gifts of advertising from her superiors, Maresse injected a little humorous reality for the crowd when she related getting zapped herself by IBM's refusal to highlight the Power i on TV. Evidently she had shared with her children that she worked with the big bad Power i computer.

Watching TV at home the weekend before COMMON, she felt defeat from the minds of a miniature crew of attackers, her own children. During one of the IBM ad segments that previous weekend, her two children, ages 13 and 11, saw an eServer homogenization piece and asked their mom, "Where's the Power i?" Hey, Cecelia, it's the marketing.

At the Fall 2003 COMMON session, it was nice that the AS/400 constituency had an opportunity to talk to the honchos and get their information directly from the horses' mouths. It's too bad that the output message of the session seemed to come from the other direction. One could only conclude that IBM's executives were not empowered to help.

At COMMON, 2003 IBM Rochester via Mr. Zollar and Ms. Maresse got the message clearly again from its customers. It is the marketing, IBM!

Will they do anything? In all fairness to both, neither probably has enough corporate power to change much about what is bothering their customers. But I do get the sense they would like to – and that's good.

What a Difference a Day Makes!

I had the opportunity to update this ending after IBM's May 4, 2004 grand Power5 announcements. While I was rethinking my ending, Al Zollar and Cecelia Maresse were back at COMMON's Spring Conference.

I am very pleased to say that Mr. Zollar brought a number of gifts with him to the "Soundoff Town Hall Meeting" at COMMON. My friends tell me that Zollar was beaming with the news he offered, and rightfully so.

Mr. Zollar introduced the new I5 machines and the new pricing and the new IBM impetus for winning the business. He would not let his superiors send him to COMMON unarmed this time. Moreover, Ms. Maresse and Mr. Zollar silenced the crowd when they announced that IBM was getting ready to advertise the Power i on TV.

Unlike COMMON 2003, IBM had armed its executives with a full chest of gifts. Nobody dared say, "It's the Marketing, IBM." At least not on this day.

Chapter 24 Homogenization Shows No Cream

I'm Nobody, Who Are You?

Randall Munson would probably describe himself in these inimitable words of Emily Dickinson: "I'm nobody, who are you?"

Yet Randall Munson is somebody. In 2003, for the umpteenth time, he walked away from a COMMON conference with a gold medal designating him a speaker of excellence. This award is one given to a very elite group. Typically two to four speakers get the gold at COMMON's semi-annual AS/400 technical conference. Munson is so good, he is always on the list.

He is a former IBMer, who for part of his 20 years, worked in the Rochester AS/400 labs in operating system development. That means that Munson cannot only talk well, he can also program and design software, as proven by his role in the architecture of OS/400 (IBM i). I had the pleasure of attending a number of Munson's award winning technical presentations over the years. I have first hand knowledge of the power in his speech and the knowledge that he puts forth when he speaks about AS/400 technical topics and personal development topics.

In early September 2003, Maryann Ratchford, a staff reporter from Power i News interviewed Munson, and the results of that interview were mailed to AS/400 supporters all over the world. I received my own copy. In this interview, the reporter asks a stirring question to Munson, the answer to which in many ways is part of the undelying theme of this book. The question and the answer are shown below:

Interview of Randall Munson by Power i News acquisitions editor MaryAnn Ratchford:

> **News/400 Reporter: If you could take Sam Palmisano's place for a day, would you do anything differently with regard to the Power i [AS/400]?**
>
> **Munson: IBM has intentionally restructured the branding for all of their platforms. They've devoted a lot of resources and a lot of work in doing that to make them appear very homogenous.**
>
> **What's unfortunate for the Power i [AS/400] is that it's a very unique platform, and when these platforms are all melded together, the uniqueness, the quality, is not coming out. Things like the Power i / IBM I architecture and its intrinsic power for database and business intelligence; the inherent security of the architecture as opposed to other systems that are constantly being hit with viruses, hacking, and so forth; the unparalleled reliability of the system -- these are being downplayed because, in contrast, they make the other servers look bad.**
>
> **So, if I were in his position, although I certainly would keep the eServer branding intact, I would take advantage of those unique attributes of the iSeries –Power i [AS/400] that could be used to my benefit in the marketplace.**

IBM has intentionally taken its product lines and thrown them into a big stew, and the individual flavors are becoming indiscernible. Munson's description of homogenization is right on.

With homogenization, the cream does not rise to the top. So if the AS/400 is part of a bigger soup called eServer, that means that it must taste like the rest of the broth and forget about adding a special zing or two that would help the guy with the spoon know that the last chunk swallowed was from the AS/400 stock.

No, in a homogenization strategy, everything is supposed to look and taste the same. In a homogenization marketing strategy, everything is advertised as being the same. So in order to be hosted as part of the eServer advertising stew, the AS/400 had to promise to leave its uniqueness at home and provide only sameness to the brew.

Those of us out here in real world know that nobody buys an eServer. You actually cannot buy the soup that is being sold. You can only buy chunks that you can find in the advertising broth.

But how does a potential consumer become aware of what chunks are in the stew? That's a good question. The answer, of course, is most damaging to the AS/400. The consumer never finds out. Hey, it's a stew!

So how do they find the other chunks? Working from the bottom of the server line up, the Windows folks have Intel and Microsoft advertising their wares. If somebody happens to be interested in IBM eServer homogenized stew, Microsoft and Intel give them enough information to spot their chunks in the eServer stew. They can have IBM or a systems integrator give them a quote. However, I can't see anybody buying an IBM PC-based server by studying the eServer ads.

At the next level of server, there are the Unix geeks, who want Unix operating system facility no matter what. Again, if these folks are inclined to want that kind of capability in an IBM product, they already know enough to spot the Unix and the Linux chunks in the IBM eServer stew.

They can then ask IBM to give them information using a tear-away from an eServer ad, or they can ask an IBM Unix/Linux integrator or business partner (if they can find one) to give them a quote on a Unix/Linux chunk of the eServer homogenized stew.

Well, that means that two out of the four ingredients can be sold separately, even though they are part of the same advertising stew. Their loyal followers will come calling. No more or no less will come calling than would have if IBM did not advertise, but, nonetheless, they will come looking for their Unix/Linux chunks, and their Wintel chunks, and when those chunks are sold, the leftover eServer stew will contain just IBM's proprietary systems, mainframes, and AS/400s.

Of course, the mainframers have no worry. The companies that traditionally use mainframes can't do without them. They are the largest companies in the world, and have the largest IT budgets.

Though IBM seemed to be ready to give up its mainframe business when *Computerworld* proclaimed that the mainframe was dead, in the 1990s, these customers continued to pressure IBM and would not let the computer giant capitulate to the unsubstantiated whining in the computer press.

So what does this mean for the homogenized soup? It means that there will always be a ton of big customers taking the biggest chunks (mainframes) out of the eServer stew. Nobody needs to advertise to these folks, because they actually have no choice but the mainframe. They must stay with IBM mainframes, and each year, they will need bigger and bigger mainframes.

There is no reason to advertise to this group at all, ever. They are going to buy because Scotty from IBM gives their enterprise more power each year. And they can't live without that power. When Scotty complains that he can't get any more power to the captain, Captain IBM always comes through. But, of course, there is a big price for custoemrs to pay—and they willingly cough up the tribute.

So now that all three types of chunks (Wintel, Unix, mainframe) have been taken from the stew, what is left? That's right. The only chunks left are the AS/400 chunks. Since the other chunks will always come out first, does this not give the AS/400 a major advantage when selling the eServer advertising stew? There's fodder for some great IBM tag lines and catch phrases for AS/400s such as "bottom of the barrel" systems or "have a salty server." The company can highlight the AS/400 by saying that it is always available because nobody else has asked for it. How about, "Get yourself an AS/400 today; it's the eServer that nobody ever asks for by name."

You may tell me that I am not close to correct, if you are familiar with the AS/400. Yes, AS/400 customers will keep coming back to IBM for the next great AS/400. But that's like saying the people who buy AS/400s are the people who buy AS/400s. Everybody knows about Wintel, Unix, and mainframes, but only AS/400 customers know about the AS/400.

Large customers buy mainframes. Unix and Linux devotees buy IBM's Unix server when the hardware must be IBM, though in most cases, they'd rather buy from Sun or HP. Windows and Intel platform devotees buy IBM's Wintel servers only when the hardware must be IBM (back when IBM still sold Intel Servers). Again, in most cases, they'd rather buy from Dell or Gateway or HP. So who buys AS/400s? Traditionally, it is small and midsized businesses that need a system to run their businesses.

IBM should understand that is the marketplace. It is not just existing AS/400 customers. So the bottom of the barrel marketing strategy for new accounts cannot work. There is no other all-IBM solution that knocks the socks off all other solutions. The AS/400 is the only one. IBM should not homogenize it so that it can no longer be sold.

I am sure Randall Munson, the gentleman, would agree that the marketplace for Power I (AS/400 is small and medium businesses. I am sure Mr. Munson would agree that IBM's lead solution for business applications should be an IBM AS/400 server. It is IBM hardware and IBM software in the form of an all-IBM, all-around solution. How much money could IBM have ever made on a PC servers when Intel happily made the processor and Windows was the most often selected operating system. How much money can they make on Unix when IBM does not own the license? How much money can they make on Linux when it is free?

If the AS/400 were a poor solution, it would be understandable. But it is a phenomenal solution. If IBM were able to remove the AS/400 from the eServer stew and call it the Super Business Server or some other interesting name, other than AS/400 or iSeries or eServer or Power i, then they'd have a name in the spirit of "Windows" that businesses could immediately recognize.

Then they could get a big share of the business back from their competitors such as Intel and Windows and HP and Dell, and others. Then maybe the AS/400 would be sure to survive, and maybe IBM stock would make a few folks rich again. Maybe, just maybe, IBM could work its way backto be ing # 1 again…and that is the message in this book.

Campaign Against Renaming Products (CARP)

While I was doing some basic research on the Internet for this book, and I was looking for information about product rebranding, I found that AS/400 zealots are not the only consumers who have been frustrated by rebranding. I came upon an organization known as CARP, which stands for the Campaign against Renaming Products. They note on their Web site that they are "a semi-militant group opposed to the renaming of popular products by large companies." CARP was formed in response to what they call the "Marathon incident of 1993." This was "when the great Marathon bar was renamed Snickers." CARP continues to fight against change on the shop shelves.

I present some direct verbiage from their Web site:

> **"For those poor souls too young to remember, there was once a time when the sweet-toothed could enter any respectable confectioner's and purchase a delicious peanut-based chocolate bar with the powerful name Marathon. Then, one fateful day, they were told, 'Oh, you mean a Snickers.' Yes, Marathon was replaced by Snickers.**
> **CARP says NO. CARP says MARATHON."**

I could not help it; I sent CARP a complaint about the eServer Power i but have not heard anything back.

CARP would like to have committed shoppers to back its campaigns. They offer the opportunity to join the organization on the Web site, http://carp.iwarp.com.

I felt a little better after I enjoyed a Marathon bar resuming my writing projects. In the United States, the bar was Snickers for as long as I can remember. But I enjoyed learning its heritage and wish the folks at CARP luck in their unbranding efforts. I certainly share their frustration.

The Rebranding of IBM's Computers

By now, we all know that on October 3, 2000, IBM underwent a sweeping server rebranding effort that the company suggested would give users a more integrated view of its multiple hardware and operating system technologies. Under the promotion, all IBM server models are sold under the same common brand name of eServer, with different model names separating the various server platforms.

Starting from the most powerful, the company's System/390 mainframes became known simply as the *eServer zSeries* line, while the RS/6000 Unix box was rebranded as the *eServer pSeries*. Similarly, the AS/400 business server became the *eServer i Series 400,* and at the bottom of the power spectrum, IBM's PC servers were renamed as the *eServer xSeries*.

Corporate IBM has had a long-term strategy to pull together IBM's different server groups under one common technology, development, marketing and sales scheme. The stated goal has been to leverage technology in a common way across all the platforms.

The move was mostly met with positive comments with some suggesting that it may help IBM grow faster because the company may be able to focus on a single line of products and be able to better communicate those products with its users. Various analysts saw the IBM announcement as a way of avoiding brand confusion by simplifying the communication of its technology strengths.

However, other analysts are concerned that this new branding may affect the ability to differentiate the renamed server lines. For example, when talking about a particular server line, or in trade press articles, the lineage of the various eServer series is given for clarity. For example, one would say the zSeries mainframe or the Power i [formerly AS/400] or the pSeries Unix box or the xSeries PC Server. Four years after the rebranding the clarification with the machine lineage continues.

The fact is that no matter how much IBM wants to have one product line, it is not about to achieve it any time soon. IBM has four hardware product lines whether the company likes it or not. All of IBM's servers differ immensely from each other, mostly by operating system or typical marketplace characterizations.

Every one of the boxes except the iSeries (AS/400)] has a natural way of being described besides by its name. Quite simply, IBM makes mainframes, powerful Unix boxes and PC Servers. These three are intrinsically different from each other in industry-obvious ways no matter how IBM would like to make them be acknowledged as the same.

The one poor system in the lot that has been hurt the most by IBM's rebranding is the former AS/400, the "Power i." Unlike the mainframe, the Unix box, or the PC Server, the AS/400 must rely on its former name for its heritage. Though IBM had always marketed the AS/400 as its midrange business system, the company chose not to describe the unit it as the IBM Business System (or Server), which is my pet name for the box. This would have been a very proper characterization of the machine.

With no IBM Business System or IBM Business Server moniker or tacit acknowledgment coming, there is concern that nobody now has a reason to walk into the IBM eServer shop and ask for an iSeries [AS/400.] For example, the clerk would not be able to say, "Well, sir, we've got mainframes, Unix boxes, PC servers, and business systems in our eServer collection. Since the Unix box will be called out by lineage, and it is the same size, power, and capacity as the AS/400, the AS/400 will be overshadowed and homogenized into market oblivion. With AS/400 unit sales decreasing substantially over the last few years since the rebranding, those fears seem to be well founded.

Power i Homogenization

The AS/400 is an elegant business machine, cast as the follow-on to the futuristic System/38 in 1988. IBM saw the AS/400 as something it called the iSeries, a member of the IBM eServer family whose sameness was more important than its greatness. IBM's marketing began to operate as if industry leading inner elegance needed to be masked to satisfy the marketing needs of Big Blue's inferior server lines to the peril of the survival of the AS/400, and the many custoemrs who believed in IBM.

Many AS/400 stalwarts have mused about life in a new homogenized eServer land. IBM seems to be willing to do anything to reduce its internal issues of having to deal with more than one product line.

From Fort Knox to eServer, the evidence suggests that IBM has always had a secret desire to have just one product line. Before IBM sold the Intel Desktop and Server line to Lenovo over the past ten years, there had been are a whopping **four** server products that the company was forced to nurture and feed. By disposing of the eSerrver X series (the PC Server), IBM managed t relive itself of a management burden.

To put this in perspective, if you are employed, ask yourself how many products your company has. How many products do you think most manufacturers have? How about the tons of distributors trying to sell thousands of different brands? With four major products in the IBM server line, the proverbial "rational man" would wonder what problem IBM actually was trying to solve.

Do you find yourself feeling sorry for IBM's plight in having to deal with four whole product lines? What if the company were forced to add two more products to its mix? That would mean two hands would be needed to count them. Is that the problem? Would the company be bogged down in countless meetings trying to decide whether three on one hand and three on the other or five on the original hand and just one finger on the second hand would be the best way to track a six-product line of producs.

Though I apologize if I am being too facetious and snippy, this is how I see it. I donot see these as "tough management decisions." The homogenization strategy for IBM apparently was one way to handle such organizational stress. Look at IBM's recent results and that tells us all it did not work, and it would be good to look again at stratagies from the past that proved they worked. How about letting the cream rise to the top? How about manufacturing first in America?

For those not deceived by IBM's lamentations, perhaps you see that IBM really had no product communications problem at all. Ther really was no big problem that had to be fixed. There was just an IBM management perception. They had a mainframe, a Unix box, and a PC server. There was no communication problem there for sure. But IBM always had a communications problem with its poorly named AS/400 product line.

What is an AS/400, anyway? There are no quick answer. It is not a generic name. It is short a product name (Application System/400) devised in 1988 for a system that could run business applications better than any system ever invented. Back then, IBM gave it a poor name but a meaningful name nonetheless. It was the Application System/400. We in the business all understood that the christened long name, the Business Application System/400 would do well shortened to AS/400.

The shortcut of the name to AS/400, despite making it easier to reference, has hurt the product, especially in the eServer era-- a time of product and brand confusion. At least a product called the Application System/400 had some intrinsic meaning in its name. Even IBM won't deny that the AS/400 was conceived and built to run business applications.

It is still the universally acclaimed best enterprise resource planning (ERP) system ever built, and it has been known to many companies as their order entry, billing, accounts receivable, etc., system for almost forever. IBM changed the meaning of "AS" a few years ago a number of times to a number of different things, including Advanced Server, Advanced System, and Advanced Series, while it let the old Application System moniker slip away. All those different names caused so much confusion that IBM itself apparently forgot that the AS/400 was the company's business system.

So I ask myself, "Why can't the AS/400 take back its traditional role in the IBM product line as the generic business server?" After all, it is the company's best business server. The best answer that I have is that the company now pushes "e-business," and all the servers are equipped for e-business, so how would it look for the other servers if the AS/400 were labeled as **the** IBM Business Server? For political correctness, and not much more of anything else, the AS/400 was made the "nothing server" in the eServer line.

It's not the Windows server, it's not the Unix server, and it's not a mainframe server. According to IBM, it's nothing but the iSereis. And coming from a name with purpose; that is nothing. IBM not only "blanded" (a cynical combo name for rebranded and blended) it into a pot with a bunch of inferior machines, the company stole its meaningful identity as the Business Application Server. While IBM suggests that all of its servers can be eBusiness servers, and they sure can, when called by someone who knows, when selected, the AS/400 is almost always selected *because* it is a business server,

An e-business server most often does not stand alone. An eBusiness server is a front end for a business server. And e-business requires a highly functional back end ERP system (a business system) to fulfill its promise. My advice for IBM is to let the three other server types be known as "eBusiness Servers." There's nothing wrong with that. They perform that function quite well. However, IBM should them remake make the AS/400 as the "Business Server." That's what it does and that's what it is and that is how it should be referenced and sold.

The AS/400 is both a business server and an e-business server. The naming burial of the AS/400 as the iSeries hurt the product in the eyes of its customers and that is a big reason why AS/400 customers are annoyed at IBM. IBM has succeeded in hiding the true identity and purpose of the AS/400 under the eServer umbrella and by not giving the AS/400 an appropriate alias, the box cannot be called out of the stew and purchased.

To repeat, for my money and for the money of many others in the AS/400 camp, IBM had no real product communication problem with its four servers using their real names. It does now, however. And the AS/400 is suffering the most from lost sales.

If Big Blue checked out some other businesses, the company would find that it's OK to have more than one product. For example, Ford has more than one car line. GM has more than one car line. The models within Ford Corporation clearly compete with each other, as do the car models from GM. Each time a new and improved product comes out of a company, it is a new product. Many are confused as to why multiple product lines are such a problem for Big Blue?

IBM is recognized as a smart company. It pulls in over $80 billion per year. Why do its products have to be the same? Why can't potential customers have a choice? Why can't IBM say the best things that it can about each of its products and let people make the decisions for themselves?

IBM would do well to bring in a panel of experts, pay them dearly for their time, and teach them all about all four products and then make them decide what type of customer should want what type of system. Maybe the experts can also point out which of the products is the best if IBM does not already know. After all, GM knows that its Cadillac line is its top line. Ford knows that its Lincoln line is at the top. What is IBM's top line?

Why shouldn't IBM have a premium brand? Why shouldn't the AS/400 be the premium brand? The company charges premium prices for the AS/400. Why not get some marketing benefit from the large prices, rather than be defending high prices all the time? How does the IBM Premium Business Server sound as a name?

Note: Can you see the ad: "You'll pay through the nose for a new IBM Premium Business Server, but, just as in *Love Story*, you'll never have to say you're sorry."

Branding, Marketing, Advertising

As noted, from the eyes of many AS/400 customers, IBM has been cheated by its eServer marketing research firms and / or its advertising agencies. The eServer campaign is an abomination. As my uncle would say, "They should fire the bums!" I sometimes ask myself in disbelief. "What agency would tell a company wanting to sell its products that it should not highlight its products?"

What agency would suggest that TV is not the best media to reach your customers while they are at home? By any chance, if the market research or advertising agency has been advising IBM to advertise on TV, then I apologize to them. In the unlikely event that IBM is getting good recommendations but is not listening to sound advice, the IBM top management team should get the boot -- and fast.

It makes sense that any company would want to tell you about its products. There's a big difference between a Ford Focus and a Lincoln, yet Ford is able to give us information, using sight and sound, so that we know the differences. You can't know that an AS/400 is a terrific business system unless somebody like IBM, its creator, tells you.

How do you know that Ford makes tough trucks? How do you know about the Maytag repairman? You don't know about any of these icons unless the creator wants you to know, and then you'll see it on television.

How do you know that an Power i is industrial strength? How do you know it is the best system for business? How do you even know what products IBM sells and why you should care? With IBM's marketing, even the product is a secret. As I have said many times in this book, none of my neighbors know what IBM makes even right after they see IBM's ads. Until my neighbors know what IBM makes, the company will be stuck below the $100 billion sales mark and they may even be overtaken by machines and operating systems that my neighbors and your neighbors have learned about on -- you guessed it -- TV.

Homogenization Is Not a Marketing Strategy; It Is a Mixology Strategy

For some time now, I have been working up a nice little anecdote about the dangers of product homogenization. I think that I've got one that does the trick and it parallels what IBM has done with its AS/400 line.

It's simple and it is a little silly, but it makes a point. It's my homogenization story, and it's coming your way right now: I think you'll find that it is both amusing and frightening.

HairHead Homogenization Story

Let's say that Joe is nuts about redheads. He dates only redheads. Let's say Mike loves ladies with black hair. We won't call them blackheads, since that word is already taken and it means something else. Mike dates the ones with the silky, shiny black hair. Sam likes blondes.
We won't say yellow-haired people here, since that is not how we know them. Sam dates just blondes. Finally, Chester cannot take his eyes off brownheads. Whoops, that's brunettes, if you please! Chester dates brunettes, and only brunettes. One day, Chester hopes to marry a brunette and have a family of nice brown-haired children.

Neither Joe, nor Mike, nor Sam, nor Chester knows whether his date uses coloring on her hair. In fact the word on the street is that only their hairdresser knows for sure. In fact, none of the daters really care if there's some gray that is touched up, as long as the ladies they date have the right color at date time. Yes, all four of these gentlemen may be described as shallow, but you probably already know who in your life I am talking about. People like this do exist.

Meanwhile, in the secret corporate laboratories of Lady HairHead, the world's largest hair care manufacturer, a new plot is brewing. Internally, the company has a big dilemma. At least it believes it is a dilemma. It is seen as the big problem of the ages. The company does not know how to deal with its major brand proliferation. It has four different hair color product lines. Wouldn't it be nice, the company officials suppose, if they could make just one hair color that fits all people.

To this end, they steal an eServer marketing person from IBM, who gives them the words they have longed to hear. They can do what they want through an innovative process known as homogenization. After all, the Lady HairHead executives already knew from the new person's bio, that IBM had became a master in the notion of homogenization, early in the 21st century.

This new marketing chief informs her fellow HairHead executives that once the homogenization process is underway, there is no turning back. The individual attributes and personality factors of the four color lines will disappear and only the new homogenized color will remain. But, what color should the homogenized color actually be? There is some "RISC" that if the homogenization is not done correctly, the project may be a flop.

For the answer, the company turned to science and technology. It seems that both **common sense** and **prudent thought** were on vacation at the time. The answer, surprisingly, was easy. While supplies of black, brown, blonde, and red still existed, the company's chief chemist guru homogenized a sample color cocktail. He added just the right amount of each color to the batch. Sure enough, the results emerged, and there was a new color, eChartreuse. The little "e" was the IBM guy's idea.

From this point on, no other colors needed to apply. Customers were not asked their opinions since the company had to do what was best for the company. The remaining stocks of the former colors were homogenized in a big vat and the product line was rushed into compliance with the "magical sameness of eChartreuse." A "hair solutions for a small planet" ad kicked off the new product line.

The executives just knew that the new eChartreuse project would make things lots easier in the plant, and they were right. It even made life easier in the office. Promotional material was reduced by 3/4. Order takers no longer had to ask that difficult "color" question. There were less purchasing and accounts payable line items. Even the work involved in physical inventories was substantially reduced. It was a business operations success, just as they had hoped.

In the plant, there was no longer the need to make small batches and the company no longer had to clean out the cauldrons after each batch. No cleaning was necessary since the process could be continuous. Economies of scale in manufacturing were achieved as four times the normal batch could be made at once.

Only a label change was necessary on the container. That was the biggest expense. The product name, "Hair Coloring," would be retained. A smiley face would be included in the new design, right where the color once was displayed. Only one set of containers was needed since all products were the same.

The new label invited all to use the product. It noted that the product was for red heads, blondes, black haired persons, and brunettes. Since there was just one color, there was no reason to put eChartreuse on the label. Why give the customer the opportunity to complain? Who would benefit from that?

The executives knew that consumers would love the new product. They needed no market research to be convinced that their decision was right on for the times. But, it did not matter anyway. There would be nothing else for customers with hair to buy. They also knew that the consumers might not understand the one-color plan at first, but, since their choices were eliminated through this shrewd business practice, they would have to buy the product anyway. After customers got used to it, the executives reasoned, they would appreciate that the company was better off than when it tried to please its customers.

This was bad news for Joe, Mike, Sam, and Chester. When they got a look at the sameness of the hair color of the full cadre of potential dates, they chose to stop dating all together. They considered taking some action, such as helping the competing brands with their product differentiation strategies or maybe starting their own company. But then they realized one couldn't fight a force as big as Lady HairHead. It would be like fighting City Hall, or even IBM.

Because there was no choice and because four products were included in a single product, sales were never better at Lady HairHead. So the company prospered. Then even before anyone's hair turned gray, the whole economy collapsed. Eventually Joe, Mike, Sam, and Chester were able to convince the rest of the dating population that the new color was bad.

When everybody stopped dating, the entertainment industry failed, as did the snack industry, the pizza industry, the CD rental business, and many others. Finally, luxury items like hair coloring could not be afforded, and HairHead had its worst quarter of all time. They had used their entire parts inventory to produce eChartreuse hair color and could no longer make the other colors. It was too late. They collapsed. It was a "hairy situation."

After awhile, strands of gray and natural colors began to appear in the population. Former HairHead customers cut their hair as short as nubs in order to be able to start dating again. Joe, Mike, Sam, and Chester, followed by the rest of mankind did not care about the length of the hair, just the color. They resumed dating with money that they had saved from before the economy crashed. They realized that if they had not helped cause the economy to collapse, things would have even gotten worse. If everybody stopped dating for an extended period, soon there would be no more births, and eventually, the end of mankind would come in a sea of eChartreuse homogenization.

By the way, the four eventually met each other and invested in a small hair coloring company that had not been able to compete with Lady HairHead in its prime and thus was on the verge of bankruptcy. The self-demise of Lady HairHead came just in time to rescue their company. Its name was SunHair. Its claim to fame was that the company had a unique idea. They gave the customer a choice. Any SunHair customer could purchase any color product as long as it was red, black, blonde, or brunette. Soon the gray all but disappeared again from the land, and the four daters and investors lived happily ever after.

Oh, by the way, SunHair went on to acquire many little companies and build its own company from the bottom up. One of the favorite company refreshments was fresh brewed coffee, which they all called Java. The employees of all companies that were absorbed loved working for SunHair because of the company's basic beliefs. Besides customer choice and a no-layoff policy (not just a practice), which were their first two basic beliefs, they also came up with three others that are worthy of note. All five basic beliefs are noted below:

1. Customer choice.
2. No layoffs.
3. Respect for the individual.
4. The best customer service.
5. Superior accomplishment of all tasks.

Now that is sure a spooky story. But at least it ends well. By the way, aren't those three items directly above (numbers 3 through 5) IBM's original written "basic beliefs?" Can you imagine that?

End of Lady HairHead Homogenization Story

Thankfully, the IBM computer homogenization will only affect folks' favorite computers. Mankind will exist long after IBM's homogenization decision. Perhaps nobody will like the new eChartreuse servers, longing for the days when there was a mainframe, a Unix box, a Windows machine, and an AS/400. Maybe the SUN will shine in different colors to help attract the four personalities from their homogenized plight. Maybe it won't be mankind that goes down when everything is so much the same that nobody wants it anymore.

Maybe IBM will become the victim of creating a bland homogenization from combining four separate, exciting, yet different concepts. Maybe IBM's four customer sets will prefer to switch than fight. Maybe there will be no IBM to dictate customer preferences in the computing future.

Of course, IBM may not bring in their top chemist to make the homogenization. Since black is such a powerful pigment, and the mainframe is such a powerful component, it is conceivable that the homogenized eChartreuse of the new IBM will be indiscernible over time from the color black. It could be that the new fully homogenized IBM computer system will be indistinguishable from the former mainframe. If this is so, there will surely be an unexpected IBM survivor: the mainframe. Maybe that's what IBM is seeking after all.

Then again, there is Linux! Maybe homogenization is not such a good idea after all!

Chapter 25 The Dead Goose That Once Laid Golden Eggs

The Rochester Pricing Story

We all know Aesop's fairy tale about the goose that laid the golden egg. Here's a possible future version, fresh from a land that looks an awful lot like Rochester, Minnesota once looked

One day Ebenezer IBM from Rochester, Minnefable, a fine countryman for sure, while going to the nest of his AS/400 goose found there an egg all yellow and glittering. When he picked it up, it was as heavy as lead, and he was going to throw it away, because he thought a trick had been played upon him. But he took it to his office and had second thoughts. Soon he found to his delight that it was an egg of pure gold.

Every morning, the same thing occurred, though the eggs were of different sizes and had strange markings. Eventually, Ebenezer noticed the different markings. One would say, **AS/400 820 hardware**, another egg would say **disk drives,** another said **memory,** and still another said **Domino.** Ebenezer soon became rich in glory in IBM by sending his beautiful yellow shining eggs to Armonk and Somers, New York, each and every day.

Then, one day as Ebenezer approached the nest, he saw that an egg had yet to arrive. He noticed a very, very large egg on its way. It was much bigger than any egg he had ever seen, golden or otherwise. The goose seemed to be struggling with it. Finally it arrived and he noticed that this egg had a marking on it that read **AS/400 interactive tax.** This egg was even larger than the goose itself. As Somers and Armonk asked for more and more, the best the poor goose could do was one egg per day. The AS/400 interactive tax eggs were always the biggest and took much longer to emerge.

As Armonk asked for more, the goose was getting weaker and poor Ebenezer felt that he was not as great a fellow as he once was, so he decided that he would please Armonk and Somers and gain great favor with a great big shipment of many golden eggs all at once. He did not really want to kill the goose but he felt so much pressure to please the corporate gods, and besides, the goose was getting tired looking and old looking, especially when giving the AS/400 interactive tax eggs.

So, one morning, the still rich in praise, and now greedy Ebenezer IBM took hold of the goose, and thinking that he could get at once all the gold the goose could ever give, he killed it and opened it only to find nothing but the markings of an unformed egg. On it were the letters E-N-T-E-R-P-R-I-S-E E-D-I-T-I-O-N.

The moral of the story, of course, is that greed often over reaches itself.

Now that's the Rochester pricing story, as Aesop more than likely would have written it.

However, if Dickens wrote it, you know that it would appear more real and yet it might all be a dream. Ebenezer IBM would look a lot like Bill Murray, and he would be accompanied by an angel of sorts each time he saw himself go after the golden eggs. After Bill Murray as Ebenezer IBM saw himself kill the goose, right before he woke up, he surely would ask the last angel, "Spirit, are these the shadows of the things that will be, or are they shadows of things that only might be?"

"Will" or "may": that is the question. The answer, my friends, is up to Ebenezer IBM in the personages (at the time this paragraph was written) of John Joyce, Steve Mills, Sam Palmisano, and the rest of the IBM executive crew. Let's hope that Ebenezer IBM from Rochester remembers his dream and that the others have a dream or two before the real AS/400 story comes to an end.

The IBM unfinished reality upon which the story of the goose is based begins in the next section. But, remember, reality can be even worse than fairy tales.

Sidebar: The AS/400 interactive Tax was real. IBM began to look at the AS/400 as a cash cow and stopped caring what its customers thought about its cleaver ways to get more revenue for IBM from the backs os AS/400 clients. This prompted pundits such as Debra Tart of Search400.com to pose a question:

"Is the Interactive Tax IBM is charging turning people away from the iSeries? Some loyal iSeries customers feel the interactive tax just gives everyone more reasons to look elsewhere. What are your thoughts?" -- Debra Tart, associate editor, Search400.com

By and large AS/400 customers felt IBM was robbing them and they felt it was bad for IBM and the AS/400 platform.

Dec 22, 2005 7:25 AM GMT
We are in the application software business and our software was written specifically for the AS400/iSeries. Most of our applications are still green screen interactive, which our customers prefer by the way. They find green screens much faster for most of their work because most of it is heads down data entry and pointing and clicking only slows them down. When we have to bid a $30K-$100k iSeries against competitors on other platforms that range from $5K-$20K for the processor, it makes it very hard for us to explain why our hardware costs so much more, especially if the IT department is populated with young kids just out of college who only know PCs

and have never heard of an iSeries. Sometimes we win, but often we lose.

The AS/400 Systems and Servers

A long time ago an AS/400 system was called a system. Then, in the mid-1990s, as Windows PCs were being differentiated by client and server designations, hoping to attract more Windows server business to the platform, IBM introduced new models specifically called servers. These were priced to be cheap enough to compete with Windows machines. Overall, these new server models were reasonably successful, but their very existence created a marketing enigma for IBM.

The question became, if the new models were servers, then what about IBM's other AS/400 models? What were they, chopped liver? What could IBM call its other models if they were not servers? The Microsoft-driven press had no problem finding something to call the leftover, non-server model IBM AS/400s. They labeled these units "legacy systems."

In the same vein that the well-known brand name Windows has helped Microsoft, the term "legacy" hurt the AS/400. The term "legacy" caught on in the Microsoft-biased press and its implication was that the AS/400 was old and stale, not even historic as the term legacy actually represents.

IBM never changed the word system on these units to "legacy system," but as noted in the chapter titled: *AS/400 Is Not a Legacy System*, IBM executives did actually begin to refer to their own systems as legacy. The name on the side of the non-server units continued to be AS/400 and the boxes were sold as AS/400 systems, not servers. However, there was a real difference in the capabilities of the servers and the systems. IBM placed big and powerful processors in the new, inexpensive server models, whereas the system models were on average substantially less powerful and they cost lots more than the servers. It made no sense to IBM's AS/400 customers either.

To ensure that its revenue stream from its traditional AS/400 shops continued to flow at normal rates, IBM did not permit the new server models to support more than a few interactive terminals. Since AS/400 programs were typically written to use "green screen terminals," AS/400 shops with requirements for more than a few terminal devices were left out in the cold. They could not use the new server models for their normal AS/400 applications. This put a black mark on the AS/400 in many IT shops.

No matter what vendor's computer system one uses, an AS/400 or another box, all traditional, "legacy" applications require terminal capabilities. The server machines therefore, were not usable by the traditional IBM AS/400 customer set. In other words, the customers who bought enough from IBM to keep the AS/400 product line alive were not able to get a price break on these new AS/400 units. However, a shop new to the AS/400, considering Internet applications or Windows GUI client server applications could get AS/400 processing capability for their type of work at a discounted rate with the new server boxes.

The message received by AS/400 shops from IBM was that they were paying a lot more for their systems than typical Windows customers. It did not go over well.

As you would expect, this created some displeasure in the ranks of the AS/400 faithful. It became obvious that, for the same price, IBM was not giving the loyal AS/400customers a raw deal. Windows type users paid less for AS/400 models.

The prices for the powerful processors in the server models were so low that the traditional users began to become unhappy with IBM because they were barred from using the machine's full power. They became concerned that they were paying much more for the processors in their "systems" than was reasonable.

Interactive Feature Cards

After a few years, IBM acknowledged the problem and came up with a fix that the company felt should solve the interactive problem and make it less expensive for IBM to provide more power and more flexibility to Windows type users. The company announced that all of its AS/400 boxes would heretofore be known as servers. Moreover, each box would be able to run interactive (traditional AS/400 green-screen-style applications), as well as client/server and Internet applications (Windows-type applications).

However, there was still an unwelcome catch. The Windows type applications would still be able to use all of the power of the processor, while traditional AS/400 applications would only be able to use a small part of the same processor. For those traditional AS/400 users who needed more AS/400-type power, IBM offered the ability to purchase more of what the company called "interactive feature cards." By purchasing the cards with more and more power, IBM would take more and more of the "governors" off the processor for traditional interactive AS/400 applications. With only a few of these interactive power boosts applied to the system, the cost of the system quickly doubled and became as cost prohibitive as the older system models were compared to the server models.

In other words, there was no real power boost for traditional AS/400 shops while Windows type shops were able to use the entire power of the AS/400 processor without buying any "interactive hardware." Windows type shops got to enjoy the full power of the AS/400 processors because IBM did not use the governors with their types of applications.

In these initial models, even if a customer purchased all of the interactive capabilities that IBM offered on a particular model, these servers would still not deliver as much processor power for AS/400 applications as the full processor that was given to Windows-type applications. Because customers viewed interactive as a necessity and IBM viewed it as optional, the customer set quickly began to call the increased cost to run their AS/400 applications an *interactive penalty* or an *interactive tax.* This was not a positive notion for IBM, and the company did not like these names at all.

The Interactive cards were measured in CPW (see Chapter titled: *No Risk with RISC* 8 for a description of the CPW performance measurement). For example, a 1999 small AS/400 Model 720 was available with a 35 CPW card for interactive, while Windows server type power of 220 CPW was provided with no extra purchase. A user could move from 35 to 70 to 120 CPW of interactive power by purchasing more powerful cards. The difference between 35 and 120 CPW was substantially more than the cost of the entire system itself. Ironically, there was no cost to IBM to jack up the power. IBM merely removed more governors. When the company came out with its 820-model line in 2000, the problem still was not fixed and it existed in all of the new 8XX models.

The Interactive Performance Penalty

When a user began to take more than the percentage of the processor than was permitted by the "interactive card," for normal AS/400 applications, governing hardware/software would kick in so that the company could not get any additional performance from the system. IBM explained it as getting what you pay for and nothing more. However, as fair as that sounds, the fact that Windows type shops got the whole processor grated on the AS/400 customer.

IBM used a trick to cause the system to slow down. When too much power was being used, the system would automatically call a nasty IBM program named CFINT. The job of CFINT's is to gobble up (waste) system power and make sure no additional benefit was given to the customer. This program could not be naturally eliminated. Its job was to steal machine cycles (performance capability) so that the user could not achieve greater (AS/400) interactive performance from the system than the amount for which they had paid. Meanwhile again, Windows type applications were never penalized. They had the maximum CPU available and never called CFINT.

AS/400 customers would get a frightful message that they were exceeding the capacity of the machine if they ran a job that needed more power than the CFINT routine was willing to give to the job. So the CFINT became disruptive to normal operations. AS/400 users began to feel that they were being discriminated against, since Windows users were able to use the entire processor capabilities with no surcharge applied.

AS/400 shops saw the issue much differently than the IBM "pay for what you use" explanation. Since Windows and Unix users paid no Interactive tax, and they also paid no Windows tax, AS/400 shops felt that they too should not have to pay the "tax."

FAST/400 to the Rescue?

Wherever there is a business problem, there is always a business opportunity. A company called Storage Solutions Group developed a product known as FAST/400. Its purpose was to prevent IBM's CFINT program from knowing that a job was running in the interactive environment. So it faked the IBM processor into giving the user all of the power with no slow-down. Storage Solutions charged a goodly sum for its program, but it was a bargain compared with the interactive tax that FAST/400 users would no longer have to pay IBM.

As you might expect, IBM was very miffed that this was occurring. So as part of the normal product maintenance fixes that IBM supplied to its customers, to repair defects, it also supplied "fixes" that crippled the FAST/400's ability to cripple the performance-killing CFINT. It was a case of the fix crippling the uncrippler of the crippler. It all was very silly in the first place that IBM would charge its loyal AS/400 customers as much as four times the cost of what it would charge the Windows customers for the same number of processor cycles.

The CFINT crippling product was met with mixed reactions. Most wanted IBM to solve the problem for them without FAST/400 so that they did not feel like criminals. Others saw FAST/400 as a performance enhancement, much like a new carburetor or some STP that would enable a standard Detroit vehicle to perform as a high performance machine. Nobody ever had to send more money back to Detroit after achieving better performance on a machine after adding some new gizmos. These same types of folks did not think they owed IBM anything after crippling its performance governor.

Besides MC Press, Power i Network, and Midrange Server, Search400 had become a very worthwhile source of Power i information on the Web in the early years of the millenioum. In May 2002, in the heat of IBM's AS/400 interactive tax and interactive penalty battle with Storage Solutions Group, the Search 400 editorial team hosted a forum where AS/400 users spoke out, pro and con, about the product.

The article was called "FAST/400 friend or foe? Users speak out." I have captured just a few exchanges from this source to show that the battle with IBM is real and that IBM's customers are being affected negatively.

You can access Search400 at www.search400.com. It is an excellent source for all types of AS/400 information.

> **"IBM would have done much better just to leave us poor, uneducated customers in the dark about their governor and Interactive pricing. They [IBM] claim they have done this for years with other models [hid things under the covers --1622 Card Reader]. But now we know that a little chip the size of PC DIMM module is controlling how much of a great system we can use. And when the little chip is upgraded, UP goes the cost of support and maintenance as it often puts the customer in another P class [Software Pricing Tier]. That is where their Interactive pricing rubs me the wrong way. Does it really cost more to maintain the system now that a different chip is in the system? Should software subscriptions [maintenance] cost so much more? Also, what if you only need the extra interactive for part of the year or part of the day? It is hard to justify the little chip for only part of a year's work.**
>
> **Can I afford to upgrade the Interactive chip? … If not, what are the alternatives? 1. Quit and take up golf. 2. Switch platforms (Give me a break!) 3. Convert well-designed, fast-executing green screen programs to some sort of GUI front end where the processing can be done in batch. (That will take considerable money and time, especially retesting of the applications in a different environment.) 4. Make a business case to IBM why Interactive pricing is wrong and loyal IBM customers should be rewarded for staying with the platform, not penalized. (YES!)**
>
> **Jef Sutherland, vice president, Information Services, KOA Inc.**

There were mixed reactions as to whether, at an ethical level, the FAST/400 product should be used to bring back cycles that some customers feel that IBM has stolen from them. The feelings were deep and mixed but most were not pleased with IBM. Yet all were not quite ready to employ the FAST/400 offering:

> **The user community has long lamented to IBM and been ignored over the ridiculous fees that seem to be targeted to rake cash out of an extremely loyal customer base. Long time AS/400 or Power i customers feel taken advantage of. What makes it worse is that it is by someone who we have**

looked up to for years. After all, it was IBM Rochester that developed such a wonderfully unique platform, garnering such fierce product loyalty that we have tolerated the penalty up until now. IBM seems unwilling to market and sell more boxes for revenue; they seem to prefer to rape their existing dwindling customer base instead.

[The goose is the AS/400 customer base]

IBM has successfully gambled that it is so expensive to shift platforms, that customers will pay the penalties for a number of years before migrating to a different system to eliminate the fees. Make no mistake: Customers are migrating to another system. They are not developing a non-penalized version of software that will run on the Power i.

Jeff Importico

Customer Dissatisfaction with Pricing

Regardless of a customer's inclination to switch systems, IBM is creating real dissatisfaction out there. One day, the golden eggs will cease as IBM cuts too far into the flesh. That cannot be good for IBM. And, as a note for the Server Division, when a business switches computers because it is angry with its vendor, especially for something the vendor should control, that business does not typically run back to that vendor for a different product or service. It goes someplace else. So, in a nutshell, the IBM Global Services Division is not about to gain if a customer leaves the AS/400, goes to Windows, and needs help. That's not to say that the HP services division may not gain from such a move.

"IBM needs to look at the amount of dissatisfaction that this is creating and act accordingly. I'm guessing that beyond lack of marketing that the pricing for certain features (AS/400 interactive features and to some degree disk and memory) is the greatest cause for customer dissatisfaction. This will lead to customers purchasing other systems. And contrary to what IBM thinks, most of them are probably not IBM platforms.

Michael Crump
Saint-Gobain Containers

The End of the AS/400 User Tax?

In early 2003, with great hoopla, IBM announced a refresh of its Model 800 Power i lines. IBM announced that it was doing away with the "interactive cards," thus the company expected the terms "interactive penalty" and "interactive tax" to disappear. IBM provided two versions of the hardware for each of the larger 800 models, though they admittedly kept the old style interactive tax in place for the baby Model 800. They called these two new AS/400 hardware versions, the Power i Standard Edition and the Power i Enterprise Edition.

If you just wanted to use the machine for Windows type or Unix type serving, you needed only the Standard Edition. But if you wanted to use the machine for traditional AS/400 applications, you needed the Enterprise Edition of the hardware.

In either case, the hardware appeared no different. However, the Standard Hardware Edition had a big governor to control its AS/400-type performance, since it provided no interactive (AS/400) capability at all. CFINT would get to run all day on this box if the user were to attempt to run a real AS/400 application. Therefore, just like the server model of the mid-1990s, a normal AS/400 shop could not use this box. The Standard Edition could not run normal AS/400 applications. Real AS/400 customers were given just one choice, the "Enterprise Edition." But it was hardly affordable.

What Goes Around!

If you add up the humungous cost of all of the interactive cards that you could add to a given AS/400 model before the Enterprise Edition, the new toll that is being demanded by IBM is about as much as the full surcharge of the most expensive interactive card. That is how much more IBM now exacts for the Enterprise Addition (spelled incorrectly intentionally for effect). So what IBM really did was contrive an all or nothing interactive model. You would either get the all the power of the machine for interactive purposes (Enterprise) or you would get no traditional AS/400 interactive power (Standard).

IBM had to consult a smoke and mirrors vendor to come up with this deal. Instead of a "pay as you go" granular notion using "AS/400 interactive tax computing," as with the "interactive cards," on the new boxes IBM offers only a maximum interactive card. Thus, the entry price for the new units is often far more than what IBM's customers paid for their older systems. Considering that hardware computing costs are going down, not up, IBM has had a hard time convincing its smaller AS/400 customers that the new machines are for them.

From my eyes, the Enterprise Edition of the hardware provides no hardware at all. The governor is completely removed so theoretically, it has less hardware than the Standard Edition. For less hardware, the customer pays four or more times what the Windows type guy pays for the same processor power. IBM seems to have designed the Enterprise Edition to spoof IBM's AS/400 customers who are ready for their next system.

The spoof is that if you want any interactive performance for any model, your bill is about what it would have been if IBM sold you the biggest, fastest interative card available. You can no longer just buy enough. You pay about the total cost of all interactive card penalties for each model. The price for AS/400 traditional customers is huge. My customers have chosen not to upgrade because of what they feel is a rip off. They are waiting until IBM comes to its senses before they buy anything.

So for all but a few very large customers, the AS/400 user tax, interactive tax, or interactive penalty is now far greater than it has ever been for every model. Yet IBMers across the globe persist in telling customers that there is no longer a penalty and there is no tax. That's because the IBMers do not have to pay it. There is just a new edition that costs four times the cost of the Standard Edition and no usable hardware comes with it. Again, it just removes the governors. You may recall in the goose analogy above, that it was the Enterprise Edition Egg that was forming, but would not come out, when the goose was killed.

To add insult to customer injury, IBM also slapped an additional $125.00 per month to the hardware maintenance cost of the Enterprise Edition versus the Standard Edition. Over $100 per month maintenance for what appears to be less hardware--there is no governor.

IBM does not like the word penalty or tax. So we might say instead that the Enterprise Edition of the hardware, which delivers a fully constraint free system, became available for a major **interactive surcharge.**

For example, if a Standard Edition machine cost about $12,000, an equivalent Enterprise Edition machine would cost $48,000. Since AS/400 applications need the $48,000 version, the surcharge is viewed as an AS/400 interactive penalty by anybody who is doing some clear thinking. Since nothing physical is provided with the upgrade other than some throwaway software, there is little evidence to suggest that the whole thing is more than just a ruse.

One can argue that the only thing that happened to the AS/400 interactive penalty was that it got much bigger for all users. It sure did not go away and it sure is a real whopper.

It is keeping IBM's AS/400 customers from buying the new models. I have at least two clients who were ready to upgrade but got blown away by the cost of the Enterprise Edition (fully AS/400-capable system model).

The IBM rep at one of these accounts examined the difference in cost between the model 825 system model and the 825 server model, and he told the customer that now he understood why Brian (me) calls this an interactive penalty.

The feature cost several times more than the rest of the system and there is a huge hardware maintenance charge on it to boot, though there is less hardware. For example, the interactive penalty on the smallest model 825 in the line is $276,000.00. That's a big tax just so that your applications can be written in the AS/400 mode. One must ask in this instance, besides wanting more money from its customers, what is IBM trying to do?

AS/400 Developers Paying the Price for Lost Sales

One of my customers showed me how the price of an 825 was not affordable by his company, and then astutely offered these observations about the IBM developer community:

> **"Don't forget that IBM is punishing the developers who have a green-screen interactive offering with a $276,000 penalty on an 825."**

In other words, if a software company writes for Unix or Windows, the same AS/400 machine that runs the software will be $276,000 less if it does not run on an AS/400. If the developer writes the package AS/400 style, the price is huge. If the developer writes it for Linux or Windows, the customer has $276,000 more to spend on the package.

That's a big incentive for a software company to want to write for a non-AS/400 platform. This kind of pricing gives developers an incentive to abandon the AS/400 in favor of a more dollar friendly environment.

Take Your Green Screens to WebSphere

There is an ad that one of the oil companies used way back that many would recognize as "Pay Me Now Or Pay Me Later." Interestingly enough, if you choose to use an AS/400 Standard Edition, you get yourself a very powerful server that can do a great job for PC clients. But if your applications are client/server oriented (considering that client/server is dead) or Internet applications, it will cost you much more in services and time to install and implement.

Now, with IBM's newest 8xx and 5xx AS/400 servers, the company is so interested in Windows-type applications always costing less that the interactive penalty is removed if a shop converts its AS/400 applications to Internet applications. Of course, the time and cost of that conversion is something to consider but with the new WebFacing tool it is much easier than otherwise.

If you run your applications through a WebFacing client server development tool, it will convert your green screen applications to run on the cheaper Standard Version AS/400 with no interactive penalty. Though WebFacing is good, however, it is certainly not good enough to convert all of your internal applications to a shape that is completely usable. Moreover, since WebSphere takes lots of performance cycles, the applications performance through a browser may very well not be as good as interactive – ven if the i5 is more powerful.

Of all the AS/400 pricing stories, the fact that IBM waives the interactive tax if you Webface applications is the best. This is the first step in the right direction by IBM on the pricing issue. The other actions were rope-a-dope. Let's hope we get some even better pricing stories in the near future.

And that's the pricing story without the goose involved, but there are other pieces left to tell. If you've had enough of the goose and the ghost, and pricing, move to the next chapter, but there is just one more little Power i pricing story coming next.

An IBM Pricing Error?

How would you react if you were an AS/400 zealot and you came across a little notice like this?

> **"IBM RAISES POWER I MODEL 800 PRICES**
> **IBM is raising the price of the model 800 Standard and Advanced editions. Standard Edition's price tag nearly doubling from $5,137 to $9,137, while Advanced Edition is going from $19,200 to $23,200. Canadian prices jumped from $8,150 to $14,500 for Standard Edition and from $30,500 to $36,800 for Advanced Edition. The new prices took effect September 5 and are valid only in the U.S., Puerto Rico, and Canada."**

In early September 2003, Power i Network ran this little blurb to announce that IBM had raised prices on its smallest system. To me, the systems were not close to a bargain in those days and they needed pricing actions in the other direction (such as the i5 announcement in May, 2004). I was disappointed in IBM and I fought back the only way I knew how. I coined a sarcastic reply to the editor, who responded quickly that, though IBM had raised the base price, the overall price was the same.

Though the announcement overall was difficult to understand, in essence, the system whose price was raised previously had to be bought with a mandatory $4,000 tape drive. Before the announcement, if you wanted a different tape drive, you had to pay twice. Buried in another IBM announcement, the company added the cost of the tape drive to the server price, and gave the choice of two "no-charge" tape drives or a third, for which the user pays a premium of $2,000.

I submitted a response to Power i Network because I could not believe IBM would increase prices on a system that had been announced for less than one year. This shows just how annoyed I really was. I recall reading this little piece to my wife Pat after I had sent it. Pat typically likes nothing I write. When she laughed as she did, I knew that it would be fun for AS/400 folks to read. But since it was a false alarm, Power i News did not run it.

Here it is. Please read this every now and then to get some relief from the stress of the day. It is completely fictitious, based on the price increase that I thought had occurred. Even if the price increase had occurred, it would still be fictitious, but fun nonetheless. I hope you get a kick out of it.

> **"In an apparent attempt to kill a product [AS/400] that continues to breathe despite no help from the corporate body to which it is attached, IBM took action today to permanently dissuade small businesses from thinking they could ever afford an AS/400.**
>
> **"Corporate spokesmen were unavailable for comment as they were involved in cashing in IBM securities while they still have value. Speculation is that, with the exception of the inimitable leader himself, the top players from the Iraqi Most-Wanted card deck, who have not yet been captured, have found refuge as executives in IBM. They were brought in as "professional hires," so that their salaries would not be constrained by the rules and grids that guide the top salaries of regular IBM employees.**
>
> **"Further speculation suggests that most of the players from other popular card decks, who have recently been seen counseling and hobnobbing with IBM top management, assisted the corporation in fine tuning the new prices to the last dollar so there would be no rounding errors that would negatively affect the company.**
>
> **"Please note the "7" at the end of the prices, not the typical 0 or 5 that a rational being would use for a large ticket item. Rumor has it that the extra $137.00 is to pay for the secret incentive. A dozen decks of autographed Iraqi Most Wanted cards are shipped with each system.**
>
> **"The iSeries was formerly known as the AS/400. The AS/400, when asked for comment on the price increases, after first spinning a disk to make an unpleasant whirring**

sound, suggested that in addition to the questionable management sponsorship, the price increase had a lot to do with the smallest Power i being a "greedy little pig." Commenting further, the AS/400 noted that the "i" in Power i stands for the "i" in P "i" G."

Chapter Epilogue

Keep in mind that the Ebenezer IBM story has not completed in our time. We did get a look at the ending that Aesop would have written. In our time, the original goose is still alive and Ebenezer has not yet done the cutting. But time is running short. Let's hope that Dickens can intervene on this one to help Ebenezer and the gods in Armonk know that when they make customers bleed, eventually there will be no blood, and then no customers.

The AS/400 pessimists see this story from the Aesop point of view and are already out buying flowers for the goose. The AS/400 optimists on the other hand hope that Dickens can save the day by showing IBM that in these pricing schemes, the IBM Company appears to be very greedy and customers do not like greedy vendors. Hopefully, the last Spirit in Dickens will overcome the powers at IBM and work them into repentance so that the AS/400 can live and that customers who buy one won't go broke.

Something for sure has to change in IBM's pricing. There are lots more outrageous pricing examples that I chose not to print. With pricing that punishes AS/400 loyal customers and rewards Windows-type customers, IBM has succeeded in creating a formula for natural resentment.

Chapter 26 Keep Your Java; We'll Take Coffee!

Java Sets the World on Fire

In May 1995, Sun announced Java at its Sun World conference. The players in the Internet world accepted it immediately. It was a natural fit. Netscape, the major browser company at the time, quickly announced that it would include Java support in its browser. Later, as Microsoft was preparing to dominate the browser world, it decided to support Java in its Internet Explorer. Java as an entity was off and running.

One of the attributes that are necessary for Java to run on any system is something called the Java Virtual Machine (JVM). This takes the Java code and makes it mesh with the actual hardware machine upon which it is running. With its hardware abstraction layer (TIMI), discussed in the chapter titled: *The All Everything Computer,* the AS/400 was an ideal candidate to be a powerful Java machine.

What Is Java?

Java is both a programming language and a programming platform. As with any language, it provides operations to read and write data, manipulate data, and call prewritten functions for specific programming tasks. As a platform it has many components that enable it to provide various services to just about all computers and all operating systems. In recent years, Java has found its niche by being the adopted environment for Web-based dynamic data applications.

In 1997 Java was announced for the AS/400 and soon after made available. AS/400 boxes at the time had just become Internet enabled two years prior. IBM was keener on Java than even Sun Microsystems, its inventor. Rochester hopped on big time and gave its Toronto lab the job of getting Java ready for prime time on the AS/400. It took several years for Java to perform well in an AS/400 environment. Now the AS/400 is known as the best Java platform in the industry. And that is the good part of the Java story and the AS/400.

AS/400 Java

A funny thing happened on the way to a superior AS/400 Java product. IBM Toronto (IBM's lab for AS/400 programmer development tools) found itself devoting substantial resources to the Java effort. From 1995, as Java began to take off, Toronto's mission was to make the AS/400 a major player, if not the major player in the Java segment. There was just one problem: The bulk of IBM's AS/400 customers want nothing to do with the Java language or platform.

AS/400 History of Java and Internet

To understand the impact of Java on the AS/400 community, just for a bit let's go back into the early 1990s to see how the AS/400 was being prepared for the Internet. As most Internet users have learned, the protocol that drives the Internet is called Transmission Control Protocol/Internet Protocol (TCP/IP).

The original TCP/IP utilities for the AS/400 were written in Pascal, a computer language that was not well implemented on the AS/400. By choosing Pascal for TCP/IP, IBM compromised the performance of the system. Instead of integrating the necessary TCP/IP stack into the base of the machine, Rochester implemented it as an add-on product. In a word, in the early 1990's, TCP/IP on the AS/400 just plain stunk. At best it behaved as a poor running application, and at worst it was missing many standard, expected functions. Overall, it did not enjoy much success.

The TCP/IP applications that were implemented were also lacking. The "well known" applications for example, such as Telnet and FTP were incomplete in function and were not built exactly to the TCP/IP specs. TCP/IP was just terrible on the AS/400.

I was with IBM during this period and the company made no excuses for the poor implementation. It was a travesty but IBM freely admitted that the only reason that TCP/IP was even built for the AS/400 was so that the AS/400 would pass government and education request for proposal (RFP) checklists that required TCP/IP but did not specify performance or functional characteristics.

If our local IBM office had gotten the business in some of these cases, I would have been embarrassed. To make a bad situation worse, IBM charged $23,880 for each copy of this unusable hunk of crap. Thankfully, none of my customers ever seriously asked for it.

From its inception, the AS/400 performed data communications naturally via a protocol called Systems Network Architecture/Synchronous Data Link Control (SNA/SDLC). This protocol was originally implemented by IBM on mainframes in the mid-1970s.

Though TCP/IP was a necessary ingredient for the Internet, and for heterogeneous computing, rather than invest in its AS/400 by upgrading the machine's ability to participate in the Internet, IBM decided that its RS/6000 (Unix box) and Windows machines would carry the day. The AS/400 would not be an Internet player by design. IBM also made the same decision about client/server for the AS/400.

IBM targeted the AS/400 as a non-participant in both the client/server and the Internet revolutions (see Chapter 28, "Client/Server and the Internet"). IBM's AS/400 competitors were thrilled that the company held back its best system from competing against them in the important battles of the day. The AS/400 customer set was not at all happy about IBM's decision. It was not the first time and it would not be the last time that IBM upset this group of loyal customers.

Gerstner Makes IBM Correct TCP/IP

It was not too long after Lou Gerstner joined IBM on April Fools' Day in 1993 that he looked at the stable of server systems and he decided that all IBM servers needed to be upgraded to participate as servers in both client/server and Internet environments. Gerstner reversed IBM's prior decision that had kept the AS/400 as a green-screen-only machine. By this time, however, with the barn door open so long, most of the horses had gone someplace else. Unix boxes had taken the lead in Internet applications, and Bill Gates had his Windows machines well honed to move right in. It was not until 1995 with the RISC boxes that IBM had a reasonably stable and high performing TCP/IP stack on the AS/400, and it was three more years before the company had most of the expected Internet applications running.

Until then, competitors had a field day knowing that the AS/400 lacked even the basics, such as Distributed Host Control Protocol (DHCP), Network Address Translation (NAT), IP filtering, and other key Internet protocols. Secure Socket Layer (SSL) and Virtual Private Networking (VPN) capabilities came even later. By the time they came out, AS/400 customers who took the Internet challenge had found another machine upon which to get them done.

For years, as AS/400 IT shops were being asked by their management to take them to the Internet, they were forced to decline since IBM had not given the machine the necessary function in time. Moreover, in the years following 1995, after IBM finally put a Web Server on the AS/400, the Toronto labs, home of AS/400 application development, offered no tools for AS/400 developers to leverage their skills on the Internet.

Because it was so preoccupied with getting Java on the machine, Toronto left AS/400 programmers, who hoped to take their company's applications to the Web, without any effective Internet development tools. Some would argue that not much has changed since then.

AS/400 shops were marking time hoping they would survive while IBM caught up to the rest of the world in functions that were clearly necessary for the platform to be competitive in the Internet environment and to perhaps even survive. In order to survive themselves, many AS/400 IT Directors and CIO's saw the wisdom of becoming a multi-platform shop for both client server and for the Internet.

At the time, Windows seemed best for client server and Unix was the best for the Internet. As noted, when Rochester was finally ready for the full Internet and client server experience with AS/400, it was already too late. The defections had occurred and the multi-platform shop became something with which IBM had to deal permanently.

IBM Says Java Is the Answer

In the later 1990s, as Java eventually become usable on the AS/400, to make up for not providing any natural Internet tools for AS/400 programmers, IBM tried to push AS/400 programmers into learning Java so that they could put AS/400 applications on the Web. AS/400 programmers did not buy in. Toronto had left the AS/400 shops with no natural tools for the platform and then tried to jam in a language that belonged in a Unix shop. AS/400 shops gave IBM a big "no" to Java.

In Chapter 19, "The Rise of the Software Division," I discussed with you the tools that Toronto finally made available in 2001 so that RPG and COBOL programs could finally be usable on the Web. After having no platform and no Internet development tools for years, in 2001, with the WebSphere Development Studio and the WebSphere Server, (two non-integrated products) AS/400 shops were staged to become full participants in the Internet. It was six years late and the revolution was already over. The dot-coms had dot-gone.

Beggars can't be choosers, so the AS/400 community slowly began to think that it had finally been empowered. But that was before the software division, as noted in Chapter 19, pulled the plug on the free WebSphere server and set Internet application development back another two years. Out of the blue, IBM dropped support on the server that was earmarked to run the applications that programmers were just starting to build with IBM's newly available development tools. The new WebFacing tool had great promise as it created Java code from existing screen panels, without the programmer having to be Java inclined.

AS/400 programmers did not have to learn Java or change any programs to bring applications to the Web. Unfortunately, because the software division had killed the free server, this was another Internet dud. It was not until April 2003 that a server (WebSphere Express) was brought forth for the AS/400 so that programmers could bring their applications to the Internet. With all this time wasted by IBM, the company could not have hurt the ability for the AS/400 to be a bona fide Internet machine if it had been the intentional corporate strategy.

Internet AS/400– Java Is the Way?

Today, the AS/400 (Power i) has been retrofitted to be one of the best Internet machines in the Industry. Though client server is dead, the AS/400 is now, also one of the best client server machines in the Industry. It's too bad that IBM waited until its competitors got the Internet business and the client/server business before arming the AS/400 with any of the capabilities necessary to compete.

With the new tools, the AS/400 uses Java to drive Internet applications. After Toronto spent five years perfecting Java for the AS/400, however, the AS/400 programming community quickly voted it thumbs down. AS/400 programmers use RPG and COBOL for their applications and are not interested in a new language, Java or Schmava. IBM knew that its AS/400 users did not like C++ and other Java-like languages, and the company had no reason to expect that AS/400 developers would embrace Java. The Java scenario was not something that AS/400 customers were asking to be built.

IBM internally supposed that AS/400 customers did not know what would be good for them, so it decided that AS/400 customers should use Java. Despite not having a customer mandate, IBM spent years making the AS/400 the beat all and end all Java machine that it is today. "But for whom?" is a big question in my mind.

The new WebSphere Studio tools for AS/400 are in many ways an answer to the Java problem. With the newly available tools, AS/400 programmers are not required to learn Java. Yet, because IBM has pushed Java for many years to the AS/400 community as its only road to the Web, many AS/400 customers still have a bad taste about Java. They don't want to hear about Java in nay way or in any form.

IBM chose to add Java to a machine instead of providing natural, major league AS/400-style Internet development tools for its traditional developers.

Toronto failed to provide the Internet development tools necessary for the integrated type of work that AS/400 developers were accustomed to producing. Moreover, when Toronto finally delivered some tools, it introduced them for the PC platform even though the natural place for many of the tools was and is the AS/400 itself.

Good for IBM, Not IBM Customers

In a nutshell, Java is another one of those areas in which the AS/400 caretakers have alienated and continue to alienate the AS/400 community. Nobody in AS/400 land asked for Java, yet IBM spent hundreds of millions of dollars on it and then just did not let it be when it was rejected. Instead the company tried to force it down the throats of AS/400 programmers.

Now that Java is actually fully implemented on the AS/400, and the system has all the tools necessary to be a top Internet server, very few AS/400 shops seem to know about it, and those that do know don't seem to care. Java need not apply.

IBM built Java into the AS/400 for some reason. Now it is there and it is very good. The AS/400 community never wanted it and still does not want to use Java. So why did IBM spend all that money building Java into the machine? There is a whole other world out there with Sun developers and HP developers and Linux developers, where a great Java presence might help attract new AS/400 customers.

If the AS/400 applies to Java developers across all other platforms, and if the Java on the AS/400 is best-of-breed, and what separates it from being used is that nobody knows about it, IBM needs to tell somebody. We're back to the same old problem with IBM management and the AS/400. As long as

IBM keeps its finest achievements hidden, the AS/400 has little chance to help IBM regain its proper share of the server hardware business. Something tells me that IBM is in for a big wke-up. Since the i5 announcements, and the Spring COMMON conference, thre seems to be a new spirit in IBM. Let's hope that the company finally recognizes its greatest opportunity and goes ahead and aggressively markets it to the world as the IBM Business System – with or without Java.

Chapter 27 Unix, Linux, and IBM

AS/400 Can Do Anything

About five years ago, IBM introduced a feature on the AS/400 that is quite spectacular. It is known as *logical partitioning*. It sounds like a lot, and it is. It lets one IBM AS/400 processor run up to 10 Linux machines on just one AS/400 processor. It is an amazing concept for AS/400 shops that also love Linux. Moreover, it has the potential of attracting new Linux customers to the AS/400 if IBM chooses to promote this new capability to non-AS/400 shops.

Just as the AS/400 does Java, the AS/400 now does Linux but the story is not over yet. With V5R3, the AS/400 also does the same Unix as the pSeries. It runs IBM's Advanced Interactive Executive, or AIX just as the RS/6000 and now the pSeries. These recent capabilities offers a nice alternative to having one or more Linux PC server type systems or Unix systems on the side that must be maintained separately from the AS/400.

Tell Somebody!

The AS/400 has been retrofitted to be able to run Linux and Unix along with its primary operating system, OS/400, on the same small machine. That is a nice capability, and if IBM ever chose to market the AS/400 to the general public, the feature would make the AS/400 more popular, for sure. However, IBM markets none of the advantages of the AS/400 to the general public. So, unless something changes, there is no reason for AS/400 folks to get too excited. There is little chance of an executive waking up one morning after REM sleep pondering what he learned by watching an AS/400 ad during a game the day before, and calling IBM looking for its AS/400. Nobody is going to learn anything about the AS/400 while watching television. The AS/400 is not on TV and it is not visible to many, even those who may need it.

For AS/400 shops it is 5 percent refreshing and 95 percent confusing that the AS/400 is getting so good at so many things that AS/400 shops really do not care about. Just like with Java, most AS/400 shops care nothing about Linux or Unix.

Barbara Chaderton, a consultant from Northeastern Pennsylvania, offers the following:

> **"...many [AS/400] IT shops are in a confused state, not knowing the 'right' way to go.**
>
> **"... This just keeps IT shops struggling to provide the means for platforms to communicate, instead of concentrating on their important business strategies. "**
>
> **... The AS/400 now means too many things to too many people. The mindset exists that thinks IBM should merge with Nike: I don't care how you do it, IBM. 'Just do it!' "**

It is a fair question to ask IBM why it is so silent about the AS/400 product in the Unix, Linux and Java community. If IBM is not looking for new customers, then bringing Unix, Linux and Java to the AS/400 makes no sense. I have no clues from IBM as to why all the fuss on the AS/400 about things that AS/400 people care little about. However, I think I know where all this is going and my speculation peaks in Chapter 39, "The Future of the AS/400."

For the AS/400 aficionado, as well for the general public, reading this book for insights on what is wrong with IBM's handling of the AS/400, it may seem a strange turn to be discussing Unix and Linux. From my eyes, the way IBM is handling Unix and Linux on AS/400 is a big part of what is wrong with the AS/400. Just as Java was pushed on the

AS/400 for years, Linux is the new push. In my opinion, AS/400 shops running OS/400 will reject Linux and Unix, just as they did Java. However, as you will note in later chapters, just like IBM stubbornly continues to push Java on the AS/400 while its customers say no, I predict the same IBM frenzy with Linux and Unix as time goes by.

I am the last one to suggest that AS/400 shops learn Java and learn Linux or Unix. In fact, I think it is counter-productive for these shops to do so, regardless of what IBM thinks. Java is not a business language. RPG and COBOL are business languages.

I would not recommend that one of my clients use both COBOL and RPG for development. RPG and COBOL are more similar than either and Java, but they are also worlds apart in terms of language syntax. I recommend a one-language shop for productivity and skill purposes. Just like you would not necessarily want oil and gas heat in the same building, a shop should standardize on one language to avoid a number of unproductive scenarios, including:

1. An RPG programmer unproductively fixing COBOL programs.
2. A COBOL programmer unproductively fixing RPG programs.

Once you throw Java into the mix, the learning curve becomes even steeper. Java is completely unlike either of these environments, and with Java, through a process called deprecation, language elements are scrapped or redone periodically so that programs must be maintained periodically even if there are no changes that help the business.

Just as I would not advocate a two-language shop, I do not recommend a two-operating system shop. As soon as Windows servers come in to a shop, trouble and down time and guffaws that never existed before become the norm.

Adding Linux or Unix to a shop is stretching resources even thinner. Who can know all thee things? Not one person that is for sure.

So, for my money, though I see Linux coming in a bigger way, pushed by IBM to the AS/400, perhaps even to the exclusion of OS/400, I would recommend resisting until you have to say "uncle." I would recommend going to a clone OS/400 if such a viable alternative is available when you feel the word "uncle" coming out.

Like it or not, Linux and Unix and Windows are all going to be around for a long time. Overall it is good that IBM brings this technology to the AS/4000. However, my concern is what the lawyers would call the "slippery slope." What I do not want to see is Unix and Linux appearing and then it becomes much easier for IBM to force all the wonderfulness of OS/400 into the background.

To an extent, though it may be a radical point of view, I view Java as my enemy. To an extent, I also view Linux and Unix as my enemies. It is probably because of my days as an IBM systems engineer, when these environments and languages were the stuff that ran on the competitor's machine. I enjoyed comparing all this low level stuff (Java, Unix, Linux) to the goodness and ease-of-use characteristics of RPG and OS/400.

The AS/400 won hands down and put DEC out of business. I find it ironic that stuff that looks more like DEC than IBM is finding its away onto the AS/400 platform, and I am supposed to welcome it with open arms. Yuck. That about sums up my thoughts.

While I was doing research for another book, several years ago, I happened to come across a number of references to the creation of the C language (lots more like Java than RPG) and Unix. I was amazed at IBM's involvement in all this pioneering work in time-sharing. This past summer, I was inspired to dust off the work and fashioned a short essay from it that gives a brief history of IBM's involvement in the creation of Unix. An abridged version was published by Power i Network in August 2003.

Since Unix is the underlying idea for Linux, and since all of this is heading for the AS/400 in a big way, like it or not, I have included the uncut version of this essay to help add a new wrinkle to most people's understanding of Unix history. I present this because it also demonstrates IBM's stubbornness in another platform area, Unix. AS/400 loyalists will enjoy the fact that while IBM is now investing billions in Unix, it never really wanted to give the operating system the time of day.

IBM's Unix History

This essay sets the stage for understanding the IBM/Unix enigma. As you will see when you get to the capstone chapter, I draw some chilling conclusions about the future role of Linux and the AS/400.

A casual observer would easily conclude that over the years, IBM has disliked Unix as much as it continues to seem to dislike its own AS/400. But don't kid yourself. This is a whole book of reasons demonstrating IBM's issues with the AS/400.

For Unix, and now Linux, there's just this one little chapter. But, as you will see through the rest of this book, whether IBM likes Unix or not, its love affair with Linux is overwhelming and all-encompassing. IBM would give up many things before it would give up its hold on Linux as the basis for its future.

This is a more complete version of an article that I wrote for iSeries Network News in the summer of 2003. This is the story of IBM and Unix. It is about how IBM could have owned Unix right from its development days with MIT to the number of times the Unix brand itself or companies who owned Unix were sold. Here goes:

[Note IBM's traditional Unix is called Advanced Interactive Executive, or AIX.]

"If IBM falls on its AIX because of its squabbling with SCO Group over Unix licensing rights, it has nobody but itself to blame. The company's seeming disinterest in whether SCO Group can put the kibbutz on its Unix game follows right along with IBM's longstanding (40-year) tradition of ignoring Unix--while cashing in on the operating system it never wanted in the first place.

"Though most Unix fans thank Ken Thompson and Dennis Ritchie for Unix, a few of those thank you's should be spent on the two organizations that gave Unix its roots, IBM and MIT. The beginnings of Unix came from the labs of MIT, and in the early development days, IBM was still its favorite partner.

"IBM's relationship with MIT goes back to 1884, when MIT Professor Herman Hollerith applied for patents for his automatic punch-card tabulating machine. This was the beginning of International Business Machines (IBM). Even without the influence of Dr. Hollerith, it made good business sense for IBM and other companies to have partnerships with universities. The companies gained the expertise of the finest scientists in academia and the institutions gained a practical perspective on how to best help their students.

"Most large companies today have affiliations with many universities. IBM history tells us that among many other reasons, one good reason for working with a number of universities is that if the relationship goes sour with one university, it can be sweetened with another.

"A case in point is the IBM Company. At one time IBM had a marvelous relationship with Harvard. In fact, IBM funded the creation of its first computer, the MARK I, by Harvard Scientist, Dr. Howard Aiken. Aiken, however, did not think IBM had given enough help and had slowed down the project. IBM founder Thomas Watson Sr. cherished his relationship with the Massachusetts Institute of Technology, even more when Harvard snubbed the company at the 1944 celebration of the IBM/Harvard Mark I, IBM's first computer system. Aiken failed to recognize IBM's contribution at the celebration. Knowing the value of relationships with the academic world, after the Harvard snub, IBM did special things to sweeten its already good relationship with MIT. No other academic

institution at the time would receive such favors. But, IBM stopped short of making itself successful in the endeavor.

"At MIT's behest, IBM developed special timesharing address-translation hardware for its mainframe-class 7090 computer -- the same type of timesharing that would later be required by Unix. Yes, before Unix and Bell Labs and even SCO, there was IBM and MIT. Unix sprang from MIT and IBM built the original address-translation hardware that proved the concept.

"MIT was more than just interested in Time Sharing. They believed in it intensely. They saw themselves as bleeding edge in Academia and had designs of connecting other Universities to their facilities through the yet-to-be-invented timesharing operating system. IBM on the other hand saw timesharing as a questionable business opportunity and one that would perhaps induce customers who shared, to not purchase their own in-house computer systems.

"Among other things, MIT wanted a degree of notoriety for its efforts. It did not want its new time-sharing operating system to run on a special purpose computer, available to a select few. IBM led the scientists at MIT to believe that its to-be-announced revolutionary new system would support time-sharing without special one-of-a-kind hardware. That would mean that any institution or organization could purchase it with no constraints.

"At the time, IBM and MIT were on their merry way to inventing Unix. Historians will look unfavorably on IBM's decision to risk its strong relationship with MIT by not honoring the university's pleas to make the same special time-sharing hardware capabilities of the IBM 7090 computer a standard feature of the new IBM System/360.

"MIT was pushing the known software technology limits to develop a multi-user timesharing operating system. This new OS needed the right hardware to perform well. Its Compatible Time-Sharing System (CTSS) software eventually grew into the Multiplexed Information and Computing Service (Multics). From this beginning, the university's efforts, with some special assistance from some individuals from Bell Labs, morphed into the Uniplexed Information and Computing System (UNICS), which soon took on the simple name of UNIX.

"The CTSS operating system in the early 1960s had great promise. IBM was first in line to benefit. But, because IBM feared that timesharing would lessen its opportunity to sell individual computers, it chose not to help MIT as MIT had asked. The university was disappointed with the

lack of time-sharing hardware of the brand new vanilla System/360. They had already made their case to IBM that the System/360 should answer the university's time-sharing hardware needs in a standard machine that anybody could buy off the shelf. They thought it was a 'Go!' When IBM didn't deliver, the scientists at MIT were humiliated -- and very angry with IBM. They sent IBM an unequivocal message when they went to General Electric for their time-sharing computer hardware solution.

"When the dust settled, the victor of the day was AT&T, through its Bell Labs division. Bell also selected the GE model, so IBM was a double loser. They lost MIT and Bell Labs' business. Ultimately, Bell Labs partnered in the project and got to take all the rights to the university's time-sharing efforts. From this original body of work, Bell Labs was able to create Unix. The success of Unix is legendary.

"Years later as AT&T wanted to be more of a long distance provider than a software supplier; again IBM got a shot at 'owning' Unix. Surely, IBM had the same chance as Novell to buy the full rights to Unix. Again, when Novell sold the Unix rights to SCO and when SCO sold the rights to Caldera, which later re-christened itself as the SCO Group, IBM was missing from the bargaining table. IBM was not looking to shore up its Unix business by owning the underlying technology.

"It's not that IBM didn't have an interest or a stake in Unix's success. The company invested heavily in its own Unix derivative, AIX (for Advanced Interactive Executive). This investment, of course, was predicated on IBM's perception that it had a paid-up license for Unix. On IBM's Web site, the company boldly states: '...Unix license is irrevocable, perpetual, and fully paid up.'

"Already having gained success with its AIX flavor of Unix, by the mid-1990s, IBM seemed preoccupied with dethroning Windows servers from their newfound preeminence in the industry. Linus Torvalds' 'free' Linux operating system seemed like just the ticket. In this regard, IBM invested heavily in Linux, an open-source Unix look-alike. Again, however, the company did nothing to shore up its Unix rights while the opportunity was still 'cheap.' IBM could have bought SCO and/or the rights to Unix for peanuts and the company never would have subjected itself or its customers to the FUD that is now permeating both the Linux and Unix worlds.

"IBM chose to fight, rather than acquiesce by purchasing SCO Group. As promised, SCO has shaken up the Linux and AIX world with its court actions -- and threats of more court actions to come. Microsoft recently threw some cash

SCO's way by buying some Unix licenses. Could this be Bill Gates' way of helping to disrupt the non-Windows world and help finance a court battle against IBM and the other foes of Windows technologies?

"One thing has remained a constant throughout IBM's 40-year history with Unix. The company has never wanted it. Even now, when it seems to be spending billions to promote Linux, and its own rights to Unix are being questioned in court, IBM doggedly, perhaps even arrogantly, refuses to budge.

"There are two classic examples of companies whose arrogance has cost them marketplaces. The most well known example may be Western Union, which tried to ignore the telephone. Ironically, Bell Telephone benefited from Western Union's arrogance. The other was IBM in two circumstances. The first was under TJ Watson Sr. who tried to perpetuate punched card processing at the dawn of the computer era. IBM was handily beat to market by Univac, the recognized computer leader in the early 1950's. To overcome the price of arrogance, Watson Jr. sent Dad on a 'long vacation' and turned the company around to become number one in computers.

The second case of extreme IBM arrogance was when the company initially closed its eyes to the revolution in personal computing. IBM paid more attention to the Justice Department suit than their business. At the time the company felt it just could not afford to monopolize another market segment.

"Either IBM managers are much smarter than those of us who would take the action that logic seems to dictate, or perhaps arrogance is again the order of the day in IBM, right up to point of self destruction in the Unix marketplace.

"Eventually, probably sooner than later, the SCO/Unix suit will be addressed by IBM. For now, both Unix (AIX) and Linux run very well on the AS/400. Maybe one day, IBM will tell somebody."

The IBM Story

The whole history of IBM is fraught with stories about how IBM had it all, had no clue that it had it, and then lost it through a guffaw or a major blunder. IBM lost the PC market, the relational database market (but got some back), the data communications market (Cisco), the CD optical market (Phillips), the Satellite Market (SBS), and so on. In many ways, Joni Mitchell's song "Parking Lot" gives the IBM story:

> **"Don't it always seem to go**
> **That you don't know what you've got**
> **'Til it's gone.**
> **They paved paradise**
> **And put up a parking lot."**

It would take a lot of time to recount all of IBM's business blunders (as well as its successes, to be fair), but it is a fact that the company has squandered its share of many opportunities. Limiting our focus on the first decade of the 21st century, we now find IBM comfortably becoming a services and software company while its hardware business is drifting away as if it does not matter.

Today, there are just four types of commercial computers in the entire world. All the others have died, including the great HP3000 and the DEC VAX. The four are as follows:

```
1. Mainframe                IBM z/OS et al.
2. Unix Boxes               Unix, Linux
3. Windows Boxes            Windows, Linux
4. AS/400 Power i Boxes     OS/400, Linux, Unix
```

Since Linux, developed by Linus Torvalds et al, is a highly standardized clone of Unix, for our purposes the term *Unix* does just fine in this context. Thus, there are just four computing platforms at the operating system level: **z/OS, Unix, Windows, and OS/400.**

IBM and Windows

IBM owns z/OS and OS/400. If IBM had paid attention to the PC marketplace that it invented, the company would also own Windows or its IBM PC equivalent. Moreover, Intel would not have been a player since IBM already had its share of PC type processors already developed. Big Blue chose Intel's 8088 processor to keep the government off its back and also to avoid the sting of the IBM bureaucracy.

With the Wintel business bringing in well over $100 billion last year, and with IBM bringing in $80 billion in the same year, it is clear that somebody made a big mistake. Considering the Wintel business now is well over $500 billion, themistake lives on.

Though all of these can be characterized by their operating systems, isn't the $100 billion something that you might think IBM would be thinking: "Don't it always seem to go that you don't know what you've got 'til it's gone." Not only is the $100 billion gone once. It's gone every year.

IBM and Unix

Now, let's take Unix, please! (Thank you, Henny Youngman.) IBM irritated a great academic partner, MIT, and did not back the university's time-sharing project that ultimately became Unix. It was MIT's project, not Bell Labs'. IBM was in the catbird seat as the vendor of choice at the time. Bell Labs, then part of AT&T, was the beneficiary of IBM's lack of vision, just as Microsoft and all the modern billionaire moguls were the beneficiaries in the PC industry.

Today as you look at the computer industry, many players are gone. You'll find that Hewlett-Packard is in the Unix hardware business. Sun is in the Unix hardware business big time, and SCO Group is in the software business as today's owner of Unix. Thus, for IBM to be in the Unix business, SCO thinks that IBM has to keep paying in dollars or frustration for Unix licensing rights. IBM's lament is that this frustration comes from an OS that the company should have owned.

IBM's posture in this market has not made much sense and has cost the company $billions. Remember, there was no Sun before Unix and Sun grabs about $10 billion per year of hardware business that could very well be IBM's own. "Don't it always seem to go that you don't know what you've got 'til it's gone?"

The Unix marketplace, considering all the little devices with burned in Unix, is worth well over $20 billion per year. With that $20 billion, IBM would have already become a $100 billion company. Right now, the only way IBM is going to make $100 billion is if the services and software divisions come up with another $20 billion. And that is actually very likely.

IBM and the Mainframe

Just a few years ago, IBM's competitors declared that the mainframe was dead. I can still remember the fight IBM put up to convince the world otherwise. It is best captured in the words of Paul Simon:

> **"And in the naked light I saw**
> **Ten thousand people, maybe more**
> **People talking without speaking**
> **People hearing without listening**
> **People writing songs that voices never share**
> **And no one dared**
> **Disturb the sound of silence."**

IBM's executive management team dared not disturb the sound of silence while its precious mainframe was being attacked. After all, the company was positioning itself to succeed in all of the markets that it served. If the mainframe didn't make it, well, it would succeed in another area of big IBM.

As luck would have it--and I mean luck--Lou Gerstner (IBM CEO before Sam Palmisano) sauntered in and changed IBM's outlook about computers altogether. Gerstner acknowledged that IBM had lost the desktop, and declared that the world was server-centric.

John Akers (the CEO before Lou Gerstner) may very well have sold off the mainframe division if he were left around for a few more years. The mainframe was preserved because of its customers. IBM did nothing radical to stave off an attack. IBM did not defend itself. But Gerstner hailed the troops inside realizing that IBM was a server-centric business, and he declared that the mainframe was--you guessed it--a server.

IBM and the AS/400

So far, in three of the four system quadrants, IBM blew opportunities or failed to defend a major revenue source. They blew it in Windows and Unix and were prepared to sell out the mainframe division rather than suggest that maybe the competition was wrong. IBM is three for three before we reach the AS/400. Two opportunities out of three are gone and not coming back, and IBM was willing to give up the third. So what will IBM do about the fourth, the AS/400?

In a few years, will somebody be writing a book about IBM as it is struggling to again surpass the $90 billion mark after losing much of the AS/400 computer marketplace and most of its hardware businsss. ? It is hard to believe that IBM never wanted to own Unix. With a track record that eliminates major opportunities from consideration, it is easy to understand why it appears that the AS/400 in its Power I reincarnation is also on its way out.

Chapter 28 Client/Server and the Internet

IBM Preferred Green Screen

As hard as it is to believe, IBM did not plan its AS/400 to be more than a green-screen business system. The visionaries dreamed too late that the AS/400 would be useful in the client/server and Internet areas. It was not until the mid-1990s that Lou Gerstner insisted that IBM begin to call its big systems "servers." Before then, the uninformed would have easily concluded that IBM made no servers other than PCs. Only after Gerstner arrived was the AS/400 permitted to participate.

Since IBM chooses not to advertise to the common person, how could the world have known that IBM was in the server business unless it called its machines servers and told the world about them. Before 1995, IBM had given Microsoft and Intel a pass, believing that its own PC business was enough to carry the day for IBM in the server space. Intel made the biggest processors for PCs popularly known as servers, notwithstanding the Unix servers.

For far too long, IBM's big boxes were not even in the server game. They were not listed. If you looked up server in the yellow pages because you wanted to buy a modern computer, you would not find IBM's AS/400 or its mainframe line.

Ironically, unlike an entrepreneurial company that remembers when it is bitten, IBM continued to trust Microsoft long after many of IBM's essential parts, including its profits, had been eaten or shipped to Redmond, Washington, home of Microsoft. IBM believed and unfortunately still seems to believe that since it sells Intel and Windows as part of its PC business that these hungry entrepreneurial guys are its partners. Intel and Microsoft on the other hand have a better perspective on reality. They see IBM as a big lumbering, unwary competitor.

IBM: No Need for Internet AS/400

With its RS/6000 in the Internet/Unix space, IBM assumed that it had the technology market covered on both the client server and Internet fronts. Thus, by management decree, IBM chose not to invest development dollars in the AS/400 to give it notable client server or Internet facilities.

No, this was not smart and it followed in the pattern of a number of other IBM product and marketing decisions. Though it was difficult to swallow during the heyday of client server that IBM would purposely keep its AS/400 from being a player, it was even more difficult to understand IBM's insistence that the AS/400 did not have to be equipped for the Internet.

Because the AS/400 did not offer Internet or LAN Server facilities, it looked like a second rate machine to the geeks and nerds who knew the AS/400 was lacking. Unix folks had a great laugh at IBM's expense and they pointed out these Internet failings as representative of why nobody should want an AS/400.

It was a far more serious marketing nightmare for IBM than a technology nightmare. The AS/400 could not support GUI e-mail systems or the new browser based World Wide Web. For a while in the early to mid 1990's it looked like the AS/400 would just fall by the wayside because of IBM's lack of vision and corporate neglect.

While working with IBM customers at the time, it was difficult for me to explain away the lack of a GUI, the lack of file serving, the lack of LAN server abilities, and the lack of Internet capability. Not only was my mission to inform my customers that the AS/400 could not do what they wanted, I also had to tell them that IBM did not believe the box needed these facilities.

After the customer asked me what to do to implement client server or Internet function, my job was to inform these loyal IBM AS/400 customers that they could find these capabilities with another IBM computer box. They were annoyed but they appreciated understanding IBM's posture that their AS/400 systems would not be equipped with the necessary computer capabilities of the day.

IBM Was Dead Wrong

My clients believed IBM was dead wrong about their needs and how they should be satisfied. IBM customers (IT managers and technicians) who attended the independent COMMON user's conference, along with most of the IBM customers of which I was aware, shared this belief. IBM ignored its customers' pleas and remained steadfast that the most advanced computer system of all time, with a price range from $20,000 to $1,000,000, would not be given facilities that were found in machines that cost no more than a few thousand dollars.

I voiced opposition to IBM's plans on many occasions. I sat through many a product positioning presentation in which the company told the field force that the PC was the LAN server and client server, and the RT/PC and RS/6000 were the client/server and Internet machines.

IBM's posture was that if its customers wanted LAN server or client/server capabilities, they should buy an IBM PC. If they wanted to have an Internet Server, they should buy an RS/6000. It was that simple. That's why even today, many AS/400 customers are still behind the curve in the newer technologies needed for e-business. Of course along the way, IBM sold its PC business and its PC Server business to Lenovo so pushing PCs v IBM's own AS/400 does not seem like a good idea in retrospect.

IBM guessed wrong about its AS/400 customers. The company was creating future competition by placing Windows boxes and Unix boxes in their most loyal AS/400 accounts. When IBM sold its PC businesses, its customers had already been trained to use Wintel systems made by non-IBM sources.

It appeared convenient at the time for IBM that the company just happened to sell PC Servers, LAN Operating Systems, and Internet capable machines. Therefore, good old IBM saw no reason to develop these things on an AS/400 or even on million-dollar mainframes, since they already had products in the stable that would do the job. The part IBM missed was that IBM's loyal customers bought Sun Unix boxes and clone PCs, rather than again trust IBM to help them.

No Plug-and-Play

If Unix boxes and Windows server machines were easy to set up and make functional, IBM's decision might have been acceptable to some of its AS/400 customers. However, AS/400 shops needed completely different skills to work with Windows and Unix and they resented IBM for not bringing the technology to their platform.

Many IBM customers reminded me of the pre-purchase AS/400 meetings when the IBM sales team had convinced them that the AS/400 was the most powerful and most sophisticated machine in existence and their million dollars would be well spent.

So what happened to these customers who had unmet technical needs? If they were very loyal, we (that is, IBM in the early 1990s) would try to get them to use an inferior product that ran on the AS/400.

If this worked, then they would not need Unix servers or Windows servers but they would suffer from slow performance or lack of full functionality. At the time, there was a product on the AS/400 for casual file and print serving, known as *PC Support*. It was primitive and slow, but it worked. Some AS/400 shops were so adamant about not bringing in another system that this "satisfied" their needs.

If the customer needed e-mail or Internet access, they had to go someplace else. The IBM recommendation was typically an IBM RS/6000 or a Windows server. The more technically savvy the account, the less they relied on IBM systems engineers to bail them out of technical issues.

So, the more technical savvy AS/400 shops began to put in Unix boxes for Internet access and email and they began to put in Windows machines for rapid file and print serving. IBM mistakenly thought it would get the PC business. In most cases, the IBM Company was the last vendor considered for PCs.

Who Buys IBM PCs?

Just because until just a few years ago, IBM sold Windows boxes and Unix boxes did not mean that its customers bought IBM PCs and/or IBM Unix machines. In more cases than not, the customer found a less expensive solution for the function than the IBM system that was proposed. Compaq and Sun were great competitors at the time and they beat IBM in the marketplace.

Sometimes, the customers got so upset that IBM chose not to provide its AS/400 with the necessary function; they did not even bother asking IBM to bid. IBM took an extremely loyal set of customers and forced them to meet and greet the competition. This was not a smart marketing move.

Once a customer began to shop instead of call IBM for its needs, the next batch of PCs came from Compaq, rather than IBM, and the next set of terminals came from Perl or WYSE or some other non-IBM source. By not having what was needed when it was needed, IBM sales in these accounts suffered and IBM lost its most favored vendor status. The customer was no longer king to IBM and very shortly thereafter the reverse became just as true. IBM was no longer king in its customers' eyes.

No Marketing Force

To make matters worse, in the early 1990s IBM decided that it no longer wanted to have a direct marketing force for anything other than extremely large customers. Some of my customers with million-dollar installations with four or five AS/400s were included in the no-support list. Without announcing it to customers, one day the company pulled the plug on its technical force.

Actually it was over the course of about two years, from 1991 through 1993, using retirement incentives first, followed by devaluing employee appraisals, and ending with a process called surplussing, IBM shrank its marketing and technical field force.

Eventually, IBM began to lay off employees all over the company. Unlike a union shop, the layoffs were permanent. IBM employees were wholesale being fired. By 1994, there were no systems engineers in the branch offices to help customers deal with the lack of product capabilities. I saw the handwriting and after landing a great position, I took IBM's best retirement option. I exited at the end of June 1992.

While IBM was chucking its sales force in the early to mid 1990s some customers did not learn for several years that their representatives–their marketing representative and systems engineer--were no longer with the company. One day, the customer picked up the phone and the extension was no longer active. IBM never announced its field support dissolution to its customers.

No decision maker in IBM wanted to be associated with the announcement of the dissipation of the sales force. They remembered the IBM president of the mainframe (data processing) division, whose name was Buck Rodgers. Buck announced unbundling as a strategic IBM move on June 23, 1969, the day I began my IBM career. In essence IBM's customers were henceforward to pay for IBM support. They never really did. Yet IBM never formally recanted.

Meanwhile, Buck Rodgers, who was very Watsonesque in his approach to business, never got to be IBM president. Buck never got to be IBM chairman of the board. More importantly, Buck never got to make another decision of consequence. IBM buried him. He appeared after a few years as the perennial guest executive speaker at IBM's annual recognition events. No IBM manager wanted to be a Buck Rodgers.

IBM demonstrated that you could not make a bad decision, take credit for it, and survive. So IBM never announced to its customers that it had eliminated its sales force. And no IBM executive from that day forward had the guts to make a real decision and take credit for it.

Dennis Grimes Sr., who passed away a few years back, was very astute. I can recall him asking his son Dennis, who was an IBM systems engineer like me, why IBM would get rid of a salesman? His assumption, as most would be, was that sales personnel do not get paid if they do not sell. So why not have lots of them? None of us understood why IBM got rid of its salesmen. The money that the company gave to business partners for fewer results was substantially more than IBM ever paid the local sales teams.

IBM Created Computer Shoppers

So IBM customers, left on their own, became better shoppers. Jiminy Cricket was no longer there telling them to buy all IBM. Some shops had enough of the IBM way and switched to Unix. Unix, of course, is the revered operating system of the technogeeks. You may know who they are. You've met them in college and afterward at cocktail parties. They live and breathe computers. They are typically very smart, and they can make a computer do things that nobody would ever expect.

But most of the things that they make computers do have no practical value, and if you could figure out how they did their work, you would not want to. Unix folks have lots of fun with their Unix boxes--about as much fun as folks do who like bowling or golfing, or happy hour.

IBM's AS/400 customers overall felt cheated by the new IBM that emerged in John Akers' early 1990s. When customers invested $100,000 to $1,000,000 for their computer systems, they did not expect to be asked for more nickels and dimes for small stuff.

Because there was no client/server or Internet facilities provided with this big, expensive AS/400, it meant IBM customers had to buy a $5,000 to $20,000 machine to do things that the big do-everything machine was supposed to do. Moreover, IBM's AS/400 customer technical shops had especially avoided low end PCs like the plague. They did not have the skills in-house to run Novell or Windows Servers or Unix Servers with native Internet capabilities.

PCs Became Important

CFOs and business managers who witnessed this phenomenon did not know how to cope with it. Should they force their AS/400 team to learn and embrace new PC technology? Most chose not to do this. Rather than fight the culture, they stopped giving the full IT budget to the IT staff and held some back for departments to buy their own PCs. Eventually little islands of computing, outside the control of IT emerged in many organizations. As these islands grew, the departments demanded support.

In some cases, IT had to accept the burden. In others, a parallel and costly support structure was formed. One thing was for certain. When it came to buying PCs, the departments did not buy from IBM. The IT budget remained constant for the most part in these shops. Thus, IBM's move to not provide needed capabilities cost the company lots in future revenue. IBM would never recover from this.

Once John Akers was ousted and Lou Gerstner came in, new thinking came. Gerstner was a computer outsider, so he saw things more like my neighbors and I would. Gerstner must have gone nuts finding out that all IBM's servers were not Internet capable. In Gerstner's world, computing was supposed to be done on the servers since that's where IBM made its money. He was smart. He believed that if a system could not work on the Internet, it wasn't even worth having.

How did a tobacco and candy guy know intuitively what the prior chairman, John Akers, with all his years of mainframe management, never learned? Until Gerstner showed up, IBM dug in and insisted that its AS/400 was a production system and needed no Internet or client/server capabilities. It's hard to believe today. Believe me, it was hard for us to believe as it was happening. But the correction was not made overnight, and the effects continue to be felt in AS/400 shops today.

Chapter 29 The Birth and Death of IBM Word Processing

IBM Invented Word Processing

One day in early 1977, before the System/38 was announced, one of my customers, Kay Wholesale, was at the IBM Bethlehem, Pennsylvania, branch office with me, attending a seminar. Al Komorek was Kay's programmer/analyst at the time, and Jim Sheehan was the DP manager. These were the types of titles that folks carried back then. Eppy Harding, the marketing rep, had cautioned me about Jack Flynn and IBM customer visits to Bethlehem. Jack was the IBM Bethlehem Branch Manager. He was quite a gentleman. Jack could not only sell icicles to Eskimos, he was also a very personable and likeable guy.

While I was busy in another area of the building, Jack shanghaied my customer and took the two unsuspecting blokes into a pristine room that had three devices inside. There was a new 6240 Magnetic Card Selectric Typewriter (MCST), an Electronic Selectric Composer, and an IBM Memory Typewriter.

When the two were finally released to me they told me they had some fun. Jack had been very cordial to them. They said that Jack Flynn was very proud of his "word processing center," as he called it, and he thought they would be duly impressed. They were not as impressed with the equipment as they were with Jack Flynn. They thought he had shown them three big typewriters. The boys were ready to buy something, but the System/38 would not be announced for still another year.

IBM coined the term and invented the whole notion of word processing in 1964. The company deployed the same type of logic chips that were in the System/360 to produce the first Magnetic Tape Selectric Typewriter (MTST). MTST units were in every IBM sales office pounding out boilerplate for proposals until the first MCST was introduced in 1969.

These units permitted documents to be stored on tape or on magnetic cards for later playback and revision. With the typical book-sized customer proposals that had to be done and the pages of boilerplate necessary to complete them, these early word processors were put to good use by the IBM sales offices.

The Electric Typewriter Company

Before these word processing units became available, IBM was the champion of the infamous Selectric (electric with the selectric ball) typewriters. The company used a direct sales force for this mission. IBM typewriters cost about as much as PCs do today, and were viewed as essential in every business. The direct sales force happened to be the best looking people in IBM. IBM had no such standards for the computer division.

After all, even I was hired. But these OP (office products) guys, as we called them, were just plain slick. They were without question the best pure sales people in the office. One particular OP salesman was so good at the game that he later left for a more difficult territory. He became a door-to-door encyclopedia salesman. I rest my case about how good these folks were at pure sales.

When I joined IBM in 1969, IBM had been known for keeping its technology around too long and not innovating enough. Though first in word processing, and clearly the company with the most installed typewriters in the world, in the 1970s IBM fell behind in its own technology, and later made some decisions that just did not make sense. This all contributed to the demise of the Office Products Division in IBM, and it contributed to IBM losing the entire word processing and office marketplace.

The Leader Falls Behind

For example, in 1972, long after IBM's early innovations, Lexitron and Linolex developed a word processing system that was everything the MTST was, plus it included a video display screen and normal tape cassettes for storage. This was revolutionary. With the video screen, typing could be entered and corrected without having to produce a hard copy. Printing could be delayed until the writer was fully satisfied with the material. Though IBM created the market, it did not know what it had. Just like IBM did not think that client/server or Internet capabilities were necessary for the AS/400, the company did not see the use of CRTs in word processing. At this time, IBM was years away from CRT-driven word processing.

Though IBM had invented the 8" floppy disk, for use in its data processing computers, in 1973, Vydec was the first to use these same floppy disks in its word processing systems. IBM persisted in using tape and magnetic card facilities in its hard copy units and eventually built an incompatible small disk for the IBM Office System/6.

In 1977, Wang introduced the first computerized word processor, which was priced at $30,000. Considering that IBM had its System/38 under wraps at the time and the System/34 was just announced, and IBM's largest customers were looking for big-time computer-style word processing, and IBM was recognized as the premiere computer and word processing company in the world, it is hard to fathom how Big Blue let Wang beat it to market. Wang not only beat IBM to market but also quickly became known as *the* word processing company. IBM had failed to tell the world that it had invented word processing. Moreover, IBM did not trademark the term when it could have.

Just as in PCs, databases, data communications and so many other areas. IBM was the leader but fell behind trying to wring the last dollar from its older technology, and from not looking ahead. Recognizing that the CRT had become the in-thing in word processing, in 1977 finally IBM introduced its Office System/6, which had a small, System/32-sized (480 character) CRT as a standard feature.

Unfortunately, it had another incompatible medium, the small special disk noted above. In 1979, the company introduced its DisplayWriter stand-alone word processing system. This unit used a CRT that was the size of the System/34 terminal that was also introduced that year. .

Though the DisplayWriter used the same 8" diskettes, as did the IBM systems of the day, IBM's Office Lab in Austin, Texas, chose to make its format incompatible with the company's standard format for system products such as the System/32 and the System/34. This made it difficult to perform database and document merges with IBM's own systems.

With the late 1970s introduction of a multi-station unit called the IBM 5520, the company was able to catch up and pass the competition, including Wang. Though the IBM workstation was the best in the business at the time, Wang had already passed IBM in terms of mindshare, and it remained as the "go to" company for word processing. IBM chose not to tell the public about its superior technology. Again, IBM was preparing to fail in an industry that it had created. The DisplayWriter and the 5520 were the last major word processing innovations developed by IBM.

It's Been the Marketing for a Long Time, IBM

Just as IBM failed to advertise the AS/400 to its potential customers, the company failed miserably in promoting its DisplayWriter and its 5520 systems, both of which were exceptional for their place in history. But word processing was not a standstill marketplace. Yet, IBM chose to stand still after these innovations. The company was always a day late and a dollar short on word processing from this time forward.

Observing that Wang had taken a business computer and had modified it to be a word processor, in the mid-1980s, eight years after Wang's breakthrough, IBM felt that it could do the same. Through offerings on mainframe, System/36, and later the AS/400, such as OfficeVision and Distributed Office System Support (DISOSS), and by devising document content and document exchange architectures, such as Revised Form Text (RFT) and Final Form Text (FFT), IBM focused on making its systems the center of the word processing universe. Unfortunately for Big Blue, IBM's customers had better ideas.

With the PC in full view, IBM also decided that the IBM PC would become its major typing head in the same universe. Though this was a good vision, the follow-up and the follow-on products again were second rate and it was easy for the competition to outclass and out market IBM in word processing. For example IBM never enhanced its DisplayWrite PC program to give it a GUI or easily handle display fonts and thus it stopped being WYSIWYG as documents became more complex.

IBM Prepares to Lose in Word Processing

Shortly after the PC came out in 1981, IBM prematurely discontinued its DisplayWriter stand-alone word processor product and substituted a PC software package noted above called DisplayWrite as a take off on the DisplayWriter. My customers fumed about the inadequacies of this PC package, compared with the nice engraved keys and easy function of the real word processor. IBM would no longer sell them the DisplayWriter.

IBM met evolutionary challenges with revolutionary decisions and tried to force its customers into new technology before the right products were actually ready. As one would expect, this customer-oriented arrogance chased many customers away over the years. There are lots of people out there who continue to say that they hate IBM. AS/400 customers are now in the on-deck circle.

At the same time that IBM was aggravating its customers, Microsoft and many other word processing software vendors were ready to steal them all. They entered the foray and their offerings were immediately better than DisplayWrite.

Though it was a while for DisplayWrite software to finally bite the dust, by the time it was discontinued in the early 1990s it seemed that IBM had let every other word processing vendor outclass its word processing products in terms of features, functions, look and feel.

If IBM had planned to give away the marketplace, it could not have executed a course of action as precisely as it did to achieve the complete loss of this lucrative industry.

The Blind Visionaries

In trying to understand how this could happen, it helps to note that IBM's visionaries had predicted that there would be a mere 275,000 PCs sold in the first five years of its existence. Computerland itself ordered 250,000 units the first day. As we all know, tens of millions of PCs are sold each year, and in the early days, IBM seemed to be the only company that could not ship a PC in a reasonable time.

By missing the forecast by a hundred-fold margin, clueless IBM was never able to gain the manufacturing/assembly facilities or outsourcing vendors necessary to bring deliveries to a reasonable level. In frustration, IBM customers who never had bought any other computer than IBM went looking for a PC from whoever could get them one.

Not understanding the tremendous irritation that it was causing its customers, IBM executives compounded the problem with more rules than any IBM employee or customer wanted to deal with. For example, the customers I supported had purchased everything from IBM, from RPG coding sheets to terminals to systems.

Yet, IBM executives ruled that they would not be permitted to buy PCs directly from the local office in the fashion that they purchased everything else from IBM. IBM would not permit easy purchases even if the PCs were going to be used as terminals to a new system that a customer was just purchasing. In essence IBM sales people had to tell their customers to buy IBM units from someplace else.

This was very disruptive and very annoying to customers. It not only hurt PC sales, it made customers want to buy everything computer related from somebody else with a passion. Because of the PC debacle and the trauma and irritation it caused loyal customers, from that point on, IBM's direct sales force had to work for sales. The easy pickings that had come in as annuities in the past were no longer a sure thing. As we say in the business, IBM stopped getting the low-lying fruit

If there were a way to chase away a customer, IBM would think of it, and implement it as another market efficiency. IBM basically told its customers that it did not have time for the small stuff, and it forced them to go out of their shops to face the aggravation of the crowds in the few computer outlets that sold IBM.

Moreover, when the local IBM office sent a prospect to Computerland or Entré in the early days, they were sold very little IBM. The PC machine they got had very little IBM in it. Sometimes the only part that was IBM was the small logo on the front. The logos were easier to get than PCs. IBM lost billions through its carelessness with its customers and its sloppiness in dealing with its "independent" retail outlets.

The clone industry was an industry waiting to happen, thanks to IBM's mishandling of every aspect of its PC business, as well as its vaunted word processing business. As soon as the clone manufacturers made it easy for IBM customers to buy non-IBM PCs, IBM no longer got the PC business. Then IBM no longer got the terminal business. Then IBM no longer got the printer business. Then IBM no longer got the tape business. Then IBM no longer got the disk business. Then IBM almost went out of business. Then Lou Gerstner saved the company.

It Was Not Just Poor Vision

Through poor vision, poor planning, and poor execution, IBM did not know how to handle the PC as the replacement product for its typewriters. I have often speculated about what would have happened if IBM had not disbanded the OP Division in the early 1980s and instead used this group of distinguished sales people to sell PCs as replacements for typewriters. They were the best pure samesmen in IBM.

Instead of not permitting customers to buy from the local branches, IBM should have enabled their elite OP marketing team to handle this new wealth of customers. These pros knew the office products better than anybody and they had all the right customer contacts. Moreover, IBM's branch office customers were crying for an IBM person to come to take their orders so they did not have to go to a computer store.

Instead, IBM forced them into the stores by refusing to take their orders. After going to the stores a few times, as one would expect, their IBM loyalty dropped off the scales. When the surprise was gone that the clone boxes actually worked, customer dependence on the rest of IBM also waned.

If IBM had used some finesse and style and the down-home approach of the OP salespeople, instead of aggravating its loyal customers, the company would still have a big chunk of the word processing software industry and IBM today would be the dominant player in the $500 billion PC industry.

If IBM used this natural evolutionary approach to achieve success in the PC area, the same IBM would be doing what is necessary to lock in and capture the whole small and midrange server marketplace with its AS/400 offering.

IBM believed it could not afford these crackerjack sales people. The fact that IBM has no real share of this multi-hundred billion-dollar market today is a testament that that IBM could not afford to let these sales people go. Yet, they let them go.

IBM had a captive market in typewriters until well into the 1980s. The PC was destined to be a success if only IBM saw it as a typewriter replacement and planned it properly. The PC was the natural single station replacement for word processing and IBM owned all the PCs in the beginning.

Instead of acting rationally, IBM executed its own game plan and then was surprised that its word processing systems, software, and PCs had stopped selling, while the clone business was mushrooming and creating new billionaires. As an IBM stockholder, IBM executives' failure to execute in each opportunity area is enough for me to vote them out of office for each lost market that they caused the company. As we are now witnessing with the AS/400, IBM executives have not yet finished making costly mistakes.

AS/400 Word Processing

In 1988, IBM still did not have its word processing game straightened out. The company began to think that big computers, such as the AS/400 were going to do well in the Word Processing game, even though there was no GUI. So IBM built a new set of word processing software that was going to run on all its platforms. As noted above, it was called OfficeVision. The AS/400 was equipped with its brand of OfficeVision right from the start, in June 1988. Its nickname was OV/400.

PC word-processing packages were beginning to get GUI and WYSIWYG interfaces and Windows was just around the corner. Yet, IBM persisted in putting green screen word processing via terminals on its largest systems, including the AS/400.

Overall, OfficeVision was successful because it did some things such as mail merges better than any other platform, but word processing was at best ugly using the AS/400, and at worst, it was lacking in function. Moreover, there were no high quality high-speed printers for the AS/400 systems to keep up with all the output that could be produced, and there were no inexpensive laser printers. HP quickly filled the void on the small side with their LaserJet technology while Printronix and others were able to outclass IBM's larger printers in creating near letter quality and barcode-capable units.

By the time the year 2000 was rolling along, nobody was putting in OfficeVision, but a lot of companies were still using it for mail merges and email. Just like IBM tried to move DisplayWriter customers to DisplayWrite and they would not budge; and just like IBM tried to move System/36 customers to AS/400 and they would not budge, and just like IBM had tried to move AS/400 programmers to Java and they would not budge, IBM had been trying since 1996 to get its OV/400 customers to move to Lotus Notes and then to Domino. But, again, many would not budge.

So in another move that infuriated its customers, in the late 1990s IBM announced that it would no longer support OfficeVision/400 as of a certain day. IBM's customers complained because Domino did not have a solution for the merge problem and Domino was not a word processor. IBM relented and extended the deadline by one year, and then, on schedule, eliminated the OV/400 product from its product line and support structure.

Now, there are just about zero AS/400 shops that run OfficeVision. IBM withdrew the product and if it isrunning anywhere today it is not supported by IBM. They resented what IBM did to them. They were forced to use older machines and older versions of the operating system because IBM took out the support for OfficeVision as promised in the current operating system releases.

As you would expect, these agitated customers who bit and IBM switched, have not been inclined to listen to IBM again about its best approaches for their businesses. Since IBM is not asking new clients to buy its AS/400 line anymore, these customers are not likely to hear IBM asking them anything anyway.

All the Cards, Played Poorly

It is a historical marvel as you review the innovations of IBM in word processing. IBM did not invent the electric typewriter, but the company perfected it. IBM invented word processing; coined the term word processing, and invented the PC. Somehow, of all the companies that should have known, IBM failed to recognize that the PC would be used for word processing and then when it did, the company had already fired or relocated its crackerjack sales force that could have won the market for them.

Today, IBM has no word processing business, other than a token attempt to keep Lotus WordPro alive, and a rejiggered Open Office version called Symphony. the company has lost most of the PC business. Lotus Domino is not word processing, in case you were wondering. It is a framework and its principal use has been for e-mail. So, now, how would IBM's OV/400 users get their mail merges done by going to Domino? They couldn't, and that's why many chose not to go.

There seems to be a pattern of IBM failures, product shortcomings, premature product abandonment, poor forecasting, and customers begging for help to a deaf ear -- throughout the history of word processing on the AS/400 until its death a year or so ago.

With all the begging, one thing remains a constant. IBM did not listen to its customers. It continues to behave as if it knows what is best -- but judging by its record, it not only does not know what is best for its customers, it doesn't even know what is best for IBM stockholders.

Through all the begging that IBM AS/400 customers did to get IBM's attention, or to do this or to do that; asking IBM to market and advertise its AS/400 product line, unlike a real marketing company, IBM ignored their message to the Company's own peril. .

Chapter 30 It's No Longer Watson's IBM

Nothing Great Lasts Forever

There is no doubt that there is a new IBM today, compared with the IBM that Thomas Watson Sr. forged almost 100 years ago. Though its roots spring back to the 1890s, the 20th century IBM began in 1915, when Thomas J. Watson Sr. became its president after 11 months as general manager.

A Watson ran the IBM that we know from then until T. Vincent Learson took over a year after Thomas Waston Jr. suffered a heart attack. Learson was a great friend of Watson, and his brief 18-month stint was more of a continuation of a Watson than the dawning of a new era.

However, when Frank Cary became chairman, in 1973, IBM did enter a new era. The company had been aggressive in the same fashion as Microsoft's early years. There was no such thing as an unimportant sale, and there was no such thing as a good competitor. Thomas Watson Sr. was the consummate manager and marketer, while Watson Jr. was much more Gates-ish, and he took some enormous risks for the ultimate benefit of the company.

When the Watsons disappeared, IBM became less agile, more sluggish and less sure and less capable of moving or sustaining a marketing battle. Besides not being as business savvy or entrepreneurial, once the Watson's were gone, the new IBM's notion of people orientation was more of a paper thing than a real thing.

Wild Ducks Are Welcome

Tom Watson Sr. had set IBM up as a company that cared about its people and their families. Watson Jr. carried on that tradition. My most favorite Watson story has to do with Thomas J. Jr.'s notion of wild ducks.

In his book *A Business and Its Beliefs: The Ideas That Helped Build IBM (*McGraw Hill, 1963), Thomas Watson Jr. described his business philosophies. Among these was the notion that if you take care of the people, the people will take care of the business. Watson meant it.

He was known and loved by mostly all employees during his term with IBM. He was especially fond of people who today we would say, "Think out of the box." Watson called them "wild ducks," and did his best to preserve the notion of wild ducks in his time with IBM. In his book, he writes:

> **"In IBM, we frequently refer to our need for 'wild ducks.' The moral is drawn from a story by the Danish philosopher Soren Kierkegaard. He told of a man on the coast of New Zealand who liked to watch the wild ducks fly south in great flocks each fall. "Out of charity, he took to putting feed for them in a nearby pond. After a while, some of the ducks no longer bothered to fly south; they wintered in Denmark on what he fed them.**
>
> **"In time, they flew less and less. When the wild ducks returned, the others would circle up to greet them but then head back to their feeding grounds on the pond. After three or four years, they grew so lazy and fat that they found difficulty in flying at all**
>
> **"Kierkegaard drew his point--you can make wild ducks tame, but you can never make tame ducks wild again. One might also add that the duck, who is tamed will never go anywhere any more.**
>
> **"We are convinced that any business needs its wild ducks. And, in IBM, we try not to tame them."**

The Irreplaceable Thomas J. Watson Jr.

On the wall in my sunroom, since 1994, I have had a page from the January 5, 1994, *Wall Street Journal* pinned up. It was cut out and hand delivered to me by my good friend and neighbor John Anstett. After a few years as a Christmas gift, my adult children had it framed for me.

Lou Gerstner's IBM remembered Thomas Watson Jr. with a magnificent tribute, a full page memorial to the wonderful man and great corporate leader, Thomas Watson Jr. My sunroom continues to be graced with this picture of the IBM person that I admire the most, though I never met him. The IBM tribute to Thomas J. Watson Jr. was as good as anything that was ever said about anybody. Thank you, IBM, for your caring and thoughtfulness in this regard: Under his picture, the tribute reads as follows:

"For all his achievements –
as a visionary, entrepreneur, corporate leader
and distinguished statesman, --
we will remember Thomas J. Watson, Jr. most
for his adventurous spirit,
his innate sense of fair play,
and the vigor of his friendship.
We mourn his passing
but we will be forever grateful that he lived".

[*Wall Street Journal*, Wed. Jan.5, 1994, Final Tribute to TJ Watson Jr., 1914 to 1993] Picture from Wall Street Journal shown in Figure 30-1

Figure 30-1 Thomas J. Watson Jr.'s Picture in IBM's Final Tribute

I loved the Watson-era IBM. I felt good working for the Watson IBM. Though starched white shirts were the order of the day at IBM in those days--and I wore mine with delight--there was tremendous pride and caring for every employee. And every employee knew the train of care did not stop until it reached the very top. Watson's IBM! That's the IBM I joined. I still miss those days.

That was the old IBM. The new IBM took awhile to take effect. Though we may speculate that it was from Frank Cary, 1973 onward, the new IBM appeared for all to see in the very early 1990s. It could no longer be hidden from public scrutiny. Seemingly, from out of nowhere, little things started to happen in the company that showed that all ducks, both wild and tame, were no longer as important to IBM. None were safe from the new IBM's employee axe.

The first signs were quite innocuous. For example, for years, IBM deposited my paycheck or gave me a check several days before the pay period ended. I can recall telling my dad about that when I was first hired. He thought that it was wonderful. I thought it was wonderful.

At the brewery where he worked, he had to wait until the Thursday after to get his weekly paycheck. Then, one day, in the 1980s, without announcement, my paycheck arrived right on time and not a minute earlier. It was that way from then on. It was not a big deal. But it signified a big change.

One another day in the late 1980s, IBM announced that it was concerned about the cost of healthcare as it affected the company. At the time, no employee contributed for healthcare in any way, and retirees' healthcare was just as good. IBM announced that it would pay no more than a specified amount for healthcare forever. It would never again be adjusted for inflation.

It was unprecedented, but it was representative of the new IBM. Because of this change, more and more of the cost of healthcare began to be born by employees and retirees. Before joining Medicare, after being retired for four years, the cost of my part of IBM healthcare had gone up to $18,000. It was as if I had no pension

For some retirees, healthcare has eaten up a lot more than half of their retirement income. Some specifics about IBM's change regarding healthcare are included at the end of this chapter.

The new IBM seemed not to have time or money to care about unimportant things like employee or retiree well-being as long as the accounting was good and it favored the company. For some this may not be a big deal, but for

IBMers who had trusted IBM with sixteen-hour days waiting for their day in the sun, it is a very big deal, and it signified a new hardened and impersonal IBM.

It is the kind of IBM of which even IBMers are no longer proud. It's sure not a Watson-like IBM. Though the new IBM "caretakers" undoubtedly feel that they pulled one over on the employees and former employees by substantially reducing their expectations, these new IBM executives will leave behind a legacy that was unknown to the Watsons. It will be one with few kind words written about them.

There are hundreds of thousands of IBM people who sacrificed family time and gave it all to the company only to find that the new IBM stopped caring and for apparent corporate profits, began to work to minimize their reward. Ironically, the new IBM seems to be working harder to claim large sums from its retirees than it is to increasing its product sales.

More Was Wrong Than Obvious

In 1992, Chairman John Akers had the company on a path to no place. He was in the process of dismantling what seemed to be everything that he could find. Nothing was sacred from the ax of Akers. The IBM Company, prior to 1992, had a strictly adhered to a "no layoff" policy. Nobody of whom I am aware ever got laid off for any period whatsoever.

If you were asked to not come to work on a given day, you would not be back. You were fired and more than likely, there was good reason. But even at that, it took several levels of management to be able to fire an employee. Watson's IBM felt that it hired right and it did not want first line managers to have simple hire and fire discretion over employees.

By 1992, John Akers began to view these "policies" more as HR practices, which they technically always had been. Therefore, he was not compelled to follow them. Rather than be the first CEO to have a formal layoff in IBM, however, Akers paid lip service to the practices.

Yet to avoid a losing year, he needed an involuntary reduction in force. He decided to reduce IBM's headcount the only way current practices permitted. He approved a plan that appeared to employees as a rigging of the appraisal system.

Rather than tapping somebody on the sleeve and laying them off because the company had to cut its workforce, Akers' IBM changed its practice of giving employees six months to improve when performance was "no longer up to par." He reduced the period to two months but it was merely a ruse for a layoff. Some managers recommended employees caught in this trap to use the two months to get another job rather than "try to improve."

The company also began to reduce appraisal levels universally and managers across the world were forced to rid the company of the lowest ranked employees in each location. But there still was no mechanism for a mass layoff, because Akers would not admit that it was a reduction in force. Therefore, there had to be a concocted reason for each dismissal. From my eyes, first-line management was encouraged to lie about employees' performance in order to fire them. IBM had become a corrupt company when dealing with its own employees. Lying was not out of the question.

The employees were not let in on the specifics of the deal. Good employees out of the blue were placed on the two-month improvement program but they were never permitted to improve. They were on their way out the door. IBM was only kidding about the two-month improvement program.

Once tapped, you were gone, but IBM would not tell its employees that was the case. They were never told. I saw terrific employees embarrassed at having their appraisals lowered and then thinking that it was for real, going through the further embarrassing improvement interviews to rescue their job after they had in fact been eliminated.

IBM was as cruel as I had seen any company ever be. Employees were crying and left without dignity, thinking that they had become poor performers rather than thinking that IBM had a layoff and merely could not afford to keep them.

In my case, I took a nice package called the Individual Retirement Option II in 1992. The package was just great. I was just a kid and just barely qualified on time. I did not know at the time how poorly Akers was managing IBM's assets, but I knew he was not offering much leadership.

I put some job feelers out, not really expecting to get what I wanted. A small college carved out a job for me and pressed me to take it. It seemed ideal so I decided to take IBM's leave of absence package offering. I got the job and life was good for me after IBM.

Over the next few years, the IBM field force was mostly eliminated via attrition and through a process that was implemented after I left called "surplussing." Through the surplus mechanism, IBMers were fired for IBM reasons and the employee was not made to feel that he or she was the blame. It was much less nasty than the older way. Other companies would simply call it a layoff.

My observations of IBM from then until now are that nobody is assured of anything at IBM. Thus IBM is no longer ensured of the same degree of loyalty that it once enjoyed from its "family." I now see bottom-line decisions affecting people all the time in IBM. From the decimation of Endicott just a few years ago to the security guards coming to Burlington, Vermont, just this year and escorting half of the workforce from the building as if they were criminals. Now, the IBM Rochester Plant is basically gone. I don't think either of the Thomas Watsons would approve.

Fire 5,000 + to Hire 5,000 +

In late 2003, IBM got some bad press as speculation about its sending 5,000 white-collar jobs overseas ran rampant on the news and in IBM circles. Obviously, IBM employees are upset about this, but it says a lot about the new IBM.

American Employees no longer seem to matter as much. People no longer seem to matter. Customers no longer seem to matter. It is understood that IBM is a multi-national company. However, leaving 5,000 employees out of work so that 5,000 other employees can be hired for one-third the cost does not list high on the human list, no matter what country is on the "from" or "to" side of the equation. Today's “to” country is destined to be tomorrow's “from” country as even cheaper sources of labor can be trained. The new IBM is very quiet about the consequences of all this.

Chapter 31 Is the Integrated AS/400 Dying?

Not on Anyone's Mind

If the AS/400 is A-okay, why is it that so many people are still asking if it is dead? Why is that even a topic? Is the AS/400 dead? From a mindshare perspective, it sure is. As far as most minds go, the AS/400 has little share. For example, my wonderful neighbors, who are all small-business people, know nothing about it. So to them, it's not just dead; it was never even born. It only occupied their minds for years when they knew that I was working someplace on the weekends, and we could not enjoy one another's company.

Besides making the platform better known for mindshare purposes, IBM needs to attract young programmers to the AS/400 platform by making it attractive to them. If IBM can't make it attractive, perhaps the company can remove the obstacles to learning the machine and remove the stigma of working on a dying platform. IBM can sure do this if it chooses.

AS/400 Folks Are Old, Windows Is Young?

To help get us thinking, I have a few questions that I ask myself. First of all, why would anybody with real blood in his veins want to stagnate with a seemingly dying computer system? Wouldn't a new entrant in the technology world have to be coerced to engage an AS/400? When I go to AS/400 user group meetings, every person is 50 or older. There is lots of white and gray on top, and for some the grass on top of their heads is completely gone.

However, when I sneak into a Microsoft sponsored session, the attendees are mostly under 30, and though I hate to admit it, there are lots more people there than at a similar AS/400 event. So the people who make no creaks and sighs when they get up and down from their seats seem to be happy with Bill Gates and Windows. It makes sense, since he makes the only system that most people even know about.

Why is there no new blood in the AS/400 area? There could be lots of reasons. (See Chapter titled "*Teach Me! Teach Me! Teach Me!*") IBM surely does not promote the box so that an aspiring programmer would ever notice that it exists. In fact if a lawyer were able to fully observe IBM's treatment of the AS/400 it would be prima facie evidence that the AS/400 must have some kind of terminal disease.

That's what causes the industry and IBM's own customers to ask all too regularly if the system is dead or dying. From a marketing perspective, if IBM were the only doctor in town, and if the AS/400 were the patient, we'd be calling in a mortician by now.

RPG Is Bad Bad Bad?

Those with a computer science background would suggest that the AS/400 is dead because its primary language, RPG, is as dead as the Dead Sea Scrolls. They would add that RPG's cohort in crime, COBOL, has had one foot in the grave for the last 20 years. The student of computer science today finds his techno-haven in Unix and Linux technology.

Those who don't fare well in the more challenging "ix" operating systems quickly gravitate to Windows, a land in which even computer dimwits appear to be smart to business managers. As I recall in my one conversation with Bill Gates, in the late 1980s, he was not a proponent of RPG and used the term "yuck" and the "language with the indicators" as his best description of RPG. I am sure you can appreciate my appreciation of such an open mind.

Was it Bill Gates who started the "AS/400 is dying" rumors? I really don't think so. He's sure crafty enough to have kicked off the campaign, but I just don't think so. However, I'd bet that he or his marketing miffintiffs had something to do with the misbranding of the AS/400, the mainframe, and IBM's Unix machines as "legacy." Now, that's a marketing coup.

Mr. Gates must be enjoying that most people in technology these days seem to understand Windows, while only a small portion know Unix and an infinitesimal portion have heard of the AS/400. With that type of awareness, maybe it would be okay if everybody knew that the AS/400 was a "legacy" system. At least they would have heard of it.

Squashing Bad Rumors About Important Things

Unlike IBM's reaction to all of its bad street news, If Bill Gates heard a rumor that Windows were dying, he would not just sit by and see what developed. "Yo, What's happening, man?" You and I both know that Bill gates would personally confront the situation and do what he had to until he was satisfied that the rumor was long gone. Judging from IBM's response to every negative label that has been placed on its systems, one could logically conclude that IBM feels the same way as the rumor indicates. Forget about Carmen San Diego; where is Sam Palmisano?

IBM offers no rebuttal to an industry press engaged in branding sabotage. The term "legacy" system burns AS/400 IT managers almost as much as IBM's response or lack thereof. RPG and COBOL are just a few more things that the Windows mongers can pick on, since they know, by recent history, that IBM will just let it happen without a whimper.

With both the AS/400 and the RPG language taking it on the chin by the computer science gurus and the Windows weenies, it serves as a double whammy for a bright young person to want to learn, either. There is always a splashy language du jour such as Pascal, C, C++, and now Java for the Unix geeks and Windows nerds to ram at the AS/400 aficionado.

The only advantage that I can see, however, for writing in one of those languages is that the number of completed programs would grow much more slowly because those languages are substantially more difficult and very inappropriate for business use. This would thereby lessen the program maintenance burden of the future. It takes lots longer to write business programs in a non-business language, so over time there would be fewer programs. Of course, I am facetious of that being an advantage.

As an aside, IBM has completely revampled the RPG language and it is the most advanced programming language in the IT world today. Of course, Big Blue enver tells anybody that as it has not ported the language to any other platform or it would be selling like hotcakes. t

RPG Productivity

With RPG especially, you can write whole programs that perform functional business routines in minutes, rather than in hours or days. A big disadvantage of this, of course, is that the program inventory increases because it is so easy to write new programs.

Again, I am facetious. Besides better productivity, there is always the probability of success to factor in programming. In the programming language du jour shop, there is always a little technical difficulty in bringing a new program into production, and so businesses can expect code inventories to grow at about one-tenth of the pace of an RPG shop. If you heard me say that RPG is 10 times more productive than Java for business applications, you heard right.

The fact, in most colleges and universities, is that RPG and COBOL are not highlighted because they are not perceived to be new, period. Yes, there are folks like Bill Gates who feel that the RPG language is so far away from the machinc that the language is no fun to work with. He's right. "English-like" and "easy to use" are terms of anathema to the pure computer geek.

RPG is not highlighted at all by anybody, anywhere. In fact, just the opposite is true in academia. Most computer science faculty members have a very negative opinion of RPG, mostly from hearsay or perhaps a brief introduction. Though students get to form their own opinions, the influence of faculty on those opinions regarding RPG would mostly be negative.

Along the way, with four years in the computer science hallways, they typically hear negatives from other students, while none of them actually has a clue about what RPG actually is. Many students and faculty members who think they hate RPG probably don't know much about it.

When I was writing this book, I helped demystify RPG for a group of students in the relational database class I taught. My objective was to show how databases are used in programs. In just 45 minutes, with student interaction, the class and I coded, compiled, and ran an RPG program in 10 clear statements. The program performed a vendor file maintenance task. My students could not bclicvc it was that easy.

They told me they had heard about RPG but never knew it could be so efficient. I told the class that this program would probably take about sixty statements in COBOL, and a student volunteered that it would be lots more than 60 statements in C++. Another added that it would be at least 160 statements in Java.

They were amazed. They told me that nobody had ever told them anything about an AS/400, and that any understanding they thought they had was way off the mark.

IBM No Longer Talks Basics

IBM no longer talks about the base AS/400 technology and its integrated facilities, nor the raw power of the RPG language in building business applications. By not talking about it, the unknowing readily conclude that all systems have the same advanced facilities. IBM treats these two technology tools as if they have no value.

Then, while its customers, who understand the value more than IBM, are using the AS/400 and its RPG more and more to solve everyday business problems, IBM just accepts the industry criticism against the AS/400 and RPG. The company keeps its responder stuck on mute, and suggests to its customers that they switch to Java.

Somewhere along the way, the AS/400, an IBM invention, and RPG, another IBM invention, have received poor reviews from people who have never worked with either. My students were duly impressed with RPG and they could not believe how something so logical and easy to write and understand would not be more popular.

For the AS/400 to survive and live, IBM has to figure out how to preempt bad reviews and false charges with positive information. Maybe this book and your many cards and letters will prompt IBM to change its ways. There are a few things somebody must be saying are good for anybody to believe that it might be true. One is the AS/400 and the other is RPG. What's so hard about the truth?

To those who know, the RPG language is very good for business applications. It would not be the language that you would use to get a rocket to the moon, but RPG would be very good for Web applications if IBM would provide the proper tooling within the operating system. IBM is the bad guy here. The company has made one mistake after another with the AS/400 in the last ten years. The biggest of all may be that the company purposely kept the RPG language proprietary to the AS/400 and the System/3X. By design, IBM made AS/400 applications non portable to other platforms.

Bill Gates Hates RPG

When OS/2 came out in 1986, there was a strong rumor that IBM was going to bring out an RPG compiler for OS/2. It never arrived. If it had, perhaps even OS/2 would be a successful operating system in small businesses today.

By design, IBM kept its most productive business programming language from its least expensive platform. And the least expensive operating system platform, OS/2, died a slow and agonizing death.

Throughout this book, we have demonstrated that IBM is not very good at estimating markets, capturing them, and keeping them. In the mid 1980's IBM had not much more than 200,000 midrange computer customers System/36 and System/38.

You may recall that IBM's total five-year market estimate for the PC in 1981 was 275,000. The company had no inkling as to how many potential customers there were for its products. With 40 million small businesses, which file tax returns in just the US today, Microsoft figures that every single one of those is a server prospect.

Would there have been one or two small businesses that would have bought a PC solution rather than a baby System/36 or an IBM 5120 DataMaster in the 1980s? Sure, but not much more than one or two. IBM was so paranoid about its secret RPG weapon that the company never permitted it to run on its small business DataMaster product–another major miscalculation.

Moreover, as a product of similar poor thinking, the DataMaster's BASIC language was built as incompatible with Microsoft's BASIC. This was to prevent IBM's DataMaster customers from easily switching to a PC. Instead it hurt IBM because the DataMaster could not use the ton of PC programs available.

It is IBM's total lack of market vision that caused the RPG language over the last 20 years to become irrelevant to all but AS/400 programmers. IBM helped RPG become "unknown" and it is doing a fine job in doing the same thing for the AS/400. To many, the term unknown equates to dying. "If it were good, I would expect to have heard about it–at least from IBM."

Back in the late 1980's, Bill Gates told me over a beer that I would never see a Microsoft RPG compiler. He kept his word. As a true computer scientist, he just hated the language. IBM at the same time was afraid that a PC RPG would cause S/3X shops to use less expensive PCs instead of AS/400's and System/38s.

Not understanding the power of its own midrange boxes, IBM was afraid that the toy PCs would overtake the AS/400 in a price battle if IBM provided the programming tools to the environment. IBM purposely kept RPG from the PC and that decision has helped keep potential programmers from being able to readily work with the AS/400. It was a big strategic mistake.

Smaller mainframes always had an RPG compiler. These shops liked RPG since it made the business-programming job easier. However, IBM never enhanced mainframe RPG to use database and workstation devices naturally.

Instead the mainframe compilers used complex structures to access databases and the CICS workstation facilities. IBM could have built the same capabilities into the mainframe as it did for AS/400, but Big Blue kept it more difficult so they could sell more software–CICS and DB2. Thus, mainframe RPG and AS/400 RPG are not the same an never were the same.

Washington Area Midrange eServer--OS/400 User Group

As I have already used up most of my euphemisms about the AS/400, I was compelled to do research to find the voices of others offering commentary about the continual life or death question regarding the AS/400 platform. The Washington Area Midrange is an active group of AS/400 users with a history of energetic and insightful presidents. The group includes AS/400 users from the Washington and Baltimore areas.

The name of this group tells a big story of Power i / iSeries brand non-acceptance. There is no Power i in this name. With OS/400 being renamed to i5/OS, it will be interesting to see if the "WAM" changes its name. Truly the differentiating factor of the AS/400 from all other machines is its integrated operating system, OS/400, and as much as I hate to say it, the AS/400 may live on with a heart transplant but its current OS/400 heart may have few beats left.

That this group of esteemed users chose not to have Power i or iSeries in their name tells their opinion of IBM's homogenizing eServer iSeries strategy. If Linux becomes the AS/400, this group is structured to let another users group worry about that.

I wonder whether these users think the AS/400 is dead or dying? Though it is not hot off the press, Peter Maher, while president of this user group a few years ago, expressed his concerns about the topic and charged his constituents to do something about it. His story follows:

February 2, 2001

Its Groundhog Day -Will the iSereis See Its Shadow?

It seems everywhere I turn these days I hear the prophets of doom and gloom regarding the Power i. If its not one company going to Unix/Linux its another going to NT. This causes me to stop and take a step back and evaluate. Is the AS/400 - Power i Dead? Will the Power i see its shadow and will we have "6 more weeks" of bad news or will the long hoped for "Spring" be just around the corner?

Those who know me well know I am the optimist's optimist (some say even say I am unrealistic at times) so I believe that the Power i has at least one more last gasp. Not because of any great pronouncements from Rochester but because I believe that the Power i is the best box going.

Now my belief in the box won't save it - no that's up to all of us banding together and fighting for the box. We have to be willing to stand up to those who want to bury it. But we must fight with logic and not emotion. Why have most of the companies that have "abandoned" the Power i left it? In my opinion those of us who were in the position to fight were unprepared. We were victims of complacency and the Power i superb track record. We stopped learning. We resisted the "new technology", the unfamiliar and the untested. Now we have a lot of catching up to do.

How do we catch up? Well each shop is different and each person is different but it is my opinion that if we want to be working on Power i boxes in the future we better get on the education bandwagon and fast

**...
Folks I'm talking about taking personal responsibility for your future. IBM won't do it. COMMON won't do it. WAM won't do it. It's all up to YOU! The next time your CEO sticks his head in the door and tells you about the newest thing he read about on the plane back from Palm Springs, surprise him and be prepared already.**

WebSphere Represents Everything Wrong with AS/400

WebSphere has been an example of everything that is wrong with IBM's treatment of AS/400 developers today. Who wants WebSphere in the shape it is in anyway? Not me! I should since I have written seven WebSphere books. I'd rather write about integrated function. The AS/400 is an elegant machine that can run lots of different things for lots of different people. But, the one thing that makes an AS/400 an AS/400 is that critical functions are integrated within. Serving dynamic Web pages is a critical function in today's Web-centric world. And, that means that a non-integrated WebSphere should have no role on an IBM AS/400.

WebSphere is a function necessary on inferior systems so that they can provide dynamic data to the Web. The IBM WebSphere server is nothing special, no matter what you may hear IBM say.

Oh, sure, it permits things to be done that are lots harder to do without it. That's a definite. But it would be lots harder to access AS/400 data without its integrated database and it would be very difficult to support interactive computing without it natural workstation interface. But, that does not mean that either of these and the many more integrated functions on the machine should become separate products. You just don't build integrated function with separate add-on products and get to call your machine integrated.

WebSphere is more important to IBM than the AS/400 community. IBM makes money on it. When an AS/400 customer buys it (Until May 4, 2004, Express costs $2,000 and Base cost $10,000), there is lots of work to do to set it up.

The right thing for the AS/400 (IBM i) is that a servlet server (like WebSphere) and a natural RPG extension for the Web should be built into the integrated AS/400. It should already be an integral part of the machine when you get an AS/400.

> **Note: On May 4, 2004, while this book was in beta form, IBM announced that WebSphere Express (IBM's most basic servlet server) would be integrated into the new OS, i5/OS. As of now, twelve years later, there still are no natural RPG or COBOL extension fot the Web.**

WebSphere Express integration looked like it would never happen. I thought that the software division would not permit it. I was wrong. The IBM software division now builds all program development tools for the AS/400, including its compilers. This fact is not necessarily a good thing for the AS/400. The Toronto Labs, the quintessential developer of all AS/400 application development (AD) tools, now works for the software division, not the AS/400 division. It is good news, however, if the IBM Software Division has begun to become come benevolent to the AS/400 division.

Since IBM's software division builds and sells products, it does not have to care what is best for the AS/400., so the relationship is tenuous. Program development for an integrated server should be integrated, but the software division earns revenue by selling software products, not integrated AS/400 function. Software division makes its money on add-on products. If the software division has a piece of rag tag code that runs on the PC that can save them the cost of developing something good to integrate into the AS/400, unfortunately they are compelled to use it. That's economics. If they build something special for the AS/400 platform, logic says that it would cost them and hurt their revenue stream.

It is both sad and ironic that today in IBM the stand-alone software king, the IBM Software Division, builds important software for the integrated AS/400. Perhaps the integration of WebSphere Express is a signal that the new software division has a way of sharing in IBM's integration revenue. My concern is that the software division controls the health of the AS/400. If the AS/400 is working under a "managed health care plan" run by the software division, that may mean that the integrated AS/400 is dying.

If there were no WebSphere and no software division, Rochester could have built a servlet server for a buck, 380. WebSphere as a product has a very small realm of function. It is merely a fee based servlet server plug-in to a free Web server plug-in (Apache) to OS/400, a free operating system. It is a plug-in once removed.

If the software group were not in charge, the servlet server function should not even have a name on the AS/400. The part of the operating system that allocates space for files or the part that checks authority or the part that loads a program from disk has no product name. Integrated function should have no name.

For 10 years, IBM deprived the AS/400 from being able to naturally run Internet applications from a browser. Then, when even Toronto had to be thinking it was time to get the AS/400 on the Web with dynamic application development, corporate IBM created a servlet server for Unix, known as WebSphere, which runs on the company's inferior servers. Because there already is a servlet server in IBM, Rochester is not permitted to build the function within the operating system, where it belongs.

The integration of WebSphere Express in the operating system hopefully signals that the AS/400 has stopped its slide down a road to being just another software piece-parts machine. The more integrated the AS/400 appears; the more the perception of death and dying can be removed from the aura of the box. Maybe this first positive action from the software group means that more can be expected in the future. I sure hope so.

Will Cinderella Survive?

The AS/400 is a lot like poor Cinderella. It's got two ugly stepsisters (Windows and Unix) and a big mean stepmother (mainframe). Midnight came and went; the ball is over. Nobody is wearing glass slippers anymore. The Fairy Godmother (Rochester) is locked in the attic, is powerless, and cannot get out. Worse than that, her stepsisters, her stepmother, and a few formerly nasty step uncles (software division and services division) control everything that Cinderella needs for survival.

Cindy knows that she must change to adapt to the times, but the best she has gotten from the family are old clothes that don't match perfectly (WebSphere, MQSeries, Eclipse). The clothes don't fit right and when she puts them on she gets sick, looks confused, and appears like she is dying.

All of the members of her family care about themselves and each other, but nobody seems to care about what is best for poor Cindy. Will she survive? She is definitely a tough lady after surviving Rochester Minnesota winters for 25 years but, for a future prognosis, you'll have to ask Sam Palmisano (the Prince) who was last seen running from the Glass Slipper and Pumpkin Cart store. Yes, it is the same Prince who runs the whole IBM show.

In other words, unless Mr. Palmisano acts, the IBM software division may have a role in calling the AS/400 integration shots from now on. Tools that in years before the software division existed would be naturally integrated into the operating system are now built on other systems (Unix and Linux) and then they are bastardized (ported) to run on the AS/400.

Integration has become a four-letter word at IBM. Even though Rochester once could have built the function necessary to give developers what they need within the framework of the AS/400, the software division, with far more revenue donated to the motherhouse each year than the shrinking AS/400 division, would say:

> **"No, you can't build your own integrated function into your machine anymore. We already have a bastardized product that does that function and we won't make any money if you do it yourself ."**

So unless we can convince the Prince that the AS/400 needs to be free from the software division's potential hold on integrated function, the old clothes that are coming the AS/400's way may continue to make it so ugly that it might as well exit stage left.

> **Note: The integration of WebSphere Express in this light is a very good sign.**

None of this, please, is the fault of the AS/400 programmer in the IT shop. Again, it is IBM's fault. Then again, with the new WebSphere integration in i5/OS, maybe the AS/400 GM has already waged a successful battle for integration.

The loss of integrated function on the AS/400 would cripple the AS/400 so that one day it would become so ugly and so non-integrated, that AS/400 loyalists would be ready to take it to the Vet to have it put down. On that day, the once spunky machine would go from dying to dead!

A rational person looking at the IBM announcements of May 4, 2004, would see no signs of death for the AS/400 anytime soon. So, there are these signs that that death is not about to set in any time soon. Integration plus telling someone about integration (TV advertising) may very well be a winning future ticket. And, nobody thinks that winning tickets are dying or dead.

Chapter 32 Suggestions for Improvement

What Can IBM Do?

At this point in the book, it is no secret that IBM's biggest AS/400 problem is that it fails to market the machine. The company has restructured its business as a services and software supplier, and that is at the heart of its problem. Hardware, including the AS/400 does not count for much anymore. Some of us think that a little care and feeding and marketing could have and could still help that. If you take a trip to IBM's main Web site, www.ibm.com, it is difficult to find anything about its hardware products, but there sure is a lot about solutions. Though solutions may include hardware, the primary ingredients are software and tailoring services.

"Solutions" is a euphemism for the things that IBM thinks customers buy when they are shopping for a computer system. IBM thinks it sells solutions in today's world. As strange as it may be, the IBM Company does not sell application solutions software. It is purposely not in that marketplace. It is not in that business. So, why would solutions be important?

IBM sells hardware, middleware, and services. The company has a dotted line relationship to its independent Business Partners and it depends on their good will as to whether IBM hardware is included in their partners' software solutions.

IBM would like to think that its Business Partners propose its products and only its products; however, this is not the case. I have been in a number of sales situations where these "loyal;" AS/400 solutions providers will gladly switch to a Unix or Windows solution if the customer balks at the price of an AS/400. They say "it is the same software, why not run it on the least expensive machine." The moral is that just like the Computerland stores of yesteryear, IBM's Business Partners are not in business for IBM's benefit; they do not sell just IBM; and they are quite **independent.**

IBM loves to sell all kinds of services, as you would see from a trip to its Web site. Since most of IBM's business is services and software, the company has apparently decided that hardware is now in the drag-along category. Years ago, IBM would sell hardware as a solution. Software products and services were the drag-along business. Now it is completely the opposite.

Though IBM still makes about $30 billion in hardware, until this year, the number has been dropping. Right now, its $30 billion hardware business is still integral to the company's success. But, in the long term, as services and software revenues climb, hardware will have less and less of an impact.

The hardware business has become less important to IBM and the company simply has not been successful in maintaining its hardware revenue or market share. In many ways the reason for its decreased sales is because hardware is just not an area in which the new IBM pays attention. In fact, IBM seems to be selling off all of its hardware divisions lately.

In late 2003, IBM announced that its software division would focus its solutions on vertical marketplaces as opposed to selling software to whomever will buy it. Since the vertical strategy is already employed in Rochester, this is not expected to affect the AS/400. However, I think that it will.

When a lumber company comes to IBM for its one stop shopping, IBM's Software Division will direct them to a software package for the industry as well as try to ensure that some of what is on the IBM software truck is sold. Since the

AS/400 software truck is not as full as the other trucks, and since its most important AS/400 middleware comes with the machine, human nature says that if the software division has a prospect, it is going to sell what it's got on its truck. Since they get less compensation for an AS/400 sale, the AS/400 will not be sold. Case closed.

Therefore, you can bet none of these companies who contact the software division will ever hear about the AS/400 -- other than perhaps an acknowledgment that it is more expensive than Unix and Windows.

The Grim Reaper

They say that in life you reap what you sew. Unless IBM re-acknowledges that it is in the hardware businesses before it fritters its server business away, just as it did the PC business, the AS/400 and its hardware sisters and stepmother will be gone before the company knows it. When that happens, the discussion about how to save the AS/400 will be moot.

Though some may argue with me about it, the best thing that can happen to the IBM AS/400 is for Microsoft to buy the whole business from IBM or for IBM to donate OS/400 to the Open Source Foundation. There would be no question that Bill Gates would highlight the product if it were his and he'd win the small and large server business by killing both Unix and the mainframe.

Eventually, he'd put a GUI on the AS/400 and would drive the box with Windows-like icons. In addition to making AS/400 customers happy this would make Microsoft happy also. Microsoft's internal IT staff would not have to be embarrassed anymore about running (or having run) the business on the AS/400 platform. Besides peace internally, Bill Gates would finally have a highly scalable and reliable platform upon which to run Windows. Intel need not apply. Don't rule it out!

A donation to the open source community would help IBM in a number of ways. AS/400 customers would get off IBM's back because the software would be open and free. IBM would not have to bear the cost of maintaining OS/400. The Open Source OS/400 may be tweaked to run on many different hardware platforms, including all of IBM's servers.

Short of action from Microsoft, or the donation route, if IBM chooses to save its AS/400 product line, this chapter has a number of suggestions. It starts with the top nine things the company can do and then generally discusses the problems that some of the nine solutions would address.

The suggestion list continues in the Chapter titled *Teach Me! Teach Me! Teach Me!* with another set of suggestions for how to attract new blood to the AS/400 and how to get them prepared for training. If IBM is ready to sell, sell, sell, there is no doubt that the AS/400 can be saved.

To the IBM Vault?

What can IBM do to prevent the AS/400 from finding its way into the IBM vault. Vestiges from IBM's glorious and ignominious past are displayed in the vault. For example, you'll find the Series/1, the 305 RAMAC, the DataMaster, the 8100, the 1620, the DisplayWriter, and the Ford Edsel? Ford has its Edsel there because it did not have a vault and Disney would not take it.

Unlike the Disney vault, the IBM vault has an entrance but no exit. Products that go to the vault don't ever get taken out for a new look – even after the kids that worked with them have grown up. The list of suggestions to IBM then is intended to help keep the AS/400 from getting tossed into the vault along with the dead products of yesteryear.

In one form or another I would suppose that others have given these recommendations to IBM over the last ten years, but perhaps not all together as the list below and the education list in Chapter 34.

When I read this list I say to myself, "of course, that will save the AS/400…yes, that's a good one, etc." But I am powerless and you are powerless other than to suggest. Suggestions or no suggestions, in the end it is IBM who must decide to what level its AS/400 has a role in its company. Based on the IBM view, the AS/400 may hit the vault or not.

AS/400 Partial Improvement List

1. Tell the world about AS/400 reliability and dependability. Since most AS/400 users believe that the most important part of an AS/400 is its reliability and dependability, IBM should tell somebody about it. Marketing is not about best kept secrets

2. Tell the world about the marvels of AS/400 integration. Since IBM thinks that the most important part of the AS/400 is its integration characteristics (as in **Power i**), again, tell somebody about it, and begin to integrate the many standalone products, such as WebSphere to keep the "**i**" in Power i from meaning "dis **i** ntegrated.".

3. Position the AS/400 as a new account business computer. Since no business expands without some new accounts, and new accounts don't come calling by themselves, again, IBM should tell somebody that they want new accounts and that they can sustain new accounts. A new accounts S.W.A.T. team would help in this regard.

4. Create a new baby sized AS/400 server / personal machine. Since the PowerPC chip line is so dominant in non-PC circles (almost all chips in game toys are IBM's), the company should use this chip to create an AS/400 style machine to sell to new accounts. There is really no reason to import OS/400 to the Intel platform if this is done.

Again, if IBM were to build it, the company would have to tell somebody about its new affordable AS/400 server and development machine. The machine should be sold as an integrated, affordable package at about $2,000.00 or less.

5. Give AS/400s away to students and to colleges. IBM should have a lottery once a week, on a different campus every week, in which they give away one or two small AS/400s to a college student and the host college.

To qualify for the lottery, a student might be asked to bid a dollar and all the dollars would go to the institution or to Student Government.

If IBM were to create this inexpensive AS/400 I would recommend giving at least one to every college and community college as a good will gesture during its kickoff period. Of course, the company would also be compelled to tell the colleges why the AS/400 should have value to them. To do this, again, IBM would have to let somebody know about the system, as in all other scenarios. Additionally, the company would have to let the general public know that these little AS/400 boxes are coming to a college close to home so the public has the opportunity to learn about the alive and well AS/400.7

6. Add a standard GUI to the AS/400 operating system box (MAC OS). Since the AS/400 looks just like the tired old legacy system that Microsoft and the trade press have it painted to be, IBM should buy the Mac GUI from Apple and adapt it as the GUI for the AS/400. The MAC and the AS/400 both use PowerPC processor technology. Academia would automatically like the AS/400 since they love the Mac. By the way, the Mac and the Apple PowerBook use the same family of chips as the AS/400. Again, IBM would have to tell somebody about this.

An alternative would be to rebuild the OS/400 front end to use an HTML or better yet, an XML driven GUI. The AS/400 command structure could also be rescued to participate in the resolution of the commands.

7. Create a hybrid futuristic Mac/AS/400 PC. Along with Apple, IBM should build a PC that has the outward look and feel of a Mac and the inner elegance and full application facilities of an AS/400. If IBM were to perform this magic, it would create another PC revolution. To ensure success, Apple would have to market the device.

8. Take advice from Mark Twain and announce that the AS/400 is not dead and that it is not even tired. Since no business wants to install a server or even upgrade one that is dead, and the trade press has declared that the AS/400 and green screens are dead, and IBM behaves as if the AS/400 actually is dead, the company, like Mark Twain should announce that the AS/400 is not dead and that the reports of its death have been greatly exaggerated. Again, IBM must tell someone about this.

9. Add generic aliases to the IBM server line, making the AS/400 the "IBM Business System." Rather than have IBM embarrass itself by discarding the eServer umbrella, add a generic primary differentiator name to the eServer brand so that the system can be known by a generic alias. Generic aliases for the other systems are already unofficially in place -- IBM Mainframe Server; IBM Unix Server; IBM PC (x86) Server. The IBM

Business System or even the IBM Business Server moniker would properly position the AS/400 and clear up its primary purpose.

10. etc. The list continues.

The Absence of AS/400 Awareness

In order to offer suggestions for improvement, you must examine the problems that the AS/400 platform is currently experiencing that makes it an at-risk-system in the 21st century. Most of my peers with whom I communicate share the thought that IBM's biggest problem with its AS/400 line of computers, besides IBM per se, is buyer awareness. Other than the AS/400 professionals, the IT folks who manage, develop, implement, and operate AS/400 systems on a regular basis, there is almost no awareness of the product. There is even less awareness of its new pseudonym, *Power i.*

Interestingly, this is not much different than the early days of computing when only the insiders knew what an IBM 1130, a System/3, or a System/38 might be like. In the early days, very few people knew anything about any computer, other than those people working directly with computers in their businesses. That is not the case today.

More people know about computers today than those who do not know about them. More importantly, ordinary people know computers today from things they do and see outside of their workplace. Just like the days gone by, not many people, other than those directly involved, know anything about the big back room computers that do the companies work every day.

Who are the people then who know little about their computer at work but are very aware of computers in the rest of their lives? You already know who they are. They are my neighbors and they are your neighbors. Four out of five of them are likely to have at least one computer at home and nineteen out of twenty are likely to have a close relative with one.

This same percentage of people is on the Internet every day or so, looking for an email from a son or daughter or parent or other loved one, or perhaps an acknowledgment that their last big purchase, such as a digital camera, CD, or cell phone has been shipped.

These people are Firemen, Accountants, Nurses, Police, Food Service Workers, Maintenance Personnel, Doctors, Plumbers, CEOs, Store Owners, Sales People, Secretaries, Street Cleaners, Teachers, Linemen, Clergy, Cable Workers, Bankers, other government workers, other school workers, and other industry workers.

Please don't forget the retirees, because many of us continue to persevere in the job marketplace. Of course we can't forget the computer geeks and the students from high school to college to graduate school. All of these people, you and I included; know much more about computers in our home lives than people ever did before.

Opinion's Count

Because we see computers in our own homes and in the homes of our friends, you and I are more likely to have formed some opinions about computers. For example, because your Windows computer locks up frequently and you lose information from time to time and you have to re-key things, you may have concluded that is a normal behavior for a computer. By the way, it is not. Because of your opinion, however, you might be inclined to think that computers that are reliable are nowhere to be found. That too is not true. Because you may run out of space in your database on your C drive and you watch your system crash, you may have already gone through a scenario that forces you to move some files to the D drive. Because of your poor experience, you may think that all computers are like that.

Again, that is not the case. Theoretically, if you never got the real answers above, your opinions might stand, unchecked by reality.

Moreover, because we have all heard the names Intel and Microsoft in our homes and in our neighbors' homes, and since we know that they make most of the computers in the world, you may think that all businesses either do or should use these very popular computers.

You may not be consciously thinking about this, but if you thought about it, you may have these types of opinions from your own experience with computers. Again, this is not true but it is the normal conclusion that one would make from being in the world of today.

The point is that you have gained an opinion of computers over time because of who you are and where you go, etc. Companies named Microsoft and Intel are part of your world, like it or not. It is probably safe to say that, as a rule, unless you happen to have an IBM PC or a friend has an IBM PC (less than 5% of the market), you don't even associate IBM with the kind of computers that normal human beings use in the course of their off work hours activities.

You may think that big companies and big government and big medical facilities might use IBM computers, but more than likely, you and others like you have not bumped into any of these behemoths in your personal life.

TV Advertising Delivers the Best Message

While you and I and the rest of the listed people above, my neighbors and your neighbors are sitting at home resting, perhaps watching a TV program or a game, or listening to music on the radio, companies of all sorts are permitted into our leisure time to give us an advertising message of some kind or another that we probably would rather not hear.

Somehow, with no effort expended on our part, we learn that Chevy is like a rock, and that the models at Victoria's secret are not what are for sale, and that beef is what's for dinner. Like it or not, they get us.

IBM is the exception. The IBM Company does not take the time to reach us at home very often, so we know little about IBM and what IBM is all about. Moreover, IBM's messages are always cryptic so we never know what they are selling. This is a major fault of IBM's since most of the general public knows little about IBM.

Therefore, why would any one of us look to IBM for a computer for our business? Microsoft and Apple and Intel, on the other hand are lots smarter than IBM. They have some great ads that help us know they are out there and they encourage us to buy their products. It follows that if IBM were to show up with a competing offer to one of these three without having spent the effort acquainting us with IBM products, you and I and the general public would be more inclined to go with one of the three.

It stands to reason that there would be an affinity with the companies that we have heard about, rather than a company that has never ever cared to tell us anything about how its products can help our businesses.

The ads from Microsoft and Apple and others that I show in the next section are very good. I present them here because IBM can and should do the same type of thing to enhance its product and company images. Have you ever seen this ad?

> **Our mission is not just to unlock the potential of today's new technologies. It is to help unleash the potential in every person, family, and business. We want to help you do the things you do every day-express your ideas, manage your finances, build your business-faster, easier, and better. At Microsoft, we see the world not as it is, but as it might someday become.**

How about this one?

> **"We stand in awe of kids and their potential. We see them as doctors, as heroes, as inventors. We see their potential and make software that helps them unlock it."**

How about this ad?

> **I'm writing to share a tragic little story.**
>
> **My Dad has a PC that my sister and I used to use for our homework assignments. One night, I was writing a paper on it, when all of a sudden it went berserk, the screen started flashing, and the whole paper just disappeared. All of it. And it was a good paper! I had to cram and rewrite it really quickly. Needless to say, my rushed paper wasn't nearly as good, and I blame that PC for the grade I got.**
>
> **I'm happy to report that my sister and I now share an Apple PowerBook. It's a lot nicer to work on than my dad's PC was, it hasn't let me down once, and my grades have all been really good.**
>
> **Thanks, Apple.**

Microsoft and Apple

Microsoft sells operating systems and personal productivity ware, such as word processing. It is safe to say that, almost everybody knows this as fact, at some level or another. Moreover, though the courts waffle sometimes about making a definite statement, Microsoft has been declared a monopoly. On the other hand, Apple is just a feisty little company taking shots at the giant every so often. You've just got to love Apple for its spunk.

In the Microsoft ads above, Microsoft is not advertising a product. They don't have to. You already know what they make. They have enough product ads in your face to tell you about their new products. When you see their Windows 2003 server ad, however, you know that they are advertising a product. You don't have to guess what they are doing as in an IBM ad. That's because they want you to go out and buy the new version of the product and they are telling you it's great, it's available, and it will save you money.

In the last ad, which is from Apple, it is clearly targeting Windows client users. The product they are selling is the Apple Power Book and the ad does a good job of letting you know what they are trying to sell. The implication is that Apple is better than Microsoft, yet they don't mention Microsoft per se, but Microsoft knows that when a PC goes down, they get the blame.

Intel gets a pass on a lock, though its processors may also cause a lock problem. That's interesting. Intel does not market to the general public and everybody, including IBM lets them get away with saying that Intel Inside means something good.

Of the three companies noted, Apple, Intel, and Microsoft, all three know what they are doing with their advertising dollars. Their ads are effective and clear and you know what product or group of products they want you to buy. If you have ever seen an IBM ad, you would not feel the same. Thus, IBM has some learning to do in this regard.

To add a little humor to this analysis, the Apple ad actually ticked off Microsoft something fierce. The big bullies at Microsoft could not let it go so they struck back with an ad of their own on their Web site. They did not take it to TV media because it did not go over too well on the Web. The ad was titled:

Confessions of a Mac to PC Convert

The ad purports to be a first-person account of a writer who decided to switch from an Apple Macintosh computer to a PC running Windows XP. It goes a little like this:

> **"Yes, it's true; I like the Microsoft Windows XP operating system enough to change my whole computing world around...Windows XP gives me more choices and**

flexibility and better compatibility with the rest of the computing world."

Microsoft copied the Apple ad style of having a real person do the ad, but then the media snoops discovered that it was not a real person. The company had commissioned the "ad" from a freelance writer who was paid for her work, although Microsoft claims her experience was as reported. Microsoft also had crow for a second course as it had to admit that the "convert" shown was really not the person who they were highlighting. It was a stock photograph.

Unlike what I would expect from IBM, Microsoft admitted that it was beaten, pulled the ad in less than a week's time when they knew that they had not gotten away with it, dusted itself off, and went after the next opportunity. The company called the ad, made by Microsoft's software marketing group, "a mistake in judgment." The company then went through the customary, "regrets the action" routine and then praised itself for removing the page. Apple declined to comment on the Microsoft snub.

What Would IBM Have Done?

First of all, IBM does not have any wild ducks any more who would consider taking on any company so the whole situation could never happen. However, if IBM approved a marketing slam-dunk on Microsoft or any other company and it was met with any negatives whatsoever, the IBM thought police would be called in to argue with the objector.

Since IBM knows what is best for IBM, the company would meet the mere suggestion that something was done improperly, with strong denials. IBM would expect that all those objecting to IBM approved thought would eventually submit. Of course, Big Blue is finding that AS/400 loyalists are as tenacious against the company's position as a bulldog on a pant leg.

I happened to see an eServer ad myself a few days ago. I almost missed it. It was the first that I had ever seen. True to form, I did not know what IBM was trying to sell. The term xSeries did appear at the end of the ad at a time when I was hoping it was not an Power i ad because it was a poor excuse for advertising. As good as the Microsoft ads, the bold Apple onslaught, and the terrific Intel Inside campaign are, the IBM eServer ads do not compare. .

No Guts, No Glory

Unlike Microsoft and Apple, from my eyes, IBM has no guts. The IBM ducks fly no more, surely to Thomas Watson Jr.'s eternal lament. Unlike Intel, with its "Intel Inside" catch phrase, IBM has no marketing creativity. When I went to the Web to find sample Apple and Microsoft ads, they were all over the place, including their Web sites. When I looked for IBM ads, neither Dogpile nor Google gave me anything other than IBM's peace and love campaign for Linux with the eServer pSeries.

Considering that Linux is not an IBM product, that's odd. Even when I surfed the IBM site itself, www.ibm.com, the company kept its ad text for all campaigns a secret. It's like they knew I was coming and they hid it all. That's how little there was about IBM and advertising. There is no apparent IBM anxiety to offer any commentary on IBM's hardware products.

Peace and Love and Linux

A funny thing happened to IBM's Linux peace and love ad party. They had hired artists to cover San Francisco's sidewalks with chalked and painted symbols for its Peace and Love and Linux eServer advertising campaign. It was a good idea. City officials, however, who obviously were not consulted, viewed IBM's artwork as more graffiti to endure and when the biodegradable material did not degrade after rainstorms; the city was looking for IBM to clean up its mess. Ironically, IBM's one eServer campaign that was noticed became a PR nightmare.

And, true to form, IBM stumbled and wondered what to do. Then almost immediately, the company was faced with another potential PR nightmare because it did not act fast enough to solve this minor dilemma. Taking advantage of a situation, Sun Microsystems, IBM's ardent competitor in the Unix space, decided that it was time to act.

Sun did its best to turn this IBM marketing gaff into a public relations coup for itself. The company announced in the middle of IBM's woes that it would rescue the City of San Francisco from IBM's graffiti and it volunteered to clean up the sidewalks that Big Blue had spray-painted.

It is heartening to find marketing departments that are still sharp and opportunistic and ready to strike at a moment's notice. It is clear that IBM does not hire people like that anymore or it tames its modern ducks to meld better with its stodgy corporate culture. While IBM was taking ten years to study the matter, Sun acted. Kudos to Sun.

IBM Can Learn From Intel

When Intel is not highlighting its company name, it has no problem telling you about how special its Pentium brand is. Unlike IBM with real end user products, nobody can actually buy an Intel. They can buy Dell and HP and Gateway, which happen to have Intel and Pentiums Inside, but they can't buy Intel brand PCs. Intel does not sell PCs. Moreover, when Intel advertises, they reach people (including CEOs) in their living rooms, not in the boardrooms. By the time the CEOs get to their boardrooms, they have a fairly positive feeling about any product that has Intel inside. And, in fact, they are probably inclined to make sure that Intel is inside, rather than take a chance on something they have never heard of.

IBM believes that it does not have to advertise its server products to regular people in their living room, though Intel finds it very effective. For about ten years IBM has promised to step up its product awareness campaign for the AS/400. The company in effect has misled its AS/400 customers on this point. That's a pretty big sin.

Al Zollar, the one-time head of the AS/400 Unit, as his excuse, said he wanted to see if advertising works. That's why IBM gets beat all of the time. IBM thinks that it must prove universal truths such as "advertising sells products." Intel just goes ahead and advertises to the public and it sets its own message rather than having it set on the street. Its customers are tickled about that and it keeps them buying Intel.

IBM acts as though its customers are wrong when they ask the company to provide some advertising support to help them prove to their management that their company made a good decision. IBM can learn a lot from Intel.

A Few Test Ads for IBM—Free of Charge

If you and I can come up with ideas as to how IBM can promote its systems, then IBM and its high paid Madison Avenue cohorts also ought to be able to do so. Here are a few neat ad ideas for the living room TV. They come from the Average Joe ad hoc department. How about a big 128-bit lion or tiger or cougar or panther with a big tongue like the Budweiser frogs, talking about its next 32-bit meal?

IBM must win the computer battle in the living room. How about an ad campaign that shows an AS/400 professional discussing the merits of the '400 with a Windows oriented computer neophyte, with the oratory -- features and functions list, in understandable terms, building to a crescendo until finally, the Windows guy says:

"Hey, you don't have to go any further; I want one of those. It's great! I even want one in my home."

The AS/400 professional says:

"I'm sorry, the AS/400 is "industrial strength." It's made to support the mission critical needs of the world. You can't get an AS/400 for your home. It's not a home computer."

The Windows guy laments:

"But I want one...."

Wouldn't it be nice to have the Windows community lamenting that it can't get an AS/400?

"You can't get an AS/400 for your home. It's not a home computer," maybe someday?

"Industrial Strength computing at its best -- the AS/400."

"The AS/400 is industrial strength"

It should be the IS/400: It's *industrial strength.*

Can "industrial strength" be the catch phrase IBM has been looking for to immediately differentiate an AS/400 from the home market units? You can buy a "blippety" dishwasher, or you can buy Maytag, which has traditionally been viewed as industrial strength. Even those that can't afford a Maytag dishwasher want one.

"Even those who think they can't afford an AS/400, still want one" But maybe you really can afford one."

The IBM Repairman Ad

How about an ad with the AS/400 computer repairman sitting in a lonely office in the same fashion as the Maytag repair man? Picture the camera moving back and the AS/400 repair office is in the middle of a repair complex, flanked by two big repair centers for PCs and PC Servers. Repairperson after repairperson are leaving the side door and coming back for more parts and bringing little PC carcasses in with them. PC users are bringing broken PC after PC through the front doors. The camera closes in on one of the repair centers and you hear... "I hope you have a backup... I understand it's your business on there but you still have to re-boot. The machine got confused"

Then the big voice of somebody such as James Earl Jones comes on and you hear:

> **"If you want to have your computer available for your business when you need it, choose the Industrial Strength computer -- the IS/400 (AS/400). Let your competition use a PC solution."**

This can be followed by a group of PC users coming from the repair center with big oversized repair tickets instead of PCs, looking up to the sky and crying

> **"We want one! How do we get an AS/400?"**

Eventually, people would know that an AS/400 is reliable and it is desirable.

The Living Room CEO

You don't have to be technical to understand this. But the computer mindshare battle - no matter what size computer -- must be fought in the living room. The living room CEO becomes the boardroom CEO again every Monday morning. They are one and the same people. People can be taught the meaning of PC, Unix, Mainframe and AS/400 in simple terms by IBM ads if IBM chooses to fight. IBM, you got that? "In the living room!" And down the road, maybe IBM can actually set the stage for something that gets IBM machines back on the desktop.

Chapter 33 A Town Without GUI

Who's the Thief?

> **"No, Steve, I think its more like we both have a rich neighbor named Xerox, and you broke in to steal the TV set, and you found out I'd been there first, and you said. "Hey, that's no fair! I wanted to steal the TV set!"**

Steven Jobs and Bill Gates have had a love/hate relationship over the years. Gates always wanted what Jobs had. In the last few years as Microsoft was fighting the government, Gates actually invested quite a few millions in Apple. Many of us thought Steve Jobs would not take the loot. He did, nonetheless!

I've mentioned in this book a few times my one encounter with Mr. Gates in the 1989 time frame. He had just delivered a speech to a roomful of IBMers at the beautiful Marriott World Center in Orlando, Florida. All of the IBM Higher Education Specialists from across the U.S. had convened for their annual update session.

Since I handled all of the colleges in Northeastern Pennsylvania at the time, I had the good fortune of being in Orlando in January. I also had the good fortune of having a few friends who invited me to the two-foot round cocktail table in the lobby bar at the Marriott. When I arrived Bill Gates himself, already a billionaire with DOS, was pontificating to a small crowd of about 10, all circled about the two-foot cocktail table filled with empties.

Gates was 31 years old at the time and had just built a new home. He was talking about all the toys and gizmos that he had in his house. He was like a kid at the table, though his speech had been very polished and perhaps even brilliant. When he mentioned the Macintosh, his eyes lit up. He absolutely loved the Macintosh, and he talked about the one or two Macs he had in his new domicile.

I must have appeared to be a dullard in his company. I was interested in RPG and the System/38 and the AS/400 at the time. I took the opportunity in the conversation to ask Bill Gates when he was going to announce an RPG compiler for the PC. He stopped dead in his tracks. He looked at me and then asked: "That's the funny language with the indicators, isn't it?" Without waiting for a response, he continued. "I worked with that in college. I hated that language! If I have my way, you'll never see an RPG compiler from Microsoft." Case closed. He kept his word.

Bill Gates Loves GUI

Over the last six or seven years, I have read a lot about Mr. Gates. In fact, I read the book *Barbarians Led by Bill Gates.* What I learned strengthened what I saw in front of me in Orlando in 1989. Gates is a man who wants what he wants and does not want to mess with anything that he thinks will be a waste of his time. Clearly he saw RPG as a waste of his time. But GUI (gooo-weee) as in graphical user interface was an area that Bill Gates absolutely loved. It was worth his time.

The initial quote that I show in this Chapter is Bill Gates' response after Steve Jobs accused Microsoft of stealing the GUI (graphical user interface) from Apple for an early version of Windows. When you read about Bill Gates you know that this historical figure wanted GUI so much he could taste it. He dreamed about GUI. He had tried by hook and crook to get GUI for his DOS operating system for years, but had consistently failed. The fact that Jobs was able to do it with both the Lisa way back in 1983, and then the Mac one year later was a big disappointment for Mr. Gates. More than five years after he announced Windows in 1983, when Gates finally had something to show, Steven Jobs whacked him, called Gates a copycat, and sued him for copyright infringement.

Note: As an aside, Bill Gates announced Windows in 1983 so he was not a full "Johnny Come Lately." But, to be fair, Windows never really worked until the late 1980's. There are some AS/400 professionals who today would suggest that Windows still does not work!

Bill Gates knew that Steven Jobs had not invented GUI. He knew that Xerox had done all of the pioneering work in the field, but the copier company had no clue what to do with its result. Over the years, both Jobs and Gates had visited the Xerox Palo Alto Research Center (XEROX PARC) and had witnessed GUI in action. In the top quote, Gates was reminding Jobs that the both of them were thieves.

Xerox Is the GUI Pioneer

The Xerox Corporation, at its Palo Alto Research Center (PARC), developed the very first graphical user interface way back in the 1970s. The first computer ever equipped with a GUI interface was the XEROX Alto, a box the company did not sell commercially. Big Xerox, like big IBM, saw no future in GUI. As dumb as IBM was for not fully embracing GUI, at least IBM did not invent it. Xerox got nothing for all of its pioneering work in GUI. Jobs saw the Xerox Alto in 1979 and was duly impressed.

From then on, he was committed to bringing GUI to Apple Computer. Gates visit is not as well documented but he saw the same thing as Jobs, more than likely several years later.

When both men were looking for the best and the brightest people on earth to help them with their GUI projects, you can guess where they went. They went to XEROX PARC, of course. Though they did not steal TV sets, each of them stole people from the XEROX PARC team to work on their historic implementations – Lisa and Mac for Apple, and Windows for Microsoft.

Inspiration or Risk Avoidance?

When Gates was at a Comdex show in late 1982, he became openly obsessed with GUI for DOS. He observed a product by VisiCorp called VisiOn. It was a GUI for PC-DOS and MS DOS. Gates was very concerned that if VisiOn was successful, and users began to use mouse clicks and icons to drive applications with DOS being invisible to the user, they would not really care if DOS was underneath it all. If DOS did not have to be underneath it all, then Gates stood to lose a lot of money to whatever operating system VisiOn chose to place under its GUI. He was right.

From then on, Gates had two missions:

1. He had to make sure VisiOn was not successful.
2. He had to create a GUI for DOS.

He theoretically solved both of these problems with the same swipe. He announced Windows in 1983 at Comdex among phenomenal fanfare, even though it took him two more years to get anything close to a working GUI from the project. Always the marketeer, Gates knew that by announcing Windows, even though it was not coming any time soon, he would hold the industry at bay.

In so doing he would crush VisiCorp's market opportunity, save DOS, and preserve a market for Windows when it was made available. As an aside, the Justice department sued IBM for doing exactly that with some of its early computer products.

By alerting the world and preserving GUI for Microsoft, it would be difficult for any other company to create a GUI for DOS. The Windows project was underway but it would take a long time to come to fruition. It's hard for me to believe that all of this began more than twenty years ago.

Gates and OS/2

In the Orlando Marriott session in which I had spoken to Mr. Gates in 1989, he was preaching his Windows while telling the IBM crowd that OS/2 was the best. But, before OS/2 was ready for prime time, Gates encouraged all the IBMers present to use Windows for program development. "After all it is just like OS/2 but it is available today." By 1991, Windows ruled the desktop. IBM and all the King's horses and all the King's men couldn't get the desktop back again for IBM. OS/2 would never be anything but a bit player. Bill Gates saw to that.

Note: OS/2 was a GUI PC Operating system that Microsoft developed for IBM in the late 1980's. Intentionally or unintentionally Microsoft did such a poor job in building IBM's PC operating system that it never worked well and Microsoft benefited by telling all who would listen that Windows was the real way to GUI. Microsoft outfoxed IBM.

Along the way, before Gates became king of the desktop, he always tried to have a mixed portfolio. He was not anxious to get IBM angry with him. So Gates came to IBM about Windows in the mid-1980s and asked Big Blue to sign up for Windows. IBM, always ready at the drop of a hat to take it on the chin from Bill Gates, wanted no part of it. Even the PC folks in IBM were not interested in GUI, though the Lisa and Macintosh had proven that the technology was feasible. How's that for adroit forward thinking?

Again a bit later in the 1980s as IBM's PC division was finally going to put a GUI on OS/2, Gates felt that IBM should partner with him and name the OS/2 product Windows instead of OS/2. Gates and IBM would share in the proceeds of the partnership. As I recall, he was playing the partner game well for a change and sincerely wanted IBM to be in on the GUI action with the best name in the business for a GUI operating system.

IBM's dimwits again rejected his plea and in fact chose to have a secret team of IBM folks build the GUI for OS/2. Rather than call it Windows as Gates suggested, the astute marketers at IBM chose to call the GUI interface of OS/2 the "Presentation Manager." Yuck! IBM sure is not good with names.

The point here is that the biggest computer company on earth, IBM who had a piece of every venture and were looking to be a $100 billion company by 1990, could not find value in GUI, even fifteen years after XEROX had made it work, and five years after the Macintosh proved that it could all be driven by a PC sized processor. Where were the IBM visionaries? Which IBM person visited Xerox PARC? Nobody that I know seems to know. IBM, including the "Little Lab That Could," was AWOL from GUI.

Still No GUI on AS/400

Barbara Chaderton, an independent AS/400 contractor from Northeastern Pennsylvania, offers the following:

> **"IBM, while struggling to remain competitive with Client Server applications, has lost all meaning of 'standards.' They've been spoon-feeding us for years with 'quick fix' solutions for every GUI application possible. Yet they have failed to create a standard GUI interface, including a GUI twin-axial console. No wonder many IT shops are in a confused state, not knowing the 'right' way to go."**

Now, everybody suspects that IBM pays for planning, as do all companies who want to have a say about their future, their market prospects, changing perceptions etc. While IBM planners and visionaries were reading the handwriting and the tea leaves looking for industry insights, I wonder if any of their high paid consultants ever told them why their traditional (proprietary) systems, such as AS/400 might not look as good in the 1990s as they may have in the 1980s?

Did anybody tell IBM what it might do with its product lines to make them impervious to attacks by Bill Gates and company? Would any paid consultant have looked at the drab green-screen panels from all of IBM's homegrown systems and have suggested they could do better?

The Difference of GUI and Green

Why should IBM feel threatened by Unix? Let's face it. Unix is an operating system that is older than the oldest mainframe operating system and older than the AS/400 operating system? Why should IBM feel threatened by Windows, which is just five years younger than OS/400? In the early to mid-1990s, Windows did not even stay up long enough to get any work done.

Let's see. One major difference visible to all is that the user interface on Unix and Windows is different from that of the proprietary IBM systems. Unix has an optional GUI for Unix workstations, called X-Windows. Windows is a GUI operating system by design. GUI artifacts drive all aspects of all Windows systems.

Could it be that neither IBM nor its consultants had noticed the difference in the way people look at the drab consoles for IBM proprietary offerings versus Windows and Unix GUI? If the paid consultants were vigilant, on duty, and wide-awake at the time, one would expect that they could see the big difference. If they did their jobs, they would have had to take a dangerous crack at telling IBM what it needed to do to address the lack of GUI problem on proprietary systems. If they took the swipe, they did not succeed enough to cause the company to take any action. IBM exercised continued GUI complacency. While I was with Big Blue and since I left, I do not recall IBM ever announcing in any way that GUI was important for its proprietary products or its future.

GUI Not Needed for LAN Serving

In the mid 1980s, when planning for GUI should have been well underway, IBM was just beginning to toy with the notion of PCs as Servers. The company made agreements with Microsoft to add LAN server facilities to DOS that could be used in an IBM PC Network configuration. Microsoft delivered with IBM versions of its LAN products. Neither the IBM versions nor the Microsoft versions of LAN Server were ever very successful in the marketplace.

Novell had invented LAN serving, and Novell was the champion of the mid-1980s. Why IBM chose to get help from Microsoft instead of Novell is another reason why IBM's LAN foray went bust. Novell was the leader, not Microsoft. But that is a story for another day.

Looking back at Novell's success at the time, it is interesting that Microsoft, the OS kingpin could not unseat Novell, the LAN Server kingpin from its dominance. Other than the Mac, all PC brands were DOS based. Novell Netware was also a non-GUI player, yet, despite no GUI, it was the undisputed king of PC servers. Just as Rochester IBM and its AS/400, there was no apparent desire on Novell's part to update its server user interface to GUI. Yet, as you will see, no GUI was Novell's major downfall.

The GUI King Aims for Novell

Microsoft, the ultimate King of GUI was already biting at Novell in the 1980s with its MS-Net and LAN Manager

Server offerings. These were all designed to loosen Novell's grip on the LAN Server market. However Microsoft could not get it right with these early volleys and they were basically unsuccessful. Gates' company needed a secret weapon and Bill Gates knew exactly what that weapon should be: GUI.

Prior to Bill Gates fixation with having GUI on the server, the industry had associated a successful LAN with the name Netware from Novell. Microsoft failed again and again during this era trying to overcome Novell's lead without a GUI offering. Novell got stronger and stronger with more and more business. Black screen and all, Novell was the darling of the LAN Server crowd until Microsoft released its GUI.

In the early 1990s, Microsoft slapped a Windows like GUI on its new Windows NT Server operating system and the world began to treat this GUI LAN Server offering lots differently from Microsoft's prior black and white entrées. NT by itself was a big, ugly, yet powerful operating system. It was nothing like the constrained DOS-based black screen offerings that Gates and company tried to use in the 1980s to overcome Netware.

This offering looked new and modern and the GUI made it look "easy." NT Server brought a new dimension and an apparent ease of use to the LAN Server world. It was an immediate success. Before long, even long-term Novell customers found themselves taking a hard look at the offering and many jumped to NT because of its inviting look and feel.

Microsoft Becomes the LAN Server King

NT was not a bolt-on LAN Server for DOS as had been the other Microsoft LAN Server attempts. It was a bona fide GUI based LAN Server, packaged as a complete bundle in the Windows NT Server operating system. If a business chose Windows NT, it could also choose Novell as the

Network Server, because the new operating system supported Novell. However, since NT handled most of what was needed internally, it really did not need to have Novell on its back.

Microsoft had gotten the LAN Server formula right this time. When NT first emerged, Gates and company may not have had the best LAN player available, but they quickly got the industry to believe that they owned the stadium and every game from then on was a Microsoft home game. The GUI of NT Server knocked the socks off the computer industry and it was not long before Novell was in financial trouble. Microsoft and Novell's fights are worth telling but that too is a story for another day.

My point in taking us here is that the GUI mattered on the server. It mattered on NT. It is missing on the AS/400. It is missing on Novell. Novell lost the LAN Server space. Today Novell has just about 7 percent of the LAN Server marketplace. Windows has almost all of the rest.

IBM Thinks GUI Is Not Necessary

GUI just does not exist on mainframes and AS/400 systems. There is no GUI interface and IBM does not feel guilty, as it should. IBM does not think GUI is needed because PCs have GUI. There are no icons on an AS/400. The IBM operating systems are not mouse driven.

The hardware does not even have a mouse port. Some may say, just as Bill Gates did with MS-Net and MS LAN Manager, that server OS's do not need GUI. But Gates did not defeat the number-one ranking LAN Server OS in the world, Novell Netware, until he turned on the icons and enabled the mouse with Windows NT in 1993.

IBM may say that it has lost no AS/400 business or mainframes business because of GUI. Yet, statistics indicate that there are well over 150,000,000 PCs in use in businesses across the world. If you give IBM credit for 10,000,000 of these shipments, which admittedly may be high, there are 140,000,000 PCs out there on business desks for which IBM was not paid.

Considering that most of those replaced IBM terminals at $1000 a pop, the IBM Company left $14,000,000,000 on the table along with countless software applications that would have been host-driven instead of client driven if IBM had the right GUI interface for its AS/400 box. You've got to be nuts to think that a modern server of any kind does not need a standard, native GUI interface.

There was lots of money left on the table that would have been IBM's if it had not chosen to lose its terminal business to PCs, for lack of a host-based GUI interface. Moreover, a green and black color combination as the only option for IBM's exceptionally powerful AS/400 and mainframe servers now contributes to the notion that they are "legacy" boxes. Windows at 20 years old gets a pass because it's got GUI.

Dave Books, a former IBM senior systems engineer in Atlanta, before systems engineer's were eliminated, then a certified senior services specialist until the mid-1990s, and now an ad hoc consultant and industry analyst, thinks IBM missed the boat with the PC revolution when the company chose not to add a proprietary GUI to AS/400, instead deferring to PCs:

> **"... what I think is the biggest mistake IBM has made in the last quarter century. IBM should have avoided the personal computer like the plague. IBM did a great job of positioning the Selectric Typewriter as a business machine, not one for personal use (even though many other manufacturers made typewriters almost solely for personal use).**
>
> **Why, then, was IBM too dumb to realize that a machine with the word "personal" in its very name was not the machine for them? By embracing the personal computer in 1979, the International Business Machines company legitimized it for "business" use, something it was never**

designed for and will never do well. If the highly overrated and hugely overpaid top executives of IBM in the late seventies had a particle of vision, they would have developed a proprietary intelligent business workstation.

How big a stretch is it to imagine a microprocessor-based workstation controller capable of running spreadsheet and word processing programs? IBM elected to play "Me, too" in an environment where technological leadership would have reaped immense dividends. If IBM had taken ownership of the business workstation marketplace, today's networks would be driven by reliable business computers (AS/400's, mainframes, etc.) and robust operating system software, not by the fragile TinkerToys currently in use.

IBM turned its back on a multi-multi-billion dollar opportunity and stood idly by while others raked in the money (you're welcome, Mr. Gates). What a squandered opportunity!"

No Terminal GUI: No Desktop

During the late 1980s and early 1990s, IBM woke up only to find that Microsoft was not really its friend. Microsoft had not only killed IBM's desktop terminals, with its Windows PCs, but by "botching" the OS/2 project, it had also killed IBM's chances of keeping the corporate desktop. IBM had to settle for the notion that it had not only lost the corporate desktop, it had lost the whole PC marketplace to entrepreneurs who really wanted to be in the business.

At best, with less than 5 percent of the PC market today, IBM has been a "bit player," an "also ran" in a market it had created. Even after losing the PC war, however, the company did not look at GUI as one of the potential causes for its demise. IBM terminals, which once were sold in the millions dropped off to the point that there was no longer enough business there for IBM to remain a player. IBM eventually stopped making terminals completely.

The cost to IBM of Microsoft's victory is staggering. For every $1,000 terminal that was replaced by a PC, IBM was lucky to get 1/20 of the action. All of that business was once

IBM's, and only IBM's. IBM did not have to win the desktop. It always owned the desktop. Before Microsoft, IBM terminals owned the desktop. IBM woke up too late to save the desktop. The company could not get a handle on what the problems may have been. For some reason, there was so much GUI in everybody else's products, IBM could not see through the "Windows," as millions were casting its mainframe and AS/400 terminals aside.

Semi GUI Is Not Anti-GUI

IBM did not think of itself as anti-GUI. The company just felt it was okay to not adopt GUI in a big way. They sold Unix (semi GUI) with IBM's RS/6000 systems, and they sold full GUI with Windows PCs. If the company considered GUI a market requirement, it already had GUI covered in two product lines and thus, IBM theoretically did not need GUI on its bread and butter systems, the mainframe and the AS/400.

IBM's high paid consultants could have pointed out to IBM that a little GUI would have gone a long way in making their internally elegant and powerful proprietary systems, externally magnificent. After all, it was because those terminals were completely non-GUI that IBM was losing $1,000 a clip.

Who Made That Decision?

After 25 years, inner elegance had made the AS/400 product, as well as its predecessor, the System/38, a clear success in the small and midsized business marketplace. Yet, as I am writing this book, there is still no GUI interface on the AS/400 and none is planned of which I am aware. Back in the late 1980s as the AS/400 was killing the minicomputer competition, IBM gave the machine a pass in terms of gaining the interface technology capabilities of the day. It did not need GUI then. Clearly the time to catch up has long past. But one must ask, where were the IBM visionaries while all this was going on?

In this instance, it was not mainframe IBM that had picked on the "Little Lab that Could." Just as Novell, Rochester had no active GUI plan for its own box. I cannot recall hearing anything from anybody in Rochester that GUI was needed on the platform. Not 25 years ago. Not 15 years ago. Not 5 years ago. And not even today. Yet Jobs was at XEROX PARC in 1979, as was Gates shortly after.

When Steven Jobs, the original GUI master, emerged in the news as a candidate for CEO of IBM around 1993, many of us were disappointed that he would not take the job. It would have been a GUI time in the IBM house if he had gotten the job. Lou Gerstner took over instead of Jobs, and his only idea of good vision was a good bottom line.

What IBM Could Have Done

First of all, it bears repeating that IBM in Rochester has had almost 30 years to dream up a way to put a natural GUI interface on the AS/400. They simply missed the boat. They did not know it was important. The consultants never told them and they did not see it themselves.

If Rochester IBM had used the years for GUI innovation and had planned to have a GUI on its product line some time in the future, you can bet that, unless big IBM would not have let them proceed, a highly innovative GUI interface would be resident on every AS/400 shipped today. It was not part of the plan, however. And so no GUI is available for the AS/400 user community other than that provided by Bill Gates.

Some time between the Future System and Fort Knox projects, Rochester could have completed a GUI interface. In 2007, the workstation controller, the part of an AS/400 that provides the green screen intelligence, will celebrate its 30th birthday. This important piece of the user interface to IBM's midrange computers uses a small low-powered microprocessor originally introduced in 1977. At that time, terminal costs approached $4,000 a piece.

Think of how much more powerful all processors have become and how feasible it would have been for IBM to have created a GUI controller and a GUI terminal by 1993. From 1978, when the System/38 was announced, IBM had more than 15 years to get it done before Windows began to take over the world, in 1993.

The fact is that IBM missed the boat by a mile. Rochester missed the boat. Other than Steven Jobs and Bill Gates nobody really got it. GUI was important. IBM still doesn't really get it or something would be in the works.

A Town without GUI

Rochester has never had a cohesive plan for graphics of any kind for the AS/400 yet the notion has been recognized as important as seen in a few scattered offerings over the years. For example, IBM offers a tool called the Graphical Display Data Manager for GUI printing that the company ported to the AS/400 years ago from the mainframe. It can create logos and the like for printed reports. There is also the Business Graphics Utility that's been around for a long time but never had any real support. Other than those two, however, there has not been much.

IBM may argue that its Operations Navigator product is the AS/400 GUI. However, I would remind IBM, if it presented that argument that Operations Navigator runs under the control of the Windows operating system, not OS/400.

In the late 1980s, IBM had a beta product called the graphical design aid (GDA), which was never released. This was a real hot tool that was modeled after IBM's successful Screen Design Aid. IBM's best graphics display at the time cost about $7,000, and at the time it was needed for GDA. So, this went no place fast.

IBM never announced it. Surely with PC color monitors achieving higher and higher resolutions, IBM could have done lots better with its graphics display and it could have introduced its GDA product when it would have made a splash.

I am sure there are some readers out there who think that IBM did its best. Well, I am sorry that you feel that way. From my trained eyes, IBM did not do its best, and worse than that, IBM Rochester did not do its best. GUI was just not part of the plan. Nobody thought it was important though it was right there in Rochester's face all the time.

The GUI Half Life

In actuality, GUI has only become important in the last ten to fifteen years. Gates first all-GUI product was Windows 95 and that did not come out until late 1995. Windows 3.0 was out in May 1900; Windows 3.1 arrived in 1992. So the GUI onslaught that many of us feel has been going on all our lives only began in the early 1990s.

The IBM that had 10 complete proprietary operating systems in use in 1985, during Fort Knox, somehow could not write one operating system for the PC that would work. IBM trusted Microsoft to this task and lost big on that bet. The company also lost its own opportunity to build its own GUI expertise.

Only Microsoft and Apple had live GUI experience. There was a lot IBM could have done but did not do because Apple and Microsoft were already doing it. Thankfully, Tom Watson Jr. did not think that way in 1952 when Univac was the only company making computers.

Web Browser: A Mode of GUI

It happens that in 1992 some very innovative GUI inroads were being made outside of Apple's influence or Microsoft's. The Internet was fast catching on. A guy named Marc Andreeson, a young man who was a student and part time assistant at the National Center for Supercomputing Applications (NCSA), had really tuned into the needs of the Internet and the fledgling World Wide Web. Andreeson and a friend, Eric Bina, built a browser that extended the use of HTML with tags for images and centering and other very important GUI notions.

The resultant "Mosaic Browser" formed the basis for a new company. Andreeson and Jim Clark of Silicon Graphics founded Netscape Communications, and the rest is well known history.

Coincidentally, IBM's Charles Goldfarb had created the General Markup Language (GML) that Tim Berneers Lee (who invented the Web Server) used for his Web server language called HTML. Andreeson's browser extended the use of HTML so that it could be a real GUI interface mechanism. IBM had invented GML, the precursor to HTML and XML.

This was in 1992. Even if IBM did not build a full-blown graphical interface from hardware, it surely could have built something like a Web server under the covers of the AS/400 to give it a nice GUI interface without an exorbitant cost. IBM again chose not to.

After all, Andreeson was just a college kid. Hey, if he could do it, and Gates and Jobs could do it, why not IBM? The answer is that IBM could have done it. However, it did not think it was worth the effort.

What IF?

What would have happened if the AS/400 had been given a real GUI interface? Wow! For one, IBM would not have lost the desktop. IT shops controlled the desktops until PC renegades were permitted to bring in their special purpose programs. IBM could have provided an inexpensive graphics terminal (less expensive than the $2,500 PCs of the day back then) that would permit spreadsheets to be run on coprocessors inside the AS/400 complex. Word processing could be done in much the same way.

Some of you may have heard of Citrix Systems. Its claim to fame is that it lets reasonably dumb PCs use Windows applications that are stored on the Citrix PC Server box. So no software must be loaded from the PC desktop. IBM could have done this with a combination of browser-ware and Citrix-like function via coprocessors or controllers, as they were called then. Instead of a LAN, the I/O bus of the AS/400 could have been equipped with as many coprocessors as necessary to execute the applications.

The coprocessors could be Intel based or PowerPC based. Though my generic suggestion and that of Mr. Books (quoted above) would certainly work, IBM really does not need us to solve this problem for them. IBM knows very well how to solve the GUI problem in the best and least expensive way. The company has clearly chosen not to.

Success Left on the Table

There are actually many ways that IBM could have solved the GUI problem. If it had solved the GUI terminal problem, IBM today would be the biggest desktop software company, providing word processing, graphics, and spreadsheet functions to PC productivity applications. They would all run in the AS/400 complex and perhaps even the mainframe. IBM left a lot of money on the table by not building GUI into the AS/400 and not retrofitting it when it was obvious that modern systems have to look modern in order to sell.

What Should Rochester Do Now?

It's only too late when a product has died. Rochester should get a team together and start moving to a server-centric world for in-house applications. Create a real GUI interface--not a client/server fat client, but an interface that runs on the AS/400. Begin to bring applications inboard, as noted above, with coprocessors as needed.

IBM surely knows how to do this better than I could ever tell them. The company just doesn't plan to do it. I think they are wrong in a big way. The sin is IBM's and Rochester's. You can't have a modern system today unless it has a modern user interface. Moreover, like Novell, you cannot rely on a GUI client to get you through the dark days. Gates' GUI was able to defeat Novell.

His GUI may one day bring down both the AS/400 and the mainframe. Hopefully IBM is secretly working on something. The GUI must come from inside the server, just as Bill Gates did with NT Server. Novell did not think GUI was needed, but after losing 93 percent of its market, I am sure that Novell thinks otherwise today. It was not needed but it was needed. It's time for IBM and Rochester to get on with the GUI.

Possible Good News

The endings of many of the chapters in this book changed as a result of IBM's May 4, 2004 announcements. Two of the things that IBM announced with its new i5 and i5/OS offering is that it added full servlet serving with WebSphere Express and it began to build a browser based GUI interface to the AS/400.

Perhaps they got the idea from the early versions of this chapter that were being emailed from friend to friend. But, I think not. I think something has changed in IBM that is permitting Rochester to change. Soon, Rochester may no longer be a "town without GUI." I sure hope this is real.

Like many of you from the AS/400 camp, I usually like what Rochester does with the AS/400. However, they missed the boat on GUI, and Rochester has become a "town without GUI." To lighten it up a bit, I took the words to Gene Pitney's famous "Town Without Pity," and I present them below, modified for GUI. (Gene Pitney wrote the song and he also recorded it. It was one of the top 100 hits of 1962.)

A Town Without GUI

When you're young and so mouse driven as we
And bewildered by green screens we see
Why do people tint us so
Only those with icons know
What a town without GUI can do

If we click to gaze upon a star
People talk about how bad we are
Ours is not a textual age
A Rochester message fills the page
What a town without GUI can do

The G-U-I has problems, many problems
But they're all solved with Ctrl-Alt-Delete
Why don't they try it, take a mouse and try it
They'd find that clicks and icons can be really neat

Take this graphical design and capture it fast
I'm afraid the interface can't last
How can we keep windows alive
How can our AS/400 systems survive
When the PF keys tear you in two
What a town without GUI can do

How can we keep windows alive
How can our AS/400 systems survive
When the PF keys tear you in two
What a town without GUI can do

No, it isn't very pretty what a town without GUI can do.

Chapter 34 Teach Me! Teach Me! Teach Me!

A Mission from the Top

Back in the early 1980s, when the System/38 was beginning to catch on, IBM made a decision that would take quite a few years to implement. By the time Lou Gerstner took over, it was, as they say, a done deal. The company was moving from a direct sales force to a distributor arrangement.

During the mid-point of the Akers years, Mr. Akers was trying to recover from having to pay for the excess plant capacity that John Opel, his predecessor CEO, had bequeathed him. One corporate and regional emissary after another flocked into the local branch offices to prepare the troops for what was coming.

As the Blues Brothers would say, they were on a mission from God. They came to help assure us that from the top of the company on down, IBM management knew that its field sales force, the very bottom of the marketing ladder, was *the* problem that needed to be fixed. Of course, by blaming the field force for a poor sales execution, it spared executive management from being blamed for poor planning.

These emissaries came to spread the corporate message that we had better get on the stick or else. They addressed us typically in formal meetings and did not spend much time working with anybody in particular. They were spreading "the word," not looking to solve any problems. They "knew" that we were the problem. Of course we saw ourselves as regular Joes, family men and women working hard in the

Branch, trying to sell and install hardware despite all of IBM's constraints.

The message of the emissaries seemed designed to shock us all into submission. It was obvious that they did not know, and our local management team could not convince them, that we were already well into submission. I can recall one of the systems engineer managers of that period, an athletic type with more gusto than most at times, hitting a cerebral high by netting out one particular emissary's visit with these words:

> **"Maybe if every now and then they'd send in a few good plays."**

The emissaries seemed very keen on making sure that we all knew that "IBM is considering the elimination of the entire field force." From the mid-1980s, almost concurrently with John Akers' reign, the big buffs in headquarters stopped trusting the little people in the field.

Before the AS/400 was announced, anyone with System/38 expertise, for example, had a price on his head. It did not take too long after I saw my price that I went to mainframe school to learn about DB2, the relational database that made the mainframe a more friendly place to be. At the time, the System/38 product line was a candidate for elimination, along with the field force.

From Fear to Short Reprieve

Then, out of no place, the rumors of Fort Knox's death and of Silverlake coming in its wake began to reach the branch offices. In June 1988, and for a few short years afterward, life as a small business systems engineer or marketing person in the field was almost good again. The AS/400 immediately did so well that DEC strongholds across the world caved in and former DEC users marched in droves to the new AS/400 box.

For example, one of my larger accounts, Commonwealth Telephone Enterprises Corporation (CTEC), during this period sold its fledgling cellular software business to Systematics, which, after a few years, sold the business to Alltel Information Systems. The company was once a do-or-die DEC account.

They had a number of DEC machines and a home-built software package called Virtuoso that they sold to startup cellular companies. At the time, all cellular companies were startup companies so there were some great opportunities. Looking at the long term prospects of success in the cellular software marketplace, the company chose to abandon the flailing DEC bandwagon, partner with IBM at a national level, and convert Virtuoso to the AS/400. Bruce Ikeda was IBM's marketing representative who covered the account for Big Blue. CTEC also used IBM's mainframe computers.

The Training and Consulting Mission

I worked with a team of DEC specialists who knew there was no returning to the DEC days. My job was to help them make the transition. Being an old buck, as my wife likes to refer to me, I understood the systems programming side and the application programming side of the AS/400. Just like anybody who is installing a new system architecture, the Alltel folks needed training, but their budgets were so tight at the time that they were not in a position to attend IBM's expensive training schools or Guided Learning Centers.

The local IBM office was not going to miss this sales opportunity for want of education. In addition to application and systems support, my role expanded to help these folks learn the system. In this vein, since the team had no systems programmer type at the time, my job was to help create one.

Kevin Goulding, a kid with more spunk and desire than knowledge, was the raw material on the systems side. Bob Cooper, a very intelligent and exceptionally nice person was the application development manager.

Bob Cooper oversaw the application conversion action and he kept his team reading one manual section after another (training the hard way) while they were converting DEC code to RPG. Goulding was getting OJT from me and at the same time he was reading a lot about AS/400 Work Management. Both Goulding and the Coopermen loved it when the "old buck" showed up. Cooper kept his five-person staff under control from making errant phone calls, but when I was on site, I was fair game. I could not leave until all of their questions were answered and those that were not answered were part of my "honeydew" list. That's how they learned.

As most IBM to DEC installations, after a few weeks, the DEC folks were so sharp that the AS/400 became a real piece of cake for the team. I would suspect that today, some of the most loyal AS/400 fans, besides ex IBM systems engineers, are the former DEC folks who, to their surprise, met a system that was better put together than the infamous and quite fabulous DEC VAX. Before the AS/400's arrival, the VAX was unquestionably one of the best and most favorite systems at the time for people who actually understood computers.

Can't Do That Today

Those days are long gone. They will never return. IBM in the 2000 era would never approach a happy customer and suggest that they would be happier with an AS/400. That was the reality of the day. There are no IBM sales people selling IBM computers today other than the nurse-mates to the aging mainframe IT management set. There's so much money to be lost in mainframe land that Big Blue can still throw people at the problem.

Nobody in the early 2000's and on to today, whther it be IBM or its very disloyal Business Partners, weree trying to sell the AS/400 to anybody who did not already know about it. That is an unfortunate reality. I got the idea that IBM simply did not care.

So when people tell me that there was a training issue at the heart of AS/400 problems, I beg to differ. Training has nothing to do with the AS/400's prospects for continued success. There is no training problem. People learn when they have an incentive. With few new AS/400 installations, one must ask, why is training needed? Many AS/400 professionals are available for hire.

In 2005, for example, I was asked to bid on a contract job for this same account, though I operate now as an independent consultant and not as an IBM Senior Systems Engineer. They needed 5 plus RPG programmers. I found five sharp guys from Northeastern Pennsylvania who were out of work and some "head hunters" found 95 more. Of the 100 individuals interviewed, the company brought in seven for a six-month engagement.

From my eyes, that means, there were ninety-three easily reachable people available for AS/400 work in Northeastern PA alone. There is no training problem when so many people are looking for work. By the way, it did not seem to matter that I had trained their existing staf pro-bono. IBM is not the only company that has forgotten how to say thank you.

When IBM had real branch offices, each time our office sold an AS/400, SEs had to make sure that the customer could make the transition to the new system. The early customers' existing staffs most often had no AS/400 expertise. Because their company was moving to an AS/400, the staff had to learn the system. It was not optional. They either attended IBM Schools, IBM's Guided Learning Centers, or like Alltel, they read manuals, asked questions, and eventually brought in some training from the outside.

There was no magic then and there need be no magic now. There was just a lot of hard work. A little MADGIC might help, however (see Chapter titled *MADGIC! MADGIC! MADGIC!*). If somebody were selling new AS/400's now, the law of natural balances would come into play and from no place, candidates to learn the AS/400 would emerge. If IBM were selling AS/400 machines like hotcakes in 2016, the industry would figure out how to fill the job placements. You bet!

IBM Systems Engineers Once Filled the Gaps

There was a time that IBM systems engineers all over the world assured IBM's customers that they would be able to do the job and then they filled in the knowledge gaps as required on the road to understanding and live operation. No time that I can ever remember was there a cadre of college graduates with AS/400 experience arriving on a regular basis to relieve the staffing burden. The same situation exists today, except with one big difference.

IBM no longer has a technical field staff to help. Business Partners do not give away services and often do not have the level of expertise that was available in the IBM offices of yesteryear. The new IBM also provides no sales team to call on small businesses. Just like a brewery, the company has turned its business over to distributors.

All of the people, who once did that work, as the emissaries had promised, were laid off in the mid 1990's or like me, they left while there was a great early retirement package on the table. Today, there is nobody left in IBM to fill in the gaps when a prospect wants to take a ride with a new AS/400.

Probably more damaging than that, there are no IBM marketing persons whose mission it is to sell IBM AS/400 gear to his or her accounts. So, the AS/400 is not on the sales table, other than to existing customers, or to somebody who, for some unexplainable reason, asks for the machine.

There is nothing out there to motivate a new client to look at an AS/400. Thus, there is no training issue as today's analysts too often report. New blood would be nice but it would only place old blood on the bench. If IBM reevaluates its AS/400 line and chooses to highlight its finest achievement, IBM can still make it to the top.

I do not want to appear to be suggesting that IBM Business Partners in the field did not try to generate business for IBM. When a customer was ready for an upgrade, Business Partners could smell the opportunity and they fought each other to get the business. They have rarely generated demand for new systems, however.

Because lazy AS/400 Business Partners call on AS/400 customers every four years whether they need it or not, AS/400 customers buy new AS/400s every four years or so. It takes too much time and effort for a lazy Business Partner to introduce somebody new to an AS/400 and actually get them to buy the product. So they don't waste their time. Nobody was out there since the early 2000's trying to bring non-AS/400 users into the fold. Thus, I repeat. There was no training issue.

Most business partners also sold Wintel and whenever it became tough to sell an AS/400 (Power i), the business partner quickly would switch totheir Windows offerings. Once the dotted line was signed, the IBM Business Partner could rape and pillage the customer for support srvices. The Windows hardware / OS software cost was minimal but making it work and supporting it afterwards cost the customer lots more than if they had selected an AS/400. Moroever, their goals were most often not met with a cheap solution du jour.

ti

In fact, as noted above, I see a glut of AS/400 developers in pockets of the world just looking for the opportunity to get a job. Barbara Chaderton, an independent AS/400 consultant from Northeastern Pennsylvania sees it this way:

> **"The developer base for the AS/400 community is already shrinking and extremely competitive. There are already too many COBOL and RPG programmers for the client base."**

More than I see new customers falling for the AS/400, I find former AS/400 companies threatening to move to the "less expensive," Windows platform, and some actually making the move. Because IBM's marketing brings in few new customers and old customers seem to be leaving the platform, at least in Northeastern PA, faster than new ones arrive, there really is no good reason for anybody to want to or have to learn the AS/400 product line. The lack of AS/400 business is the problem, not the lack of resources in AS/400 accounts.

George Farr: "Get Used to It!"

George Farr, a highly technical development manager from IBM's Toronto labs, a person who I respect deeply as a technician but not a marketer, once told a group at COMMON that there will be no enhancements to RPG/400, and then he added briskly, "Get used to it!" To keep sane, I must tell myself at times that there will be no AS/400 marketing--get used to it! By the way, George was wrong. IBM has enhanced its RPG language so that it is now the most advanced programming language in the world.

Hey, George, because I like the sound of your message, but not the message itself, I would like to say the following words to you and to other IBM people who seem to wonder where the new blood is in the AS/400 ranks:

There is no new blood, IBM. Get used to it!

There will not be any new blood, IBM. Get used to it!

If you don't have a thin dime to invest in advertising the AS/400 on TV, nobody will be drawn to the AS/400, no matter how good it is and no matter how bad companies need people. Get used to it!

New generations of programmers are not coming to the AS/400. The legions are graduating and heading out for jobs in Unix, Linux, and Windows camps. This is s stain not only for this generation of kids, but for generations to follow. They're not coming. Get used to it!

IBM decided it was OK to snub MIT years ago, and all academic institutions knew from that day forward that they could not trust Big Blue to keep a promise.

Kids grow up to be adults and on the way they go to school to learn things, including computers. If they never hear about an AS/400, they won't be inclined to learn about it. IBM does nothing to convince the best Academic Institutions in America that its AS/400, now Power i is worth another look. So, students of these universities never learn an iota about what IBM has to bring to the table. Hey IBM, Get used to it!

Nobody Loves What They Don't Know

Why would anybody spend good money to learn about something that they have never heard about? The IBM AS/400 for twenty-eight years and counting has been completely missing in any academic computer scientist's depth chart of systems. It's not missing the point. It's just missing. As long as the AS/400 message is missing from the technologists ear and from the public's ear, the world will know nothing about the AS/400 and will choose to know nothing if asked to learn.

IBM advertising honchos may think they have no reason to tell ordinary citizens about the AS/400 -- Power i since it is a business system—though a great business system. However, business people, such as my neighbors are also ordinary citizens and they know nothing about the AS/400, because IBM chooses to tell them nothing.

When they go for a new system to run their businesses, would they even think to call IBM? For what? That's the training "problem" in a nutshell. It's a ruse. Nobody new is buying and that's why nobody new needs to learn about IBM's AS/400 system. Eventually IBM will **get used to it!**

Tell Somebody About An AS/400!

There is a company whose message is always heard. Wherever you go, the Windows platform is close by. Every one of my neighbors has one or more PCs. I have six PCs. Even I can't afford an AS/400. My son Brian was an IT major in college. He got the Science Award at his university.

He never once saw an AS/400 at home or at school. He got out of IT and when I originally wrote parts of this book, he was his second year of law school. He is now an accomplished lawyer far from IT. He still does not know what an AS/400 can really mean for a business.

Now, law is a career I would recommend. I have two lawyers as sons. They do no thave to worry about what IBM does or does not do. IBM offered my son, who had received the Sceince Award at his university no opportunities as an IT major to see the AS/400 at school or even on a field trip to IBM.

IBM should not wonder why there are no new bodies learning about the AS/400 when the company does nothing to attract new interests. We're not talking about TV advertising here. IBM's AS/400 message, if it was ever spoken, was certainly not put out to assure that it was heard.

Just a few years ago, at the university where I once taught on the IT faculty, my students told me that the institution was no longer going to teach RPG, because it felt the language had become irrelevant. I am a consultant and a professor at this university, and I know that I never told them that! The trade press has never had a love for IBM or IBM's special products.

There is no question that RPG is the language of the traditional AS/400 implementer. This one-time all-IBM university's decision was made without consultation, and it will go unchallenged by IBM because nobody from IBM will care enough to object.

In fact, it took IBM many years to know that the university had made the "no RPG" decision, because nobody from IBM was calling on this university to find out what was cooking on the IT education front. There was no IBM representative whose mission it is to call on faculties to help them with their curricula, and there was no IBM calling on the top officials to make sure they enjoyed their IBM relationship.

If IBM thinks that AS/400 education is an issue, they could do a lot better job of addressing it as a problem. I don't see IBM doing anything–not just in TV advertising but where the rubber meets the road. George Farr taught me how to talk to IBM about this. You are reaping what you sew, IBM. Get used to it!

How Could IBM Help in Education If It Chose To Help?

In many ways, the things that IBM could and should do for the AS/400 are things that occur naturally to help the Windows server platform. If IBM were inclined to sell new AS/400 accounts and spread the word about the AS/400 and make it easy for people to learn, there are a few things that Big Blue could work on to help make the AS/400 a desirable system to learn. Though there is some overlap with the recommended improvement list in the chapter titled: *Suggestions for Improvement*, these recommendations pertain to the "training issue" per se if there really is one. A non-prioritized, numbered list follows:

1. Introduce a mini AS/400 for one-person businesses and for the home.

There are hundreds of millions of PCs across the world. Ninety nine percent of all PCs are Windows PCs. The rest are Linux. You may know that Linus Torvalds invented Linux because DOS / Windows was such a sloppy operating system and Unix was too expensive. A PC-based AS/400 would help expand mindshare, which is the biggest detriment to AS/400 style computing.

2. Hire a SWAT team of good-will ambassadors who can give short seminars at local colleges, universities, and town halls.

Use this team to conduct one-day AS/400 seminars at least twice a year in all areas of the world and invite all the business people. Run half-day public seminars (town hall meetings) for anybody wanting to come.

3. Stop treating AS/400 education classes as a profit-oriented business.

Education should be bundled with system sales so that one or several people can be trained for free.

4. Provide a free, AS/400 self-learning center over the Internet.

Using this center, IBM customers or anybody wanting to know, can come and be assured that a person will be there for questions, using a form of Chat to answer questions within a reasonable period.

5. Sponsor public debates on Educational TV.

All factions, Windows, Linux, and AS/400, should be presented and debated.

6. Create AS/400 memorabilia and a fun-to-watch demo CD.

Attractive cartoon-like, give-away AS/400 dolls could be commissioned to give the platform a friendly face. A well-done "AS/400 as a business system" CD or DVD could also spark some interest.

7. Start a "you, too, can know the AS/400 campaign" for kids.

Bring back Captain IBM and Captain 400 to tag team the kids att heir schools or after school. Meet them on their turf in grade school, high school, and college, and tell them what the AS/400 is all about. Invite the press to special events

8 Encourage former systems engineers and marketing reps and former Rochester people to help educate the masses on the AS/400.

IBM treats folks like mc more as competitors than as hands willing to help. Maybe some ex IBMers, such as me, would volunteer their time. IBM has never asked its ex employees with AS/400 expertise for anything, including the time of day. At any rate, IBM can take advantage of their former employees' willingness to help by treating them with some dignity.

Note: When IBM dismantled its field force, thousands of local IBM Systems Engineers went off into the sunset. This was a potential army of loyal AS/400 types. At the time, local management was happy just to get rid of their employ, never to see them again. In retrospect, this

intelligent herd could have been unleashed with a positive message to IBM customers. IBM could have also helped systems engineer's keep abreast of the system to be in a position to help customers. This is still a good idea.

In my particular case, IBM was so paranoid that they viewed my helping my clients as competing with the local office. In my first summer, I received a notice from corporate counsel. I construed this to mean cease and desist. One of my former peers had turned me in for helping my clients, who were AS/400 shops, and may also have been IBM's services clients.

The local office then insisted that I get approval for every engagement or seminar that I was to run just in case that they decided to do the same thing. It wasn't nice and it certainly did not help IBM's AS/400 customers. IBM went so far as to send an IBMer to teach a seminar onsite at one of my clients, after I had asked permission, rather than permit me to gain the business. IBM never charged for this particular seminar.

9. Conduct a wake-up, one-time, three-month marketing blitz from IBM branch office sites or hotels close by the former site.

Bring back as many former IBM marketing reps. systems engineers, and former local managers as part-time temporary employees to conduct such blitzes. A person working for IBM should visit every customer and prospect (especially K-12 schools and colleges) at least once during this period, offering special deals on systems bought under the program.

AS/400 Memorabilia and the CD/DVD that demonstrates powerful AS/400 features should be provided. Free AS/400 education should be available at the IBM Branch Office or a rented site for the entire blitz period. The visit to all IBM customers and non-customers can help them know that IBM is in town and the AS/400 really is not dead.

For added support, a direct mail campaign to local businesses should precede the blitz along with all the details of what customers and prospects should expect from the visit. Figure out how to make the Business Partners help by paying them for sales made during the program.

10. Change the name of the AS/400 or Power System for IBM I or the Power i (whatever it may be called) from its current name to *The IBM Business System* with no numbers. If this change is made, the two tag team captains could be captain IBM and captain IBS. Change the name of the RPG programming language to the Business Language and make it available on all platforms.

Just a Start

These are just a few ideas to help generate a demand for training and to get some training accomplished. If IBM decides to market the AS/400, I'm sure the marketing experts at IBM would add many more items to this list. Until then! It surely would help IBM to achieve #1 again to get started on the list. Make it a 10 to 15 year rollout with a roadmap.

Chapter 35 No Stork and No Baby AS/400!

IBM Announces New Power i Pocket Rocket -- Baby AS/400

On April 1, 2003, April Sfole of the now-defunct iSeries News staff scooped the whole computer industry with her fabulous research and discovery piece about IBM's new Power i Pocket Rocket. In a piece titled "IBM Prepares Power i Pocket Rocket," this contributing writer to the talented iSeries Network news organization, a division of Penton Media, provides this compelling and crisp introduction and analysis of this potentially fabulous new IBM undertaking. (See back of chapter epitaph on Penton.)

> **April 1, 2003**
>
> **Although the Power5 processor that's expected to debut in the Power i next year promises to bring more refrigerator-sized, power-hog iSeries boxes to the market in 2004, the big news comes in a much smaller package.**
>
> **By 2006, IBM says, Rochester will release a revolutionary new machine code-named the iPocket - which will undoubtedly be renamed upon GA to something with a more "IBM" ring, like "iSeries Miniature Business Computer." The machine will be built on a molecular computing model made possible by IBM's carbon nanotube technology.**
>
> **The machine, IBM says, will crunch data-mining transactions at a blistering pace while dissipating less heat than a wristwatch--all in a package the size of a PalmPilot. (The iPocket, of course, would be much costlier to replace if misplaced, with an estimated price tag of $15,000 for an entry version.) The technology would bring a whole new meaning to 24/7 support, with OS/400 administrators literally able to take their work home with them.**
>
> **Power i marketeer Malcolm Haines is already dreaming up attractive new packaging to appeal to the under-40**

> **crowd he wants to lure to the platform. "Imagine an Power i in the shape of a Coke can," he says. "Not only would it draw upon the 1970s nostalgia that's so hot, but it would be a great collector's item in 2007 when new technology makes it obsolete."**
>
> **April Fools!**

Some of the most serious things are said in jest. I thank Power i News for presenting that piece for us and if you read it in their space in April 2003, I bet you also said, "Holy Cow! It's about time." I can see my neighbors plugging into a coke can for their computing power.

I love the idea of a nice little AS/400 so that I too can have an AS/400 instead of having to borrow time on customer machines to do work related to their needs. Many small businesses, which IBM would not necessarily consider candidates for the AS/400, would love to run their businesses on a little AS/400. They would be able to do more than keep their books in Excel spreadsheets. They could do anything. I'd also like to be able to develop solutions for my customers on a little AS/400. There are lots of people who feel the same as I, but not as many as there would be if IBM actually came through with a product with April Sfole's specifications. You may read all about this notion at http://www.itjungle.com/tfh/tfh121106-story03.html.

Barbara Chaderton, an independent AS/400 consultant from Northeastern Pennsylvania, offers her thoughts:

> **IBM needs to scale down the pricing structure to be more marketable to small businesses. For example, when I went independent, I considered getting a small box to keep my skills fresh and to possibly do a little outsourcing. The lowest price I could obtain was in the range of $10,000 on a refurbished [AS/400 Model] 270, and that was for a single user! I was looking for something comparable to the old Baby 36. Too pricey for my pocket!**
>
> **A large percentage of IBM's potential customer base is comprised of small businesses, including independent developers. Naturally this group will seek alternative business solutions, which are more affordable and the developers will go along with them.**

An Apple and IBM Product Partnership

Perhaps IBM can get the little AS/400 out the door through Apple. There is always the Apple Possibility. Considering that Apple was able to run its Mac OS-X operating system on the G5 PowerMac models that ran on tailored IBM PowerPC chips, the technology is definitely there. Apple switched to Intel but you can bet those OS links to come back to IBM Power are still there.

If IBM and Apple partnered above the processor line, the end result could be that the OS/400 (operating system) now known as IBM I could run nicely on a PowerMac. A side benefit is that a nice Mac GUI could theoretically drive it.

With the capabilities of logical portioning on one of these babies, IBM and Apple could make the partition connection invisible between the two operating systems and the Mac could be on every OS/400 big box and OS/400 could be on every little Mac. That again is wishful thinking. Only things that IBM wants to happen with regard to AS/400 will happen. If IBM decides that it is time, all impossible tasks would again become probable.

On the same day as the Power i Pocket Rocket article above. Ms Sfole, the contributing writer who put the above piece together, published another brilliant article called "Haines to Market Power i Cool." By the way, Malcolm Haines (or a guy or gal just like him) is a very spirited marketeer who, if empowered in his day, could have won the day for the AS/400.

April 1, 2003

Malcolm Haines, the wily Brit behind the Power i' most memorable marketing campaigns, recently revealed radical new plans--for Big Blue, anyway--to rescue the world's best-loved platform from obscurity. Haines is crafting a new image for the Power i designed to appeal to the 40-and-under crowd--especially those folks in their mid-thirties who are rapidly ascending the corporate ladder to technology-buying positions (and impending midlife crises) yet who still harbor delusions of being on youth's cutting edge.

The key to reaching these trend-conscious 20- and 30-somethings is to make the iSeries [Power i] seem cool - and On/Off Capacity Upgrade on Demand isn't enough to do the trick. So Haines has lined up celebrity endorsements to bring a hip yet respectable cachet to the platform. The premier TV spot features serial pitchwomen Catherine Zeta-Jones and Jamie Lee Curtis bantering coyly about how the iSereies is the greatest contribution to humanity since Dr. Scholl's Exercise Sandals and Ben & Jerry's ice cream.

Future ads will feature basketball star Yao Ming, posters Queen Latifa, Nora Jones, Marc Anthony, and the Dixie Chicks, and actors Morgan Freeman and Gene Hackman. (Actor Martin Sheen had been scheduled for the slot Hackman filled, but he was axed for being too morally centered to fit the image of a large corporation.)

To give the Power i the "underground cool" factor favored by many tech savants, Haines also had the idea of building a video game around the platform, much like car companies often debut new models in racing games to build buzz. Though the game is still in co-development by Rochester's Linux team and the creators of EverQuest, Haines leaked a few details. The game is set in a gloomy, futuristic world where combatants battle to "assimilate" the greatest number of operating systems. One of the characters, a Borg-queen-like marauding mama with braids, bears a striking resemblance to former IBMer Janet Krueger.

April Fools!

Kelly's Law is a euphemism for things that I have found in life that are so obvious nobody ought to have to be told. Among other things, Kelly's Law would say that good marketing and advertising sells, that poor marketing and advertising sells just a little, and that no marketing or advertising sells nothing. IBM has done the latter.

Once Bill Gates builds an AS/400 clone, even Malcolm Haines, IBM spokesman exemplar, will not be able to put IBM Dumpty's pieces back together again. The moral of this story is when the ducks are lined up, it's time to bring them in. A few baby AS/400s would help get the ducks heading in the right direction.

Why would iSereies News Network run little April Fools things like this? Maybe they are written for their readers' enjoyment, and maybe there is a dual purpose, like this book, hoping IBM reads them and does something about the mess it's created. These things do get great reactions. Sometimes thoughts come from apparently no place and yet they stick. Eventually IBM may feel the need to do something or be compelled to explain the notions away. That's why I stay at it.

The New Sony AS/400?

There is lots of speculation about IBM's interest in the new account area for AS/400 or the new account sized AS/400 system. Certain IBMers (Frank Soltis) have even suggested that the new PowerPC chip that IBM designed for the Sony PlayStation may be the basis for a smaller, less expensive AS/400 business computer in the future.

There are few people who are aware that IBM has any role in the chips that go into any video games, yet IBM is the leader in all chips for all purposes other than Intel PCs. Early in 2003, there was a strong rumor that IBM was working on porting the AS/400 operating system, OS/400 to the Sony PlayStation? It was a natural rumor for two reasons: The PlayStation will soon be using a new IBM PowerPC Chip, and Dr. Frank Soltis said that it would be so.

Though Soltis, the Power i' chief scientist until his retirement at the end of 2008, likes having fun with the crowds in his "future talks" at COMMON user group conferences, he was compelled to respond to the PlayStation rumor with a resounding "no!" In fact, he called the PlayStation rumor nonsense. Soltis admitted that he had joked about it himself and may have been the real source of the rumor but he defended his statement as a simple "joke."

The reaction to the rumor was telling of AS/400 sentiments. People were excited. Most AS/400 aficionados would love to see an affordable AS/400 in IBM's sales book. It would certainly help my neighbors enjoy AS/400 technology, but more importantly, it would provide a vehicle by which young people could be attracted to the platform. If IBM could retrofit a *PlayStation* with a bit of OS/400, it would certainly be more effective exposure for the AS/400 than all the advertising spots available on all TV channels.

Come on, Frank, what's wrong with the idea? Think of the free PR upon announcement. There would be nobody who had not heard of OS/400. Of course, an IBM executive with some heavy mettle would have to stand up and be counted for that to ever happen.

With the current conservative, no-risk crop of executives in IBM, I would not expect something innovative or market startling from IBM any time soon.

Prickett Morgan Prods IBM

Timothy Prickett Morgan, a noted AS/400 industry analyst, likes the idea of a little AS/400. He espouses the notion that a powerful but inexpensive IBM "Cell" Power processor chip or the Apple PowerPC 970 "G5" chip should be usable in an inexpensive Baby IBM AS/400 box. Prickett Morgan is one of the folks in the AS/400 media who goes toe to toe with IBM to help the company do its best.

In 2005, it was IBM's Enterprise Systems Group that designed chips for the AS/400 line and other units in IBM's server group. The Technology Group designed chips for the Apple computers and also makes the chips used in various gaming machines. IBM merged the two divisions to gain greater synergies. Prickett Morgan had been blasting IBM for having excluded needed components from the new inexpensive chips that could have been used for a new, inexpensive AS/400 box. Basically, the Technology Division was doing its own thing without discussing its plans with the Enterprise Systems Group. Important features that would have benefited the AS/400 could have been done cheaply yet were not done.

In a March 1, 2004 article in *The Four Hundred*, Prickett Morgan fired a constructive volley at IBM about assuring that its Power PC chips are built with OS/400 capabilities:

> **"IBM should have a PowerPC 970 line of entry tower and rack-mounted Unix servers to go after Sun Microsystems, but it doesn't, because IBM's systems people thought that Power4 and Power5 would be sufficient to compete. It is not. Further, Technology Group created the PowerPC 970 chip to give Apple a hot chip, and it definitely succeeded, but it did so without adding the special PowerPC AS instructions that would allow the chip to run IBM's own OS/400 operating system. That is 1980s IBM thinking, and it is as unacceptable as it is short-sighted."**

Baby/400 et al.

The chapter title may very well have made some knowledgeable industry watchers a little nervous. There actually is a company in California originally called California Software Products, (now Infinite) which in 2005 released its newest version of something it once called BABY/400 (now Baby/iSeries). IBM has no Baby/400 product in the works, and could not have one, because it does not own the name.

FYI, Infinite is the global leader on IBM AS400 Application Migrations, and has performed thousands of successful AS/400 migrations. Infinite has developed and launched many successful products and service packages AS/400-based designed to migrate applications written. Somehow, they can make a Baby/400 but IBM cannot? Hmmmmm!!!!

Infinite acknowledges that AS/400-based applications are stable, reliable, and more function-rich than many of their Windows-based competitors. The company built its AS/400 emulator because it felt that maintaining a competitive edge and realizing continued growth for some companies may require a multiplatform strategy. Its BABY/iSeries offering allows companies using AS/400s to achieve the goal of a platform independent system in a fraction of the time, without having to redevelop homegrown applications.

The product maintains the lifeblood "legacy" applications of an AS/400, notably those written in RPG/400, RPG IV or COBOL/400. The company offers its package for Windows, Unix, and Linux, and suggests that the source code is exactly the same for the Power i. Isn't it too bad IBM did not think of that! And isn't it too bad that IBM does not support this little company more than it supports Microsoft.

The migration to these little guys occurs quite simply. Existing source code is downloaded to the PC, recompiled, and executed on a Windows or Unix or Linux box. California Software, for one, has been in the business a long time doing these types of migrations. Its customers obviously use the products because they work.

From the mid-1990s, there was another promising company called CrossWorks, which offered something close to Baby/Power i. In January 2004, unfortunately, CrossWorks folded its tent and left the business. However, there is some speculation that its product and development assets may very well be purchased by some high profile vendors out there, such as Sun or HP. If this were the case, there might not just be a nice little PC based AS/400 running CrossWorks, there might also be a real AS/400 clone to help HP and /or Sun fight IBM in the AS/400 space. If that happens and a clone system faces IBM in this once all-IBM market, historians might suggest that, "for want of a "baby," the whole family was lost. I can see many defections.

Back in the Baby/400 days, the price of a 10-user license was $4,999. This is still too expensive for massive acceptance from the Windows "on-the-cheap" crowd, but perhaps when a penetration strategy is announced, there may be some room for California Software to provide the environment that Bill Gates is looking for to run his own company. (Microsoft for years used 23 AS/400s to run the company.)

The Baby IBM Should Bring Forth!

With 40 million small businesses in the U.S. alone, there is great potential for a small business machine at about $2,000 per unit that does the job, does not lock and hang, and can provide absolutely superior and stable business applications.

IBM has at least three hardware choices if it wants to capitalize on this market with an IBM solution. Its first choice is to port the IBM i operating system (formerly OS/400) to Intel so that any PC can use it, just like Linux.

Its second choice is that, as long as the specific Power chip has the extra bit to handle single level storage, a new baby IBM AS/400 could use a PC-like chassis driven by a Sony PlayStation-like or Apple-like PowerPC processor running OS/400.

Its third choice is a little sneakier, and it also depends on the chip supporting Single Level Storage. The company can add a PowerPC chip on a PC card for the existing PC chassis, enabling any PC to become an "AS/400" and be able to run OS/400 applications through the existing PC hardware. Any of these solutions would be acceptable as long as IBM i (formerly OS/400), the AS/400 operating system personality, were in control.

There is a lull in the action in computerdom right now. Nobody seems to be making a big splash about anything. There is no question that timing is everything in marketing. A big splash right after somebody else's big splash is not as big of a splash. So, if there is any spark left in IBM's marketing, the "Little AS/400" would be a groundbreaking, spectacular marketing event. My neighbors would love it.

If April Sfole can get major reaction to announcing it and it was not even real, and California Software / Infinite can actually do it, and CrossWorks once did it, surely, IBM can do it. However, Big Blue has to be inclined to again dirty its hands on the small business market that the company once "owned." Come on, IBM! Don't let April Sfole down.

April Sfole of course is fictional but iSeries News, here employer, was once real but not any more.

IT Jungle's Dan Burger wrote an epitaph on iSeries News, News/400 etc. titled Penton Media's IBM i Sites Cease Publication. The date was April 7, 2014. This is just another bad signal on the AS/400 (IBM i) platform as there are not enough users to support a support business.

Here is Burger's piece from IT Jungle. Out thanks to Timothy Prickett Morgan and Dan Burger of IT Jungle for this article.

Penton Media has discontinued its two digital publications for the IBM i community--iProDeveloper and Power IT Pro. iProDeveloper was a website with technical content for developers on the IBM midrange systems known as the IBM i, System i, iSeries, and AS/400. Prior to the digital version ofiProDeveloper, there was a printed magazine version previously titled System iNews, iSeries News, and News/400.

Power IT Pro was a website that expanded the IBM i technical content to include the Power Systems family that includes AIX and PureSystems.

Contributors to the two publications were informed of the decision in an email dated April 1. The email, authored by Megan Keller, Penton's online training and conference director, informed contributors the company would "no longer be acquiring and posting new content to these websites, or producing an iProDeveloper digital publication."

These moves were explained as allowing the company to "focus more closely on our online training initiatives."

In recent years, the editorial staff for the IBM i publications was reduced, and advertising sales were outsourced to contract representatives. Several IBM i vendors contacted by IT Jungle last week were unaware that the Penton publications had stopped publishing. Chris Maxcer, the editorial director for these pubs, was laid off April 1. All content on the website has been locked down and the Keller email advised that "we are taking our iProDeveloper and Power IT Procommunities private."

It is unclear whether that means paid subscribers would have sole access to existing "premium content." Attempts to obtain additional details from Sanjay Mutha, senior vice president of the Technology Division at Penton, were unsuccessful by the deadline of The Four Hundred.

The historic time line leading up to what became iProDeveloper began with Duke Communications, which started publishing News 3X/400 in the early 1990s. That magazine became News/400, which was sold to Penton Media in 2000, along with a book publishing business called 29th Street Press.

News/400 eventually was renamed iSeries News, then System iNews, which was the last of the printed magazines in the lineage. The electronic prodigy was then named iProDeveloper.

Many people in the IBM i community remember Wayne Madden, the longtime publisher of Penton's IBM i publications and a part of the editorial team from the Duke Communications ownership, parted ways with Penton a little more than a year ago. Madden also served as president of COMMON and was a member of the COMMON board of directors.

Penton Media filed for Chapter 11 bankruptcy protection in 2010 and reorganized to reduce debt by $270 million, and it remains one of the largest B2B business publishers in the world.

Chapter 36 Maybe IBM Should Be More Focused?

Cut Your Losses IBM!

When Lou Gerstner was asked in his first year about IBM being broken up into pieces by plan and was badgered about his vision statement on the situation, his response is often quoted: "the last thing IBM needs right now is a vision?" Three years later, after the fires were out and the embers were well watered, Gerstner quipped in the annual report:

> **"It's with enormous sense of irony that now, almost three years later, I say this: What IBM needs most right now is a vision."**

Annex interpreted Gerstner's Words to mean he would like to recant his decision about keeping Big Blue as one big company. They think he meant:

> **"Make IBM smaller -- Make it smaller to boost its value? Precisely!"**

Annex offered a number of supporting reasons why it might be best to keep a smaller IBM around in order to boost its value, and to get rid of the "dead wood."

They concluded that the upshot of a well thought out and well-executed IBM break-up could be a $43 billion bonanza for its shareholders. It would lead to a smaller and a bigger Big Blue - smaller in revenue (about $46 billion) and bigger in market value (about $103 billion).

The Crown Jewels

Here's how Annex believed that IBM would achieve $180.00 stock value immediately

They suggested that IBM examine the worth of its crown jewels. They saw the crown jewels and their bottom line contributions in 1995 as the following

1.	IBM Global Services / Maintenance:	$1.8 billion
2.	System/z -- System/390 (Mainframe):	$1.3 billion
3.	Power i (AS/400):	$600 million
4.	IBM's non OS-IBM software:	$500million
5.	RS/6000 (RISC Unix Machine):	$500 million

Annex enjoyed referring to these five businesses as the IBM "crown jewels." Ironically, the PC Division is not on the list. "If valued as separate companies with shares priced in line with their leading competitors, the 'five IBM musketeers,' as Annex quipped would likely be worth double the value of the entire Big Blue on Jan. 18, 1996--the day its 1995 results were announced!'

They saw the services business as being a phenomenon of success and gave Gerstner his "A" for the work. At the time, in 1996, IBM stock was selling for between $83 and $129. This made its P/E 15 and its P/R ratio .81. They looked at IBM's competitors such as EDS and CSC and saw that they were at 28 -- 32.5 and 1.18 – 1.05 respectively. This indicated that there was a lot more to be had if the rest of IBM were not holding the division's ratios captive.

Let's go through these numbers again. Annex went through the numbers carefully and found that if IBM operated in just its crown jewels, the value at the time would be $103 billion or $43 billion more than the entire value of IBM, based on its average 1996 stock price. They estimated that without the rest of IBM, the stock price would be $180 per share, compared with an average 1996 price of $106. Revenues would become $46 billion versus the $72 billion for the losers/winners combination IBM had been enduring.

Annex's Six Point Plan for IBM Success

They concluded that a smaller, nimbler IBM would mean increased market value, and they offered the chairman six steps to get the job done:

Step 1: Spin off and report separate financial results for the IBM Global Services, including the Integrated Systems Solutions Corp., its outsourcing subsidiary, as well as maintenance.

Step 2: Sell the PC Division and the other low-margin hardware operations, such as OEM, and/or other low-margin hardware products. [This has been done.]

Step 3: Consolidate the remaining high-margin product businesses - S/390, AS/400 and RS/6000 into a single IBM Server company. It should include the respective OS software (OS/390, OS/400 and AIX).

Step 4: Evaluate the feasibility and desirability of spinning off the non-OS software into a separate business, such as the network-related (Lotus+), or other IBM software (e.g., middleware; VisualAge, systems management tools/Tivoli, etc.).

Step 5: Aggressively market the new IBM market value proposition - "smaller is better" to some Wall Street "stoncagers."

Step 6: Increase the IBM dividend as the financial benefits rise (i.e., the shareholders' value).

Is Lou the Man?

Annex flet that if Lou Gerstner possessed two attributes, he could make their dream a reality. The two attributes needed were "courage" and "humility." They posed the question in their report: "Does Gerstner Have What It Takes?" "Does Gerstner have the courage and the humility to do it?" History has given us the answer.

Chapter 37 Fort Knox II – The New IBM eServer

Get Out the Old Gold

Maybe there is a good reason for Linux and Unix on the AS/400, but if IBM were moving to having just one server line, my choice would be the AS/400. Though IBM lost hundreds of millions of dollars on the Fort Knox project, the current direction smacks like a return to the days of the gold standard project.

Unlike those days, instead of accommodating both hardware and software, today's consolidation efforts are not as ambitious. With better and better PowerX technology expected throughout the IBM non-Intel product line in this decade, from a hardware perspective, other than logos, it should be hard to tell the IBM servers apart.

By the time the server group is ready to do its Fort Knox II consolidation, the IBM Services and software divisions will represent an even greater share of IBM's revenue stream and they will have that much more to say about what happens to the hardware line. Logic suggests that a services group or software group in control of hardware would not want an AS/400 style machine as its basis for the consolidation.

The AS/400 is integrated and it is very simple to use. Though these attributes are perfect for businesses, they also mean that a lot of software won't get sold by IBM and thus, there would not be a lot of services needed. That would not be good for either the software division or the services division. If these two divisions control the purse strings of the corporation, it would be unlikely that they would sign off on anything that would hurt their revenue streams?

Mainframe at the Camel's Base

Regardless of coulda, woulda, and shoulda, based on my sources, IBM has announced in various forums its plans to take the PowerX processors and shape them in such a way that the mainframe, the Unix box, and the AS/400 will all be using the same PowerX chips. If the hardware is destined for a Vulcan mind meld then what about the software? That's a big question. Without the software, there cannot be a full Fort Knox II consolidation.

Let's look at a few factors that indicate that the mainframe is being prepared for consolidation:

1. Logical partitioning already exists in the merged hardware.
2. The authors of logical Partitioning are from mainframe IBM.
3. The mainframe division is expected to use the Power 8 or Power 9 platform or a derivative.

Therefore we can expect some modifications to the hardware box that now is used by Power i and pSeries so that the zSeries can also use the same hardware box. The physical model will have to be re-designed to support the mainframe. That fact brings out big fear in AS/400-land.

But, if this is so, and one box with a mainframe shaped hypervisor to control the logical partitions is likely to emerge, that would explain why the IBM Global Services Division is not complaining. A box with that power and complexity would demand substantial installation services.

The fact that this seems to be happening indicates that there will be a consolidated mainframe and there is less of a chance that we will see a Fort Knox II box running just OS/400 with Linux and Unix in guest partitions. It is also very likely that Bill Gates may promise IBM a stable Windows 10 or Windows du Jour for the PowerX architecture so that all four operating systems of today would run on the new IBM Fort Knox II box. Yes, that would be more than even Fort Knox would have been if it were developed. All operating systems on one hardware box, including Windows has got to be the major goal of the consolidation set inside IBM.

Segregation Is More Profitable to Big Blue than Integration

The original Fort Knox, as you may recall, was geared to help IBM with its perceived and real server consolidation problems of the 1980s. It was never expected to be easy and the machines that would flow were destined to be caricatures before they were ever successful. Hopefully, Fort Knox II will be better planned and IBM will be better prepared with answers that fit each customer set.

When IBM brings all of its servers to one box, and that one box also runs IBMi, (OS/400), there is one way that it would not threaten the profit margins of the software division and the services division.

If the software division gets to design the software architecture, IBM's only integrated system known as Power i, iSerie, and AS/400 would have its software segregated (de-integrated) to match all of the other servers. Theoretically, IBM could take the "i" from 'i" Series and solve its dilemma with the software division. By making all software more difficult on all platforms, IBM would get to sell lots of software and lots of services. An integrated system would greatly reduce those prospects and their resulting profits.

With the "i" removed, the software division could sell DB2 and CICS and/or Tuxedo Workstation Support for the

AS/400. Single Level Storage could also be a Fort Knox II option, rather than a built-in. That would solve a big IBM problem in file systems compatibility. Meanwhile, since reassembling Single Level Storage and DB2 and workstation code would require services, there would be no complaint from the services division. There's profit there for everybody if IBM has the guts to squeeze that little "i" from its eServer line. If they do that, there would be no more reason to care about the AS/400. It would be no more!

Chapter 38 It's Time for New Management at IBM?

Some IBM Managers Are Very Good

I am reminded often of an IBM executive from World Trade Corporation who graced an IBM Family Dinner at the Radisson Hotel remake of the Erie Lackawanna Railroad Station in Scranton, Pennsylvania, a few years before my retirement leave of absence. Every five years or so, IBM would take all of its local families to a fine restaurant or banquet hall and put on a family feast. My wife and I arrived a bit early for this event and we ponied up to the libation counter for a "McDuff." I whispered to Pat that the very well-dressed person next to us was probably the evening speaker. I was right.

In short while, he introduced himself, and we had a very nice conversation. I can recall in my days with IBM that any conversation with an IBM executive that ended without anybody getting reprimanded or fired was a good conversation. While we were talking about odds and ends and IBM, he made sure he had my attention and then he thanked me. He thanked all of the salesmen and systems engineers and administrators in the field that evening who present a much nicer face to IBM's customers than the decisions made by the executives often warrant. This executive lamented that IBM had to do what it has to do business-wise so that it can survive.

Later, he gave a wonderful speech in which he thanked the IBM husbands and wives for their support of their spouses when the going gets tough at IBM. From my experience and this person's overall demeanor, I would suspect that he was a fine manager, caring and cunning, and that he motivated those who worked for him to do their best.

Taking the Heat

The fact that IBM's corporate executives appreciated that their orders and decrees got softened or ignored before they reached customers stayed with me while I continued to wirk for IBM. Why couldn't good executive managers just do the right thing, rather than depend on subordinates to do it for them?

I found that to be a major systemic IBM executive management weakness. It is a sign that IBM executives are very concerned about taking business risks so much that they appreciate it when smaller managers and even non-managers in the organization take the risk and the heat by doing the rigt thing even if counter to corporate dictates.

For my money, that is a major reason why IBM is viewed as a pussycat and not a tiger in its business dealings. The companies out there who still have the original entrepreneurs running the company are not the milquetoasts and pushovers that IBM's style and culture breeds. Most of today's successful IT industry moguls are self-made billionaires. They love taking IBM for a ride but it must not even seem a challenge for these entrepreneurs to engage IBM when victory is almost always a certainty. By the way, in spring 2016, I wrote another book you will like titled *"Thank You, IBM-- The Story of how IBM helped today's technology millionaires and billionaires gain their vast fortunes." At 774 pages, it tells the whole story. Available at www.bookhawkers.com*

IBM Management History

Thomas Watson Sr., who joined IBM when it was the Computing Tabulating and Recording Company (CTR) in 1914, is often credited with being the founder of IBM, because he ruled the company from his arrival as if it were his company and his company alone. Watson had learned much of his visionary notions from his early experience with the NCR Corporation, at the time headquartered in Dayton, Ohio.

He was very concerned about building the IBM Company based on sound principles, and though many of the principles he championed in IBM were borrowed from NCR, they remained integral to company operations until Thomas Watson Jr. turned the reins over to a non-Watson in the early 1970's.

Throughout its history, the company was known for making reliable products and IBM's service was recognized as good as service could possibly be. Though never fully bleeding edge, IBM's products were always well made and there was a radical element to IBM's pro-customer service. Good products and excellent customer service were fundamental to the building of the company itself.

IBM grew to be a ten billion dollar company by the time Watson Jr. left after his heart attack. While a Watson was in control of IBM, however, there was a sense that the company was still entrepreneurial in how it engaged the marketplace. With their pockets full of IBM stock, the Watsons ran the company as owners, not as paid managers or simply as "charismatic" leaders. It was their company.

Thomas J. Watson Sr's principles carried over to Thomas Watson Jr. The Watsons had so much power that it permitted IBM to do things by top management decree without much concern for 'board approval." For example, it was T.J. Watson Jr. who built the country clubs that helped IBM encourage employees to socialize among themselves. The IBM Family Dinner that we discussed above was another IBM socialization "scheme" from the Watson playbook. The Watsons wanted IBM to be a family and a business with family values. It was.

The Watson's were not without their share of outlandish ideas. Long time IBMers still remember the required incantations within IBM's sales training programs. IBMers sang songs from the "Songs of the IBM," such as "Ever Onward IBM" and "IBM Is Thoroughly Modern."

Though many of us recognized that we had to give up a small amount of individual identity to survive IBM, until the last days of John Akers rein most IBMers believed it was two ways. Few felt that IBM would not always be there to do the right thing for us, for any employee who needed it, for almost any good reason. "

The End of Risk

Real innovation, risk taking and entrepreneurism managed by the corporation ceased with the departure of the Watsons' direct influence. The non-Watson era brought forth executives who were once good salesmen or accountants, not business owners and certainly not entrepreneurs. Executives, who seemed to look over their shoulders three times for every glance forward, managed the post-Watson IBM. IBM had few bold, original thoughts after 1973.

There are some who have categorized Frank Cary's decision to build a PC as a big risk-taking venture in the order of Watson's $5 billion gamble with System/360. There was no comparison. No big decisions, of which I am aware, were made in IBM from the time the last Watson retired. The truth about the PC's development is that IBM executives were getting sick of having Apple and Radio Shack being rubbed in their face by their own grandkids. It made IBM look inept. The company was the target of ridicule. For want of a unit that could be built with corporate petty cash, Apple and Radio Shack were beating the biggest computer company in the whole world in the public mindshare battle.

Note: Cary was appointed Chairman in 1973, one and one half years after T.J. Watson Jr. T. Vincent Learson was interim CEO right after Watson retired.

The IBM PC Project

So it was more for pride than business that Cary commissioned the group of ten with a mission to build a PC within a year. Considering that he saw a five-year market of no more than 275,000 unit sales tells a great tale about how much Frank Cary was prepared to invest in this "toy" technology.

At that small manufacturing volume and with a cast of just ten employees doing the design work, Cary did not put much investment capital at risk. IBM was more surprised than any company on earth when the PC was such a success. Its market forecast missed by a gazillion.

Yearly sales estimates of 55,000 units per year were nowhere close to the actual numbers that were in the tens of millions. With such poor PC executive management, it is no wonder that IBM today is little more than a bit player in the $100 billion PC marketplace that the company created. IBM once had it all, but its top executives could not manage its fortunes.

A different breed of cat manages the companies that sprang from nothing during the formation of the PC industry. These guys are real entrepreneurs. They are not caretakers of somebody else's ownership. They are the owners. When the company earns a penny, they feel it. When the company loses a penny, they feel it even more.

Everybody's Getting Rich

There are tons of examples of real entrepreneurs who made $billions and who continue to run their companies. Larry Ellison (Oracle), Bill Gates (Microsoft), Ted Waitte

(Gateway); Scott McNealy (Sun), Michael Dell (Dell), etc. are all billionaires who acquired their money because Frank Cary had such a poor forecast that IBM could never build enough PCs. Even after sales volumes were well understood, John Opel, Cary's successor never adjusted the business model to win the PC market.

Along the way to being billionaires, the PC entrepreneurs became hundredaires, then thousandaires, then millionaires, and then billionaires. They got there by doing things that IBM, with all of its billions could not or would not do. Because the team of billionaires had the entrepreneurial spirit, and were not salesmen rewarded for consistently huge sales as in IBM's case, these startup companies were able to grow rich and make their founders rich while IBM's executive managers were content to "manage" the business.

Who Took Blame for Business Failings?

The PC legacy as a story of IBM executive mismanagement has not gotten enough criticism in the press or inside IBM. It seems that the failure to execute in this area was never held against the CEOs of IBM. Therefore, one could conclude that there are other PC-like stories locked in the inner chambers that will never be seen by the public or by the stockholders.

Bye Bye Disk

IBM has failed miserably with its post-Watson, pre-Gerstner executive leadership in many areas. Consider that IBM invented the revolutionary disk drive in the 1950's and was consistently recognized as having the best disk technology in the industry. More and more IBM disk drives were sold each year. The business appeared to be very successful.

Little more than a few years ago, while Lou Gerstner was still on board, IBM boasted of the extraordinary recording head technology that the company had pioneered. Its microelectronics division sold millions of these disk heads to IBM competitors and PC suppliers. IBM was the unquestioned disk drive champion of the entire world.

Then, all of a sudden, like a bad dream, Swoosh -- IBM decided to get out of the disk drive business. They sold it, lock, stock and barrel, to Hitachi for $2 billion. The company claimed that it could not make any money at it. Let's look at this premise just a bit. IBM held the patents on the technology so nobody else could build it. IBM theoretically could charge what it wanted since no other company had this top technology.

IBM set the price based on volume projections, costs, and expected profit. IBM executives ran the business. If the company could not make a thin dime in its disk drive business then who is to blame? Look no further than IBM's post Watson Management team. In this case, the culprit was Lou Gerstner whose interests were to bolster stock prices, rather than manage a hardware business.

Bye Bye Typewriters

Throughout the 20th century, until about 1985, IBM's typewriters were the best and IBM sold lots of them. The typewriter business began to change in the 1980's to the PC printer business. In Chapter 29, I discussed how IBM chose not to use its crackerjack direct typewriter sales force to sell PCs. Additionally, the company chose not to make high quality, inexpensive printers that could be used on PCs, even though, in most businesses, these printers were the replacement product for the typewriter. Hewlett-Packard, on the other hand, decided that there was a big market for printers and it created one innovative PC printer product after another, while IBM relied on OEMs to supply its printers.

IBM had once owned the electric typewriter and the big laser printer business, yet the company's forecasters did not see enough reason to develop printer families such as the HP

DeskJet and the HP LaserJet. Before Lou Gerstner took over, John Akers sold the whole typewriter business for a song to the investment firm of Clayton, Dubilier & Rice Inc., which became an independent company, Lexmark Inc.

To put this in perspective, HP makes about $4 billion each year of an $8 billion market on these little printers. Since HP believes that the printer supplies business is one that they want to be in, they make about twice that sum per year on computer supplies. So, if you take just HP's share of the printer market, Akers' sale cost the company about $10 to $12 billion per year. That's not a product of good executive management.

Executives Get Lots of Chances

Industry Analysts agree that the AS/400 is the best IBM computer for business and its architecture is the most outstanding. The Rochester Laboratory in IBM built the System/38, the AS/400's predecessor, on the quiet, using the leftover technology secrets from the IBM Future Systems (FS) project. IBM executive management was shortsighted enough to cancel its own FS project after spending hundreds of millions on research. This was an unthinkable mistake that kept IBM mainframes at reduced technology levels until just recently. Without telling the corporate executive management that the Lab was building a machine with an architecture far superior to that of the mainframe, The Little Lab That Could (IBM Rochester) just went ahead and did it.

IBM corporate executive management had already voted no on the project, so Endicott and Poughkeepsie did not get its Future System in the form that it had hoped. But Rochester, because of its clandestine project, tricked the corporation into thinking that the System/38 was going to be a small business system to replace the 1969 vintage System/3 line. There are countless anecdotes depicting how, for many years, IBM's mainframe-biased management did its best to undermine the System/38, the AS/400, and now again the Power i.

IBM executives just do not seem to learn from their business mistakes. This whole book is about post-Watson corporate executives who have squandered opportunity after opportunity regarding the System/38, and AS/400 product set. IBM executives are clearly interested, even today, in selling PCs more than selling AS/400s.

Yet, IBM has failed miserably in the PC business and more than one analyst has suggested that IBM sell its PC business and just get out. You don't need a business degree to understand that one. Yet, IBM executives persist in downplaying the superiority of its all-IBM AS/400 line while exalting its mostly OEM PC line.

"See What Sticks" Management

IBM literally throws one thing after another against the wall that enough sticks to keep the company afloat. Industry analysts and other independents have evaluated IBM's AS/400 and Power i computer lines and its capability to grow businesses into the future. This unique product that we have discussed in this book remains in a back-seat status in IBM's marketing plans. Ironically, the same PC line that is in the red each year gets more attention than the IBM-built, one-of-a-kind, best computer in existence.

IBM's non-entrepreneurial management team has hedged its bets by hiding its products in the hedges. In the mid-1980s, John Opel, Mr. Cary's successor, brazenly announced that IBM would be a billion dollar company by the end of the 1980's decade (1990). If there was a plan to do this, Opel and Akers failed miserably in its execution. Twenty years later, and IBM is just above $80 billion.

Bye Bye Rental Business

Not only did $100 billion not happen, but also while John Opel was building plant capacity in anticipation of the $100 billion mark, he continued Frank Cary's slick little deal of selling off the rental inventory for cash and apparent profits. Opel's plant anticipatory expansion program placed IBM in an over capacity position and huge excess product inventories appeared in the normally capacity constrained IBM plants.

Though it was not yet apparent in the mid 1980s, when John Akers took over, the excess plant space and inventory began to eat up IBM's cash while the company was moving from a rental base to a purchase base. In other words, these CEOs overbuilt and then sold rental machines that were generating annual revenue to pay for the plants as they came on line. IBM gave massive incentives for companies to purchase their rental equipment, often for less than one whole year's rental.

Tom Watson Jr., an IBM CEO who was always successful, did not particularly like Frank Cary's switch from rental to purchase. He noted in his book:

> **"It bothered me because rentals traditionally had been crucial to IBM's success. Rental contracts wedded us to our customers, gave us a powerful incentive to keep the service top-notch, and made IBM stable and essentially depression-proof. Once the stream of rental payments dried up, IBM became far more volatile and vulnerable to fluctuations in demand."**

Burning the Cash

After years of poor results after poor results, John Akers burned up IBM's entire cash reserve. In 1992, for the second year in a row, Akers' IBM was in the red. This time it was $5 billion. In 1993, the year he was replaced by Lou Gerstner, Gerstner made sure that all the bad press would be removed from 1994 earnings as he brought in an $8.1 billion loss in his first (partial) year at the helm.

John Akers did not get to benefit from Frank Cary and John Opel's careless selling of the rental business for cash. The rentals were already gone. Akers needed lots of cash and he needed new revenue sources. With the rental sale revenue boost all gone, Akers had to find new revenue just to keep IBM afloat.

In fairness to Akers, no CEO in IBM had ever been saddled with that big a job. Moreover, there was far too much plant capacity for what IBM could sell and the drag on profits by these new plants kept hurting Akers' plans for good financial results.

Back in February 1990, some astute analysts saw many weaknesses in John Akers management style and took on IBM's wrath for reporting about it. Bob Djurdjevic of Annex Research (www.djurdjevic.com/Bulletins/ibm-corporate/91-31.htm) writes:

> **Time for Change at the Top? "In other words, one has to wonder if the company leaders know what they are doing. And question why IBM isn't "unfreezing" itself, as the chairman of one of its customers put it. By that, he meant thawing out the company's mindset. He thought that it was time the progressive-thinking 'young Turks' took over the reigns of power from the 'IBM establishment.'" 'As an American, I would really like IBM to be successful,' this executive said. 'But, I am afraid that the company is wasting the competitive edge which it once enjoyed.' That is why, he argued, it was time for radical changes within the company."**

Bye Bye Rolm & Disco Vision

IBM also got acquisitions and joint venture happy during the 1980s, spending millions to form or assimilate companies such as Rolm (made Telephone Computerized Branch Exchanges), DiscoVision (a pioneer in CDs and Laser video technology) and Satellite Business Systems (a long distance communications business). The executives who made these purchases forgot one major point. The stodgy IBM corporate culture was a hard fit for any company with entrepreneurial spirit. It was a killer.

The company saw its investments turn to sludge as one by one, IBM caused these companies to fail and then sold the companies and their assets at fire sale losses. IBM executive management could not make them work; yet nobody of whom I am aware in IBM upper management paid the price.

CEO Tunnel Vision

Of all the stories in IBM history, the Fort Knox debacle is one of the most well known. There is a lot more to it (see Chapter 15 for Fort Knox details). I tell it only in how it demonstrates the penchant in IBM executive management to get the Rochester labs out of the computer business, though it was IBM's most innovative plant.

I had spent a number of years in IBM's elite DPD marketing division (sold mainframes) in the post System 360 / pre System/370 era, and I had worked with IBM's small business customers as a systems engineer since 1969. I observed the narrow focus and the downright tunnel vision, of every IBM chief executive who followed Tom Watson Jr. to the plate regarding their propensity toward mainframe computing.

Everybody that I know in IBM loved T.J. Watson Jr. Vincent Learson, a great friend of the Watsons, was CEO for a very short while right after Watson Jr. stepped down. This was more or less at a time when IBM was sorting out who should run the company after Watson. The CEOs after Learson had few of the defining characteristics of Watson. The days of bold decisions were gone. The Post Watson IBM CEOs ruled the roost in IBM, but their sense of business and their sense of fair play was never as good as when a Watson ran the company. They were more concerned about government suits than running their own business.

Whenever something goes wrong, you've got to go to the top to cast blame. Whereas Frank Cary humored the Little Lab That Could in the middle of the Justice Department Suit, he secretly planned to turn it all over to the government to ransom IBM's mainframe business from the Justice Department. Cary saw little value in small systems and viewed the possible expunging as an IBM saving solution.

Cary saw that IBM was in the mainframe business, and the company also sold typewriters. Those two businesses were so far separated that it took a long time for conflict to emerge, and for the record, when it did, IBM's executives got rid of the IBM typewriter division. But, the mainframe division remained.

If you look at the history of IBM from before Watson Jr. through the present, you might conclude that the last original thought may very well have been by Tom Watson Jr. As noted in Chapter 10, the mainframers always behaved arrogantly inside IBM. They were the Kings. Many in the press have attributed the word "arrogant" to the IBM Company during this time period because of the notion that everything was second to the mainframe. If you were on site in IBM to watch the action, you'd call that an understatement.

Bye Bye Rochester

It is a documented fact in IBM the mainframe executive management team had designs to eliminate the Rochester Laboratory and all its systems, the System/36 and the System/38. Over the last ten years, their wish has come true.

Some believed that the elimination of the successor AS/400 system was their goal. The AS/400 and the mainframe are the only all-IBM general business machines that IBM markets. However, executive management's fear that Rochester might be able to make a better mainframe than the mainframe, coupled with their long-standing disdain for the Little Lab That Could, added to the corporate parochial instincts.

In the early 1990s and to today, when PC and Unix based companies are attacking all IBM proprietary systems, the mainframe contingent has never sought Rochester as an ally, even when the press declared that the mainframe itself was dead.

The attacks from the Open (Unix) community and then from the PC Server contingents became more and more threatening to IBM's traditional computer lines. Yet rather than have a crow dinner and advance the notion of the AS/400, executive management hid under rocks and seemed to disappear. No IBM executives appeared on the scene to tell the world that the press was wrong and that the mainframe was not dead.

IBM management seemingly believed the press reports that mainframe computing was dead. The lack of a real IBM response to these attacks measures among the grossest business management errors of all time. Rather than fight, IBM management was ready to cash it in just like DEC and all the other minicomputer vendors who died or were absorbed by stronger companies. One could conclude that IBM's executives believed the handwriting on the wall that was clearly written by its competitors.

Other Thoughts on IBM Leadership

On April 13, 2001, Wayne Madden, publisher of the one-time highly popular *iSeries News* magazine wrote an article titled "IBM and Lotus What Could Have Been." In the article Madden supports my contention that IBM does not manage its business well and often makes poor executive decisions. He notes IBM's uncanny ability to squander many of its opportunities. Madden's topic is software, an area that, along with services, the company is currently focusing. Madden offers less than positive comments on IBM's executive management decisions:

You've always heard that hindsight's 20/20. It's only been a few short years since IBM bought Lotus, and now that they're finally integrating the company into IBM, I'm going on the record to say that they're making a huge mistake on this one. Lotus is a software company -- in fact, a good software company. Integrating Lotus into IBM's Software Group is the exact opposite of what a true visionary would do.

...in past decades, [IBM] products such as Mapics, DMAS, and CMAS dominated their respective segments (manufacturing, distribution, and construction). Honestly, those applications had little competition. As a whole, IBM's history as an application/tools software company is widely viewed as less than stellar. In more recent endeavors such as OS/2, the San Francisco application framework project, DB2/UDB, and products such as VisualAge and WebSphere software, IBM generally finds a way to undermarket and committee-manage its software to death. VisualAge and WebSphere have a chance, but only if IBM can overcome its track record.

The Lotus acquisition presented IBM with a golden opportunity: ... Lotus is small enough to escape the suffocating bureaucracy that IBM has layered onto its creative processes over the years. ...Lotus executives who were accustomed to fluidly taking a project from idea to execution must now endure IBM's infamous conference calls -- many organized only to schedule more conference calls. Their once-elegant plans must be repackaged to fit IBM's corporate requirements, their words must be approved by more lawyers, and their future must be tied to the "good of the whole."

Just think of what could have been. Don't get me wrong. I'm bullish on products such as WebSphere, but I'd be outright ecstatic if it belonged to a true software company that could compete uninhibitedly in the wild against the likes of Microsoft's .Net blitzkrieg. Change would have caught people off-guard, rocked the world a little, surprised those who sleep through most of IBM's predictable actions and perfectly scripted press briefings. Shame on IBM's "visionaries" for not seeing this.

How about that for an indictment of IBM's management by bureaucracy? Can the person at the top be held blameless?

On January 1, 2002, Carson Soul of Power i Network wrote a piece titled: "How Will IBM's Crown Prince Value the iSeries (Power i)." A short while later, Gary Zalaoras, in a reader feedback, offered his commentary about Carson's Article. I include the feedback here because it is right to the heart of the continuation of IBM management issue post Akers re AS/400. It also is a sample of the consensus of the iSeries (Power i) community about how IBM's CEOs value the AS/400 product line. Gary was motivated to write:

> **I just read your article "How Will IBM's Crown Prince Value the iSeries?" and the feedback from Mike Russell. Very interesting. But I just don't get it that Gerstner is suddenly the semi-white knight of the AS/400. I have never seen a press release or anything else where he has missed an opportunity to NOT support the iSeries.**

On October 30, 2002, the Power i Network News Staff broke the news that Sam Palmisano was about ready to be named IBM's Chairman as well as CEO. In the article, the staff took the opportunity to list Palmisano's accomplishments since taking over as CEO in March 2002.

> **During Palmisano's short tenure as CEO, the 29-year IBM veteran has rid IBM of its unprofitable hard disk drive division, spearheaded the acquisition of PricewaterhouseCoopers (PwC) Consulting to beef up Global Services, realigned the microelectronics unit, outsourced PC manufacturing, and laid off more than 15,000 employees, or 5 percent of Big Blue's workforce.**

The Palmisano Future

Such a legacy for such a short time in office! The troubling part of the tribute is that it can also be read that Palmisano gave up on a major IBM hardware tradition and sunk the hard drive business rather than try to make something of it. He also bought an existing services company, degraded the microelectronics division, got rid of PC manufacturing, and told 15,000 IBM employees that they no longer had jobs. One might wonder based on the corporate advertising budget if the AS/400 is next for the Palmisano ax?

Many AS/400 loyalists including yours truly think that idea would not be all that bad for the AS/400 line and its prospects for success, as long as IBM sold the line to a viable company such as Microsoft or HP. However, it might be a very bad move for IBM. Would IBM really be able to compete against the AS/400?

Lou Gerstner Rescued IBM

By 1993, the homegrown, post Watson non-entrepreneurial executive management team had just about put IBM out of business. For the first time, the board looked outside of IBM for a replacement. They could not take a chance on the IBM internal executive management system. Although he was not the first choice, IBM hired Lou Gerstner of RJR Nabisco for the top job.

As noted, IBM had just lost $5 billion and was about to lose another $8 billion. The company had already "laid off" 45,000 employees, and Mr. Gerstner got to lay off another 35,000 before the end of his first year. During Gerstner's predecessor, John Akers' tenure, IBM's market share had dwindled to all-time lows. The company that once many described as "the best-run company in the world" had become the piñata of the IT industry. Competitors, customers, and loyal employees wondered if IBM as a company could survive.

Many expected that Gerstner would continue the chop-up plan that Akers had begun in order to stop the flow of blood. But he did just the opposite. He saw some good in IBM's bigness. Under his leadership, IBM was resurrected -- not as a computer company, but as the technology organization that overall still leads the industry. Gerstner concentrated more on perception than reality. IBM no longer had to try to be the best. As long as the company made money and Gerstner could move up the value of the stock that would be more than enough. Considering that the company was on a death spiral prior to his arrival, Gerstner gets full credit for the IBM rescue.

When I was working on my umpteenth plan to leave IBM and start my own billion-dollar business, many a friend cautioned me as I prepared to visit venture capital firms. The message was don't fall in love with the company. Venture capitalists do not care about the company. They care about making a buck. The objective is to sell the company when its stock price grows. If the company became successful, Fine! If not, OK! The Gerstner years can be described in this same way.

He did nothing to strengthen IBM's traditional business. But, by concentrating on profitability, he kept the company going while he orchestrated $36 billion in new revenue from services to make up for IBM's lost preeminence in hardware. Now, IBM is profitable but it has an identity crisis. It seems that the company has no idea in which business market it is to operate.

Timothy Prickett Morgan on IBM

When I wrote this piece initially in 2005, I had never met Industry Analyst Timothy Prickett Morgan but I did speak with him a few times and I have read with deep interest many of his interesting commentaries over the years. Prickett Morgan is editor of *The Four Hundred* and other industry publications. I have since met with him numerous times and we both seem to like a certain golden beverage which Tim brews at home. In this pre-2002 quote, he offers his own brand of insight about IBM's management and their propensity to avoid risk:

> **If all of IBM's executives, including Chairman Louis Gerstner, were compensated based on server market share and revenue growth, customer satisfaction, and employee moral, rather than on IBM's share price, I think IBM would be behaving a whole lot differently. Then again, after having failed with the Future Systems project to unite its disparate mainframe and minicomputer lines in the 1970s (which lead to the development of the System/38 in the 1980s), maybe IBM just figures that it got lucky once in 1964 and that its luck has run out and it should not make any more bold moves. The fact is, IBM didn't get lucky with the System/360. The company performed an incredible marketing and technical feat, and even if IBM didn't engage in questionable monopolistic behavior, IBM deserved to reap what it had indeed sown with the System/360 and its kicker, the System/370.**

Ditto for the System/38 and for the AS/400. While not exactly the same bold move, the fact that an orphaned division of IBM has been able to get an excellent product out the door for twenty years running is a stunning accomplishment, especially considering the environment inside IBM is at least as hostile to the AS/400 as the midrange market outside of IBM's walls.

Maybe I expect too much from IBM. Maybe we all do.

While I was doing research for this book, I exchanged emails and spoke to a number of people in the computer industry. Most were very willing to speak about their poor opinion of IBM's executive management team and especially its poor treatment of the AS/400 product line. Because a number of the folks that I spoke with cannot risk IBM's displeasure since their business depends on their IBM relationship, not as many permitted me to quote them. However, without citing this author, I do want you to see most of the following email since it is very compelling:

"... This all sounds terrific...but you are giving IBM exec's way too much credit by calling them [@#$&%#]. If you think these guys actually sit down and think about what they are doing you're dead wrong. Everyone that I have met at IBM with very few exceptions is really concerned about doing the right thing. It is probably one of the most moral companies I have ever seen.

The problem is an old archaic way of doing business -- endless meetings with as many as 100 people on a conference call to review something that you and I would make a decision on instantly without thinking. No one and I mean NO ONE is responsible for anything.

Did you know that Al Zollar does not control development or sales? He has marketing period, end of story. Marketing allocates money to products and features via something they call the "line item" file. The line item file is literally that -- a list of proposed features for a product reduced to one line of text. These items can be multi-million dollar projects or a 10-minute project. Hundreds of people are involved in reviewing and prioritizing these items. That's just to develop products. When it comes to pricing it's even worse.

Politics are everything at IBM. Executives starting at the Director level and up are gods and not to even be talked to

by the mere mortals that work in the company. There are over 500 Vice Presidents and probably over 2000 Directors. A director usually has between 500 and 5000 people under their control.

No matter how good the people are the system eats them alive.... No one can do anything or make a decision. Then the culture is such that no one dares to make a decision or go against what they perceive the corporate objectives are. IBM is also more like Somalia with warlords than a modern corporation. Each of the Sr. VP's like Zeitler in Server Group or Mills in software group or the Sales guy, Services guy, or the corporate marketing [person] run their own kingdom and heaven forbid they ever talk to each other let alone work together.

So it's more like the 3 Stooges meet the Keystone Cops.."

Chapter Summary and Conclusions

Today, thanks to Lou Gerstner, IBM has grown a tremendous services and software business, while it has let its traditional hardware business go to the dogs. Though IBM makes the best hardware, just as the company pulled out of the disk drive business, IBM executive management, while concentrating on software and services, has not paid adequate attention to the server business. Once upon a time, the hardware business alone was one of the biggest companies in the world. Now, this portion of IBM's "empire" is not even as large as Microsoft.

When a company makes costly marketing decisions, its leaders must answer to the stockholders. That's what the management textbooks say. Yet, in IBM, only when John Akers almost put the company under did the Board of Directors ever address a top management problem. Lou Gerstner may have saved IBM from itself, but in so doing, he also destroyed all of the Watson era people principles in the process. Even with this, IBM still is not the big powerhouse it should be. The entrepreneurial companies are still pushing Big Blue, the "Rough Tough Cream Puff," around at will.

If the executives won't change this very capable company to get some more juice from its hardware offerings, then maybe it's time that IBM stockholders change the board of directors and corporate officers. IBM's stubborn corporate advertising policy is built on the premise that large computer decisions are made in the board room and not the living room. This is way off the mark. If this were ever a good idea, times have changed and IBM's competitors are coming at the company with intentions to defeat IBM in its own game.

IBM's do-nothing TV advertising gives them a free shot. IBM may think the Microsoft brand passed IBM in popularity because the company (Microsoft) is in everybody's home. This may be partially true. But, they are on everybody's TV also in advertising and with MSNBC. The IBM "no-response policy" permitted Microsoft and Intel products to be known by every executive in the world. Yet, the man on the street, including the CEOs of SMB and emerging large businesses, as well as my neighbors, have no idea whether IBM has a server solution that is better for them. If IBM wants its server business back, it will have to reach its potential decision makers where they live.

Would IBM be better off without Sam Palmisano, Ginny Rometty, and the IBM executive team? I guess I am really not sure of the answer to that one.

Considering that services grew from $4 billion to $40 billion in ten years, credit must be given to IBM's leaders as due. So, it may not yet be time to start looking to replace the IBM team with some industry entrepreneurs, such as the PC, database and Unix billionaires.

However, to the extent that their companies consistently beat IBM in its own game, it is that type of executive spirit that is needed to turn IBM's server business around and to help the AS/400 get its due as an IBM product. For AS/400 zealots, the idea of a smaller company taking over IBM would mean that the Watson spirit of entrepreneurism could be re-injected into the company.

Yes, that would mean that Sam Palmisano would have been on the carpet partly for the sins of prior regimes. Mr. Palmisano is a 30-year IBM veteran, trained by the services-oriented Lou Gerstner for IBM's top position. During his tenure, he did not changed anything major of which I am aware to help the AS/400.

If it is right to recall Palmisano, Sam might need some help from Gray Davis in the unemployment line, but Gray can handle that job. I don't think that I would see any global lament from the IBMers. After all, Sam and Lou have given their share of pink slips to many IBM loyalists so the weeping and gnashing won't happen when and if Mr. Palmisano ever sees his pink slip.

Anyway, it is too late for a recall. Ginny Rometty is IBM's new CEO and she has managed a revenue slip for IBM for seventeedn quarters in a row. She took Palmisano's $100 billion revenue achievement in 2011 to less than 90 billion. That sure is the worong direction. Whatever Rometty's server strategy had been it sure was not working. At least she sold the PC server division to keep IBM focused on IBM.

So far, nothing she has done seems like IBM has chosen to move IBM's hardware business from the road to oblivion to the top of the pack. In fact, she is talking about selling both the hardware and the service divisions. What happens when there is nothing left to sell?

So, it does not look like stockholders will have to be rallied to take back the company anytime soon. Services are helping revenue at least for now. Rometty can begin to help by aggressively marketing IBM's "AS/400" server line. Besides SuperComputers, it's the only unique thing IBM has today.

Chapter 39 The Future of the AS/400

Software and Services First?

When I began writing this book fourteen years ago and as I was finishing it up in its first publishing eleven years ago, I felt the much frustration. Like many technicians and consultants in the AS/400 land, I once thought corporate IBM just did not know that it had the best system in the world and that is why it was not being showcased. As this whole project unfolded for me, I became disheartened in that I began to think that IBM does know, but does not plan to change its ways.

I had seen IBM unabashedly offering at COMMON that the AS/400 did not need advertising and I saw the services division and the software division bringing in almost seventy percent of IBM's $90 billion in annual revenue. Though I was not asleep ten years ago, IBM's corporate makeup has changed so much that I am at shocked at how IBM actually makes its money. The IBM Company now refers to itself as a Software and Services Company, not a hardware company, and no wonder with those numbers. The new IBM has given me a completely different view of the "AS/400 marketing problem."

Looking at the IBM revenue of the last thirty years, IBM has not grown substantially as a company. Yet, two divisions, software and services, which did not exist twenty years ago when I was with IBM, now are about as big as IBM was when I left the company. So, I ask myself, "What happened to the hardware business?" Just like the PC business and many other potentially wonderful IBM businesses over the years, Big Blue is not holding on.

The services division and the software division literally saved IBM from its impending death as a corporation when Lou Gerstner took command. On April Fools Day, 1993, upon arrival for his first day of work, the new Chairman found himself in a life raft looking at John Akers' former team sawing off major pieces of the big IBM boat. Since the IBM cah hordes were on "E," with no regard to whether what was left could float by itself, Akers, planned to sell those pieces one by one for cash. His team was merely preparing the pieces for sale.

From the official IBM lifeboat, Gerstner could see what would happen if huge pieces were indiscriminately taken from the big IBM boat. Since he was not interested in watching all of IBM sink, he chose to halt the dismemberment. Then, since the till was empty, he scrounged up some nails, some putty, and some gum, and tried to hold the big IBM boat together while he figured out what to do.

Surely Gerstner noticed the hundreds of IBM captains all over the boat trying to steer their little sections to safety and success, regardless of which way he chose to take the boat. Many have speculated that no matter how hard he tried, after keeping the pieces together, he could not get all the captains together to move the boat in the same direction. His view from the lifeboat was compelling.

He knew the game was survival and he had to create a new underbelly for the huge boat before it came apart by itself and sunk under its own weight. He picked services and software, two-also-rans in the once mainframe hardware dominated IBM and he used those to prop up the big IBM boat while he figured out what he needed to do about the rest of it.

The services division and the software division have been growing revenue numbers in real terms ever since while the server division has been losing revenue over most of the last twenty years. The new percentages amazed me when I examine IBM's current revenue makeup. It took a lot to convince me that IBM was not a hardware company. I am now convinced. IBM is no longer a hardware company. It is mostly a services company. Yet, software is a vital element of the mix for the future.

At just above 30 percent of revenue, why should IBM care about any of its servers? It is clear that services and software literally saved the company? Survival will make a company do strange things. Perhaps this is the root of all of what I see as IBM's marketing problem with the AS/400. Has IBM's survival strategy caused more than a loss of AS/400 mindshare? That's a topic for somebody else's book, but it gives a proper perspective on what's happening to the AS/400 in this new IBM context.

If I were sitting at the top of IBM right now, having watched about $30 billion in hardware business disappear since Lou Gerstner's arrival, I would look to recapturing that $30 billion that is no longer mine. Those dollars, however, are not going to come from PCs. It's too late for IBM in the PC area. Those dollars however, can certainly come from displacing PC servers from Dell, and from HP. Moreover, they can come from displacing Sun gear.

There is also a tremendous opportunity for IBM in new accounts. IBM knows how to get that engine started up again. As many already know, there is one machine that is even more uniquely qualified to be IBM's lead dog in its revenue reclamation project. The same trusty AS/400 that killed DEC can again be used as the secret weapon to bring back all that lost cash.

Corporate Strategy or Accident?

Twenty-five years ago, IBM built a beautiful Thunderbird, and over the years, its marketing team has transformed its public shape into that of an Edsel. The Edsel façade does nothing for the product but dissuade prospects from buying it. There are few who would not argue that the AS/400 of recent times is built with the external face of yesterday and marketed as if it does not even exist.

I hate to think that through all of its denials and promises, IBM's treatment of the product is intentional and strategic. But, it sure has looked that way. Right now at least, IBM does not have a valid reason to want the AS/400 to completely disappear, but for many years, it seemed to be going out of its way to ensure that the box did not accidentally become extremely successful.

About a quarter million IBM customers already know about the AS/400. IBM's most pressing marketing problem appeared to be how to limit the exposure of the AS/400 so that it would not become a must-have system. One might conclude that a successful AS/400 could interfere with the revenue objectives of the software and services businesses.

Those of us who think rationally and who had been unaware of how big software and services had become had convinced ourselves otherwise. Most AS/400 watchers had been observing the AS/400 as IBM's best-kept secret and most assumed that the company would like nothing more than to have everybody know about it, as long as its other servers were not put down. The natural conclusion was that IBM had not yet figured out how to do that.

In retrospect, for me it sure was a warm and fuzzy hypothesis that IBM had been really looking out for the best interests of its AS/400 constituency, and the company just was not smart enough to figure out how to help. However, that logic is non sequitur.

IBM is a $90 billion plus company. The several million AS/400 professionals out there individually have annual revenue substantially less than IBM’s. This group is not organized and it cannot pay for any big marketing analysis yet when this group is partially assembled, led by industry gurus at conferences such as COMMON, the voice of the AS/400 community is unified: "It's the marketing, IBM." How can IBM, with all its resources not know as much?

Most of the AS/400 followers are deluding themselves that IBM does not know how to help the AS/400 be more part of its mainstream-computing scene. IBM does know how. It must know how. Yet the AS/400 has remained a back room after thought. IBM knows what to do to make the AS/400 line popular. It has chosen not to do it. The more a rational person chews on that thought, the more he or she must conclude that the original hypothesis cannot be true.

IBM knows exactly what it is doing and IBM knows the effects of what it is doing on the AS/400 customer set. Logic also suggests that IBM cannot wholesale eliminate the AS/400 from the mix because it would be a PR nightmare and for a time it would be a revenue nightmare. Cynics may see that may be the company's only reasons for keeping the system alive. The AS/400 is surely not part of a secret growth strategy or we would have heard of it by now.

The IBM Company for years spendt all of its eServer (Power System) dollars pumping up the eServer brand, rarely, if ever, mentioning the AS/400. When there would be an IBM ad message, the best a TV viewer sees is something about IBM or an IBM PC Server. IBM cares only about the IBM name and now, the eServer brand. But make no mistake about it: IBM does not the AS/400 (Power i) on its hot list, and perhaps not even on its warm list.

Prove to Me You Love Me

If IBM had to go to court tomorrow and testify about what it has done for the AS/400 or Power i lately, despite the collective opinion of its customers, its testimony would actually be impressive. After all, from 1995, the same time period when its customers had become agitated with its marketing, IBM has invested tons of money in the platform.

For example, it transformed the AS/400 server from a 48-bit hardware platform running on CISC architecture to a 64-bit hardware platform, first in the industry, running on RISC architecture. Through the 1990's IBM has walked the system through many iterations of Power chip technology and brought to today awaiting the Power8 level, which is the envy of the industry. Moreover, IBM has discussed its vision of the Power Architecture on to 2020. Now, that sure does not appear like a company that has abandoned the flagship.

But, AS/400 watchers would argue, IBM buried this special machine / OS combo in its marketing. The AS/400 is still never highlighted. Under oath, again IBM would come out shining like a rose. In the last part of the 1990s the company included the AS/400 in its "magic box" ad campaign and highlighted its unique capabilities, such as Domino support. In the year 2000, again IBM spent tons of marketing dollars on the AS/400 as it re-branded the unit and it included (not excluded) the AS/400 under its massive eServer umbrella. But, IBM has bnever suggested to the world that its AS/400 line was special.

But, IBM can argue, that when someone sees the eServer brand, they can carry that on down to the specific models and there it is, the Power i, one of the included brands. A rational and prudent judge would find in IBM's favor. Yet you and I (if you are an AS/400 watcher) know that is not true and IBM's treatment of AS/400, no matter how much it spends, is counterproductive. We just can't take our arguments to court.

Only if you get under the eServer umbrella and under the covers of the AS/400 do you see its uniqueness and elegance. Who is going to be motivated to do that after seeing an eServer ad? We spent the early part this book highlighting those wonderful features but IBM does not even mention them anymore to anybody.

Though no other system has capability based addressing or single level storage or a full object orientation, or an integrated relational database, these are no longer highlighted by IBM because they are part of OS/400, an operating system for which IBM, as a company, has mixed emotions. IBM has not highlighted the unique attributes of its AS/400 for years because these are properties of OS/400 and OS/400 is not the company's strategic direction; Linux is. Many fear that OS/400 under the name of IBM i is being sent to the pastures.

AS/400 OS—IBM i Is Not Going Away

Let's take a guess that there are over 200,000 IBM AS/400 customers. Let's take a second guess that there are over 400,000 AS/400 systems of various sizes in operation today. And, let's take a third guess that there are more than 1,000,000 AS/400 professionals who earn their living in the AS/400 space. Let's take a last guess that there are more than 10,000 mainframes out there, just to put the box numbers in perspective. These numbers are definitely not 100 percent accurate but they are good for ballpark purposes.

To conclude that IBM i and the Power System are going away, one must buy into the notion that IBM is hopelessly stupid. No matter how many wrong-headed things IBM has done over the years, many of which I have captured in the chapters preceding this one, IBM is not stupid. IBM may not be very entrepreneurial at times. IBM may be too trusting at times. IBM may not be adroit at times. And IBM may not be agile at times. But IBM is not stupid.

A company would have to be stupid to eliminate the major advantage that permits it to charge well over market price for AS/400 technology. To test this thesis, take a look at what companies are willing to spend for Linux boxes and compare your results with what they have been spending for AS/400 boxes. The delta for hardware has been as much as five times that amount.

OS/400 provides the ability for the AS/400 to be what the IBM sales office once called a system-managed system. If a computer system is not system managed, then who or what manages it? The answer is "people." It is therefore fair to say that Linux, mainframe, Unix, and Windows servers are people managed systems. Everything costs lots less on these boxes, but you need a larger number of people with various skills to make it all work. Thus, overall, the total expense is much greater.

You need more people and each person that works in the non-AS/400 world is more like a computer scientist than a businessperson. Business people who understand business and computers typically run AS/400 shops. The computer science talent in the AS/400 shop does not have to be at the same tech level as non-AS/400 shops because the system itself manages much of the system. Thus, AS/400 machines traditionally cost more than all others but the cost to the business is most often less with an AS/400. IBM's pricing model for AS/400 is keenly aware of those business savings.

The fact that IBM can exact a premium for its AS/400 is not lost on the few marketers that exist today in IBM. If IBM removes IBM i from the AS/400 mix, the premium, which is mostly profit, is also removed and IBM loses. Since IBM does not like to lose revenue, IBM i (formerly OS/400) stays.

Having said that, as you continue to read and you get a perspective on where IBM is taking all of its servers, that does not mean that the company will continue to enhance IBM i if it can provide the function in other ways. It does mean that your investment in IBM i (OS/400) applications is safe, and that IBM will continue to exact large sums for your right to use those old applications. Moreover, when IBM can begin to slip technology into the non-IBM i parts of an AS/400, and yet still make it easy for you to run your IBM i (OS/400) based applications using that technology, you will see less new function being ported to IBM i (OS/400).

Linux is IBM's eServer OS

Under this backdrop, it is very logical to conclude that IBM's treatment of its AS/400 product line must be conscious. It must be intentional. We can't think that IBM is dumb just because it does not do what we think is rational. I take that back. It is actually more comforting to think IBM is dumb, but the company is smart like a fox.

The facts about what IBM is up to are becoming more and clearer and the facts explain quite a bit of the apparent irrational IBM behavior. There is a major assimilation agenda at work at IBM in hardware, software, and branding. As discussed in the Chapter titled Fork Knox II, there is an informal, un-labeled Fort Knox II project underway within IBM today, and this time it is moving unimpeded.

Just the other day I attended an IBM presentation in which the speaker highlighted the new Power models as being that much better because he would not need OS/400 to run Linux applications. Hah! The new "hypervisor" for AS/400 does not need the AS/400 operating system, IBM i (OS/400). What the speaker did not say, however, was that an AS/400 without IBM i (OS/400) is not an AS/400. Yet that is the new message.

The AS/400, a system that demonstrates its value through its uniqueness, not its sameness is not necessarily the system that Fort Knox II architects want to find at the heart of their new system. Therefore, they have found a logical way to handle this sticky issue. The only part of an AS/400 that is unique to the AS/400 is its operating system, now called IBM i.

It is the defining characteristic of an AS/400. When I use the term AS/400, I mean a computer running OS/400, i5/OS or IBM i. I don't mean a computer capable of running an AS/400 OS but it is running Linux or Unix without an AS/400 OS.

In today's IBM, that is a big difference. If IBM no longer is forced to invest in OS/400 as a prime operating system, there will be big savings for the company. Always interested in its bottom line, I have concluded that IBM will figure a way to get those savings. As long as I don't have to see a different personality on my AS/400, I really don't care how IBM implements function.—even if the AS/400 used an integrated Linux OS under the covers as a hypervisor to get things done on IBM i's behalf.

Linux Can Make Development Cheap at IBM

If you are IBM, and if you become able to build software just once for the Linux environment, since Linux runs on all of your platforms, even the pesky AS/400 hardware platform, your development job for all platforms could be just about done. With function made available through Linux and partitioning, there would be no z/OS version or OS/400 (i5/OS) version or Unix version or Windows version of IBM software required. If you are IBM and you make your software (DB2, CICS, WebSphere) work for Linux, and you have made Linux work on all your servers, it follows that your software works on all your servers.

What a deal for IBM? It's so good that even an AS/400 buff can see its logic, though not necessarily be pleased. In the Linux scenario, IBM would build once for Linux, put Linux on every eServer (i5 and others), and save the huge development dollars required for three operating system ports. That is a lot of money. For the AS/400 aficionado, the loss may be OS/400 control and integration unless IBM does it right – and as long as Rochester is in tact, it will be done right.

So maybe there won't be a high price or any user price to pay for IBM's savings. IBM i (OS/400-i5/OS) would remain stable and gain new function by adding APIs for Linux cross partition support. In other words, IBM would only have to build a few hooks so that OS/400 would seamlessly cross over to the Linux partition to gain access to any new, apparently non-integrated functions. To the AS/400 user, they would appear to be integrated (woven) into the machine itself.

There is another possible advantage to IBM that might be a negative for the AS/400. Since IBM would have its software working on Linux, and Linux is an ala carte operating system (you build it), IBM's software division could get to sell the same one product across four different platforms without anybody asking for integration. Even AS/400 shops would have to buy the software. But if the WebSphere integration is a forerunner of things to come, the new Linux software and the IBM i APIs would be integrated ahead of time by Rochester or Rochester's replacement in the new world.

I would not want to see the software licensed to Linux even though it may run under Linux. In that world, OS/400 integration would soon become passé. It would be superfluous, and nobody could blame poor IBM. Hey, that's just how Linux is! That's why Rochester integration with IBM i is so important.

IBM's own software development costs would become less than half of what they otherwise would be, plus there would not be three or four different labs trying to keep software versions bug-free and up-to-date. When IBM hauls the mainframe personality to the PowerPC architecture in the next several years, all of IBM's three operating systems will be hardware and software compatible.

The mainframe will be the Linux box. The IBM Power System will be the Linux Box. The AS/400 will be the Linux box. The Unix box (RS/6000, pSeries) will be the Linux box, and the PC Server has been a Linux box all along. There is nothing to say that IBM could not slip the Intel Instruction set on the chip even if IBM is not selling Intel systems.

No wonder IBM is pushing Linux on the AS/400! Even if it does not make sense for your business because you see no value in Linux, you can see how this is a logical, coherent strategy for IBM. It is not a product of ad hoc helter-skelter thinking. Therefore, you can almost expect that this is a lot more than rumor. This must happen.

Schizophrenia

In the November 12, 2003, Power i Network News Wire Daily, Earl Perkins, vice president of the Meta Group is quoted under the heading of:

> **Schizophrenia**
>
> **"If you look inside IBM today, they have a schizophrenic nature to them. The problem with most of the big companies now is to know when is the right time to, essentially, change your bet. This is the same company that has mainframe and iSeries (Power i) and a lot of legacy stuff that they've hung onto because, as far as they're concerned, the timing's not right. There're still enough customers and there's still enough money to be made in their respective environments. ... They'll make money on AIX as long as they can, but when they can actually perceive the tide shifting for a majority of their customer market -- because there will always be people who buy AIX, no matter what -- you'll see a consequent move to support ... Linux more and more."**

IBM's mantra is changing from the best possible customer service to "Linux on my shoulder makes me happy!"

The IBM Animal Thinks Rationally

Try to imagine how the IBM animal actually thinks. This company spent hundreds of millions of dollars trying to converge five product lines and 10 operating systems with

Fort Knox in the early 1980s. This kind of expenditure was folly but it was not accidental. It was planned, but not well planned.

In the 1980s, IBM was invincible, so it used bravado, not patience. It used revolution, not evolution. It used disruption, not harmony. For its hundreds of millions and all the turmoil it caused, and for its big failure, IBM came home with its early homogenization objectives unaccomplished.

Though Big Blue was clearly unsuccessful with Fort Knox, its goals of having just one system capable of all functions never left the corporation. In its latest iteration, the fox, played by IBM, has been using harmony, evolution, and patience in achieving through time, what it could not do by decree. It's not there yet, but it is well on its way. Will Chair Virginia Rometty let it happen?

Let's look at the evidence. From a hardware perspective, the AS/400, the Unix box, and the Linux box have share the same processor for years. They also shared the hardware chassis, and major components. They were both made in Rochester, Minnesota for years. The machines looked almost identical coming off the line. This happened quietly, post Fort Knox, over the last 16 years or so.

In a few more years, the mainframe can easily be part of the Power hardware mix. The mainframe integration and convergence project that we call Fort Knox II actually has a code name in IBM. It is the "universal" or "Mach 5" server. Components in all three systems are basically the same already.

Note: As a humorous aside, if and when the mainframe is included in the Power processor mix, I doubt that we'll ever see a mainframe processor coming off the line in Rochester. Though IBM eliminated its Endicott plant that was way over on the other side of the state [NY], Poughkeepsie is just too close to Somers and Armonk for mainframes to ever be made in Rochester, Minnesota. It would not be good for IBM people to lose jobs and have to

move out of this NY area. Hey, IBM executives live nearby. You don't think they'd do anything that would lower the values of their own homes! As a reminder, IBM is dismantling operations in Rochester Minnesota as I write this line.

No Marketing Problem for IBM!

On the marketing side, IBM's marketing department has performed its job letter perfect. AS/400 folks think there is a big marketing problem but inside IBMers know the execution has been perfect. IBM marketing successfully created the eServer umbrella brand, which for a time at least, made all systems the same from a marketing perspective.

That is part of the overall unifying Fort Knox II strategy. The AS/400 became an eServer and nothing more. IBM advertises eServers, though there are no such things per se. The products exist in the series names but Power I is never the focus of an ad.

However, if all IBM hardware boxes actually became the same, and if Intel instructions were made to run on the IBM Power chips, there would be no need for series names. Even Intel's processors and PCs would be irrelevant in IBM's "golden" plans.

The All-In-One-Hardware eServer

The most important element that having the same hardware would provide is that the eServer could actually be a hardware product. There would be no need for a small letter series of computers. The eServer would actually be the Fort Knox II do-everything-machine that IBM dreamed about in 1981 but could not make happen then. There would be no need for co-processors since all of the "guest operating systems," z/OS for mainframe, IBM i—OS/400, i5/OS for AS/400, Linux and AIX (Unix) for the Unix box, and Windows for former PC Servers, would run on the same IBM Power-based processors.

Though this may seem an IBM dream outside of the realm of possibility, the ingredients are all in place. Why would IBM ignore its AS/400 customers' requests for help if the company did not think it had a better idea?

Even if the hardware and the marketing were the same, the thing that separates the systems is their respective operating systems. The mix includes

Mainframe	z/OS (formerly OS/390), VM, VSE, Linux
AS/400	IBM i, OS/400 (i5/OS), Linux, AIX
Unix Box	Unix (AIX), Linux
PC Server	Windows, Linux

The All-In-One-Software eServer

As noted above, each of these boxes also run one common operating system. You guessed it: Linux. If IBM were to concentrate its future on Linux in more ways than you could imagine, the primary OS for the all-in-one eServer box would naturally be Linux. All other operating personalities that were necessary could be worked in with guest services running in logical partitions of the big Linux eServer.

That is a super technical achievement for IBM and it would make Fort Knox II a resounding success, however, it would have to be done very carefully to preserve the AS/400 as we know and understand it.

The AS/400 is known by its operating system, IBM i—OS/400-i5/OS, not by its hardware. IBM has shown over the years that, other than reliability and speed, the hardware does not matter. In the new Linux all-everything world, real AS/400 users would have to press IBM for enhancements to the AS/400 personality (IBM i—OS/400- i5/OS) under the eServer scenario, even if the eServer machine were called a Power i.

The AS/400 personality is not the defining characteristic of Fort Knox II. The original eServer branding pretended that all machines were the same but a future IBM AS/400-like RISC box can actually be the homogenized server running all personalities and running Linux as the homogenization factor. From IBM's perspective, that would complete the successful building of Fort Knox II. Though IBM's accomplishments will have been done surreptitiously, for the AS/400 crowd it would be quite serendipitous. For joe S. the plain old AS/400 IT manager, the box for its core functions, would provide it all with the same old AS.400 personality we all have come to know and love.

The Big Three

If you get your checklist out, the three big convergence items for Fort Knox II are in process. (1) The convergence hardware is on its way. (2) The marketing piece is done. (3) Linux has gotten the call.

With the long-term strategy in place and firing on all four cylinders, what can IBM do in the meantime to soften the blow to an unwary constituency? Well, you might not be surprised that the company has actually been doing it for years. That's part of the reason that many AS/400 shops have been concerned for some time.

The IBM AS/400 message has not been IBM i (OS/400-i5/OS) oriented for a number of years. The only time IBM showed an AS/400 box in any form of IBM promo, the message was not the AS/400's fine OS or integration.

The message has been Linux, Java, on-demand computing, and logical partitions. This is not by accident. IBM is not advertising to its own customer set per se, though it should. They are advertising to the AS/400 professionals to get ready for the big day when OS/400 and Linux get to live together on all eServer boxes. A better ad would be to say that the AS/400 is so immune to technology changes that just like CISC to RISC, moving to a hypervisor based machine will be no more difficult, and more than likely a lot less difficult.

A Rose by Any Other Name

AS/400 loyalists will resist IBM's call to view the new fish as a rose. Since operating systems give a computer its personality, having Linux control a machine on which AS/400 (i5/OS) is emblazoned will not easily convince the AS/400 crowd that the machine is an AS/400. If it is running Linux, it is a Linux machine.

f it is not running OS/400 as its primary OS, no matter what IBM calls it, is it really an AS/400? IBM will need a new marketing department to convince AS/400 shops that the new Fort Knox II computer is their ever-faithful AS/400.

Look at how stubborn System/36 customers were for years until IBM saw it their way. Having their venerable S/36 operating system emulated in an AS/400 environment did not cut it for the S/36 crowd. Look at how obstinate AS/400 shops have been in resisting Java and WebSphere and the language du jour. It will take a tremendous marketing effort for IBM to sell the notion that Linux driving a PowerX box is really an AS/400. I

f recent attempts to convince AS/400 customers to follow blindly to Java are an indicator of how IBM plans to convince AS/400 shops to accept Linux-driven Fort Knox II boxes, you might want to hold off on buying any more IBM stock for a while. With full knowledge of its stubbornly loyal AS/400 constituency, I think IBM will be smarter this time.

IBM's recent message has not been resonating with its untrusting customers. If you read IBM's AS/400 message, you see the great new words all lined up about the eServer

Power i--Linux, Java, on demand, and logical partitioning. I can tell you this. My small and midsize customers have seen the lineup. None of my customers are asking for any of that, and quite frankly they don't want it. IBM has not convinced them.

Sure, AS/400 customers are intrigued that their AS/400 can be made to do all that great stuff. But if IBM persists in this marketing style, the new Linux based AS/400 that replaces the real AS/400 will be greeted as warmly as identity theft. I am encouraged, however, that IBM seems to be getting the message slowly but surely from its customers. The very positive May 4, 2004 i5 introduction hopefully was just IBM's first response. If it was it still is!

IBM had been using the Linux advertising for AS/400 shops to get its message out and after awhile, the company seemed to hope that AS/400 professionals will soften and "accept the inevitable." The IBM smart-like-foxes crowd has been on this same bandwagon for six years or more pushing Java.

The IBM plan is that the more AS/400 shops that adopt Java, the less customer pain there will be for IBM to move these shops to a new Linux-driven Fort Knox II box. IBM has had to rethingk that one.

Move from RPG to Java

The AS/400 community is aware that IBM has been subtly and not so subtly trying to move its AS/400 loyalists towards Java and open systems for years. Even IBM's own RPGIV language, supposedly devised for RPG fans now looks surprisingly like Java.

There is good reason. The more IBM can get AS/400 folks moving to Java as Luddites following the light, the easier it will be to throw a Linux/Java environment on them with Fort Knox II and call it the future. Despite what some would call IBM's best efforts, the almost 20-year-old RPG IV language has not been adopted as blindly as IBM would have thought.

Since IBM could not make its AS/400 followers adapt or even like Java, through the back door, Toronto, which is now owned by IBM's software division, has been making RPG IV more and more like Java. IBM has not been very happy that this plan is not working. The big failing for Big Blue is that the IBM Toronto software lab, under immense corporate pressure, seems to have forgotten who its customers really are.

Computer scientists do like the new RPG more than the old RPG, but they like Java more than RPG IV. The AS/400 is not for computer scientists. AS/400 business programmers on the other hand have never like Java at all from their first cup and therefore, they are not too impressed with the Java-like facilities in RPG IV.

The RPG language was not written for the scientific community. So one must ask why IBM changed the RPG language to accommodate a group of programmers who will never want to use RPG IV. They don't need it since languages such as Java and C++ are already available, even with OS/400. RPG was written in the 1950s for business programmers who understood business. The other languages were written for machine language coders looking for something just a bit easier.

Though it is not working in AS/400 shops, the IBM plan has been to get AS/400 programmers accustomed to how life would be under open systems - Linux and Java. Placing Java features in RPGIV is just part of the transition mechanism so that eventually, OS/400 developers would find it easier to move to the substantially more difficult to use Linux platform.

Though AS/400 "Pro Developers" would have you think otherwise, there is little danger in that happening naturally.

Based on IBM's predisposition to spend no more development dollars than necessary to help AS/400 customers make such a transition, there is little risk that it would happen as a real life IBM project.

The only danger to IBMi—OS/400—i5/OS going away completely is if IBM moved some AS/400 and program development function to Linux to make a conversion easier. I can't see that happening for several computer generations, if ever.

If IBM were willing to spend some real money on software development, building Single Level Storage, a Library subsystem, CL compiler, and RPG/COBOL compilers for Linux would be a smart concession to the AS/400 loyalists and it would help the eServer move to Linux as its microcode with fewer complaints. That's real scary for those of us who want more OS/400 integration and not less.

Don't worry! IBM is not interested in spending money for the convergence. The new IBM is not interested in spending money on anything unless it absolutely must. It is interested in saving money. AS/400 compatible RPG, COBOL and CL as other languages to maintain under Linux are <u>not</u> what IBM is seeking. Less is more and has always been more for IBM.

Java Is Part of the Linux Game

IBM's "push Java" approach for AS/400 over the years is completely logical when placed in the Fort Knox II light. Consider this IBM logic. RPG and COBOL run mostly on the AS/400 platform and the mainframe platform. Mainframe developers don't need the mainframe for their Web applications because they have no problem putting them in a separate Unix box with its own staff for the Web.

AS/400 developers like to do all development and execution on one machine type to save the company hardware and support costs. The tiebreaker is that what IBM wants wins. IBM has told its AS/400 developers to use Java for the Web. So IBM i—OS/400—i5/OS has already been excluded unless you are into Java. Since the preponderance of AS/400 shops have rejected Java, despite IBM's push, AS/400 shops have no other OS friendly tools for Web development, and there seem to be none coming.

In this scenario, IBM has proven that it is interested in saving its own development dollars, not in making the AS/400 a better Web development machine. Just like the AS/400 was an afterthought in the client server and early Internet revolution, until Lou Gerstner demanded it be included, AS/400's OS has not been retro-fitted with any natural mechanisms for Web application development.

IBM's WebSphere Studio, which takes as much as a day to install on your PC and then unmercifully hangs after you spend a day coding your Web application, is certainly not yet the trick to bring IBM i up to Web snuff. Moreover, WDSc is a PC product, not an OS/400 extension.

After 20 years of requests and complaints, there still is no natural Web development or GUI integration for AS/400 even through IBM i. One could easily conclude correctly that is IBM's plan and that it did not happen by accident. IBM was not ready to pay to do it. Why would IBM take on such a big effort for a proprietary machine (AS/400) or operating system to make it a Web machine when it thought that it could move AS/400 programmers to use WebSphere (already written for Unix) and the Java language?

Prior to the release of i5/OS, I would have said, "Don't expect Web integration tools for AS/400 any time soon." I've changed my mind. If AS/400 customers hold out, just like S/36 customers before them, IBM will change the game. In IBM i for example, WebSphere servlet serving is integrated and the company is now building a Web based GUI interface for the platform. But, IBM is stubborn.

The Java and WebSphere approach would be far less expensive for IBM's development labs. Of course it is far more expensive for AS/400 shops to use a non-AS/400 operating system or a language (Java) and a servlet server (standalone WebSphere) that have little if any OS/400 affinity. Sam Palmisano's IBM and now Ginny Rometty's may be a little different from Lou Gerstner's. Gerstner's dictate would have been to "sell what you've got on the truck." With IBM i, I see a different IBM unfolding and that may be very good for us in AS/400 land.

In the future, an eServer itself with Linux as the champion operating system or hypervisor may very well unfold. In such an environment, WebSphere would no longer have to be ported to the OS. It would already run in the standard eServer Linux partition and use the high tech virtual LAN to grab data from the IBM i partition. As long as installation is seamless and appearance is integrated, I see no problem with Web servlet serving running under Linux in a pre-configured no-brainer partition on a friendly AS/400 box. From my vantage point, IBM i—OS/400—i5/OS will not miss it one bit.

Such a complete metamorphosis is highly unlikely in the short term, however, since it would be quite costly. Moreover, if done abruptly, it would put companies with AS/400 shops using IBM i out of business. However, it will be the next subtle push once the eServer box is in place and selling well. If IBM management can figure how to give the software division a share of the software revenue from products that are placed under the covers of the AS/400, there can even be division harmony within IBM.

The AS/400 can become a favorite of the software division. IBM Global Services Division can get its AS/400 business by adding application functions to the scenario, rather than building the Linux or Unix operating system in the customer shop. It's up to IBM. But, there is great hope that this "different Palmisano IBM" is not interested in having IBMi—OS/400 (i5/OS) labeled a legacy operating system in another five to 10 years.

Can Linux Be OS/400 and More?

When I worked for IBM as a systems engineer, I had the pleasure of working with customers who had IT staffs. Marketing representatives would often ask me to make a sales call on a prospect that was running his business on non-IBM or non-AS/400 equipment.

I always tried to steer the company into a migration / conversion / rewrite scenario rather than a package because eventually I knew it would work and quite frankly the package route often pushed the customer into looking at "industry leading solutions" that ran only on non-IBM systems.

I believed and still believe that through application programming or database views or SQL or Queries, any conversion or migration quirk can be solved without having to get the package vendors into the act. The most important element is that the application does the job and that the customer's technical team understands how the software operates and how it is put together.

Can Linux ever be OS/400 and more? Sure it can. Just as application programming makes all things possible in terms of application features and functions, systems programming can take an OS such as Linux and make it like any other OS, even OS/400.

If IBM plans to save development dollars (costs) rather than sell the integration capabilities of OS/400 (revenue), there is no logical reason why it can't donate OS/400 to the Open

Source Foundation or the Open OS/400 On Linux Foundation, so that major OS/400 facilities can be ported to Linux.

As long as the Linux contingent would not be upset having single level storage, object orientation, capability based addressing, integrated database hooks, and a top-flight programming environment, as part of its underpinnings or extrapinnings, Linux has the potential to become as powerful as OS/400. And wouldn't that be a coup.

Nothing in life worth having is easy. The biggest mistake that IBM can make is to undo the present before the future has arrived. For example, IBM discontinued its System/36 before its customers decided that its emulation services worked. Several hundred thousand potential AS/400 customers were immediately alienated. IBM discontinued its OfficeVision/400 product before it had a valid substitute for data merges, thereby alienating a number of loyal AS/400 shops.

IBM stopped making terminals and terminal controllers before its customers were ready to give them up, thereby alienating even more AS/400 shops. IBM stopped providing important OS/400 features in the native interface long before all of its customers were migrated and/or pleased with its PC / GUI (Power i Navigator) implementation.

IBM has a penchant to cancel what somebody is using to get them to do what IBM wants them to do, even if the new IBM function is not stable. The System/36 is the most flagrant example. If IBM thinks that its AS/400 customers should move to Fort Knox II before it is rock solid and easy to do, the company will make a big time mistake that will be tough to undo.

If I had my way, I'd force IBM to continue to develop on IBM i rather than move to a more complicated hybrid platform. With the recent positive signs from Big Blue,

AS/400 customers should not have to show some muscle and unite to do some outrageous things like boycott new IBM AS/400-like offerings.

If IBM persists in changing the platform, and its customers are willing to hold position for a year or so, they would certainly gain IBM's attention at such a sufficient level that real customer objectives could be accomplished. I am encouraged that the customer set will not have to force IBM's hand to listen and act. The 2004 announcement, as I saw it, was IBM's first installment of a great future. Yet, nouch has been done since then.

What's It All about Alfie?

So what does this all mean to an AS/400 RPG shop and IBM stockholders? Prior to the 2004 i5 announcements, I would have said that IBM has dug in and that IBM i—OS/400—i5/OS enhancements would be few and far between. I would have said that the company will not put a GUI on OS/400, and it will not integrate necessary Web functions into the RPG and COBOL environments.

I would also have said that there will not be any teeny weenie AS/400s that would cause more users to like the platform, and I would have said that there would be no integrated OS/400 Web development environment. Remember this is a partial remake of another book that talked about similar issues. I am looking at the promise from 2004 and I regret to say that in 2016, IBM has delivered nothing. I am sorry I ended the prior book on such a positive note. I spoke to Division Heads, I lectured to the Rochester Developers as a Marywood Instructor. I was promised certain things that simply did not happen.

If I had not believed in IBM at the time, I wrote a predecessor book about whther the AS/400 could even survive IBM, I would have said what I felt. I did say what I felt at the time but I was wrong. IBM let me down.

I would have ended the prior book on a note of gloom suggesting that AS/400 developers who want in on the Web will just have to buy something from the software division's truck, even if it is difficult to install and operate. I would have painted a similar picture for stockholders.

I would have cautioned that the days are getting darker and that AS/400 shops will have to be concerned about piece parts software installation problems with IBM's many separate (non-integrated), off-the-truck software offerings.

I would have pointed out that AS/400 shops may not be able to get all these things installed easily and I would have suggested that IBM was making it tough on purpose so that you would have to buy plenty of IBM services to help you get the job done.

I would have reminded the reader that services are where the new IBM makes most of its money. I would have capped off my caveats by concluding that the next AS/400 might not be bult in Rochester and the one after that would be assembled in your shop just like the systems of the 1970s.

Then, just to get you as angry as I am, when I was thinking all those bad things, I would have come up with some cutesy saying that would have gotten you outraged at the predicament in which IBM had placed your AS/400 shop or your stock portfolio. I probably would have said something like: "*If your heart is with the AS/400, you had better position your wallet someplace else. IBM is not about to do it for you.* " Sorry, but that's how I see it. You can bet IBM will do little to prove me wrong. But, I sure hope that Tom Watson Jr. appears in somebody's good dream and gives some intructions.

Then, in case that was not enough to get your juices flowing, I probably would have added something like this, "In the biggest case of identity theft since the Application System/400 became the Advanced Server/400, Fort Knox II (the eServer) is taking the place of the beloved AS/400, and Fort Knox II will be driven by Linux, not OS/400."

Sorry, I can't say those things now. On May 4, 2004, IBM began its campaign to prove me wrong. At least I hope. Prior to May 4, Big Blue had not shared with me that their plans for the AS/400 were to make it even better and even more affordable and to enhance integration and usability all at the same time.

I love IBM's campaign to prove me wrong because I love the AS/400 and so do my customers. When Big Blue begins to advertise the AS/400 on TV around the world to educate the masses subtly about this wonderment of modern computing, even my neighbors will start to love the machine.

The AS/400 will survive IBM! You bet! IBM will be # 1 because it will embrace its finest technology and drive it to success. But, the IBM AS/400 of the future will be different and better. Yes, it will be running Linux! But, unless you want to see its ugly face, Linux will be hidden.

Yes, until I tell you othersise, it is OK to hold onto your IBM stock and your AS/400s. Unless IBM changes course again, the future has a shot at being bright indeed.

LETS GO PUBLISH! Books: (sold at www.bookhawkers.com etc.). All books are written by famous author Brian W. Kelly

LETS GO PUBLISH! is proud to announce that more AS/400 and Power i books are becoming available to help you inexpensively address your AS/400 and Power i education and training needs. Email letsgopublish@kellyconsulting.com for ordering information. Our general ttitles are pretty good including two one of a kind football books about Notre Dame and Penn State. They are followed in this list by AS/400 and technical books.

Great Moments in Penn State Football Check out the particulars of this great book at bookhawkers.com.

Great Moments in Notre Dame Football Check out the particulars of this great book at bookhawkers.com or www.notredamebooks.com

WineDiets.Com Presents The Wine Diet Learn how to lose weight while having fun. Four specific diets and some great anecdotes fill this book with fun and the opportunity to lose weight in the process..

Wilkes-Barre, PA; Return to Glory Wilkes-Barre City's return to glory begins with dreams and ideas. Along with plans and actions, this equals leadership.

The Lifetime Guest Plan. This is a plan which if deployed today would immediately solve the problem of 60 million illegal aliens in the United States.

Geoffrey Parsons' Epoch... The Land of Fair Play Better than the original. The greatest re-mastering of the greatest book ever written on American Civics. It was built for all Americans as the best govt. design in the history of the world.

The Bill of Rights 4 Dummmies This is the best book to learn about your rights. Be the first, to have a "Rights Fest" on your block. You will win for sure!

Sol Bloom's Epoch ...Story of the Constitution This work by Sol Bloom was written to commemorate the Sesquicentennial celebration of the Constitution It has been remastered by Lets Go Publish! – An excellent read!

The Constitution 4 Dummmies This is the best book to learn about the Constitution. Learn all about the fundamental laws of America.

America for Dummmies!
All Americans should read to learn about this great country.

Just Say No to Chris Christie for President!
Discusses the reasons why Chris Christie is a poor choice for US President

The Federalist Papers by Hamilton, Jay, Madison w/ intro by Brian Kelly
Complete unabridged, easier to read version of the original Federalist Papers

Kill the Republican Party!
Demonstrates why the Republican Party must be abandoned by conservatives

Bring On the American Party!
Demonstrates how conservatives can be free from the party of wimps by starting its own national party called the American Party.

No Amnesty! No Way!
In addition to describing the issue in detail, this book also offers a real solution.

Saving America
This how-to book is about saving our country using strong mercantilist principles. These same principles that helped the country from its founding.

RRR:
A unique plan for economic recovery and job creation

Kill the EPA
The EPA seems to hate mankind and love nature. They are also making it tough for asthmatics to breathe and for those with malaria to live. It's time they go.

Obama's Seven Deadly Sins.
In the Obama Presidency, there are many concerns about the long-term prospects and sustainability of the country. We examine each of the President's seven deadliest sins in detail, offering warnings and a number of solutions. Be careful. Book may nudge you to move to Canada or Europe.

Taxation Without Representation Second Edition
At the time of the Boston Tea Party, there was no representation. Now, there is no representation again but there are "representatives."

Healthcare Accountability
Who should pay for your healthcare? Whose healthcare should you pay for? Is it a lifetime free ride on others or should those once in need of help have to pay it back when their lives improve?

Jobs! Jobs! Jobs!
Where have all the American Jobs gone and how can we get them back?

Other IBM I Technical Books

The All Everything Operating System:
Story about IBM's finest operating system, its facilities; how it came to be.

The All-Everything Machine
Story about IBM's finest computer server.

Chip Wars
The story of ongoing wars between Intel and AMD and upcoming wars between Intel and IBM. Book may cause you to buy / sell somebody's stock.

Can the AS/400 Survive IBM?
Exciting book about the AS/400 in a System i5 World.

The IBM i Pocket SQL Guide.
Complete Pocket Guide to SQL as implemented on System i5. A must have for SQL developers new to System i5. It is very compact yet very comprehensive and it is example driven. Written in a part tutorial and part reference style, Tons of SQL coding samples, from the simple to the sublime.

The IBM i Pocket Query Guide.
If you have been spending money for years educating your Query users, and you find you are still spending, or you've given up, this book is right for you. This one QuikCourse covers all Query options.

The IBM I Pocket RPG & RPG IV Guide.
Comprehensive RPG & RPGIV Textbook -- Over 900 pages. This is the one RPG book to have if you are not having more than one. All areas of the language covered smartly in a convenient sized book Annotated PowerPoint's available for self-study (extra fee for self-study package)

The IBM I RPG Tutorial and Lab Guide – Recently Revised.
Your guide to a hands-on Lab experience. Contains CD with Lab exercises and PowerPoint's. Great companion to the above textbook or can be used as a standalone for student Labs or tutorial purposes

The IBM i Pocket Developers' Guide.
Comprehensive Pocket Guide to all of the AS/400 and System i5 development tools - DFU, SDA, etc. You'll also get a big bonus with chapters on Architecture, Work Management, and Subfile Coding.

The IBM i Pocket Database Guide.
Complete Pocket Guide to System i5 integrated relational database (DB2/400) – physical and logical files and DB operations - Union, Projection, Join, etc. Written in a part tutorial and part reference style. Tons of DDS coding samples.

Getting Started With The WebSphere Development Studio Client for System i5 (WDSc) Focus on client server and the Web. Includes CODE/400, VisualAge RPG, CGI, WebFacing, and WebSphere Studio. Case study continues from the Interactive Book.

The System i5 Pocket WebFacing Primer.
This book gets you started immediately with WebFacing. A sample case study is used as the basis for a conversion to WebFacing. Interactive 5250 application is WebFaced in a case study form before your eyes.

Getting Started with WebSphere Express Server for IBM i Step-by-Step Guide for Setting up Express Servers
A comprehensive guide to setting up and using WebSphere Express. It is filled with examples, and structured in a tutorial fashion for easy learning.

The WebFacing Application Design & Development Guide:
Step by Step Guide to designing green screen IBM i apps for the Web. Both a systems design guide and a developers guide. Book helps you understand how to design and develop Web applications using regular RPG or COBOL programs.

The System i5 Express Web Implementer's Guide. Your one stop guide to ordering, installing, fixing, configuring, and using WebSphere Express, Apache, WebFacing, System i5 Access for Web, and HATS/LE.

Migrating to WebSphere Express for Power i: Your Roadmap for Migrating Applications to WebSphere Express
A Comprehensive guide designed to be your roadmap for moving to WAS Express for Power i. It is loaded with examples and structured for easy learning. Through an easy to understand sample case study, you experience a real migration, and you learn the gotchas before they getcha! This book is designed to be a companion to all of your WAS Express migration efforts in the Power I environment

Joomla! Technical Books

Best Damn Joomla Intranet Tutorial Ever
This book is the only book that shows you how to use Joomla on a corporate intranet.

Best Damn Joomla Template Tutorial Ever
This book teaches you step-by step how to work with templates in Joomla!

Best Damn Joomla Installation Guide Ever
Teaches you how to install Joomla! On all major platforms besides IBM i.

Best Damn Blueprint for Building Your Own Corporate Intranet.
This excellent timeless book helps you design a corporate intranet for any platform while using Joomla as its basis.

IBM i PHP & MySQL Installation & Operations Guide
How to install and operate Joomla! on the IBM i Platform

IBM i PHP & MySQL Programmers Guide
How to write PHP and MySQL programs for IBM i

Made in United States
North Haven, CT
04 November 2026

21766918R00323